Genders and Sexualities in History

Series Editors: **John H. Arnold**, Joanna Bourke and **Sean Brady**

Palgrave Macmillan's series, **Genders and Sexualities in History**, aims to accommodate and foster new approaches to historical research in the fields of genders and sexualities. The series will promote world-class scholarship that concentrates upon the interconnected themes of genders, sexualities, religions/religiosity, civil society, class formations, politics and war.

Historical studies of gender and sexuality have often been treated as disconnected fields, while in recent years historical analyses in these two areas have synthesised, creating new departures in historiography. By linking genders and sexualities with questions of religion, civil society, politics and the contexts of war and conflict, this series will reflect recent developments in scholarship, moving away from the previously dominant and narrow histories of science, scientific thought, and legal processes. The result brings together scholarship from contemporary, modern, early modern, medieval, classical and non-Western history to provide a diachronic forum for scholarship that incorporates new approaches to genders and sexualities in history.

Missionary Masculinity, 1870–1930: The Norwegian Missionaries in South-East Africa is a groundbreaking study of Norwegian male missionaries and constructs of masculinity. In this original book, Kristin Fjelde Tjelle provides a meticulously researched, incisive, and fascinating analysis of Norwegian Lutheran missionaries, and questions what kinds of men they were, and also what kinds of masculinity they represented, in ideology and in the lived experience. This book reveals the significance of Scandinavian religious missions in Colonial Africa, an aspect of African history neglected in Anglophone scholarship. The complexities of Norwegian male missionary masculinity are revealed through encounters in South-East Africa with African masculinities, settler masculinities and Imperial masculinities. In common with all volumes in the Genders and Sexualities in History series, *Missionary Masculinity, 1870–1930: The Norwegian Missionaries in South-East Africa* presents a multifaceted and meticulously researched scholarly study, and is a sophisticated contribution to our understanding of the past.

Titles include:

John H. Arnold and Sean Brady (*editors*)
WHAT IS MASCULINITY?
Historical Dynamics from Antiquity to the Contemporary World

Heike Bauer and Matthew Cook (*editors*)
QUEER 1950S

Cordelia Beattie and Kirsten A. Fenton (*editors*)
INTERSECTIONS OF GENDER, RELIGION AND ETHNICITY IN THE MIDDLE AGES

Chiara Beccalossi
FEMALE SEXUAL INVERSION
Same-Sex Desires in Italian and British Sexology, c. 1870–1920

Raphaëlle Branche and Fabrice Virgili (*editors*)
RAPE IN WARTIME

Peter Cryle and Alison Moore
FRIGIDITY
An Intellectual History

Lucy Delap and Sue Morgan
MEN, MASCULINITIES AND RELIGIOUS CHANGE IN TWENTIETH CENTURY
BRITAIN

Rebecca Fraser
GENDER, RACE AND FAMILY IN NINETEENTH CENTURY AMERICA
From Northern Woman to Plantation Mistress

Dagmar Herzog (*editor*)
BRUTALITY AND DESIRE
War and Sexuality in Europe's Twentieth Century

Robert Hogg
MEN AND MANLINESS ON THE FRONTIER
Queensland and British Columbia in the Mid-Nineteenth Century

Andrea Mansker
SEX, HONOR AND CITIZENSHIP IN EARLY THIRD REPUBLIC FRANCE

Jessica Meyer
MEN OF WAR
Masculinity and the First World War in Britain

Meredith Nash
MAKING 'POSTMODERN' MOTHERS
Pregnant Embodiment, Baby Bumps and Body Image

Jennifer D. Thibodeaux (*editor*)
NEGOTIATING CLERICAL IDENTITIES
Priests, Monks and Masculinity in the Middle Ages

Kristin Fjelde Tjelle
MISSIONARY MASCULINITY, 1870–1930
The Norwegian Missionaries in South-East Africa

Forthcoming titles:

Matthew Cook
QUEER DOMESTICITIES
Homosexuality and Home Life in Twentieth-Century London

Melissa Hollander
SEX IN TWO CITIES
The Negotiation of Sexual Relationships in Early Modern England and Scotland

---

Genders and Sexualities in History Series
Series Standing Order   978–0–230–55185–5 Hardback
                             978–0–230–55186–2 Paperback
(*outside North America only*)

You can receive future titles in this series as they are published by placing a standing order. Please contact your bookseller or, in case of difficulty, write to us at the address below with your name and address, the title of the series and one of the ISBNs quoted above.

Customer Services Department, Macmillan Distribution Ltd, Houndmills, Basingstoke, Hampshire RG21 6XS, England

---

Missionary Masculinity, 1870–1930

The Norwegian Missionaries in South-East Africa

Kristin Fjelde Tjelle

Director, School of Mission and Theology,
Stavanger, Norway

First published 2014 by
PALGRAVE MACMILLAN

Palgrave Macmillan in the UK is an imprint of Macmillan Publishers Limited, registered in England, company number 785998, of Houndmills, Basingstoke, Hampshire RG21 6XS.

Palgrave Macmillan in the US is a division of St Martin's Press LLC, 175 Fifth Avenue, New York, NY 10010.

Palgrave Macmillan is the global academic imprint of the above companies and has companies and representatives throughout the world.

Palgrave® and Macmillan® are registered trademarks in the United States, the United Kingdom, Europe and other countries

ISBN: 978–1–137–33635–4

This book is printed on paper suitable for recycling and made from fully managed and sustained forest sources. Logging, pulping and manufacturing processes are expected to conform to the environmental regulations of the country of origin.

A catalogue record for this book is available from the British Library.

A catalog record for this book is available from the Library of Congress.

To Lars Sigurd, Hans, Erling, Ingeborg and Marie

Contents

List of Illustrations

List of Abbreviations

BMS	Berlin Missionary Society
CIM	China Inland Mission
CLM	Cooperating Lutheran Missions in Natal
CSM	Church of Sweden Mission
FEAM	Free East Africa Mission
KS	Kamp og Seier (Victory and Struggle)
MA	Misjonsarkivet (Mission Archive)
MC	The Missionary Conference
MHS	Misjonshøgskolen (School of Mission and Theology)
MKF	Missionslæsning for Kvindeforeninger (Women's Mission Readings)
NMS	Det Norske Misjonsselskap (Norwegian Missionary Society)
NMT	Norsk Misjonstidende (Norwegian Missionary Tidings)
SMR	Sykepleiernes Misjonsring (Female Nurses' Missionary Association)
SVM	Student Volunteer Movement for Foreign Mission
YMCA	Young Men's Christian Association

1
Introduction:
Missionaries and Masculinities

This book examines male missionaries and constructs of masculinity. A missionary can be defined as someone who attempts to convert others to a particular doctrine, programme or faith. Although it is not always the case, a missionary is often seen as someone 'going to' or being 'sent to' a 'foreign' place to carry out a mission. The group of men scrutinised in the current study served as Christian missionaries between 1870 and 1930, representing the Lutheran mission Norwegian Missionary Society (NMS), which was established in 1842. The first NMS missionaries reached the shores of south-east Africa in 1844, arriving at the coastal town of Durban, which was situated in a region that had been proclaimed the British Colony of Natal in the previous year (1843). The target group for their missionary activity was the Zulu ethnic group.[1] In addition to establishing a 'mission station'[2] in Natal, the NMS missionaries also settled in Zululand, a sovereign African kingdom on the eastern frontier of Natal.

What kind of men were these Norwegian Lutheran missionaries? What kind of masculinity did they represent, in ideology as well as in practice? What kind of processes obtained when a missionary masculinity was constructed? Presupposing *masculinity* to be a cluster of cultural ideas and social practices that change over time (history) and space (culture), and not a stable entity with a natural, inherent and given meaning, this study seeks to answer such questions. First, it examines how a missionary masculinity was constructed in the NMS. Second, it looks at how a missionary masculinity was represented in the Norwegian Lutheran mission discourse. Finally, it explores the practical implications which the construction of a missionary masculinity had for the male missionaries themselves as well as for other groups of men and women participating in the Norwegian–Zulu encounter.

This book suggests that Norwegian Lutheran missionary masculinity was constructed in the tension between modern ideals of male 'self-making' and Christian ideals of 'self-denial'. It was also constructed in the tension between missionary men's subjectivities as modern professional breadwinners in an enterprise with global interests, and their subjectivities as pre-modern housefathers in an enterprise that expected their private and domestic lives to be integrated into their professional missionary lives. Finally, missionary masculinity was constructed in the tension between powerlessness and power. On the one hand, inappropriate missionary masculinity, or missionary unmanliness, meant powerlessness. This study reveals that not all missionary men lived up to the standard, and the personal costs of 'falling' into missionary unmanliness in some cases meant catastrophe and death. On the other hand, however, appropriate missionary masculinity meant powerfulness. The missionary men were originally from humble social backgrounds. Through their engagement in the missionary enterprise they were empowered, moving from being 'nobody' to being 'somebody'. When they encountered African masculinities, settler masculinities and imperial masculinities in south-east African societies, the complexity of Norwegian missionary male subjectivities was further increased, and in the context of late nineteenth-century and early twentieth-century South Africa, Norwegian missionary masculinity meant power, not powerlessness.

The case and the context: Norwegian missionaries in south-east Africa

The NMS's mission in nineteenth-century south-east Africa was known in Norway as 'the Zulu mission' (*Zulu Missionen*). From 1844 to 1930, 56 men and 76 women served as labourers in the Norwegian 'mission field of Zululand and Natal', an endeavour which from 1910 after the creation of the Union of South Africa from the previous Cape and Natal colonies as well as the Orange Free State and Transvaal republics was defined as 'the NMS's mission in South Africa'. Norman Etherington claims in his classic study of missionaries and Christian communities in south-east Africa that no other parts of nineteenth-century Africa were so thickly infested with Christian missionaries as this region.[3] Besides the NMS, other bodies working in the field included the American Board of Commissioners for Foreign Missions (Congregational and Presbyterian) from 1835, the Church Missionary Society (Anglican) from 1837, the Wesleyan Methodist Missionary Society from 1841, the

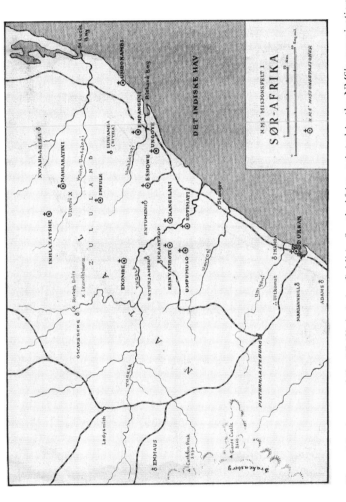

Figure 1.1 A map of the NMS's 'missionfield' in South Africa, printed in the NMS's organizational history published at the centenary in 1942

Source: Mission Archives, School of Mission and Theology, Stavanger.

Berlin Missionary Society (Lutheran) from 1847, the Oblates of Mary Immaculate (French Roman Catholic) from 1852, the Society for the Propagation of the Gospel in Foreign Parts (Anglican) from 1853, the Hermannsburg Missionary Society (Lutheran) from 1854, the Scottish Presbyterian Mission from 1864 and finally the Church of Sweden Mission (Lutheran) from 1876.

With the purchase of Umphumulo Mission Reserve in 1850 the NMS, like the other missions in the region, first settled in the colony of Natal but the Norwegians were eager to get a foothold in the heart of Zululand, and as the first Western missionary the NMS pioneer Hans Paludan Smith Schreuder received King Mpande kaSenzanga-khona's permission in January 1851 to establish permanent mission stations on royal land.[4] John William Colenso, the Anglican Bishop of Natal from 1853, was granted the same permission in 1859.[5] From 1851 to 1871 nine Norwegian mission stations were established in Zululand at Empangeni (1851), Entumeni (1852), Mahlabatini (1860), Eshowe (1861), Nhlazatsche (1862), Imfule (1865), Umbonambi (1869), Umizinyati (1870) and Kwahlabisa (1871). The Anglo-Zulu war of 1879 resulted in the fall of the independent Zulu state and introduced a colonial system of indirect rule through 13 chiefs under the guidance of a British Resident. The lifespan of the 1879 'settlement' was brief, however. A new division of Zululand in 1883 resulted in the outbreak of civil war, and was followed by British annexation of all of Zululand in May 1887.[6] In 1898, effective administrative control of Zululand was transferred from the metropolitan authorities in London to the self-governing settler colony of Natal, which had gained its independence in 1893. The NMS's mission stations of Umizinyati and Kwahlabisa were 'lost' during the time of political turbulence, but land at Ekombe (1880) and Ungoye (1881) was offered as compensation by the new rulers. Later, the NMS also established mission stations at Eotimati (1886), in Durban (1890) and at Kangelani (1915).

There have been some previous studies on the NMS missionaries in south-east Africa. In the early 1970s, the Norwegian historian Jarle Simensen initiated a research project whose aim was to exploit Norwegian missionary material from South Africa and Madagascar in the nineteenth century in order to shed light on local African history. Significant contributions were made by six master's dissertations covering the African side, three of which concerned South Africa,[7] and one covering the Norwegian background of the missionaries.[8] The main findings of the project regarding South Africa were presented in 1986 in the edited book *Norwegian Missions in African History*.[9] The introductory part contained an analysis of the geographical, socio-economic, religious and family backgrounds of the nineteenth-century NMS missionaries and concluded that the majority were recruited from farmers and middle-class craftsmen engaged in revivalist movements in the coastal areas of south-western Norway. The main part of the book focused on the political and social interaction between the missionaries and the African people concerned. The book addressed the NMS missionaries' role directly in relation to the British colonial enterprise and indirectly in relation to the steady incorporation of Zulu society into European forms of modernisation. Simensen's comprehensive project attracted much attention, not least because it was the first time scholars outside the NMS's internal circles had examined the political and social role of Norwegian missions in African societies. The project can be regarded as part of a Marxist-oriented, anti-imperialistic tendency in historical research, following the processes of post-colonialism in Africa and Asia.[10]

Meanwhile, the church historian Torstein Jørgensen's doctoral thesis *Contact and Conflict: Norwegian Missionaries, the Zulu Kingdom and the Gospel 1850–1873* (1990) examined the encounters between the NMS missionaries and the Zulus.[11] Although social and political aspects of the encounter were considered in this work as well, Jørgensen's intention was to emphasise the processes of religious transmission. Given that the Norwegian mission among the Zulus produced few converts in the first three decades, Jørgensen assumes that both 'contact' and 'conflict' characterised the process. The NMS missionaries' attitudes towards a rising African nationalistic movement in South Africa in the 1920s, as well as towards the internal independence efforts of Zulu pastors in the Norwegian mission church, were examined in Hanna Mellemsether's doctoral thesis of 2003.[12] Mellemsether finds that close relations with the white settler establishment, which had Norwegian roots, influenced the missionaries' standpoints and decision-making in a regime practising extensive politics of race segregation. The intimate relations between Norwegian missionaries and settlers are also documented by the South African historian Frederick Hale.[13]

The NMS was the first missionary organisation established in Norway, and 'the Zulu-mission' was its pioneer enterprise, before a second mission was established in Madagascar in 1866 and a third in China in 1902. As in other Western countries, the extensive interest in foreign missions emerging in early nineteenth-century Norway was above all a product of voluntary commitment on the part of individuals and groups related to evangelical revivals and lay movements, who had transnational networks.[14] Although some pastors in the official Evangelical-Lutheran

Church were enthusiastic about the project, the modern idea of mission, that it was the task of Western Christians to bring the Christian faith to the masses of non-Christians abroad, was unfamiliar to the majority of the high-church clergy. Inspired by the readings of German and British missionary magazines, men and women started to form local missionary associations in the 1820s and 1830s. In August 1842, 82 male representatives from 65 of these associations, as well as 102 other men interested in missions, made their way to a mission council in Stavanger. The meeting ended with the establishment of a national society, the Norwegian Missionary Society, which was actually the first national organisation of voluntary local associations in the country, and introduced an era of immense growth in voluntary religious, political, economic and cultural societies and organisations, on both a local and a national level.[15]

Whereas the British missionary movement was founded on the pillars of denominational missionary organisations (Anglican, Baptist, Methodist, Congregationalist, Presbyterian, etc.),[16] the Norwegian missionary movement was far more homogeneous. Although the NMS was a private and voluntary enterprise and not initiated by any church organisation, its Lutheran denominational foundation was accepted without question The NMS constitution of 1842 declared that its representatives in the mission fields should teach in accordance with 'The Holy Script and the Church of Norway's Confessional Scripts'.[17] Schreuder, a university-educated theologian from an upper-class family, was himself ordained in accordance with the rituals of the Evangelical-Lutheran Church of Norway. His aim was to establish a Lutheran Church in Zululand in line with the Scandinavian folk-church model, which also explains why in an introductory phase of the mission work he put great effort into converting those in the upper strata of society, beginning with the king and the royal household.[18] Schreuder acted, however, in accordance with the NMS as a Lutheran mission organisation and was in 1866 consecrated 'missionary bishop' of what was defined as 'the Church of Norway's Mission Field'. Although the majority of the NMS missionaries, unlike Schreuder, were recruited from the lower social classes, and the education they were offered at the NMS's theological seminary never qualified them for employment in the State Church of Norway, they were ordained to serve as missionary pastors by state-church bishops. The relation between the NMS and the official Lutheran church continued to be close. Other mission organisations established in Norway in the last decades of the nineteenth century, both Lutheran and non-denominational, had a more distant relationship with the state church.[19]

In 1842 Norway was still under Swedish rule, but nevertheless had its own constitution, parliament and government. Although the nation can hardly be defined as a colonial power in the strict sense of the term – contemporary Norwegian nationalists claimed that the nation itself had a long history of being 'colonised' – Norwegians nevertheless participated in colonial encounters as sailors, soldiers, surveyors, ethnographers – and missionaries. The Norwegian historians Hilde Nielssen, Inger Marie Okkenhaug and Karina Hestad Skeie claim that missionaries not only participated in activities that had culturally and socially transforming effects on indigenous societies, but also that the missionary movement involved considerable activity at 'home' including representation of the people and cultures they encountered.[20] Norwegian missionary activity must be studied in a colonial and post-colonial context, they claim, and they refer to recent scholarship which has pointed out that the 'colonial culture' had an impact on the European imagination of 'self' and 'other'.[21] In the course of the nineteenth century Norway had the highest number of missionaries per inhabitant in the world. The mission movement cut across boundaries of class, gender, occupation and education, and included people in the rural as well as the more urban areas. The number of subscriptions to NMS's monthly magazine *Norsk Missionstidende*, which rose from about 2,000 in 1850 to 6,500 in 1870 and 10,000 in 1885 among a population of 1.9 million, shows impressive support for the mission enterprise. In comparison, one of the most influential Norwegian newspapers, *Morgenbladet*, had just over 2,000 subscribers in 1873.[22] Through books, pamphlets, mission magazines, photographs, films and expositions, not forgetting missionary tours throughout the country, Norwegian missionaries' representations of 'other' people and cultures, and also their 'self'-representations, reached a vast audience.[23]

Missions and gender

Women constituted a majority in the international Protestant missionary movement, both in the supportive home organisations and among the missionary staff. Women were also a central object of missionary ideology and practical work. A number of studies focusing on issues of women, gender and Christian missions have contributed decisively to the understanding of both missions and missionaries.[24] Several studies conducted on Norwegian missions have a gender perspective. Whereas my own master's thesis charted the growth of a female missionary movement in Norway,[25] Kristin Norseth examined the women's democratisation process in Norwegian missionary organisations,[26] Line Nyhagen Predelli scrutinised issues of gender, race and class in the NMS in both Norway and Madagascar,[27] and Inger Marie Okkenhaug has in several studies examined the life and works of individual female missionaries, both British and Norwegian.[28] Other works have dealt with Norwegian female missionaries and their work in South Africa. Hanna Mellemsether performed a cultural-historical analysis of the missionary life of Martha Sannes, who represented the Free East-African Mission among the Zulus from 1884 to 1901,[29] and Rannveig Naustvoll examined the lives of the missionary wives in the NMS in South Africa between 1900 and 1925.[30]

Although there is an extensive body of literature on women, gender and missions research has rarely focused on masculinity whether that of the missionaries themselves or of their missionary subjects. Recent publications discussing the relationship between men, masculinities and missions imply,[31] however, that in future we will see more research on this issue – and this book makes an initial contribution. It should furthermore be regarded as part of the field of gender studies in general and studies of men and masculinities in particular. Recent gender research understands men as gendered beings and as part of historically and culturally decided gender systems. A research tradition where men have been regarded as the standard, the norm or the neutral is challenged. Essentialist definitions of masculinity as stable and something with a natural, inherent and given meaning are questioned and discussed. Masculinities are seen as variable and changing across time (history) and space (culture), within societies, and through life courses and biographies. From this perspective masculinities, as well as femininities, are understood as socially constructed, produced and reproduced.[32] The term *masculinity* is in this book used as an analytical term for a better understanding of men's gendered lives and gendered social systems. It is further used to analyse institutional practices and cultural patterns. Although in everyday speech it is usual to use the term *masculinity* to describe men's biology, men's physical attributes, men's identity marks, men's psychological dispositions, and so forth, this is not how it is used here.

This book presents and discusses two theoretical approaches to the study of men and masculinities: the first rooted in the research tradition of social sciences, the second rooted in the humanities. The first approach emphasises the relational aspects of masculinities – namely, the relations among types of masculinities and relations between masculinity and its 'others'. The essential issue of masculinity and power is thus included. The second approach emphasises masculinity within the context of the male body which we can call the masculine identity. Alternatively, Todd W. Reeser's term 'masculine subjectivity' is used.[33] 'Subjectivity' is a less stable equivalent of 'identity' and suggests complications and a closer relation to cultural and psychological influences. As previously suggested, masculinity as a concept, ideology and practice is inherently many-faceted and unstable.

Masculinities and power

The theoretical perspectives of the Australian sociologist Raewyn Connell have strongly influenced international research on men and masculinities.[34] Connell rejects the single concept of masculinity. The interplay between gender, race and class suggests the need to recognise multiple masculinities: black as well as white, working class as well as middle class, heterosexual as well as homosexual, and so forth. Recognising a plurality of masculinities is only the first step, however. The next is to examine the relations among them, 'to unpack the milieu of class and race and scrutinize the gender relations operating within them'.[35] This analysis should be dynamic, and Connell introduces a model to analyse gender practices and the relations between masculinities in current Western gender order.[36] A key concept is that of *hegemonic masculinity*. In any era, one form of masculinity is culturally exalted above the others. Hegemonic masculinity, moreover, presupposes the male domination of women and dictates a patriarchal system. As far as a particular masculinity is hegemonic, it presupposes that others are subordinate. In Connell's definition, hegemonic masculinity is 'the configuration of gender practice which embodies the currently accepted answer to the problem of the legitimacy of patriarchy, which guarantees the dominant position of men and the subordination of women'.[37]

Connell's theory of masculinities has influenced gender studies across many academic fields, but it has also attracted criticism.[38] She is primarily criticised for taking for granted the premise that men profit from patriarchy. Her model does not allow for groups of men wanting and working for changes towards gender equality, a development actually taking place in the Nordic countries.[39] The theory is further criticised for its universality and generalisation. Cultural, geographical and historical studies on constructions of masculinity reveal a complex and diverse picture, but these variations are not taken sufficiently into consideration. Although it was meant to be a dynamic model, some have claimed that it readily becomes static when practised. Finally, the concept of hegemonic masculinity, which assumes that power relations and power structures are fundamental in any gender system, is too rational and functional, according to some critics. Men's personal emotional and bodily experiences are underestimated.

The Norwegian sociologist Øystein Gullvåg Holter, one of the critics of Connell's theory, asserts that gender research should be careful to distinguish between a patriarchal structure, which he defines as the general character of the oppression of women and the linked oppression of non-privileged men within a given society and culture, and a gender system, a partially independent and dynamic framework of meaning.[40] A gender system is not simply an echo of the structures of inequality or patriarchy. It develops its own dynamics, sometimes acting on its own, often in tense and conflict-filled relation to patriarchal structures. Holter's core idea is that we have to distinguish between patriarchal structure and gender system developments, and then look at the changing connections between them.

Yet following Holter in making such a distinction does not necessarily disregard the fundamental feature of Connell's concept of hegemonic masculinity, the combination of the plurality of masculinities and the hierarchy of masculinities.[41] This fundamental understanding of the concept is therefore a theoretical presupposition for my research on missionaries and masculinities. First, Connell's theory on hegemonic and subordinated masculinities is helpful in spotting the processes of male individuals and groups of men representing different ideas and ideals of masculinity and struggling for influence and positions within the NMS. Whether the 'gender system developments' of the NMS were characterised by 'patriarchal structures', to borrow Holter's terms, is a question that needs to be discussed further. Second, according to the original understanding of the concept of hegemonic masculinity, it does not necessarily need to refer to the most common pattern in the everyday lives of boys and men. Rather, hegemony works in part through the production of exemplars of masculinity, symbols which have authority despite the fact that most men and boys do not fully live up to them. As already discussed, the missionary movement in Norway was socially transformative and culturally influential. Like Norwegian polar explorers, the missionaries were the idols and heroes of thousands of Christian men. It is therefore of interest to trace dominant masculinity ideals in the NMS. Third, Connell's persistent emphasis on the importance of power in analyses of masculinities is in fact an adequate perspective. The group of Norwegian men scrutinised in this study left a relatively homogeneous societal and cultural milieu for a south-eastern African region of highly complex mixed-gender regimes and gender identities. According to South African historian Robert Morrell, Connell's ideas on rival masculinities and the gendered claim to power, not to mention the interplay among class, race and gender, have inspired recent South African gender research.[42] A range of masculinities can be identified and defined in nineteenth-century South African history. Morrell lists three main groups: white colonial masculinities (British, Boer, etc.), African rural masculinities and black (multi-ethnic) urban masculinities. White supremacy suggests that the white ruling-class masculinity was hegemonic.[43] The group of Norwegian missionary men who landed in southeastern African communities should be studied from this perspective.

Masculinities and subjectivity

Claes Ekenstam, a Swedish historian of ideas, is responsible for striking new approaches and theoretical perspectives on masculinity in Nordic milieus from the 1990s onwards.[44] Ekenstam prefers the term *manliness* (in Swedish *manlighet)* to masculinity, which he claims also reflects a tendency in Nordic research to focus more on men's lives in a broader sense (work, family, organisational life) and less on power relations between masculinities and femininities in a gender system. Ekenstam is critical of certain aspects of Connell's theoretical framework, first and foremost the tendency to reduce masculinity to a question of power. He credits the theory for breaking down static and monolithic ideas of manliness, but asserts that it does not give a complete understanding of the complex processes in the construction of masculinities.

Ekenstam introduces a model built on the dynamic between diverse masculinities while also including the relation between the ideas of manliness and unmanliness. Manliness and unmanliness are relational phenomena; just like manliness and womanliness, they constitute each other in a continuously ongoing process. Manliness and unmanliness must be understood in a plurality in which different forms of manliness and unmanliness have a dynamic, changeable relation to each other as well as to ideas of womanliness. Manliness should not be understood as an archetype, a cultural dominant ideal in a fixed period, but more like a changeable cluster of attributes and practices wherein certain elements can be replaced, strengthened or added depending on ideological or social influences.

Ekenstam refers to the Swedish historian Jonas Liliequist, who argues that the concept of unmanliness is relevant in men's history.[45] Ideas and concepts of unmanliness (the immoral man, the alcoholic, the feminine man, the homosexual, etc.) have had a great impact on the creation of masculine ideals and have been used to confirm certain dominant masculinities as well as marginalise those men who diverge from the standard. Moreover, the concept has methodological advantages. Although ideas of manliness in history can be diffuse, the ideas of unmanliness often seem to be well articulated, and by contrast they endow clarity and distinction on the concept of manliness. The rhetoric of unmanliness is helpful in pointing to the core of masculinity constructions. The concept of unmanliness further helps us to understand the processes of exclusion, which are often important in the constitution of masculinities. In the rivalry and competition between diverse forms of masculinities, describing the counterpart as a bearer of unmanliness seems to be an efficient strategy. The counterpart (i.e. the other) can also be accused of having less manliness than the self, thereby declassifying, degrading or minimising it. These phenomena of exclusion occur on an individual as well as a collective level.

Ekenstam's concept of unmanliness corresponds with the British historian Georg L. Mosse's thesis of 'countertypes'.[46] Modern Western masculinity was created as a bulwark against several stereotypes that lacked masculinity. According to Mosse, the countertypes were needed as contrasts (i.e. as others) to strengthen the normative ideal of manliness. In addition, the Swedish historian David Tjeder, in his examination of nineteenth-century middle-class masculinities, displays how ideals of manliness were defined in relation to opposites or countertypes. Tjeder's findings reveal a greater complexity in the construction of the countertypes than was previously assumed by Mosse. First, several concepts of manliness and unmanliness existed side by side throughout the century. Second, the category of age was of some importance, since ideals valid for youth differed from the ideals concerning mature men. Finally, a fear of demasculinisation, or stooping to unmanliness, worked as an internal guardian against improper behaviour in every single man. Not even the 'manly man' could be sure of his manliness; he continuously had to prove and be confirmed in his value as a man.[47]

When using the model of manliness–unmanliness, Ekenstam claims that it is possible to obtain a better understanding of what emotional and personal costs certain masculinity ideals have had for individuals and groups of men in history. According to Ekenstam, a tendency has existed in studies of masculinity to create distance from or even oppose what have been labelled as therapeutic or psychological approaches. It is often claimed that by viewing individuals and groups of men as 'victims' in one way or another one is in danger of underestimating the fact that men have a privileged and superior role in most societies compared with women. Ekenstam, on the other hand, advocates a psychological approach to the study of men and masculinities. He regrets that the priority of power relations in gender studies represents a continuation of a Western rational logic whereby feelings are contrasted with reason, masculine is contrasted with feminine and sociological perspectives are contrasted with psychological perspectives. This polar thinking reduces and minimises the complexity of the phenomena of masculinity constructions, creating a rigid dichotomy. The question of gender is not a simple but a rather complex issue, and Ekenstam argues that the model of manliness–unmanliness allows for a more concrete phenomenological and process-oriented understanding of masculinity than Connell's theory does.

With regard to my research, Ekenstam's theory of manliness–unmanliness provides a useful tool for disclosing the construction of a missionary masculinity within individual missionary men – to identify the 'masculine subjectivity', in Reeser's terminology.[48] One concern is to chart the practical consequences, social as well as psychological, which the construction of a particular missionary masculinity had for particular men and other groups of men and women in the Norwegian–Zulu encounter. The idea of countertypes can be traced in the NMS discourse. One countertype was the 'heathen', polygamist Zulu man, and another the secular, immoral, white settler. In addition, within the community of missionaries, ideas of unmanliness – of inappropriate missionary masculinity – were prevalent. Finally, fears of demasculinisation (i.e. stooping to unmanliness) could affect the individual missionary himself. The missionaries were religious men of high ethical standards, devoted to their Christianising task. We can assume that they lived in a constant fear of failing – or falling.[49] They could commit sin, fail to recruit new converts or lose their faith in God.

Christian masculinity and modernity

As previously stated, gendered studies of men in missions are still not very numerous. The same could be said about research on the relationship between religion and masculinity. In a recently published interdisciplinary handbook of gender research in Norway, issues like identity, family, labour, politics, health, violence, ethnicity, aesthetic, technology, media and sexuality are all discussed in relation to gender.[50] Surprisingly, though, the handbook has no chapter dealing with the relation between religion and gender. As religion has been and still is a dynamic force in human history, and as religious movements in Norway like elsewhere have been and remain culturally and socially influential, this is regrettable. The interdisciplinary research project 'Christian Manliness – a Paradox of Modernity', initiated in 2004 by the Swedish church historian Yvonne Maria Werner, has thus been of particular relevance to my research on a particular group of religious men. By focusing on Northern European conditions, Werner's project aims to illuminate the link between Christianity and the construction of manliness in the 1840–1940 period. Ten researchers have been engaged in the project, and collections of essays in both Swedish and English have been published.[51]

Werner claims that two main concepts are of special interest in any discussion of gender and religion in modern Western society: the feminisation of Christianity and the re-confessionalisation of Western societies.[52] The 'feminisation thesis' is based on studies on liberal-bourgeois milieus in the second half of the nineteenth century, during which time a belief in science and social progress gradually replaced Christianity as a normative guideline among Western men.[53] According to Belgian historian Tina van Osselaer, the feminisation thesis has a quantitative side, pointing to the preponderance of women in the religious field (e.g. mass attendance, female participation in charity and missionary activities, a rise in Catholic female religious orders). Yet it also has a qualitative side. Religion developed 'feminine' traits, and researchers have pointed to the 'softening', 'sentimentalisation' and 'emotionalisation' of its content. Furthermore, a 'discursive feminisation' of Christianity took place. Hand in hand with the growing division into the private and the public sphere so characteristic of liberal-bourgeois society, religion became 'domesticated' and associated with femininity, thereby assuming no or little relevance to men.[54]

Although gender historians find an increased religious commitment among women in this period, they tend to regard modern masculinity and religion as incompatible. From this perspective, Christian masculinity appears to be 'a paradox of modernity'. Werner's team of researchers nevertheless challenges historians' common assertion of religion as irrelevant to modern men by referring to other distinctive features of nineteenth-century Western society, namely the revivalist movements and the revitalisation of the confessional churches.[55] They argue that confessional identity continued to be an important factor in the construction of nineteenth-century European national identities, and that links exist between confessional or denominational culture and national identities. In sum, processes of secularisation as well as processes of religious revival, church mobilisation and confessionalisation were dominant cultural trends in this period. Werner's general hypothesis is that church mobilisation and confessionalisation can be interpreted as strategies used by the churches to counteract the secularisation of society and the feminisation of religion, further restoring and reinforcing male domination within the religious sphere. She worked out her theory in collaboration with the German church historian Olaf Blaschke who, in addition to claiming a 'second confessional era' in Europe from 1830 to 1960,[56] launched the theory of a religious re-masculinisation in the wake of the tendency to re-confessionalisation.[57] In his research on Protestant and Catholic churches in Germany, Blaschke finds processes of re-masculinisation to be latent in the last part of the nineteenth century, but more openly expressed in the early twentieth century. Werner and Blaschke are actually not alone in pointing to trends of 'masculinisation' within various confessional and national contexts, which all tried to make the religious experience and religious life more attractive to modern men.[58]

Sources

This section will present and discuss the sources used in this study of Norwegian missionaries and constructs of masculinities as well as the context in which the sources were created. In terms of reading and interpreting the sources, the focus has been on linguistic definitions and expressions or metaphors for men, male attributes or manliness/masculinity. The study has further explored explicitly or implicitly expressed thoughts, ideas and attitudes regarding gender systems and gender practices in the NMS. Finally, I have searched for narratives and anecdotes describing the male missionaries' lives as sons, brothers, husbands, fathers, friends, colleagues, farmers, employers and employees.

Mission magazines

Written accounts of life and work in the mission field were regarded as an integral part of a missionary's mission. As NMS was essentially a non-governmental, democratic and national organisation of local 'mission associations' (*Missionsforeninger*), the missionaries represented all those women and men who defined themselves as 'mission friends' (*Missionsvenner*). The mission friends felt ownership of the mission enterprise, in which they invested money, commitment and prayer. The representatives were obliged to report to their guardians. According to the 1867 revision of the missionary directory, a missionary who managed a mission station had to send quarterly reports to the NMS's Home Board (*Hovedbestyrelsen*) in Stavanger. All missionaries, whether they were station managers or not, had to write annual reports. The superintendent of the mission field was required to send reports every third month.

The Home Board's affairs were administered by a secretary (*Sekretær*), known as the General Secretary (*Generalsekretær*) from 1916, who received and archived the missionaries' reports. The secretary, who by 1870 was the only administrative staff member in Norway and in practice managed the organisation, was also the editor of the NMS magazine *Norwegian Missionary Tidings* (*Norsk Missionstidende*) (*NMT*). Missionary reports formed the basis of the *NMT*'s content. Lars Dahle, who became secretary and editor of the magazine in 1889, stated in his first editorial that the NMS's constitution 'demanded' that all mission friends should actively seek information about mission work.[59] The mission friends should be fully prepared to take part in discussion and decision-making at the NMS's annual district assemblies (*Kretsforsamlinger*) as well as the general assembly (*Generalforsamling*) arranged every third year. Furthermore, mission friends, apart from demonstrating empathy and interest, should direct their daily prayers towards the missionaries' 'struggle and fight' in the mission field. The *NMT* was the most important source of information. It was originally a monthly magazine but was published twice a month from 1878. The number of subscribers rose from about 2,000 in 1850 to 6,500 in 1870 and 10,000 in 1885 (in a population of 1.9 million).[60] In 1900 the *NMT* had 15,000 subscribers and around 20,000 in the 1920s; however, the number of subscribers declined to 13,600 in the 1930s, partly because of the economic depression. The number of subscribers subsequently rose again, reaching 26,000 by the NMS's centenary in 1942.[61]

When the missionaries wrote their reports, they were aware that extracts could be reprinted in the *NMT*. Thus, their texts had to be understood as tools for communicating with both the Home Board and a broader audience of mission friends. Ultimately, the mission leadership, represented by the secretary/editor of the *NMT*, selected the texts to be published. Karina Hestad Skeie has rightly criticised previous historical research on the NMS for not being fully aware of the fact that the material printed in the *NMT* was selected and edited for a particular target audience.[62] The reprinted reports and letters in the magazine are not necessarily representative of the incoming letters and reports more generally. Skeie systematically compared the archival letters and the printed versions in the *NMT* and found that editing practice extended to the selection of actual texts as well as the language (i.e. spelling/grammar) and content. She also found that the missionary report, or mission account (*Missionsberetning*), is merely one of several genres of written texts left by the missionaries. Actual events and issues were presented differently according to genre.

In my reading of the missionaries' texts, I employed Skeie's genre consciousness. Texts by missionaries printed in the *NMT* were until 1925 mostly edited extracts from the obligatory missionary reports. From 1925, the *NMT* was published as a weekly magazine in a larger size with more illustrations. In addition, the editorial style changed as the missionaries were now encouraged to write shorter narratives or thematic articles particularly suited to the new format.[63] This new genre of missionary texts, the short mission article or narrative, had for a long time been the standard in two other NMS publications – namely, the women's magazine and the youth's magazine, which were both closed down in 1925 and integrated into the *NMT*.[64] The magazine *Mission Readings for Women's Associations* (*Missionslæsning for Kvindeforeninger*) (*MKF*) was established in 1884 with the objective of providing female mission groups with information about NMS mission work. It was edited by Bolette Gjør, an influential leader of the female mission movement in Norway, and its content consisted largely of extracts from private letters or short narratives and articles written by female missionary workers.[65] The *MKF* was published from 1884 to 1925 as a monthly supplement to the *NMT*. Gjør aimed to present the missionaries' domestic life in more detail in order to complement the *NMT*, which mainly concentrated on the ministerial and business side of the mission project. NMS's illustrated magazine for youths, *Battle and Victory* (*Kamp og Seier*) (*KS*), was published monthly from 1900 to 1925. The establishment of a youth magazine reflected the growing organisational concern to recruit young people to supportive mission groups,[66] but it should also be understood as part of the international youth movement within Western missions.[67]

Mission literature

The mission organisations in Norway produced a remarkable volume of literature related to work in the mission fields. These books were quite popular, with thousands of copies being printed. Odd Kvaal Pedersen broadly defines *mission literature* as 'any written or printed testimonies of the Christian mission – from the times of the apostles until today'.[68] He provides a narrower definition as well, however, and characterises mission literature as literature that first develops themes and topics from work in the mission fields and then aims to stimulate and encourage the reader to donate funds and to further support the organisation. The social anthropologist Marianne Gullestad, in an analysis of published photographs in the NMS mission literature from North Cameroon, speaks of *mission propaganda*.[69] She observes that this concept was occasionally used by the missionaries themselves to describe their marketing efforts; furthermore, an element of propaganda is almost inherent in any general definitions of documentation and information. For the purposes of her study, she defines mission propaganda as 'the communication of experiences and information from the field arranged in ways that are meant to touch people emotionally and spiritually and propel them into supporting the mission'.[70] Lisbeth Mikaelsson, who has analysed Norwegian missionaries' autobiographies, asserts that the mission literature in Norway was primarily published by the mission organisations or by publishing houses specialising in religious and mission literature.[71] The mission literature was produced in a context with definite rules and norms of its purpose and content – norms that were shared by the majority of the readers. Mikaelsson claims that in religious publishing one finds 'a communicative relation between institutional co-players'.[72] When discussing the religious institution of literature, one has to recognise the readers as a specific and prominent group; indeed, tight bonds existed between authors, publishers, distributors and receivers.

In my study, the NMS's and other mission organisations' published mission literature from 1870 to 1930 serves as a source of information; I have thus collected and studied all available mission literature related to NMS's mission in South Africa. Some of the books were written by the missionaries themselves, whereas others were written by church historians or authors with a close connection with the NMS. As the mission literature consisted of several genres, they will be briefly presented herein. One should be aware, however, that a mixture of genres characterised the mission literature. One single text could borrow from the genres of travel, ethnography, history, autobiography, fiction or religious literature.

The missionary autobiographies and biographies constitute an important and popular part of the mission literature. The books in this genre are seldom labelled as 'autobiography' or 'biography', as terms like 'memoirs', 'diaries' or 'glimpses' are preferred. Mikaelsson listed as many as 228 published missionary autobiographies in Norway from 1843 to 1994, most of them dating from the post-war period from 1940 to 1960.[73] She identified three styles which were common in the genre of missionaries' autobiographies: accounts from the mission field, lifetime narratives and religious testimonies.

The missionary travel account is a secondary genre of mission literature, although elements from it were also incorporated into the missionaries' ordinary reports when they described geography, climate, people, society, culture and religion. NMS representatives other than the missionaries who visited the mission fields also published reports and travel accounts on returning home. The emerging field of ethnography and geography from the early nineteenth century onwards has been described as a 'culture of exploration'.[74] Hilde Nielssen claims that the ethnography of Norwegian missionaries 'should be seen in relation to the forms of knowledge production and consumption which formed a part of the cultural production of the colonial era'.[75]

A third genre of mission literature is the mission narrative or the mission novel. Although most of the mission literature was non-fiction, Johannes Einrem (NMS missionary in Madagascar from 1893 to 1933) published *Ravola* (1918), a Malagasy novel. Einrem was known for introducing this new genre (i.e. the mission novel) into mission literature and for revitalising it, making it especially popular among younger generations.[76] Einrem's huge literary production, as well as Racin Kolnes's (NMS missionary in China, 1925 to 1947) many children's mission novels,[77] reached a vast Norwegian audience. The mission narrative was a shorter version of the novel. Collections of narratives from the mission work, both non-fiction and fiction, were a popular genre.

A fourth genre of mission literature is the mission study book. The historical background and development of this genre illustrate the extensive transnational networks within Protestant missions. The American Student Volunteer Movement for Foreign Missions launched in 1893 provided outlines for mission study circles and encouraged the creation of mission libraries.[78] The mission study movement escalated after the ecumenical and international World's Missionary Committee of Christian Women, established in 1888, started to publish annual textbooks and arrange summer schools for mission circle leaders.[79] The Norwegian female mission leader Henny Dons participated in a mission summer school in Mundesley in Norfolk, England in 1909.[80] After returning home, she approached the administrators of several mission organisations, and the first Norwegian mission summer school was arranged at Framnes in 1911, with 500 youths, both males and females, participating.[81] The first mission study book in use in Norway was a translated version of the American student and mission leader John R. Mott's book entitled *The Decisive Hour of Christian Mission* (1910).[82] In the years to come, the NMS, among other mission organisations, published annual study books to be used in mission study groups and at the mission summer schools.

A fifth genre of mission literature can be labelled mission histories. As the NMS histories were initiated, financed and censored by the NMS's Home Board, they are central texts in the mission discourse. In 1854, after merely 12 years of existence, the Home Board engaged the young pastor Halfdan Sommerfelt to write a history of the first 20 years of the

Zulu mission.[83] In 1865, 5,000 copies of the book were published.[84] At the NMS's fiftieth anniversary meeting in 1892, a second NMS history was published. It was written by Lars Dahle and Madagascar missionary Simon Emanuel Jørgensen.[85] In 1915, the retired missionary Ole Stavem wrote a history of the NMS's 70 years of mission work among the Zulus.[86] To celebrate the centenary in 1942, a five-volume organisational history was published. Several authors were involved in the project, all of them theologians and all involved with the NMS either as former missionaries or as active mission supporters. Olaf Guttorm Myklebust, a missionary in South Africa during the 1930s, wrote the section on South Africa.[87] The theologian and church historian John Nome wrote two volumes on the history of the NMS in Norway.[88] Nome's books sparked a methodological debate concerning historical research on church and mission. Church historian Erling Danbolt criticised Nome's sociological perspective on church history, among other things,[89] and the secular historian Jens Aarup Seip described the books as 'outstandingly interesting' scientific works.[90] Yet Seip criticised Nome for adding an additional set of explanations to his historical analyses – namely, the spiritual work of God. Nome was further criticised for his 'conscious will to subjectivity' and his defence of every historian's right to be influenced by their own bias and prejudice. The intense debate in the 1940s introduced a phase in Norwegian research on mission which Jarle Simensen characterised as 'the theological paradigm'; it was marked by the establishment of missiological research institutions, journals and professorships.[91]

Unprinted sources

Tomas Sundnes Drønen's study of the encounter between NMS missionaries and the Dii ethnic group in Cameroon distinguishes between 'frontstage' and 'backstage' information in the NMS.[92] Frontstage information – namely, official printed material published and distributed by the NMS – was issued to the supporting group of mission friends as well as prospective groups of supporters. Backstage information included letters and reports written mainly to keep the NMS's secretary and Home Board in Stavanger up to date with events; such information was unofficial.

Only some of the missionary accounts/reports/letters were printed and made public through the mission magazines, but a complete collection of the obligatory reports is available in the mission archive. The missionaries also wrote to the Home Board on other occasions: correspondence included formal requests for private loans, permission to get engaged or married, and furlough. The letters could also be of a more private character, including accounts of personal or family matters, accounts of one's standpoint on certain issues, and expressions of personal frustrations or sorrows. Every missionary commissioned as a mission station manager was obliged to register sacraments like baptisms, Eucharists and weddings in a church ministerial book. The ministerial books were regarded as church property and were usually not sent to the NMS archive. In addition, the missionaries were encouraged to keep a station diary, and the mission archive has preserved several of these.

Another archival source of great relevance to the current research is the missionary conference minutes. An annual conference of all-male missionaries was, according to an NMS general assembly decision of 1876, 'the highest advisory, decisive and controlling authority' in the affairs concerning the mission field.[93] Decisions made at the annual conferences were either ratified or turned down by the Home Board in Stavanger. At the missionary conferences, all issues regarding the mission work – practical-administrative as well as ideological-theological – were thoroughly discussed and voted upon. As the minutes from the missionary conferences are extremely detailed, naming individuals and their contributions, they are indeed interesting sources. The reliability of the conference minutes naturally depends on the reporters, but they were usually very careful to note both agreements and disagreements among the missionaries. When an annual conference took place, both a chair and two secretaries were elected by and from the missionaries. When the negotiations were formally settled, the missionaries waited several days for the final copies of the minutes, which were passed by everyone before being passed to the Home Board. The minutes from the missionary conferences are handwritten, some of them consisting of several hundred pages. Starting in 1905, the NMS made printed copies of the minutes; however, they were still regarded as unofficial documents.

The superintendent's inspection reports after visits to the various mission station districts constitute further interesting source material. According to the 1876 arrangements for administration of the mission fields, the missionaries themselves had to elect a superintendent. It was the superintendent's task to regularly inspect the work carried out at the different mission stations. His reports were presented at the missionary conferences and finally sent home.

Outline

This book is divided into two main parts. 'The Construction of Norwegian Lutheran Missionary Masculinity' examines the relational aspects of masculinity and how a missionary masculinity was constructed in the homosocial community of men. Although the theoretical term *hegemonic masculinity* has been contested, my research nevertheless displays traits of a culturally influential and socially dominant missionary masculinity that can be labelled as hegemonic. Missionary masculinity was constructed in the relationship between types of masculinities and in relationship to its 'others', and the discussion begins with the processes of interaction among the missionary men in South Africa and those between the missionary men and the leading NMS men at home. Second, the discussion focuses on how the ideal missionary masculinity was represented in official and unofficial mission discourses. By focusing on five particular examples, these case studies reveal, third, the social and practical implications which hegemonic missionary masculinity could have both for the missionary men themselves and other groups of men and women participating in the Norwegian–Zulu encounter.

Chapter 2 considers whether the missionary Hans Paludan Smith Schreuder's resignation from the NMS in 1873 meant the breakthrough of the modern ideal of male 'self-making' in the Norwegian mission movement. In Chapter 3, the 1888 exclusion of Christian Oftebro from missionary service in the NMS is the point of departure for an investigation of ideas of appropriate and inappropriate missionary masculinity in mission discourse. Being a man and a Christian was a challenging task for missionary men, as notions of 'manliness' and 'Christian' could be seen as irreconcilable. In Chapter 4, the relationship between masculinity constructions and confession is investigated. The case of Karl Larsen Titlestad, who was called home from the mission field in 1891 by the NMS's Home Board because of his personal confessional doubts, serves as the starting-point for the discussion. Masculinity and race are discussed in Chapter 5, which focuses on the relationship between Norwegian missionaries and Zulu pastors. The events and processes preceding the ordination of the first Zulu pastor in the NMS in 1893, Baleni kaNdlela Mthimkhulu, as well as the dismissal of the very same pastor ten years later are analysed. Finally, Chapter 6 demonstrates how missionary masculinity was constructed in relation to missionary femininity. The Norwegian mission enterprise in nineteenth-century southeast Africa was never a clean-cut masculine project; quite the contrary. From the pioneer days onwards, both men and women participated in the mission enterprise; by the early twentieth century, women outnumbered men in the missionary community. The case of the missionary wife Marthe Nicoline Hirsch Borgen, who in 1886 was refused admission to the missionary conference as a professional, although she was the housekeeper at a boarding school for missionary children, is a telling illustration of the internal gender system of the NMS.

Masculinity is constructed relationally in the homosocial community of men, but how is it constructed as masculine identity or masculine subjectivity? How did hegemonic or other masculinity constructions influence the lives of individuals? What was the relation between the missionaries' professional subjectivity and their private lives? Rhonda A. Semple focuses a gendered lens on the private actions of male mission professionals in British Protestant missions for a better under-standing of 'the ways in which their personal lives were regulated by their professed faith, and how that activity shaped their professional identity and work'.[94] Semple asserts that the new scholarly interest in women's contribution to the modern mission movement has resulted in a critical view of the traditional strict gendering of the public/private divide, whereby men were publicly regarded as 'real missionaries' and women were part of the private sphere and thereby 'outside' official mission history. Light shed on the private sphere of mission revealed the unsung work of missionary wives and daughters; in addition, it was demonstrated that women were actors in the public sphere much more often than expected. But what about the importance of the Christian husband and father, Semple asks? The male missionaries balanced the professional and the private, a juggling act which Semple claims has not yet been properly examined by either historians of church and mission or social historians of gender and imperialism.[95]

A second part of this book, 'Missionary Masculinity between Professionalism and Privacy', examines how missionary masculinity was constructed in the lives of individual men. It discusses the relation between male missionaries' professional and public life as employees in the NMS and their domestic and private lives as sons, husbands, fathers, brothers, friends and civil citizens. Methodologically, a biograph-ical study of three male missionaries is carried out to highlight three different generations – namely, a father, a son and a grandson. Karl Larsen Titlestad (1832–1924), Lars Martin Titlestad (1867–1941) and Karl Michael Titlestad (1898–1930) all served as NMS missionaries in South Africa. The biographical method allows for an in-depth description of how the private lives of the Titlestad men influenced their professional subjectivity and, similarly, how their private lives were affected by their professional work. A biographical family history makes it possible to register long-term changes and continuities in missionary masculinity in the period under investigation. According to John Tosh, masculinity is constructed in three areas of a man's life: at work, at home and in all-male associations.[96] This division is followed in the design of the second part of the book. Chapter 7 discusses the interaction between the personal and professional in missionary masculinity subjectivities. Chapter 8 examines the missionaries as family men. Finally, Chapter 9 discusses the missionaries as male civil citizens in the context of southeast African societies.

Part I

The Construction of Norwegian Lutheran Missionary Masculinity

2
Missionary Self-Making

Introduction

In the summer of 1866, a remarkable happening took place in the Norwegian town of Bergen. Hans Paludan Smith Schreuder, the NMS's first missionary to the Zulus, was consecrated as bishop of what was defined as 'The Church of Norway's Mission Field'. The Church of Norway's Bishop of Bergen conducted the ceremony; approximately 30 priests assisted him.[1] It was the first time since the establishment of the NMS in 1842 that one of the society's missionaries had visited the homeland, and everywhere Schreuder and his wife, Jakobine Emilie Adelheid Løwenthal, went, people gathered in their hundreds and thousands.[2] The prime minister invited the couple to a dinner party, and the King of the Union of Sweden–Norway donated presents. National and regional newspapers covered their three-month tour, and poets wrote romantic epics hailing Schreuder as a great Norwegian pioneer. The NMS subsequently published a booklet recounting the ordination service that contained a selection of sermons and lectures given by Bishop Schreuder during his six-month stay in Norway.[3]

In 1873, Bishop Schreuder resigned from the NMS, an act that marked the end of seven years of episcopal rule in the organisation. A system granting the 'mission bishop' the highest authority in the mission field was replaced by a system distributing power partly to the Home Board of elected members in Stavanger and partly to the missionary conference in the field. According to the new system of administration, finally settled by the NMS's general assembly of 1876, the annual conference of missionaries was 'the highest advisory, decisive and controlling authority' in affairs concerning the mission field. Decisions made at the missionary conference could, however, be ratified or turned down by the Home Board. Church historian John Nome characterised this shift of regime in the NMS as a change from a 'clerical regime' to 'church democracy'.[4] Nome interpreted the case of Schreuder's resignation as a final breakthrough of democratic principles in Norwegian mission. In the nineteenth-century NMS, however, democracy was still the privilege exclusively of men. Moreover, it was the privilege of Norwegian men, as South African and Malagasy church personnel (evangelists, teachers and pastors) were excluded from the mission's decision-making bodies. In addition, not even all Norwegian male missionaries possessed the privilege of democratic rights. It was primarily the male theologians (or missionary pastors), who participated in the missionary conferences with the right to speak and vote. Skilled artisans, employed by the NMS and assigned to construct the mission buildings, were described as assistant missionaries but were not regarded as members of the missionary conference. In other words, the rule of the bishop was merely replaced by the rule of another group of clergymen.

This chapter explores whether the case of Schreuder's resignation can also be understood as the breakthrough of a certain masculine ideal within the Norwegian mission movement. Since the establishment of the NMS in 1842, men representing various social backgrounds and advocating diverse religious and cultural ideas and ideals had been struggling for influence and positions within the fast-growing organisation. The outcome of the Schreuder case was that a certain kind of masculinity became more central in the NMS and, likewise, that another lost its authority, or hegemony, in terms of Connell's theory of hegemonic masculinity. Michael S. Kimmel's concept of the self-made man, which he claims was an influential masculine ideal in industrialised societies from the first decades of the nineteenth century, is central to the current discussion. The term *self-made man* is an American neologism, first used in the 1830s. The economic boom of the post-revolutionary new country's first decades created a range of possibilities for American men. According to Kimmel, 'men were free to create their own destinies, to find their own ways, to rise as high as they could'.[5] As the emerging capitalist market freed individual men, it simultaneously destabilised them, however. The self-made man was born anxious and insecure, uncoupled from the stable anchors of landownership or workplace autonomy. Now manhood had to be proved. The self-made man was ambitious and anxious at the same time, both 'creatively resourceful and chronically restless'.[6]

Erik Sidenvall, in a study of non-educated, lower-class Swedish missionaries to China, asks in what ways missionary work and male self-making coincided during the late nineteenth century. Could religious activism

Figure 2.1   The consecration in 1866 of Hans Paludan Smith Schreuder (1817–82) as bishop of 'The Church of Norway's Mission Fields' in South Africa and Madagascar. Schreuder is number two from the right in first row

Source: Mission Archives, School of Mission and Theology, Stavanger.

Photographer: Meyer and Nicolaysen.

be understood as a road to self-making? Sidenvall concludes that the theme of social advance was contested among the missionaries. It first and foremost emphasised the middle-class concept of the 'Christian home', ensuring that social advance and self-reform became integral parts of the missionaries' lives. Another self-making effort, according to Sidenvall, was the yearning to acquire a 'priestly' identity; paradoxically, this took place 'within a religious environment that championed the spiritually endowed lay preacher'.[7] Sidenvall asserts that the adoption of middle-class patterns, already sanctioned and prescribed in mainstream Protestant missionary discourse, harmonised with the ambitions of missionaries from humble backgrounds.

Following Sidenvall, this chapter examines the issue of missionary self-making, starting with an account of Schreuder's breach with the NMS in 1873, followed by a demonstration of two traditional interpretations of the Schreuder case among mission historians. The dominant representations of Schreuder in the NMS discourse, and those of his younger opponent Lars Dahle, helped to create images of ideal missionaries as men who, despite their humble background, succeeded in mission work. This chapter further presents examples of how ideas of social advancement were present in the self-understanding of male NMS missionaries. Finally, it suggests that the concept of religious and secular male self-making was central in Western Protestant missionary strategies towards 'heathen' men in south-eastern Africa in the mid-nineteenth century.

The case of Hans Paludan Smith Schreuder

Hans P. S. Schreuder was born into a family of state officers. His father held a position as procurator.[8] Many of his forefathers had served as pastors in the official Evangelical-Lutheran Church of the pre-1814 regime of Danish supremacy. The young Schreuder decided to take up theological studies at the university in the Norwegian capital Christiania (renamed Oslo in 1925). In 1841 he passed his theological exams with excellent results. To the surprise of his teachers, mentors and peers, who imagined he would have a great career in the state church, in 1842 he published a pamphlet in which he announced that God had 'driven' him to become a missionary among the 'heathens'.[9] Moreover, in the pamphlet he reminded fellow Christians of their duty to bring the Christian religion to 'pagan' regions of the world. Schreuder hoped that the Church of Norway would integrate foreign mission work in its strategy and consequently consecrate him and regard him as its representative abroad.

In Christiania, a group of prominent pastors formed a committee to raise funds for Schreuder's mission. The established Norwegian church during this period was not interested in foreign mission, however. The extensive interest in overseas mission work emerging in Norway from 1820 to 1840 was above all a product of the voluntary commitment of individuals and groups rich in initiative and receptive to new impulses.[10] In certain revival and lay movements, like the Moravians and the Haugians,[11] groups of women and men developed an interest in Protestant European mission enterprises. Inspired by international mission magazines, they started to form local mission associations in the 1820s and 1830s, and in 1842 the national organisation of the NMS was established in Stavanger, a small town on the south-west coast. The mission society was a private enterprise; its formal and economic foundation rested on small groups of volunteers and its actual management was overseen by a general assembly and a board consisting of elected members.

Thus, in 1842, two different initiatives were taken: one in Christiania supporting the theologian candidate Schreuder, and the other supporting a private mission society in Stavanger. The former initiative stemmed from a group consisting primarily of clerics serving in the capital whereas the latter had its basic support among middle-class businessmen, craftsmen and farmers involved in the Moravian and Haugian lay movements who lived in the coastal areas of the south-west. The board of the NMS immediately made efforts to unite the scattered forces, approaching Schreuder and his supporters to this end. Negotiations between the two parties were arranged during the mission society's first general assembly in 1843 and eventually resulted in NMS's support of Schreuder's mission. Agreement implied, however, that if the NMS became 'a nationwide, general mission society' in the sense of a close connection with and acceptance by the official church and national public approval, Schreuder's mission would amalgamate with the NMS. In subsequent years it emerged that the popular and fast-growing NMS was far more capable than the committee in Christiania of supporting Schreuder's mission financially. Schreuder's original supporting committee eventually resigned in 1846.

John Nome defines the first decades of the NMS history as the 'time of a clergy-church regime'.[12] He finds that clerics were strongly represented in the Home Board and dominated the discussions at regional and national mission conferences. He suggests that the alliance between groups of men representing the upper-class high-church clergy and the middle-class lay movement in the cause of mission was a success. The clergy element contributed the required authorisation and the industrious lay movement provided a broad social network which together gave the new mission organisation a powerful lift-off. The ordination of Schreuder to the position of mission bishop in 1866, a happening that in fact was celebrated by the whole nation, symbolised the alliance between the official church and the lay movement.

In 1873, Schreuder resigned from the NMS. There had been a number of disputes between Schreuder and the Home Board in the 1850s and 1860s, but the final decisive conflict was a discussion on the status of the local missionary conference.[13] Lars Dahle, a young, brilliant and ambitious missionary serving in the NMS's new mission field in Madagascar, envisioned more power for the missionary conference. Frustrated at being under episcopal authority, he sent a proposal of statutory reform directly to the Home Board in Stavanger in 1872, bypassing his bishop in Zululand. The Home Board reacted favourably to Dahle's proposal, consequently provoking open conflict with Schreuder. Schreuder claimed that a local missionary conference with the right to make majority decisions by vote was irreconcilable with what he regarded as proper church order. The authority granted him as bishop was deprived of power, he claimed, and his position would be reduced to 'an executive agent of a majority government in our mission society'. He hinted at parallels with the political struggle for parliamentary government in contemporary Norway, admitting that he strongly disliked the 'self-willed, levelling spirit of the age' and the 'eager-to-rule spirit of democracy'.[14]

At the 1873 general assembly of the NMS, the Schreuder case and the 'conference question' were on everyone's minds. As a result, 384 delegates representing mission associations from all over the country discussed a response to Schreuder's letter of resignation, voting on a number of proposals. The assembly's final resolution was an acceptance of the Bishop's resignation. As Bishop Schreuder had gained a huge following in Norway, public reactions to the final decision in the case were mostly negative, and a contribution to the influential newspaper *Morgenbladet* attracted more than 60 responses.[15] To prevent further speculations about what actually happened in the Schreuder case, the NMS Home Board published some of its correspondence with Schreuder from the Bishop's ordination ceremony in 1866 to the final breach in 1873.[16] Although Schreuder resigned from the NMS, he did not resign from missionary work in Zululand. He retained the mission station at Entumeni and continued to operate a separate mission referred to as 'The Church of Norway's Mission by Schreuder'. After Schreuder's death in 1882, his work was carried on by the pastors and brothers Nils and Hans Astrup. Schreuder's mission developed a close relationship with Norwegian congregations in the United States and was finally taken over by the American Lutheran Mission in 1927.

The self-making spirit of the Norwegian mission movement

For the first three decades of the history of the NMS, Schreuder was more or less identified with the Norwegian mission enterprise, and his pioneering work among the Zulus was public knowledge. Schreuder was celebrated as the first Western missionary to establish a permanent Christian mission in Zululand, permission for which he received from King Mpande ka Senzangakhona at the end of 1850. He was seen as the one who 'probed into the core of the proud Zulu aristocracy' and 'opened' up the 'heathen' Zulu kingdom to Christian influence.[17] A statue of Schreuder was erected on his grave at Untunjambili in Zululand, but he never had a monument in Norway. Meanwhile, a statue of Lars Dahle was erected at the campus of the NMS's mission school in Stavanger. Olav Guttorm Myklebust, previously a missionary to South Africa and a scholar in theology, questioned this in his biography on Schreuder, which was published in 1986.[18] Myklebust claimed that, while writing the section on South Africa in the NMS's official centenary organisational history in 1942, he was put under strict censorship by the NMS management.[19] His positive evaluation of Schreuder's life and work was disliked,[20] and he was asked to modify it. During the rest of his time as Professor in the Science of Mission at the Norwegian School of Theology (Det teologiske Menighetsfakultet), Myklebust spent considerable time researching Schreuder and collected an abundance of related source material. After his retirement, he published two monographs that aimed both to present Schreuder's theology and to give a deeper understanding of his personality in an attempt to restore Schreuder's reputation in the history of Norwegian mission.[21]

Mission historians in Norway have maintained contradictory views on Schreuder and his breach with the NMS. The dominant view within the NMS, which also became the organisation's official version, was that of Schreuder as a 'difficult personality' representing an orthodox theology of church and mission irreconcilable with the theology of the NMS. This version was not least nurtured by Lars Dahle, who had challenged the episcopal system in 1872; in 1877, he was elected as the first superintendent of the NMS's mission field in Madagascar.[22] Dahle was subsequently appointed as the NMS's general secretary, a position he held from 1889 until 1920. Otto Emil Birkeli, missionary in Madagascar (1903–19) and later Professor in Church History at the NMS's mission school (1923–44), strengthened the impression of a high church-oriented, orthodox Schreuder in both his teaching and his writing.[23] The above-mentioned John Nome, editor and co-author of the NMS's centenary history, wrote in the tradition of Dahle and Birkli when explaining the breach in 1873 as being partly caused by ideological contradictions between the mission's 'democratic church view' and Schreuder's 'episcopal church view'. Terms like 'high churchly', 'monarchic', 'aristocratic' and 'strictly orthodox' were commonly used to describe Schreuder's theology. Nome furthermore claims that Schreuder's difficult personality, his uncontrolled temper, his obstinacy and his arrogant, polemical writing style could also explain why the NMS eventually chose to separate from its Bishop.[24]

Historians with no connection to the NMS sanctioned the organisation's official view of Schreuder. Oscar Handeland, in a popular history of the Norwegian mission movement, described Schreuder as follows: 'Look at his picture. The nose is square, his face is square, the whole man is square! ... He was edged, stiff and stubborn.'[25] Jens Aarup Seip shared an obsession with Schreuder's physical appearance: 'He had a strange, dogged nature (you should see his portrait!), with a tendency to unlimited sacrifices, but also to unlimited power.'[26]

Another trend in historians' descriptions of Schreuder tended towards hagiography.[27] Myklebust's works definitely follow this tradition. His explanations of the breach between Schreuder and the NMS are nuanced, however.[28] According to Myklebust, the theological disagreement between Schreuder and the members of the Home Board was less profound than previously presumed.[29] According to Myklebust, to explain the conflict one also has to look at the personal clashes between Schreuder and Dahle, on the one hand, and between Schreuder and the secretary Christian Dons, on the other. Furthermore, the conflict should be interpreted from the perspective of power, as the central management in Stavanger and the regional leadership in the mission field were competing for influence and authority. According to Myklebust, however, the most important explanations are to be found in general ideological and political trends in mid-nineteenth-century Norway. Ideas of liberalism, individualism and democracy were gaining growing support and influence on political as well as church life. Although Schreuder rejected modern ideas of democracy, the NMS was essentially a democratic organisation. This view is supported by the historian Roald Berg, who claims that 'the fall of Schreuder' in 1873 illustrated how deeply the Norwegian mission movement was attached to political and ideological trends of modernity. Berg claims that the fall of Schreuder was, moreover, one of several premonitions about the 1884 fall of 'the regime of the state officials' (*Embetsmannsstaten*) in Norwegian politics.[30]

There are obviously reasons to believe that the post-1873 regime of the NMS was influenced by contemporary ideas of liberalism, individualism and democracy.[31] Thus, from a gender perspective, it is interesting to examine how the modern concept of male self-making – in this chapter called 'the spirit of self-making' – influenced the construction of a Norwegian missionary masculinity. A spirit of self-making in the Norwegian mission movement is also evident from religious, cultural and sociological angles. First, an element of self-making is traceable in the revivalist lay movements of the time, particularly in the Hauge movement that emphasised the importance of individual conversion, individual spiritual development and every Christian's (clergy as well as laypeople) opportunity and right to engage in religious or temporal enterprises.[32] Whereas Schreuder's forefathers were ministers in the official Danish Evangelical-Lutheran Church, Dahle was a third-generation Haugian. From the very beginning of the NMS's co-operation with Schreuder, leaders of the lay movement questioned Schreuder's spirituality. There was no doubt about his excellent theological qualifications, but was he a true Christian? At the NMS's general assembly in 1855, the personal conflict between Schreuder and Lars Larsen, a missionary with a Moravian background educated at the mission school in Stavanger, was officially discussed. A local mission group from a rural district commented on the conflict as follows: 'We know Larsen to be a spiritual man, but as regards Schreuder, we don't know him ... '[33] During the discussion of the Schreuder case in 1873, the baker Bottelsen stated that the divine power who had once called Schreuder would surely find his successor and that the mission was not at all dependent on its Bishop.[34] This self-confident attitude in religious matters, even among non-educated farmers and craftsmen, was part of the Haugian heritage.

Second, the spirit of self-making in the Norwegian mission movement was related to nationalistic ideas of cultural formation and education. The upper class – the state officials – based its political power on university qualifications. Throughout the nineteenth century, a 'Norwegian-rooted' ideal of formation emerged in opposition to dominating traditional but 'foreign' (European) cultural ideals. The growing nationalistic opposition to the cultural influence of Christiania's monopolistic political and educational institutions was furthermore rooted in old regional diversities between western and eastern Norway. The 1843 establishment of a private mission school in Stavanger, on the west coast of Norway, is interesting seen from this angle. The NMS frequently discussed whether the organisation should run a private theological seminary or whether its missionary candidates should be recruited from university-educated theologians.[35] The Home Board received a letter from a mission association in the rural village of Valle expressing the desire for 'a Mission School in our own country, not abroad, but preferably in Stavanger'.[36] In addition to NMS's private missionary preparatory school in the 'periphery' of Stavanger, regional teachers' seminars were established in several rural areas from the early 1830s. Although the aim was to qualify talented farmers' sons to teach in state primary schools, these institutions simultaneously became think-tanks for nationalistic cultural ideals of education and formation. Educated schoolteachers, recruited from and identifying with the rural population, appeared as the new cultural elite, reducing the university-educated pastors' authority and influence in many communities.[37] Teachers were often elected as chairs of local mission associations, and as the numbers of their delegates to the NMS's general assemblies increased remarkably during the 1850s, so the number of pastors decreased.[38] Lars Dahle was in fact a student at the teachers' seminar in Klæbo from 1861 until 1863, entering the mission school in Stavanger in 1864.

Third, the spirit of self-making in the NMS was, as previously discussed, closely related to upcoming middle-class views and values. Scholars in the field of studies on men and masculinities consider the process of modernisation and industrialisation in nineteenth-century America and Europe as a period in which new forms of masculinities were constructed. The early nineteenth century was an era in which merit began to replace birth and class began to replace estate as the foundation of society. Old aristocratic models of masculinity were questioned when representatives from the middle classes proclaimed that every 'real man' had to earn his own fortune, create his own position and deserve his own reputation in society. Upcoming craftsmen, traders, landowning farmers and schoolteachers constituted the social basis of the nineteenth-century mission movement in Norway.[39] With a few exceptions, including Schreuder, the first generations of missionaries were also recruited from the same social classes.[40] The middle-class men in the NMS were sceptical of Schreuder for several reasons. His 'strange' German name, his social background as the son of a state official, his cultured and educated manner and his arrogant self-consciousness all confirmed that he was not 'one of them'.[41] Schreuder represented a dying regime, a regime that based its hegemony on inherited titles and property. The 'self-made' men in the new upcoming mission enterprise no longer regarded it as a drawback to lose a bishop who showed no respect for their egalitarian, democratic, Norwegian-rooted organisation. By contrast, Lars Dahle was 'one of them'.

In 1873, NMS representatives shared a common understanding of Schreuder's reassignment as inevitable. No one really tried to stop him from leaving the organisation. Still, the gap left after his resignation was formidable, and the mission supporters at the grass-roots level missed him.[42] Nome concludes his historical account of the Schreuder case by acknowledging that, ultimately, 'the great thing about Schreuder was that he had character'.[43] Even Dahle in his memoirs suggested that 'The Man' might be a suitable term to describe Schreuder.[44] Their admiration and respect for Schreuder, and simultaneous rejection of his 'theology' and derision of his personality, reveal an ambiguity in the NMS men's perceptions of the pioneer missionary. In addition to the narratives of the 'aristocratic', 'monarchic', 'stubborn' and 'difficult' Schreuder, other alternative narratives continued to circulate in the NMS discourse, something that Myklebust's 1942 history on the NMS's mission work in South Africa exemplified.[45] According to Myklebust, Schreuder was 'born to be a chief', he was 'a man of character', 'a man of willpower' and his life was 'an epic of energy'. In terms of physical appearance, he was a giant; he even had enough muscular strength to conquer an attacking leopard.[46] He was also, however, a man of faith. His faith was the 'secret' and the 'stronghold' of his life, which may also explain his 'perpendicular obedience to God's calling'. As Myklebust opined, he was a Norwegian version of the legendary missionary David Livingstone, who unfortunately was born into a minor nation that was too 'small and narrow minded' to understand his greatness. In 1942 Myklebust represented Schreuder as an exceptionally strong and independent man, but also as a man of faith, obedient to and dependent on his God. Schreuder was characterised as an amalgamation of human abilities/ambitions and subordination to a divine cause, of 'hardness' in human matters and 'softness' in spiritual matters. In this regard, he continued to be a masculine hero in the Norwegian mission movement even after his break with the NMS.

Subjective missionary self-making

What were the Zulu missionaries' view of the breach between Bishop Schreuder and the NMS? Ole Stavem, a new missionary in 1873, said several years later that they were left 'like a ship without its captain'.[47] In retrospect, Stavem regarded the breach as a crisis with disastrous consequences as the remaining missionaries were few and lacked experience in management.[48] It seems likely that the missionaries deplored Schreuder's withdrawal from the NMS. In February 1873, ten of them sent a letter of support to 'his highness Mr. Bishop Schreuder', in which they expressed their gratitude for his work and their regrets about his announced resignation.[49] Yet once the separation became a reality, none of Schreuder's colleagues followed him. They preferred loyalty to the NMS to service in the Church of Norway's Mission with Schreuder. Among mission supporters in Norway, rumours had circulated for years that Schreuder suppressed the missionaries and treated them like 'children'. It was claimed that the missionaries in Zululand lacked independence, influence and authority.[50] Minutes from the missionary conference in July 1872 suggest that the rumours might have been true. Lars Dahle's proposal of statutory reform for the NMS missionary conference was discussed. As previously mentioned Dahle challenged the episcopal rule and suggested more power for a missionary conference governed by democratic principles. The discussion at the conference was quite tense. Schreuder was alone in his rejection of the proposal. The rest of the missionaries argued that they had for years 'longed' for 'real conferences', like the mission conferences back in Norway, where important issues were 'freely' discussed in plenary and then voted on. They supported reforms that would grant them influence and put an end to their days as 'schoolboys'. In response to Schreuder's accusation that Dahle's proposal was influenced by 'the spirit of time', the missionaries answered that it was only 'by freedom a man could reach maturity'.[51] Indirectly, they hinted at years of suppression under Schreuder's patriarchal rule – years in which they had been treated as boys, not men.[52]

Most of the NMS missionaries were men from humble backgrounds. Ole Stavem, a missionary in South Africa from 1869 to 1912, recalled the group of young men who first met at the mission school in 1864: 'We were mostly young craftsmen and farmer's boys with little previous education.'[53] According to Vidar Gynnild's study of nineteenth-century NMS missionaries, 70 per cent came from an agricultural background, but they were seldom the oldest son with allodial rights to inherit the family farm. Most of the applicants lacked formal secondary education, although 40 per cent had acquired some additional education (one year of middle school courses, teacher training, etc.). The great majority of the applicants were already 'on the move', both geographically and socially, and were swept up in the comprehensive demographic and socio-economic changes of the time.[54]

The NMS's mission school was the first private institution in Norway to offer higher professional education without requiring upper secondary examinations.[55] Until 1874, the school had two courses: one for missionary pastors and one for assistant missionaries. Starting in 1864, missionary candidates who decided to pursue pastoral service received ordination according to the rituals of the Evangelical-Lutheran Church of Norway. Their service was restricted to the mission field, however, and they were not permitted to serve in the Norwegian state church. Nevertheless, these men succeeded, as they had come from humble origins and ended as respected missionaries. The farmer's son Ole Stavem, who was a printer's apprentice before entering the mission school, is but one example of those who both geographically and in terms of class made considerable strides. In 1911, he was appointed Knight of the Order of St Olav for his long-term service as missionary pastor in the Zulu mission and for 19 years of management of the same mission (1887–1901, 1907–12).[56]

Figure 2.2 Lars Dahle (1843–1925), who challenged the episcopal rule in the NMS, served as a missionary in Madagascar, 1870–88. He was in 1889 appointed as the general secretary of the NMS, a position he held until 1920

Source: Mission Archives, School of Mission and Theology, Stavanger.

Photographer: Carl Kørner.

Contemporary commentators ridiculed the self-making spirit of the mission movement and the fact that most of the missionary candidates were poor farmer's sons, with no real prospects. Novelist Alexander Kielland claimed that the mission was a shortcut to 'worldly comfort' and priestly status.[57] Although the NMS's management, represented by Lars Dahle, in this case denied the charge of materialistic motivation, the theme of social self-making was in fact present in missionaries' self-representations. Hans Christian Martin Gottfred Leisegang migrated from Schleswig-Holstein to Norway as a poor young carpenter. He was accepted as a student at the mission school in 1859 and ordained a missionary pastor in 1864. After 46 years of service in the Zulu mission, he delivered a farewell speech at the missionary conference in 1911. He made it clear to his colleagues that it was through missionary activity that he had moved from the status of being 'nobody' to being 'somebody': 'I came to Norway in my youth as a stranger. I was nobody. I became a Christian in Norway, and by the help of God I became a missionary.…The dreams of my youth have been realised out here.'[58] Perhaps Lars Dahle himself is the most outstanding example of a man of humble background who became a pastor, researcher, Bible translator and national mission leader.[59] According to Lisbeth Mikaelsson's analyses of his monumental autobiography, Dahle appears as a modern, rational actor. His self-presentation is of a man driven by a thirst for knowledge with a sense of duty and great ambition. Dahle was a man who grabbed the opportunities that the democratic organisation of the NMS offered him, but Mikaelsson claims that his driving force was still an inner, individual will.[60]

Erik Sidenvall found that, for contemporary advocates, the ideal of male self-making was more than a materialistic ideology of individual or financial success. It was also a question of independence and respectability.[61] Sidenvall refers to the American historian E. Anthony Rotundo's remarks regarding the nineteenth century as a time of self-making both in the economic sense and 'in the sense of shaping the desires and talents of the inner self to fit the proper moral and social forms'.[62] The financial rewards offered to the Swedish missionaries in Sidenvall's study were limited, but evangelical religiosity still had much to offer men of humble origin 'who "made it" in the religious world that the evangelical world knew, and held in highest esteem'.[63] The Swedish missionaries recruited by the New York-based Christian and Missionary Alliance were sent to the mission field without any educational preparation whereas the NMS offered four to five years of professional education. Still, the social background of the Swedish men in Sidenvall's study and the

Norwegian missionaries in my study are similar, as is their consciousness about how – through a missionary career – they experienced a social upgrade. These anonymous, non-educated young men were recruited from the lower classes to become respectable theologians and pastors, serving as heroic missionaries overseas.

Self-making as a mission strategy and theory

When Schreuder and his assistant E. E. Thommesen[64] arrived in Durban in Natal in 1844, they were welcomed by the British Methodist missionary James Archbell, who immediately introduced them to Congregationalist and Presbyterian missionaries representing the American Board of Commissioners for Foreign Missions.[65] For the next 18 months, the two Norwegians lived at the American mission station Umlazi in Natal while they studied the Zulu language and local customs. The American Zulu Mission, as it was later called, started a mission in Natal in 1835. The missionaries arrived with a grand, optimistic plan for quick conversion of the African people to Christianity and Western culture. The strategy was based on an utterly negative view of African culture combined with an optimistic belief in the capacity of Africans to progress along Western lines, in both religious and temporal terms. In addition, the Wesleyan Methodist Missionary Society, in Natal since 1841, was over-optimistic in its belief in the capabilities of African evangelists as itinerant preachers in their congregations, following in the tradition of Methodist lay activity. Pioneering American Congregationalist/Presbyterian and British Wesleyan missionaries preached a muscular, agrarian faith, where work and education were emphasised alongside worship.[66] The mission stations became enclaves in which an emerging middle class of African landowners – the *amakholwa* (believers) – found agricultural and service opportunities within the colonial, capitalist economy.[67]

The nineteenth-century Western idea of male self-making can be recognised in the Anglo-American mission strategies regarding indigenous men. The male Zulu converts were often detribalised men who had fled to the mission station from suppressed patriarchal societies. After their conversion to a 'new life' as Christians, they embraced many of the evangelical tenets of self-improvement and self-help advocated by the missionaries. It would be interesting to ascertain if the idea of male self-making can be traced to mid-nineteenth-century Anglo-American mission theories of 'three-self'. The three-self theory was systematised in the United States by Rufus Anderson, Secretary of the American Board of Commissioners for Foreign Mission, and in Great Britain by Henry

Venn, Secretary of the Church Missionary Society.[68] The goal of the missions was to establish native churches characterised by self-support, self-government and self-propagation or self-extension. Church historians and mission theologians regard the three-self theory as the most important church-centred corpus of Anglo-American mission thought in the nineteenth century.[69] Mission historian Dana Robert claims that the idea of 'the Christian Home' was another cornerstone of Western mission thought and practice.[70] In addition to establishing churches, nineteenth-century missionary theorists were concerned with 'civilisation', the idea that Christian conversion would lead to improvement of the totality of people's lives, including social structures, political systems and gender relations. Christian homemaking was part of a gendered mission strategy, and female missionaries in particular were responsible for converting mothers and transforming indigenous domestic life. Indigenous women were to be educated and their social status improved.

Chapter 5 will further discuss the Norwegian mission's gendered mission strategies in Zululand. Meanwhile, the question here is whether the widespread three-self theory can be understood as more than merely a theory of institutional church independence. If we look at the theory through a gendered lens who are actually the 'selves'? After all, were not the indigenous churches supposed to be governed by men – indigenous, converted men who were expected to uphold the Western masculine ideals of self-support, self-government and self-extension? Both the mission theory of (female) Christian homemaking and the mission theory of (male) Church self-making can in a sense be interpreted as gendered mission theories. The theories were based on missionary experience and practice, but as mission theories they also influenced mission priorities and long-term objectives.[71]

South African historians have described how the *amakholwa*'s struggle for economic success and political rights were met with growing constraints imposed by the Natal government and an advancing ideology of racial segregation.[72] In the mission organisations operating in South Africa, original ideas of democracy and equality within the church structure were abandoned as the missions leaned towards the policy of advancing segregation and racial exclusion.[73] In addition, the three-self theory was by the turn of the century more or less abandoned in international missions.[74] In the case of the NMS, historians like Sigmund Edland and Karina Hestad Skeie have described how Lars Dahle, during his inspection trip to Madagascar in 1903, cancelled the internal process of self-government in the Malagasy Lutheran Church, which in this case had been encouraged by the missionaries.[75] According to Skeie, Dahle's intervention in 1903 marked the end of what she defines the 'Malagasy era' in the Norwegian mission and the beginning of the 'colonial era'. Chapter 5 will return to the relationship between male Norwegian missionaries and male Zulu pastors within the NMS to determine if the original idea of Christian brotherhood was eventually replaced by paternalistic and racist discourses.

In Kimmel's research on nineteenth-century self-making men, he claims that the hegemonic masculinity ideal in the United States was 'grounded upon the exclusion of blacks and women, the non-native-born (immigrants) and the genuinely native-born (Indians), each on the premise that they weren't "real" Americans and couldn't, by definition, be real men'.[76] The connection between male self-making and male exclusion of 'others' may seem paradoxical. As previously mentioned, however, although the missionary pastors in the NMS favoured a democratic system that distributed power equally between them, women and non-Norwegian church men were excluded from all powerful positions in the mission.

Conclusion

This chapter has examined the outcome of the Schreuder case of 1873, arguing that it indicates that new masculinity ideals had become more central in the NMS and, likewise, that the other had lost its authority or hegemony. The new masculinity ideals in the NMS were related to modern, middle-class notions of masculinity, particularly to the concept of male self-making. In the case of the NMS, this 'spirit of self-making' had religious as well as cultural and social dimensions. In post-1873 NMS discourse, Schreuder has mostly been represented as anti-modern and an obstacle to democratic initiatives espoused by upcoming missionary men. As demonstrated, however, the picture is far more complex, not least since narratives of Schreuder as a missionary hero continued to circulate. Claes Ekenstam, in his critique of the theory of a hegemonic masculinity, asserts that masculinity should not necessarily be understood as an archetype, a cultural dominant ideal in a fixed period, but more like a changeable cluster of attributes and practices, in which certain elements can be replaced, strengthened or added to according to ideological or social influences. From this perspective, it is possible to understand why certain elements of the Schreuder type of missionary masculinity could survive even after the emergence of a new missionary masculinity in the NMS.

3
Proper Missionary Masculinity

Introduction

In January and February 1888, the head of the NMS, Secretary Ole Gjerløw, visited the mission field of Natal and Zululand.[1] This was the first inspection of any mission field by the mission management, and it was necessitated by a long-term conflict between the missionary community and the Home Board. The conflict had escalated after a certain resolution was passed during the 1887 extraordinary missionary conference at Eshowe mission station.[2] When Gjerløw arrived, he immediately convened another extraordinary meeting, during which he severely reprimanded the missionaries. They collectively accepted his accusations, repented and promised subordination to the Home Board.[3] Gjerløw also replaced the superintendent – Ommund Oftebro since 1877 – with Ole Stavem, known to be loyal to the leaders in Stavanger.[4] Finally, at the meeting Gjerløw officially announced the Home Board's decision to dismiss the medical missionary Christian Oftebro, Ommund Oftebro's nephew and son-in-law, from service in the NMS. This had tragic consequences for the individuals involved. Christian Oftebro became seriously ill soon after the Secretary's return to Norway. He never recovered, dying from rheumatic fever at 48 years of age. As well as his humiliating dismissal, Ommund Oftebro suffered a personal loss in the death of his close relative.

Although the two Oftebro missionaries were supported by the majority of their colleagues,[5] Christian Oftebro in particular represented ideas, principles and attitudes that were unacceptable to his superiors in Norway. In addition, his personal character was highly question-able. His dismissal was controversial but what caused the Home Board and Ole Gjerløw to exclude him was a complex mixture of motives. In the last decades of the nineteenth century, disagreements on mission theory and mission practice emerged within the NMS, including definitions of appropriate male missionary ideals. Christian Oftebro became an outstanding representative of what was regarded as inappropriate missionary masculinity. Oftebro was accused of not only introducing 'new' theories on Christian mission that were irreconcilable with Evangelical-Lutheran principles, but also of being a 'worldly' man, lacking an inner spiritual life. He was ultimately charged with violating vows of loyalty and obedience to his superiors.

The previous chapter concluded that masculinity ideals in the Norwegian mission movement resembled modern middle-class notions of masculinity, particularly the concept of male self-making. In this chapter I will continue my investigation of the Norwegian Lutheran male missionary ideal. Erik Sidenvall found in his study of Swedish evangelical missionaries to China a contradiction between rival ideals and discourses in the lives of the missionaries: a discourse emphasising the subordination of human ambitions to a greater divine cause as well as a contemporary gender discourse about what true manhood was, emphasising close ties between masculinity and self-making.[6] The dismissal of Christian Oftebro in 1888 is an interesting case in the context of the diverging ideas and ideals of mission and male missionaries in the late-nineteenth-century NMS. By analysing the Oftebro case, we can probe the internal NMS processes that resulted in the marginalisation of certain men and certain masculinity ideals. Discourses on appropriate missionary masculinity, and likewise discourses on inappropriate missionary masculinity, became part of the rhetoric used in the intervention against Oftebro. To the winning part in the conflict, Oftebro was portrayed as the outmost example of an inappropriate missionary. He was represented as a 'countertype', to refer to Georg Mosses' concept, or an 'unmanly man', to refer to Claes Ekenstam's. In fact, his negative example impacted on the creation of ideal missionary masculinity as it clearly articulated what a missionary should not be.

The Oftebro case concerns the scholarly discussion on Christian manliness in the era of modernity. I have already discussed the tendency among gender historians to interpret nineteenth-century feminisation of religion and secularisation of society as evidence of the decline of religion among modern Western men. As historian Yvonne Maria Werner points out, modern masculinity and religion seem to be incompatible and Christian manliness appears to be 'a paradox of modernity'.[7] Recent gender research, however, has emphasised how Christian men mobilised to counteract the separation of the spiritual from secular life and shape a new synthesis of contemporary masculinity discourses and Christian practice. The NMS missionaries were men who never saw Christianity and manliness as incompatible. The question was more of what Christian masculinity should look like in the age of modernity.

This chapter will first present a short biography of Christian Oftebro's life and career as a medical missionary. Second, it will present the controversial discussion on how to balance the 'evangelising' and 'civilising' aspects of mission, a controversy that was actually related to ideas of ideal missionary masculinity. Third, with the Oftebro case as a starting-point, the discussion will explore to what extent the Lutheran concept of the spiritual and temporal realm influenced the missionary masculinity ideal. Finally, the dilemma of combining modern masculinity ideals and Christian values and virtues in the case of the NMS will be discussed.

The case of Christian Oftebro

Christian Tobiassen Oftebro was a farmer's son who was born in Berge in Lyngdal in 1842.[8] After church confirmation at the age of 15, he signed on as a seaman in a Stavanger-based shipping company. He continued his maritime career until he contracted typhoid fever during a voyage in 1865 and was hospitalised in Port Louis, Mauritius. After three and a half months, he finally recovered. While planning to sign on to another vessel, he was unexpectedly visited by Hans Paludan Smith Schreuder, who was in Port Louis on a tentative expedition to Madagascar to investigate whether the island could become a new mission field.[9] While waiting for a vessel to Madagascar, he was told that a few young Norwegian seamen were hospitalised nearby, so he went to visit them. Realising that the nephew of his colleague Ommund Oftebro, an NMS missionary in Zululand since 1849, was among them, Schreuder visited Christian Oftebro and persuaded him to join him on the journey back to Africa.

Christian Oftebro assisted his uncle at the mission station of Eshowe for the next two and a half years. He obviously enjoyed it, as in February 1866 he submitted his application for admission to the NMS's mission school in Stavanger: 'From the time I came here the desire to work in the mission has grown stronger, and now I do not wish for anything else than being educated a worker for the promotion of the Kingdom of God among the heathens.'[10] His application was accepted, and he entered the mission school in August 1868,[11] graduating in June 1873. Unlike the rest of his class who became ordained mission pastors to Madagascar in

1874, the Home Board sent Oftebro to Scotland to study at the medical school operated by Edinburgh Medical Missionary Society.[12]

After three years of medical studies, Oftebro travelled back to Zululand, and in January 1877 he arrived at Eshowe. His uncle reported to the Home Board that 'it was very precious for us to have him back. He immediately became busy seeing patients, because as everywhere else, here are plenty of sick and feeble people.'[13] Oftebro soon moved to the

Figure 3.1 Christian Oftebro (1842–88), a theologian and medical doctor, represented ideas and practices controversial to the missionary management and was dismissed from missionary service in 1888

Source: Mission Archives, School of Mission and Theology, Stavanger.

mission station of Mahlabatini, where he was assigned a post as medical missionary. The Mahlabatini mission station had been established in 1860, close to the previous King Mpande kaSenzangakhona's homestead, Nodwengu. The location was regarded as strategically important as it afforded 'splendid opportunities to those wishing to reach the whole Zulu nation with the word of God'.[14] When Prince Cetshwayo kaMpande succeeded his father in 1872, he built a new homestead, Ulundi, on the same Mahlabatini plain.[15] It served as his chief homestead and a political and administrative centre of the kingdom, where state meetings and national ceremonies took place. King Cetshwayo took advantage of Oftebro's medical services[16] as well other Norwegian missionaries' various construction works.[17] In April 1878, all the NMS missionaries stationed in Zululand were evacuated because of the expected war with the British colony of Natal. Until the Anglo-Zulu war ended in the summer of 1879, Oftebro lived with his uncle's family at a farm on the Natal side of the Tugela River.[18]

Oftebro moved back to Mahlabatini in December 1879 to reconstruct the mission station buildings, which had been totally destroyed and burnt by Zulu warriors.[19] He married his cousin Johanne Guri Mathea (Hanna) Oftebro in January 1881, and their daughter, Gudrun Katrine, was born the following year. Since no ordained pastor was sent to Mahlabatini after the war, Oftebro was asked to act as station manager as well as provide medical services. Because of his theological education at the mission school, he was regarded by the NMS as capable of taking care of the station's daily devotions and the Sunday services. He was also permitted to teach catechisms and elementary classes in reading, writing and arithmetic. Sacraments like the Eucharist, baptisms and weddings, however, were, according to the Lutheran understanding of the office, to be performed by an ordained pastor. In such cases, an ordained missionary serving at a nearby mission station came to assist.

The Anglo-Zulu war of 1879 resulted in the fall of the independent Zulu state. Moreover, the British post-war political arrangements introduced a period of political turbulence and internal civil wars between the king's loyal Usuthu party and the rival chiefs Hamu kaMpande Zulu and Zibhebhu kaMaphitha Zulu. The wars had disastrous consequences for the Zulu people. Thousands were killed or hurt; thousands suffered from hunger when their homesteads were burnt, their cattle stolen and their grain plundered or despoiled.[20] When Zibhebhu attacked the king at Ulundi in July 1883, Oftebro welcomed hundreds of Usuthu refugees to the mission station. At one time he hosted 18 queens and six princesses, accompanied by their court servants and relatives.[21] Upon Zibhebhu's withdrawal, neighbouring people who feared attacks and robbery by Usuthu troops took refuge at the mission station. Most of them belonged to the tribe of Mfanawendlela Zulu, a chief who tried to remain neutral in the conflict. When Mfanawendlela was killed by Usuthu troops on 14 December 1883,[22] aggressive Usuthu legions patrolled the mission station during the following days, claiming cattle and property. At this point, Oftebro decided to escape. Together with his family and about 30 to 40 of the Zulu mission station settlers, he left the station on 17 December and arrived in Eshowe three days later.[23] In the days to come, the rest of the mission station settlers followed. For the next four years he lived in exile with 'his people', approximately 100 Zulu refugees, at the Eshowe mission station. While he waited for peace in upper Zululand and further decisions regarding his future service, he established a colony with considerable farming and industrial activities. This was the situation when the NMS's Secretary visited the mission field in January 1888 – a visit that resulted in the expulsion of Christian Oftebro from missionary service.

The NMS's official information channels include few comments on the dismissal of Oftebro. The *NMT* informed readers of his death in June 1888, but no obituary, as was normally the case in the death of missionaries, followed.[24] Observant readers would note that, by the time of his death on 30 April, Oftebro was no longer in the NMS since it was stated that he served as a medical missionary 'until the beginning of the present year'. The dismissal of Oftebro was not mentioned in the superintendent's 1888 annual report.[25] Although most of the documents in the 1873 Schreuder case were made public in 1876,[26] the NMS management did not intend to do the same in the Oftebro case. A central document – the Secretary's inspection report – was dispersed in wider mission circles, however, although it was meant exclusively for the members of the regional boards.[27] As a result, the Oftebro case was discussed unofficially among mission-friends throughout the nation, and rumours of Gjerløw's report soon reached the missionaries in South Africa. When they asked for a copy, the Home Board refused.[28] The management in Stavanger argued that the report had been written by the previous Secretary (Lars Dahle replaced Ole Gjerløw as Secretary in 1888),[29] that it was controversial and could revive old disputes, and that it was never meant to be official. Yet the report was somehow sent to the missionaries by other channels, as Hans Christian Leisegang in 1904 ironically refers to it as 'the black book; since all in it is black with one exception, and this person's whiteness beams even more in the black surroundings'.[30]

For many years mission historians were reluctant to comment on the delicate Oftebro case. The case was not particularised in the memorial volume published for the NMS's 50-year anniversary in 1892, although the doctor's sudden death was mentioned.[31] In the same book, Gjerløw's inspection was described as a trip during which several 'administrative affairs were settled'.[32] Although it was not published by the NMS, Madagascar missionary Anders Olsen edited the anthology *Home from the Battlefield* in 1906, which contained biographies of 30 late NMS missionaries. In the anthology, a short biography on Christian Oftebro's missionary life was written by his colleague Marcus Dahle. Dahle confirmed that Oftebro's career ended with his dismissal from missionary service, but he hesitated to comment on it further. [33] The same was the case in Ole Stavem's historical overview of the NMS's 70 years of mission in Zululand, published in 1915. Stavem admitted that he was a party to the conflict of 1888 and stated that 'the judgment shall, by the way, be left to exterior historians of mission'.[34] Ole Gjerløw's inspection report has been an essential source for historians' subsequent discussions of the Oftebro case. John Nome described Gjerløw in 1942 as a man who acted like a bishop, 'with authority and power',[35] and Olav Guttorm Myklebust was the first to give a critical account of Gjerløw's inspection of the mission field and the dismissal of Oftebro.[36] Myklebust asserted that the main reason why the NMS acted against him was Oftebro's 'independency efforts', as he defended the local autonomy of the missionary conference and contested the authority of the Home Board. Yet Thomas M. Børhaug and Per O. Hernæs suggested that it was Oftebro's theory and practice of mission that mainly explained why he was expelled. Whereas Børhaug was critical of what he saw as Oftebro's pro-imperialist and pro-colonial attitudes,[37] Hernæs found Oftebro's ideas of local Zulu ownership and self-sustainability interesting.[38]

'By Word or by Plough?': contested theories on mission

In the British Protestant missionary movement, there were from the early nineteenth century debates about the best missionary methods and the relations between Christianity, commerce or civilisation.[39] In similar discussions in the NMS, Christian Oftebro was accused of introducing new and un-Lutheran principles of mission. Ole Gjerløw described his intentions to reduce mission work to general colonial activity, emphasising the 'plough' and not the 'Word' (the Christian Gospel).[40] From their pioneer days, the Norwegian missionaries made distinctions between direct and indirect mission work. Direct or 'real' mission work, as it was also called, referred to the evangelising task. Everything related to this superior aim – such as praying, preaching, religious education and religious counselling – was regarded as direct mission work. Indirect mission work was related to the 'exterior' or 'outward' sector of the mission project. Construction of buildings like churches, schools and assembly places as well as missionaries' dwellings fell under this category. The same was true of services related to the well-being of the missionary and his family, like nursing and medical care, midwifery services, housekeeping, farming and the education of his children. Another category of work – namely, missionaries' services towards the indigenous people of a non-evangelising kind (e.g. health, education, industrial and agricultural services and enterprises) – was also defined as indirect mission work. This category of work was alternatively called 'civilising mission work', and was based on the idea that Christian mission would lead to an improvement of the totality of people's lives, including material conditions, social structures and political systems.

In Oftebro's opinion, however, Christianisation and civilisation – or direct and indirect mission work – should be combined and regarded as equal elements in mission.[41] In 1886, he asserted that the contemporary mission in Zululand, to a greater extent than during the pioneer period when preaching the Gospel was the essential requirement, should encourage practical working abilities and industrial handcrafts among the 'uncivilised' people. The indirect mission work should no longer

Figure 3.2 Ommund Oftebro (1849–93), number three from the left in second row, and the inhabitants at the mission station at Eshowe, Zululand

Source: Mission Archives, School of Mission and Theology, Stavanger.

be regarded as peripheral, but rather as central, and therefore systematised and integrated into the NMS's mission strategy. Oftebro argued
that the Norwegian missionaries had practised from their first days in
Zululand what he called the 'station method'. They had established
Christian communities by employing young, unmarried apprentices
and servants who lived and worked together with them, subsequently
settling with their own families on the mission station land. When Zulu
men and women lived and worked at the mission station, they were
influenced by its Christian life and spirit; when they regularly attended
Christian devotions and classes, many eventually became converted.[42]
In Oftebro's opinion, the establishment of mission stations was the most
effective way of recruiting converts, although the measure needed to
be further developed. In addition to the soul-winning objective, the
mission stations should be 'civilised' enclaves where male converts were
educated and trained in agriculture, handcrafts and commerce. The long-
term goal was to create independent farmers, artisans and traders – men
who could support themselves and their families in a growing capitalist
economy. In Oftebro's theory of mission the idea of male self-making
was evident.

Oftebro practised his theory of mission by employing 'everyone' who
came to the mission station and asked for work; he offered them accom-
modation, a salary and security. Yet he also expected the mission station
like any commercial enterprise to become 'self-subsisting' or 'self-
supporting' in the long run, not dependent on mission donations.[43] At
Mahlabatini mission station, where he employed 60 to 70 people, he
cultivated a field of approximately 40 acres and grew maize, potatoes,
beans and peas.[44] He had a herd of about 100 cattle and between 50 and
100 sheep and goats, in addition to hens, ducks and pigs. In missionary
debates concerning land achievements, Oftebro advised the NMS to buy
as much mission land as possible as it could give opportunities to practise the ideas of self-supporting mission stations. Furthermore, Christian
colonies that offered Zulu farmers the chance to buy private land and
become freeholders could be established on the mission land.[45] His view
of the mission as an essential 'civilising' force in Zululand persuaded
Oftebro that the NMS should invest in higher educational institutions
and industrial schools at the expense of theological seminaries.[46]

Mission theory and mission practice were frequently discussed at
the Norwegian missionary conferences in south-eastern Africa in the
1880s. Whereas Oftebro enthusiastically promoted the methodology of
'mission-station mission' and the ideas of 'industrial mission', Ole Stavem
became a devotee of 'evangelistic outreach',[47] a point of view he shared

with the Home Board. In 1884, the Home Board requested that missionaries discuss the establishment of out-of-mission station preaching places or satellite stations as well as an extended use of Christian Zulus as evangelists and teachers, supervised by the missionary pastor at the central mission station.[48] The Home Board frequently referred to the NMS's other, but still younger, mission field in Madagascar, where these methods had been practised successfully. Although the missionaries in inland Madagascar in 1882 could report an impressive 1,111 baptisms, 38,000 church attendants, and 33,000 students in the mission schools, the Zulu missionaries reported merely 66 baptisms, 870 church attendants and about 500 students in the schools.[49] The relation between evangelisation and civilisation in mission was even discussed at the NMS's regional conferences in Norway in 1886, and the Home Board received massive support for its accentuation of what was defined as the Evangelical-Lutheran mission practice: to preach the Gospel.[50] In the NMS's letter of dismissal addressed to Oftebro, Gjerløw stated that a Lutheran missionary was not free to invent 'new principles' of mission as they 'were given in his faith and in his church's confession'; if he practised anything else, he should leave mission service.[51] In his inspection report Gjerløw emphasised that Oftebro lacked an 'evangelical attitude to and understanding of mission' and that he had behaved like 'a grand employer' rather than an Evangelical-Lutheran missionary.[52]

Oftebro's theory of mission gained much support among his colleagues in Natal and Zululand, but it clashed with the theories of the Norwegian management, which also meant that his notions of ideal missionary masculinity clashed with the missionary masculinity ideals advocated by the Home Board. This will be further discussed in the following sections, but first the discussion will briefly speculate on Oftebro's sources of inspiration. Oftebro was primarily inspired by his observations of the work of American and British missionaries in Natal and Zululand. He referred particularly to Congregationalist missions, like the London Missionary Society and the American Board of Commissioners for Foreign Mission, and to the Presbyterian Free Church of Scotland, but claimed that the high-church Anglican mission had also recently applied the same theories of 'industrial mission' to its work.[53] As a student in Edinburgh, Oftebro was greatly interested in the 1875 expedition of the Free Church of Scotland to Lake Malawi.[54] The expedition sought to 'to fulfil the mission of David Livingstone', and established a Christian settlement named Livingstonia. Livingstonia's expeditionary party included only one theologian along with five artisans: a sailor, an engineer, a gardener, a blacksmith and a carpenter.[55] Oftebro was obviously attracted to the ideas advocated by the famous mission doctor David Livingstone – namely, that betterment of the Africans' 'uncivilised' state did not lie so much in individual conversions as in a general improvement of social and economic living conditions, which would naturally result from the opening-up of the continent for free trade and its incorporation into a capitalist world economy.

Oftebro's view of mission was also influenced by his background as an educated physician, the first in the NMS's Zulu mission.[56] The development of medical missions was hotly disputed in British missionary societies, according to Esme Cleall.[57] The first educated physicians sent to the mission field in the nineteenth century had the twofold task of caring for sick missionaries and their families as well as the indigenous sick[58] but their primary duty – as was the case with all evangelical missionaries – was to evangelise. According to Norman Etherington, a medical missionary in the nineteenth century was strictly speaking a 'missionary trained in Western medicine'.[59] In 1834, Peter Park, who is reckoned to be the first Protestant medical missionary, opened a hospital specialising in eye disorders in Canton, China. He was employed by the American Board of Commissioners for Foreign Mission. Parker visited Britain in 1841 and inspired physicians in Edinburgh to establish the Edinburgh Medical Missionary Society, the first medical mission in Europe.[60] It was to the medical school run by this mission that the NMS decided to send its missionary candidate Christian Oftebro in 1867. In the NMS, the importance of medicine for the success of mission had been acknowledged ever since the days of Hans P. S. Schreuder, who paved the way for the Norwegian mission in Zululand in 1850 by responding to King Mpande kaSenzangakhona's call for medicine. The NMS missionaries all had some rudimentary training in medicine from the University of Oslo, and they had their own medical kits and provided medical advice.[61] In fact, most Western missionaries in Natal and Zululand did elementary dentistry and surgery, such as pulling out teeth and removing cataracts and tumours. They also practised small-scale vaccination programmes.[62]

Oftebro was thus inspired by Anglo-American efforts at both industrial and medical mission. Implicit in his mission theory was a critique of what he regarded as the unbalanced emphasis on the spiritual side of the Christian gospel and neglect of the social side. Missionaries should heal bodies as well as souls, and they should build civilised communities as well as Christian churches. In the latter half of the nineteenth century, several cultural and political movements that aimed to counteract the separation of Christian spiritual life from secular life emerged in Britain and America. One example was Muscular Christianity, which spread as a literal, social and cultural movement among Christian men in Great Britain and America from the 1860s, promoting a way to combine robust, physical strength with Christian ethics.[63] Another example was the Social Christianity movement, which historians describe as new religious tendencies within Protestantism that gained growing support from the 1880s and that advocated the duty of the church to engage with social challenges.[64] Recent scholarship, as previously discussed in Chapter 1, has interpreted these movements as reactions to the image of religion as unmanly and feminised and as efforts to find spiritual dimensions in what was regarded as typical and traditional male activities. Oftebro's theory and practice of mission, as well as his notions of ideal missionary masculinity, thus corresponded with contemporary and influential trends in British and American Christianity.

The missionary caught between the spiritual and the secular

In the 1874 House Order (*Husorden*) for the NMS's mission school in Stavanger, which was a boarding school, it was emphasised that the school was 'an institution for the work of the Holy Spirit' (*en Anstalt for den Helligaands Virksomhed*). The school should therefore test the sincerity of the young candidates' vocation to missionary service and, 'by the Holy Spirit', educate and train prospective missionaries 'to preach the Gospel among the heathens'. During their stay at the mission school, the candidates were obliged to exercise daily 'self-denial' (*Selvfornægtelse*), 'world-denial' (*Verdensforsagelse*) and 'fear of God' (*Gudfryktighet*).[65] The Lutheran concept of the 'Two Kingdoms' or the 'Two Realms' – the temporal and the spiritual – was central to Norwegian mission discourse. The same was true of the Lutheran idea of the three hierarchies – or 'orders' – within Christian society: the household (*oeconomia*), with the father as the head; the state (*politia*), where the princes and magistrates exercised secular authority; and the church (*ecclesia*), where the clergy exercised spiritual authority. A missionary pastor, like all clergy, acted within the spiritual realm; evangelising and congregational work were his main tasks. Nevertheless, the Lutheran doctrine did allow, and also expect, a male missionary to exercise paternal authority as father of the missionary household and secular authority as manager of the mission station land. Although a church man, he was never free from temporal responsibilities, a discussion we will return to.

The Oftebro case clearly illustrated that, in the nineteenth-century NMS discourse, a missionary was regarded as a 'man of the Word' and not a 'man of the plough'.[66] There was little approval of Oftebro's engage-ment in commercial and social projects, and he was repeatedly accused of being secular or 'worldly'. One accusation levelled against Oftebro was his undesirable involvement in gold-mining companies. On one occa-sion, he bought a share in a gold-mining company, and he also estab-lished a minor gold-mining enterprise at the Eshowe mission station land.[67] The missionaries received an annual wage from the NMS and, although it was not articulated in the missionary instruction, there was a common understanding of mission work and commercial activities as being irreconcilable. This issue was frequently discussed by the mission-aries in the 1880s,[68] as it was actually expected that they should have some income from their agricultural work (e.g. by selling corn, cattle or sheep).[69] Gold-mining activity, on the other hand, was definitely not tolerated and was regarded as an inappropriate activity for a mission-ary.[70] Gjerløw claimed that Oftebro's involvement in mining enterprises further affirmed his close relation to the British settler community. In his report he commented that the Oftebro missionaries were known for their persistent pro-British attitudes during the Anglo-Zulu war as well as in the ensuing political turmoil.[71] Missionary instructions demanded neutrality in internal political conflicts in the host country.[72] Although the NMS's Home Board, like the majority of missionaries, had welcomed the British conquest of the Zulu monarchy,[73] Gjerløw asserted that this was not the same as choosing a side in the tense post-war political disputes. He had noticed that the Oftebro family had British officers, magistrates and farmers among their acquaintances, and that Christian Oftebro attended gentlemen's social events.

Gjerløw found all of these examples to be evidence of Oftebro's worldly manners and attitudes.[74] When he officially announced the Home Board's decision to dismiss the doctor at the 1887 missionary conference, he further stated that 'serious doubts about his suitability for mission service' had been raised since Oftebro's days at the mission school. The NMS management, according to Gjerløw, thought he had 'always lacked Christian seriousness and a Christian life'. In Stavanger Oftebro was known as a 'boastful, worldly man', and certain mission men still remembered 'the debaucheries' in which he participated during his student days.[75] Gjerløw's insinuations about Oftebro's worldly life-style and the lack of an inner spiritual life, all printed in the report, caused speculations in the years to come in Norwegian mission milieus. What kind of debaucheries did Oftebro participate in during his youth? Oftebro himself found Gjerløw's insinuations hard to accept, claiming that he never had any complaints from the school's management during his stay at the mission school.[76] In the 1940s, Olav Guttorm Myklebust thoroughly researched the issue, examining the available textual sources and conducting interviews. As he failed to find any evidence of Oftebro's immoral lifestyle, Myklebust concluded that the accusations must have been false.[77] Myklebust also found it hard to believe that the NMS leadership, if it truly had doubts about Oftebro's spiritual life and was suspicious about his lifestyle, would take the risk of sending him as its representative, much less invest in a second medical education.

Myklebust was probably right. It is hard to believe that Oftebro could have engaged in acts regarded as immoral or participated in local scandalous 'debaucheries' without being expelled from the mission school. The rules of the boarding institution were extremely strict even for its time, and the school earned the popular nickname of 'the cloister'.[78] In the period when Oftebro attended the school, several students left either because of their own or management's doubts about their suitability for mission service.[79] The candidates' relationships with women were particularly controlled. In 1868, a mission candidate was expelled from the school because he admitted to having shown 'carelessness' in his relationship with his fiancée, something which provoked anger and indignation among the girl's relatives.[80] In 1872, four of Oftebro's peers were reprimanded after conducting 'negotiations about marital relations' without informing or involving the Home Board of their plans.[81] The students admitted their failure, repented and broke off friendships with the young girls in town. The regulation of private lives applied to all intimate relations between women and men, and courtship, engagement, marriage and sex were all areas in which the NMS thought it legitimate to intervene.[82] The missionaries were not allowed to marry until they had served at least two years in the mission field. Permission for engagements as well weddings was to be provided by the Home Board. Pre-marital sexual relationships were naturally not accepted. For example, Superintendent Ole Stavem expelled a newly arrived assistant missionary in 1890 because of his fiancée's pregnancy.[83] Line Nyhagen Predelli, who researched missionaries' marriages in the NMS in Madagascar in the 1880–1910 period, found some examples of adultery among the male missionaries. Such incidents were kept 'top secret' within the NMS system, and the men all had to resign from missionary service.[84]

At the mission school, candidates learnt that 'a pious, God-fearing mind' resulted in 'respect and obedience towards superiors' and 'mutual brotherly love'.[85] Vows of loyalty to the NMS's laws and instructions and obedience to both the Home Board and superiors in the mission field were taken by all missionaries before they left Stavanger for the mission field.[86] In addition to accusations of introducing non-Lutheran theories on mission and of being a 'worldly' man, Oftebro was also charged with acts of disrespect and disobedience towards his superiors. On several occasions he had apparently expressed 'outrageous accusations and scorning utterances' against both colleagues and the NMS leadership.[87] It was above all the missionary Nils Braatvedt who was offended, as Oftebro accused him of acting 'falsely', 'cowardly' and 'untruthfully' in an internal conflict that arose when the veteran missionary Martinius Borgen was relocated from Madagascar to South Africa. Borgen, who followed Braatvedt as principal of the school for missionary children at Umphumulo, demanded radical changes in the organisation of the school.[88] Instead of following the normal procedure by raising the issues at the missionary conference, Borgen wrote personal letters to Secretary Gjerløw and received the Home Board's permission to put the reforms into effect. This provoked a protest by the majority of the missionaries, as the Home Board – by approving Borgen's proposals – had undermined the authority of both the superintendent and the missionary conference.

At an extraordinary conference at Eshowe in February 1887, when 'the affairs of Borgen' (*de Borgenske affærer*) were settled, a resolution regarding the power balance between the missionary conference and the Home Board, authored by Christian Oftebro and Ole Zephanias Norgaard, was passed.[89] The missionaries argued, referring to the NMS constitution of 1842, that the general assembly was the organisation's highest authority and that both the local missionary conference and the Home Board received their power and authority from this body. Although the constitution granted the Board authority over the NMS's general affairs, the missionaries asserted that § 18 in the missionary instruction granted the missionary conference 'the highest advisory, decisive and controlling authority' in all the affairs concerning the mission field.[90] The missionary resolution of February 1887 concluded as follows: 'We cannot at all grant the Home Board any right to intervene directly in the administration of the mission field.'[91]

Oftebro and Norgaard's resolution overlooked § 17 in the same missionary instruction, which proclaimed missionary obedience to the NMS's Home Board – 'the highest governing and decisive authority'.[92] The resolution was therefore perceived to be a provocation that resulted in the Home Board's decision to send Gjerløw to the field in order to demonstrate its authority and clear up 'administrative affairs'. It definitely put an end to all ambitions for local autonomy, somewhat ironically since the break with Schreuder fifteen years earlier had been provoked by the Home Board's demand that the local missionary conference should be strengthened. The inspection trip was among Gjerløw's last commissions before he left the NMS to serve as a minister in the Church of Norway. In his report, he concluded that the inspection had been a success and that similar complications would not in all likelihood arise in the future. He further asserted that the problems in the field were rooted in the 'unauthorised and unfavourable influence' of a certain individual member of the conference, who had 'set the administrative machinery and the workers on the wrong track'.[93] Gjerløw singled out Oftebro as the one who had influenced the majority of the missionaries to engage in acts of disloyalty and disobedience.

Christian Oftebro was represented as a secular man by the NMS management: 'A missionary who has lost the Spirit's fire in his work, is in fact a caricature of what he should be.'[94] In the revivalist-oriented NMS, statements describing Oftebro as a worldly oriented missionary lacking an inner spiritual life were met with shock. His sudden death did not decrease the speculations about the state of his soul. Ole Stavem, in a report of the 'unexpected and strange' death of Christian Oftebro, wrote that he 'hoped the best for his spiritual state', but still had some doubts.[95] On the other hand, missionary Karl Larsen Titlestad reported that he had engaged in deep, spiritual conversations with Oftebro only weeks before his death. Oftebro was ready in spirit to meet the Lord, Titlestad stated.[96] Ommund Oftebro further assured the Home Board that his nephew had 'frankly proclaimed his faith' before taking his last breath.[97] Ommund had consistently supported his nephew's ideas of mission. In a private letter to Christian's father, in which he tried to explain why his son had been dismissed from mission service, Ommund regretted that the NMS misunderstood Christian. Ommund wrote that Christian did not intend merely to 'civilise the heathens...but he wished, by keeping many as employees, to pull them into the influence and effect of the Word of God'.[98] Ommund further claimed that Christian had won many converts through his medical service. Most of his longer-term patients had abandoned paganism to become Christians. In contrast, he continued that – without mentioning any name – 'the missionary here, who always was his enemy and always proclaimed that evangelising, and nothing else, was our main task, cannot point to a single soul who is won for the Kingdom of God'.[99] Christian's father need not have worried about the sincerity of his son's faith. Oftebro cited the Anglican missionary Robert Robertson, who had exclaimed that 'the angels were crying and the devil laughing' when such an extraordinary man was expelled from mission service.

Missionary masculinity: a paradox of modernity?[100]

The NMS missionaries were men who never regarded Christianity and manliness to be incompatible. The question was more what they should look like in the age of modernity. Several historians have claimed that, towards the end of the nineteenth century, notions of Christian values and qualities no longer corresponded with what were regarded as prevailing masculinity ideals. Norman Vance, in his book on Victorian Christian manliness, found vigour, physicality, strength, robustness, toughness, heroism, militarism, powerfulness and self-reliance to be examples of secular masculinity ideals. Christian virtues included patience, self-denial, confidence and restraint; Christian men were also expected to resist worldly pleasures and enjoyments.[101] Anna Prestjan, in her study of 'priest manliness' in Sweden from 1900 to 1920, claims that the priest was 'the Christian man personified' – at least until female ordination was introduced by the church. According to Prestjan, this group of men 'ran the risk of being seen as less manly than other men, or even unmanly'. In contrast to masculine values of activity and action, Christian virtues were regarded as passive, and in contrast to modern masculinity values of rationality and sense, Christian virtues such as tenderness and compassion were seen as sentimental and emotional. Christian spirituality understood as indifference to worldly matters was criticised by modern men for its lack of commitment to social life.[102] Prestjan finds that Christian values were often understood as the 'opposite to modern masculinity' and suggests two types of 'strategies' were needed for Christian men to represent Christian manliness in the age of modernity. In the first type, qualities and values perceived as masculine were added to the Christian character – 'a Christian, *but to that*, a man'. The other type of strategy focused on *uniting* a prevailing ideal of masculinity and Christian virtues at the same time as the latter were masculinised and described as true manly virtues. Christian qualities, ideals and values were recoded to correspond with secular masculinity – namely, 'a Christian, and *therefore* a man'.[103]

If we apply Prestjan's model to the Oftebro case, it seems fair to say that Oftebro himself practised the first strategy. The masculine qualities so valued in the settler society in which he lived – physical strength, robustness, toughness, self-reliance, energy, activity and vigour – were obviously regarded by him as positive attributes and added to his identity as a Christian man. Although he was accused of being a secular man, there is no reason to believe that Oftebro ever rejected the validity of the

Christian virtues in which he had been trained at the mission school. The 'House Rule' lists the kind of Christian spiritual virtues and values that were to be nurtured in missionary candidates: 'fear of God' (*Guds Frygt*), 'self-denial' (*Selvfornægtelse*), 'world-denial' (*Verdensforsagelse*), 'reverence' (*Ærbødighed*), 'obedience' (*Lydighed*), 'brotherly love' (*broderlig Kjærlighed*), 'calmness' (*Stilfærdighet*), 'faithfulness' (*Troskab*), 'gentleness' (*Varsomhed*), 'frugality' (*Sparsommelighed*), 'indulgence' (*Overbærenhed*), 'patience' (*Taalmodighed*), 'vigilance' (*Aarvaagenhed*) and 'zeal' (*Nidkjærhed*).[104] Nevertheless, this brief study of the life and career of Christian Oftebro demonstrates that virtues like 'self-denial', 'world-denial', 'calmness' and 'patience' hardly characterised him. Moreover, Oftebro was critical of a Christian spirituality that advocated indifference to secular matters and reluctance to engage in societal issues.

Ole Gjerløw's ideas of Christian manliness were perhaps more in the direction of Prestjan's suggested second strategy: uniting Christian virtues and prevailing ideals of masculinity by defining Christian virtues as true manly virtues. Gjerløw obviously defended traditional Christian values like self-denial, world-denial, brotherly love, obedience, patience, modesty and carefulness, yet the strategy he used to advocate them – at least in the Oftebro case – was to single out men who lacked these values. Oftebro was portrayed as a 'caricature' of a missionary, a countertype of ideal missionary masculinity. Claes Ekenstam asserts that, although ideas of manliness can be diffuse, the ideas of unmanliness often seem to be well articulated and, in contrast, offer clarity and distinction regarding the concept of manliness. The concept of unmanliness further helps explicate the processes of exclusion, which are often important in the constitution of masculinities. In the rivalry between diverse forms of masculinities, describing the counterpart as a bearer of unmanliness seems to be an efficient strategy (see Chapter 1).

In Gjerløw's report, Oftebro was described as a verbally uncontrolled man who used 'conceited allegations and great words' and answered with 'a certain pathos'. His 'little dash of English posture' combined with 'agitation and attempts to tyrannize and terrorise' had succeeded in influencing his co-workers. His methods were regrettably used at the missionary conferences that, according to Gjerløw, were supposed to be meetings characterised by 'calm, passionless, brotherly treatment of cases'.[105] Gjerløw furthermore described a situation in which Oftebro, during a private conversation, enquired as to the possibility of a new contract with the NMS. Gjerløw answered that a change of mind was necessary, and Oftebro admitted 'his weaknesses, his anger and violence of expression', sins he thought could be repented and forgiven. To

Oftebro's disappointment, Gjerløw stated that his sins were rather to be regarded as 'pure evil'. In his report, Gjerløw scornfully commented that, towards the end of the private conversation, there was nothing left of 'this great, superior man': 'He was almost like the Knight of Sadness, when he sat there holding a napkin in front of his mouth.'[106] The metaphor of a passionate, if slightly feminine, knight was used to describe Oftebro's final state as a fallen man. In the nineteenth-century middle-class discourse of masculinity, this was not an honourable term – indeed, it was quite the opposite. To modern men, aristocracy symbolised an old-fashioned, shallow and artificial model of masculinity.[107]

In his diatribe against Christian Oftebro, Ole Gjerløw turned to contemporary hegemonic masculinity discourses. Oftebro was represented as a man unable to control his passions, a man without character. Historian David Tjeder finds the concept of passion to be central in the nineteenth-century discourse of middle-class masculinities. Passion was understood to be the impersonal, threatening forces residing within men; thus, a real man should be able to withstand, discipline and control his passions. The struggle to master one's passion was, moreover, grounded in power. Control over one's passions meant not only power over the basic impulses of the self, but also power over others. Tjeder claims that it was men's varying successes in mastering their passions that decided why some men should have power whereas others should not.[108] According to Tjeder, another crucial concept in masculinity discourses was the concept of character, or the inner nature of man. Character was believed to be a hidden potentiality within all men, one that could only be realised through hard work. It was also a true reflection of the individual's self – a self that had always been a potential within the man. Character was therefore both the true self and the effect of hard, enduring work. Developing character meant developing inner, hidden potentialities. A man of character naturally had to control his passions.[109] In Gjerløw's report, both Christian Oftebro and his uncle Ommund Oftebro were portrayed as men without character – the younger as a man unable to control his passions, and the older as 'the less oriented and most characterless' of all the missionaries. Consequently, they were no longer worthy of their power positions. The younger Oftebro, who used to be an unauthorised leader among his colleagues, was dismissed from service, and the older, who used to be superintendent, was replaced by Stavem, 'a man of solid character'.[110]

It is a paradox though that the type of masculinity Christian Oftebro represented – the vigorous, tough, strong, active, self-reliant man – was a necessary ingredient in the mission enterprise. The traditional Christian virtues taught at the mission school, in the 'cloister', could perhaps work in the family-like surroundings of the boarding school but when the missionaries arrived in the mission field other qualities were needed as well. The NMS, like most Western missions, needed physically strong, practical, vigorous and creative men like Christian Oftebro.[111] Historian John Tosh asserts that, more than most areas of British national life, the empire was seen as a projection of masculinity. He finds a striking convergence between the language of empire and the language of manliness; both made significant use of struggle, duty, action, will and character. Overseas expansion depended on manpower and on the supply of men of a certain type – namely, those who were practical, resourceful and self-reliant.[112] Although the NMS missionaries in Natal and Zululand did not represent any imperial power, they still shared the imperialist understanding of service as 'life at the frontier'.

We have seen that the pioneer Hans P. S. Schreuder was described as a man with extraordinary masculine virtues in popular mission literature: a powerful giant who could conquer leopards, a practical man who raised mission stations and churches with his own hands in the wilderness, and a self-reliant man of strong will (Chapter 2). Schreuder was obviously strong and independent, but he was also a man of faith, a man obedient to and dependent on his God. Schreuder lived up to the Victorian image of muscular Christianity that can be defined as 'an association between physical strength, religious certainty, and the ability to shape and control the world around oneself'.[113] 'Self-making' and 'self-denying', which at first glance seem to be diametrically opposed, were central elements in missionary masculinity. Yet every missionary had to strive to find the right balance between the two; consequently, 'self-control' was also needed. Learning to master one's passion and developing a strong and sturdy character were central to modern masculinities. Perhaps the difference between the secular and the Christian man was that, whereas the first strove to achieve control over himself and the world around him on his own, the latter continued the Christian tradition of daily exercises in self-denial, self-reform and self-control with the help of divine forces outside the individual.

Conclusion

The dismissal of medical missionary Christian Oftebro in 1888 is an important case for the investigation of ideals of missionary masculinity in the NMS. The Home Board's decision to exclude Oftebro, however, stemmed from a complex mixture of motives. Oftebro was first accused of introducing principles of Christian mission irreconcilable with Evangelical-Lutheran ideology. Second, he was accused of being a worldly man lacking an inner spiritual life. Finally, he was charged with violating vows of loyalty and obedience to his superiors. In the NMS intervention against him, Oftebro was represented by the NMS Secretary Ole Gjerløw as a man unable to control his passions and a man without character – both common definitions of unmanliness in the nineteenth-century bourgeois discourse of masculinity. Oftebro was portrayed as an unmanly man, a 'caricature' of a missionary, an extreme example of inappropriate missionary masculinity. Claes Ekenstam's assertion that ideas of unmanliness are often better articulated and, as a contrast, offer clarity and distinction to the concept of manliness is confirmed in the current examination of the Oftebro case. The concept of unmanliness also helps to uncover the processes of exclusion and marginalisation of certain men and certain masculinities. In the rivalry between diverse forms of masculinities, describing the counterpart as a bearer of unmanliness seems to be an efficient strategy.

The missionary enterprise was a modern phenomenon, and men who lived up to contemporary masculinity ideals were much needed in the mission field. To survive in the 'wilderness' and to be able to construct Christian communities on the 'borders of civilisation', the missionary men needed to be physically strong, tough and robust; they had to be handymen who could manage a variety of crafts as well as self-reliant men who were rich in initiative and energy. On the other hand, the missionaries were Christian men, and as pastors they were 'the Christian man personified'. They had been trained in a range of virtues that were regarded as Christian, such as world-denial, self-denial, modesty, patience and calmness. Moreover, the Lutheran theology restricted their engagement to the spiritual realm (i.e. the Church) and forbade them from becoming extensively involved in secular projects. My examination of the Oftebro case has demonstrated that this combination of masculine 'self-making' and Christian 'self-denial' could in fact be quite challenging.

The previous chapter concluded that, although the outcome of the 1873 Schreuder case meant the emergence of a new cultural hegemonic missionary masculinity in the NMS, certain elements of the Schreuder type of missionary masculinity survived. The memory of Christian Oftebro also lived on in the mission milieus in South Africa. His dismissal from missionary service was strongly criticised by the Christian Zulus at the Eshowe mission station as well as in the British settler community.[114] He gained much support in the missionary community, and most of his colleagues contributed financially when British settlers at Eshowe suggested the erection of a memorial at his grave.[115] As late as 1926, missionary Peder A. R. Strømme described the dismissal and death of Christian Oftebro as an 'unhealed wound in our mission'.[116] Nevertheless, NMS's Zulu mission became less of a 'medical' or 'industrial' mission after 1888 and more of a confessional 'Church mission', something which will be further investigated in the next chapter. An industrial school was established at the Eshowe mission station in 1887, but this project was never a success, ultimately closing in 1905.[117] Consequently, all-male missionaries employed by the NMS in South Africa from 1900 to 1945 were theologians and ordained pastors. Oftebro was not replaced by another medical missionary. Some of the missionaries regretted this, and the issue was occasionally brought up,[118] as both the mission fields in Madagascar and China were well equipped with physicians, nurses, deaconesses and deacons, and the establishment of health institutions had been a priority.[119] In 1921, Lars Martin Titlestad again raised the issue of a medical mission in Zululand, and in the following years this became a subject of negotiation between the missionary conference and NMS's Home Board – something we will return to in Chapter 6.

4
Confessional Missionary Masculinity

Introduction

In 1924, after the death of Karl Larsen Titlestad, who had served as a Zulu missionary from 1865 to 1891, an obituary was written by his colleagues Ole Stavem and Anders A. Olsen, a former missionary to Madagascar. In the obituary, Titlestad was praised for his qualities of 'gentleness', 'patience' and 'modesty'. However, regarding the genre of the obituary, the conclusion was somewhat surprising: 'Except for the scruples he for a while suffered from, he was a faithful son of our Evangelical-Lutheran church.'[1] What kind of 'scruples' did Titlestad suffer from? According to Olsen and Stavem, 'the kindly Titlestad' experienced a spiritual crisis at the end of the 1880s. He was exhausted after many years of hard missionary work that had resulted in almost no converts. Unexpectedly, a revival arose among Africans as well as European colonists in the north-western part of Natal, close to Titlestad's working field. Olsen and Stavem labelled the movement very briefly a 'Baptist Lammers-revival in miniature'.[2] Some of Titlestad's missionary friends became influenced by the religious movements and joined a 'free mission'. To Titlestad, this period was 'spiritually stressful', according to Olsen and Stavem, and doubts about the Lutheran confession and the dogma of infant baptism (*paedobaptism*) evolved within him.

This chapter will examine the relationship between masculinity and church confession in the NMS. The case of the missionary Karl Larsen Titlestad, who in 1891 was actually ordered by the NMS's Home Board to return immediately to Norway because of admitted doubts about central Lutheran dogma, provides the starting point for this discussion. In Olsen and Stavem's text, Titlestad's confessional scruples were represented as heretical ideas that unfortunately influenced him, partly because of his disillusion after a long, fruitless missionary service among the Zulus and partly because of his 'warm' and 'kind' personality. The religious revivals in Natal and Zululand at the end of the 1880s were further reduced to a marginal phenomenon – namely, 'a Baptist Lammers-revival in miniature'. Yet Titlestad was in touch with influential non-denominational religious movements – the international faith missions and the movements of Independent African Churches. Confronted with a fast-growing number of transnational and local mission agencies in south-east Africa, we find a group of Norwegian missionaries with an accelerating consciousness of their own Lutheran identity and a growing will to defend and fight for 'the church of their fathers'. As we saw, Olsen and Stavem assured their readers that the missionary Titlestad conquered his confessional doubts and ended up as a 'faithful son' of the Norwegian Evangelical-Lutheran Church.

Based on this discussion on the relation between confession and masculinity in the Norwegian mission movement, the chapter continues to explore the character of missionary masculinity in the NMS. It will examine how a particular aspect of the missionary masculinity – namely, the Lutheran identity – was strengthened from the 1890s. When facing Christian revivalist movements, whether African or Western, that advocated faith theology, millenarian theology, prophetic and spiritual talents, interdenominationalism, or non-confessionalism, the NMS missionaries increasingly emphasised confessional, institutional church building.

Although a missionary was expected to be a spiritual man, not a worldly one, there was a limit even for his spirituality. Interestingly, the millenarian, faith-oriented and interdenominational movements of the late nineteenth century were regarded as *too* spiritual, too emotional and too soft in the NMS discourse, and men engaged in these movements were portrayed as feminine and unmanly. In the discursive mobilisation against religious movements and 'other' confessions that could threaten the Lutheran church-building process in south-east Africa, a 'masculine' language of heroism and militarism was activated. The missionaries regarded themselves as 'soldiers' in the global struggle for World Lutheranism. Likewise, the gendered metaphor of 'faithful sons' was used to emphasise expatriate Norwegian men's affiliation with the Evangelical-Lutheran Church – 'the church of the fatherland'.

The case of the Norwegian Lutheran missionaries is interesting in light of Yvonne Marie Werner's hypothesis of church mobilisation and confessionalism as Christian men's strategy to counteract the secularisation of society and the feminisation of religion as well as further restoring and reinforcing male domination within the religious sphere (Chapter 1). Werner's team of researchers challenge historians' common assertion of religion as irrelevant for modern men by referring to other distinctive features of nineteenth-century Western society: the revivalist movements and the revitalisation of the confessional churches. They argue that confessional identity continued to be an important factor in the construction of nineteenth-century European national identities, and links exist between confessional or denominational culture and national identities.[3] Moreover, links exist between the processes of re-confessionalism and re-masculinisation in nineteenth-century European Christianity. Olaf Blaschke – in addition to his claim of a 'second confessional era' in Europe from 1830 to 1960 – launched the theory of a religious re-masculinisation in the wake of the tendency for re-confessionalism.[4]

This chapter will first look at the Norwegian Lutheran mission enterprise in a denominational, church-organisational context. It will then investigate the denominational disturbances that took place in the NMS's mission field of Natal and Zululand in the late 1880s – disturbances that actually resulted in the establishment of a Norwegian Evangelical-Lutheran Church in Durban as well as in Karl Larsen Titlestad's withdrawal from the field. Finally, it will discuss to what extent the confessional aspect was part of a Norwegian missionary masculinity construction.

The denominational context of a Norwegian Lutheran mission in south-east Africa

When Hans P. S. Schreuder and his assistant E. E. Thommesen arrived in the colony of Natal in 1844, they were welcomed by the British Methodist missionary James Archbell, who immediately introduced them to Congregationalist missionaries representing the American Board of Commissioners for Foreign Missions. For the next year and a half, the two Norwegians lived at the American mission station Umlazi, in Natal, while they studied the Zulu language and local customs. As soon as they had acquired some language abilities, they carried out a first excursion to Zululand, still a sovereign kingdom on the eastern frontier of the colony. Schreuder obtained an audience with King Mpande kaSenzanga-khona in Nodwengu and asked for permission to establish a Norwegian mission in the kingdom. As his request was persistently rejected by the king, Schreuder decided to sail to China in 1847 in search of a more promising mission.[5] Why did he not consider establishing a mission in Natal? In Schreuder's view, Natal was already 'occupied' by other missionary societies.[6] He advocated an 'apostolic praxis of mission', meaning the preaching of the Christian gospel in areas where it was unknown (i.e. not already introduced by any missionaries).[7] However, as it turned out, China was also an inappropriate alternative. Schreuder returned to Natal in 1848, convinced of God's calling of him to preach the gospel among the Zulu people.[8] As the first Western missionary, Schreuder finally received royal permission to establish permanent mission stations in Zululand in January 1851.[9] The NMS also remained one of a few missions in nineteenth-century south-east Africa with its 'nerve centre' in Zululand, not in Natal.[10]

As we have seen, Schreuder accepted the 'domains' of other missionaries of diverse denominations and did not want to interfere in their areas. On the other hand, he was highly conscious of his own confessional background. As an ordained pastor in the Church of Norway, he was obliged to teach in accordance with the confession of Augsburg, even in remote 'pagan' areas of the world. Schreuder's aim was to establish a Lutheran church in Zululand in line with the Scandinavian folk-church model.[11] However, he acted in accordance with the NMS and its profile as a Lutheran mission organisation. The NMS constitution of 1842 declared that its representatives in the mission fields should teach in accordance with 'The Holy Script and the Church of Norway's Confessional Scripts'.[12]

Olav Guttorm Myklebust asserts that the NMS arose in a decade marked by the 'victory of confessionalism' in church and mission, foremost on the European continent, and particularly in a Lutheran context.[13] Modern Protestants' overseas mission was originally a fruit of eighteenth- and nineteenth-century evangelical revivals. The goal was 'universal redemption' – namely, that all people of every nation should get to know the Christian Gospel. Myklebust defines this early Protestant missionary activity as a 'subjective' one.[14] More important than establishing church organisations that reflected the missionary's denominational belonging was the individual soul-winning activity. A majority of the Protestant missionary societies established from the 1790s was thus interdenominational[15] or interdenominational oriented.[16] However, this changed starting in the middle of the nineteenth century, and the denominational question became more important in Protestant missions established from the 1840s onward. According to Myklebust, the missionary organisations became more 'objective' oriented. Confessional doctrines were accentuated on behalf of missionaries' inner spiritual life and church tradition on behalf of missionaries' personal experiences.[17]

Even if the pioneer missionaries of the NMS had a distinct confessional identity as Lutherans and aimed to establish an Evangelical-Lutheran Zulu Church, reality could sometimes be more complicated than expected. As previously noted, Natal and Zululand were areas that attracted missionaries from diverse denominations and nationalities. Norman Etherington claims in his study of missionaries and Christian communities in south-east Africa that no other parts of nineteenth-century Africa were so thickly invested with Christian missionaries as this region.[18] Against this background he finds it peculiar that the number of converts were very few. By 1880, the African Christian population in Natal did not exceed 10,000 people, accounting for considerably less than 10 per cent of the total population. In Zululand, where the Norwegians worked, converts numbered in the hundreds. According to Etherington, most missionaries, independent of denomination, lost confidence in their organisations' particular abilities and methods in recruiting new converts among the resisting Zulu people. Similarities in mission theory and practice outweighed the differences.[19] On the local level, missionaries from diverse denominations approached each other. There was frequent contact between Norwegian missionaries and missionaries from other Protestant denominations and nationalities.[20] Three assistant missionaries even left the NMS for service in the Anglican Society for the Propagation of the Gospel in Foreign Parts.[21] Missionary families living far from colleagues apparently appreciated social contact and Christian fellowship with other Westerners, and confession and nationality were in those cases subordinated. It is also very likely that the turbulent decades of the 1870s and 1880s, with British imperial intervention, Boer expansion and Zulu civil wars destabilising the area and on several occasions forcing missionaries to leave their stations, called forth a kind of solidarity and common understanding among white Western missionaries.

In May 1887, the once-sovereign Zululand became a British possession. In 1898, it was incorporated into Natal, which had been a self-governing colony in the British Empire since 1893. In the NMS organisational history writings, the years of 1887–88 are regarded as a watershed. The 'proud' Zulu monarchy was 'humiliated and crushed', and the British colonial rule in Natal and Zululand brought 'peace' and 'progression'. Western missionary organisations profited from the new political situation, as the colonial rulers encouraged the 'civilising' efforts of the Christian missionaries. Missionaries could finally live and work in peace at their stations, and the number of converts increased from year to year.[22] However, as the years of 'trials and hardship' were over, according to mission discourse, and a new era of consolidation and growth in the mission work started, we also find an increased emphasis on church organisation and church confession among the NMS missionaries.

The political events of 1887 introduced a period in which the NMS in south-east Africa strengthened its confessional identity and developed strong and enduring bonds to other Lutheran missionary organisations. In 1889, the first co-operation between Lutheran missions working in Natal was initiated.[23] Annual Lutheran conferences sought to promote collaboration on publications like hymn books, catechisms and religious literature in the Zulu language as well as the Lutheran church periodical *Isitunywa* from 1897. A more fixed co-operation became reality from 1912 through the organisation Cooperating Lutheran Missions (CLM) in Natal, a joint venture between the NMS, the Church of Sweden Mission (CSM), and the Berlin Mission Society (BMS). The three missions sought to establish an Evangelical Lutheran Zulu Church and authorise their missionary conferences to work for this purpose. However, the immediate result of the CLM was an extensive financial and administrative co-operation involving three educational institutions: the theological seminary at Oscarsberg, the evangelist school at Emmaus, and the teachers' college at Umphumulo. Other Lutheran missions joined CLM, and in 1939 there was agreement on a new objective: 'To establish a self-supporting, self-propagating and self-administrating Lutheran Church among the Zulus and kindred tribes, preserving their characteristic traits as far as possible.'[24] The Lutheran unification process continued after World War II, supported and encouraged by the Lutheran World Federation from 1947, and in 1975 five regional churches, each reflecting various mission influences and traditions, united to form the Evangelical Lutheran Church of Southern Africa (ELCSA).[25]

Denominational disturbances

In the same period that we find a Norwegian missionary organisation in south-east Africa strengthening its identity as a denominational mission, religious waves that moved in completely opposite directions swept over the country. First, a range of Western, interdenominational faith missions reached the African continent in the last decades of the nineteenth century.[26] Second, in the 1890s, the phenomenon of African Independent Churches came to light; these churches were generally established in opposition to mainline, denominational mission churches. Regarding the latter, historian Robert Edgar claims that colonised people through the founding of independent churches challenged mission Christianity, as Christianity was 'interrogated, challenged, reinterpreted, and assimilated'. Sometimes the vehicle for challenge was an established mission church, at other times it was independent religious movements.[27] In the case of south-east Africa, the ordination of indigenous clergy in mission churches encouraged a small group of black professional churchmen to expect equal treatment from their white colleagues. However, their expectations were not met, and from the 1890s onward numerous Ethiopian separatist churches were founded by African clergy and evangelists, many of whom were the missionary societies' most trusted and admired men.[28]

Markus Dahle was the first NMS missionary to report substantial revivals among Africans in the area of Greytown in northern Natal.[29] According to Dahle's 1889 report, the pastor of the Dutch Reformed Church in Greytown, Mr Turnbull, was a mission-oriented pastor who had acted as a supportive mentor to African revival leaders.[30] Dahle himself regularly visited a group of converts in the same area and had received permission to construct a simple chapel at the farm of a German settler. When missionary Karl Larsen Titlestad also reported revivals, the Secretary Lars Dahle exclaimed in the *NMT* that 'glimpses of light' were finally visible 'in the Zulu-Kaffir's night'.[31] These initial reports of revivals and awakenings in south-east Africa were received as wonderful and exciting news among mission supporters in Norway. However, soon thereafter, both missionaries and mission management realised that the religious movements could actually challenge the Lutheran church-building process. In Lars Dahle's report from his inspection of the mission field of Zululand and Natal in 1902–03, he commented on the issue of the independent Ethiopian churches and warned against the 'degrading and uttermost dangerous forces'.[32] It was not until the 1920s that some of the ordained pastors in the Norwegian Lutheran Zulu Church resigned from service either to join an African independent church or to establish their own separate churches.[33] White missionaries' fear of black pastors' independent church movements is an issue that will be further discussed in Chapter 5. Meanwhile, this section will concentrate on the NMS's response to transnational, interdenominational missionary movements.

A Scandinavian 'free mission' in Durban

In 1889, a group of interdenominational 'free' missionaries belonging to the newly established Free East Africa Mission (FEAM) (Den Frie Østafrikanske Mission) was established in Durban.[34] FEAM was a pan-Scandinavian group consisting of five female and four male missionaries;

unlike the NMS, FEAM considered all of its representatives – women as well as men – to be missionaries. The brothers Olaf and Jacob Wettergren were the group's spiritual leaders. They were both born in Zululand, where their father, Paul Peter Wettergren, served as an NMS missionary from 1861 to 1870. Through the presence of FEAM in Durban from 1889, NMS missionaries in south-east Africa had their first encounter with the international wave of faith missions. Historian Klaus Fiedler defines faith mission as a mission that traces its origin, or the origin of its principles, directly or indirectly back to the China Inland Mission (CIM), founded by Hudson Taylor and his wife Maria in 1865. The 'faith principle' of financial support meant that no home organisation or home church was responsible for providing missionaries with fixed financial support. Faith missions were interdenominational and otherwise characterised by holiness theology, a pragmatic approach to church order, an egalitarian structure (ordained and unordained female and male missionaries shared an equal position), cultural identification with the host country, a priority of evangelism for institutional work and field-directed mission work.[35]

FEAM was one of several faith mission-oriented organisations whose origin lay in the wake of the Swedish-American evangelist Fredrik Franson's global missionary ministry.[36] In 1883, Franson visited Norway, coming into contact with the already mentioned Paul Peter Wettergren, a previous missionary to Zululand who was one of a few university-educated theologians on the NMS staff.[37] After the death of his wife, Wencke von der Lippe Knudsen, Wettergren left the mission field in 1870. While working as a pastor in the Church of Norway, he became involved in the church reform movement that later led to the founding of the Evangelical Lutheran Free Church of Norway in 1877. Wettergren accepted the calling to serve as the first pastor of the denomination's newly established congregation in Arendal. He left the state church in March 1877 and published an official defence of his move.[38] Franson, who campaigned in Norway in 1883, was invited to Wettergren's congregation in Arendal. In 1888, Wettergren also attended Franson's 'evangelist course' in Kristiania. Wettergren's affiliation with Franson was not appreciated in the Evangelical Lutheran Free Church, and he resigned from his post in 1888. In December of that same year, Wettergren was baptised (or 're-baptised'[39]) in the icy waters of Skagerak. By then, he had already made his preparations for a new, interdenominational Zulu mission, which in 1889 was constituted as the FEAM. His sons Olaf and Jacob, who had both been students at the famous Moody's Bible school in Mount Hermon in Chicago, joined their ageing father and travelled widely in Scandinavia to raise funds for the mission. The magazine *The Missionary* (*Missionæren*) was launched in 1888 in support of the new venture.[40] Wettergren never realised his dream of going back to Zululand. In March 1889 he suffered a disabling stroke that led to his death five months later. He was buried in Arendal, just one day before his sons and their companions disembarked in Durban.

The Wettergrens and their FEAM colleagues soon initiated a co-operation with the Swedish missionary Otto Witt, who was sent to Zululand in 1877 as the CSM's first missionary.[41] Unlike the NMS and most Protestant missionary organisations in the nineteenth century, this Swedish mission was not organised as an independent society inside the frame of the state church, but was in fact the official church's mission enterprise. Witt, who was welcomed by Schreuder and provisionally stayed at his Entumeni mission station, purchased the farm 'Rorke's Drift' in 1878 and renamed it the Oscarsberg mission station.[42] Witt's theology and theory on mission underwent fundamental changes during the mid-1880s. He rejected Lutheran confessional theology and became a spokesman for non-denominational Christianity. Furthermore, he criticised the well-established strategy of most missions in south-east Africa – namely, to construct mission stations or mission villages and educational institutions. As he was influenced by millenarian ideas, he regarded itinerant evangelism, in order to reach as many 'unconverted' as possible before Jesus Christ's predicted second coming, to be the prime object of mission.[43] Witt broke with the CSM in 1890. Afterwards, he moved from Oscarsberg to Durban, was baptised by Olaf Wettergren, and joined the FEAM's missionary staff.[44]

In 1889, the FEAM missionaries started to arrange evangelical revival meetings in the Scandinavian congregation in Durban. In their preaching they criticised denominational Christianity for being 'spiritually dead'. They further rejected infant baptism and started to baptise Scandinavian 'converts'.[45] Since 1880, Lutheran Scandinavians in Durban had organised divine services in a rented Wesleyan school house. As the congregation lacked its own pastor, lay ministers or NMS missionaries visiting Durban were often asked to preach and administer the sacraments.[46] In 1883, the fellowship was officially constituted a Lutheran congregation based on the Augsburg Confession. However, as the group consisted of both Lutherans and Baptists, and as the non-Lutheran faction had a growing influence, the references to 'Lutheran' and the 'Augsburg Confession' were removed from its constitution after only three years. In 1887, the congregation purchased a house that was consecrated as a sanctuary and given the denominationally neutral name 'Scandinavian Chapel'.[47]

The Lutheran part of the Scandinavian congregation in Durban was alarmed by the development after the arrival of FEAM missionaries. Thirty-two Norwegian male immigrants sent an application to the NMS asking for assistance to establish a separate Lutheran church in the city. The letter of request from the 'brothers in Durban' was copied and circulated amongst all the NMS missionaries, who were asked to comment on it.[48] Ole Stavem travelled to Durban in January 1890 to investigate the circumstances, subsequently sending a thorough report to the Home Board.[49] The issue of an NMS enterprise in Durban was further discussed at the missionary conference in May 1890.[50] The Home Board eventually sanctioned the establishment of a Lutheran church in Durban, and Stavem was asked to be its pastor.[51] However, it was made clear that the NMS was a 'Heathen's Mission', not a mission with a call to serve emigrated Scandinavians. NMS missionaries should therefore give priority to the Zulu migrant workers dwelling in Durban. As it turned out, the missionary stationed in Durban had in fact two separate fields of work. First, he should establish a mission among the rapidly growing black, mostly male migrant population working on the docks and temporarily living in wretched barracks. Second, he should serve as a Lutheran pastor among Scandinavians (most of them Norwegians) in the city, who consisted of both established immigrants and visiting seamen. Chapter 5 will further discuss the NMS's mission work among male immigrant workers, and Chapter 9 will return to the issue of the missionaries' pastoral service of Scandinavian immigrants.

Confessional disturbances did not hit the Scandinavian community in Durban exclusively. Some of the NMS missionaries were also influenced by the new religious trends. At the end of 1890, superintendent Stavem reported to the Home Board that missionary Karl Larsen Titlestad had recently spent a lot of time together with 'the re-baptised' Otto Witt. Moreover, Titlestad had admitted to having serious doubts about the Lutheran theology and practice of baptism, as he no longer believed in the dogma of regeneration through baptism.[52] Some months later Stavem was worried that Witt and Wettergren, who were currently touring Zululand, would visit 'the weak Titlestad and the even weaker Mrs. Titlestad and that they will not give up until they have had the pleasure of bringing this Norwegian missionary into the water'.[53] Stavem's comment reveals a fear of 're-baptism' even among the NMS staff. The members of the Home Board reacted resolutely, sending a letter to Titlestad that ordered him to immediately prepare for his homecoming.[54] The Home Board admitted that Titlestad's spiritual development had both surprised and hurt them. As a student at the mission school in

Stavanger he had been regarded as 'the most mature and solid also in a spiritual sense', and in numerous reports from the mission field he had given the impression that he was a reliable Lutheran missionary. The Home Board members expressed their hope that, if Titlestad could come home and again 'inhale the air of our church in our dear fatherland', he might possibly be able to return to 'our dear Lutheran church, which we know for certain is founded on the Scripture'. After receiving the letter, Titlestad started the preparations for his return to Norway.[55] On 17 August 1891 he left Zululand, never to return.

Denominational disturbances at home

The spiritual journey of Titlestad, Witt and Wettergren – all presumed to be solid Lutheran pastors – and the establishment of a free interdenominational Scandinavian mission among the Zulus shocked and worried the missionaries in the field as well as the management at home. In 1889, the issues of 'Missionary societies and free-missionaries' were discussed at all of the regional conferences of the NMS in Norway.[56] A majority of the conference participants supported the Home Board's proposal that the classic model of missionary societies – Christian men and women canalising their support through a missionary organisation that educated and sent out missionaries – should be regarded as the most qualified mission method.

FEAM was a fruit of Wettergren's affiliation with Franson's global evangelistic ministry, which came to be another point of concern for the NMS leadership. After Hudson Taylor's celebrated call for 1,000 new missionaries for China at the 1890 Shanghai Missionary Conference, Franson launched a recruitment campaign in which he promised to deliver 200 missionaries from the Scandinavian countries.[57] He established the Scandinavian Alliance Mission of North America and soon started to send missionaries to China, Japan, the Himalayas, Mongolia, and East and South Africa. A lot of enthusiasm for Hudson's China mission emerged in Norway as well, especially among the younger generations. Some Norwegians had from the mid-1880s started their careers as CIM missionaries, and by 1890 China committees were established in several Norwegian towns.[58]

When the China committee of Bergen assembled for a China conference in October 1890, Secretary Lars Dahle was invited as one of the main speakers. However, the committee, who was seriously interested in a close collaboration with the NMS regarding future mission work in China, was disappointed.[59] Dahle's attitude towards an NMS venture in China was extremely negative. He emphasised that Madagascar was the mission field that should have priority. Referring to reliable, scientific mission statistics, Dahle further argued that China was a high-cost mission field with unsatisfactory results and that too many Western missionaries were already working there. Finally, the Norwegian China enthusiasts were, in Dahle's opinion, a dissimilar group with loose relations to the Lutheran church and confession; thus, for the NMS, it was out of the question to co-operate with such groups. At the conference in Bergen, Ole Næstegaard, who had served as a CIM missionary in China since 1888 and whose letters and reports had trigged 'China fever' in Norway, was officially interrogated by Dahle, who was especially concerned about his confessional standpoints. According to several conference reports, Næstegaard made a bad figure and was totally overrun by Dahle's brilliant polemics.[60] Despite Dahle's authoritative position and his strong opposition against a Norwegian mission in China, he could not prevent the Norwegian Lutheran China Mission from being established in 1891, consequently challenging the dominant position of the NMS in Norway. When commenting on the establishment of a new China mission, Dahle was pleased by its Lutheran character.[61] However, during the 1890s, he continued to reject any further collaboration with the organisation, which he still found to be too influenced by Reformed Christianity. In 1901, the NMS established its own China mission.

'Heroic soldiers' and 'faithful sons': re-confessionalisation and re-masculinisation in the NMS

The departure of a new band of NMS missionaries to the Zulus in February 1864 was quite an event in the little town of Stavanger.[62] Enthusiastic mission supporters had for some years donated funds for the mission ship *Elieser* that could now make its maiden voyage.[63] The ship was named after the servant of the Old Testament's patriarch Abraham, who was sent to Abraham's homeland to search for a bride for Isaac, his son. Analogous to the Old Testament narrative of Elieser, the New Testament metaphor of Jesus as the bridegroom searching and waiting for his bride was central in the descriptions of *Elieser*'s mission.[64] 'The bride' was in this case a metaphor for 'the heathens' in Africa, who did not know the bridegroom's love for her. *Elieser* should bring this message of love to Zululand, and the missionaries should be the messengers. This example from the mission discourse of the 1860s reveals what some historians have labelled 'mission romanticism'.[65]

Towards the end of the nineteenth century, the discourse of 'soft and sweet' missionary love became increasingly rare, and an alternative 'harder' discourse of missionary conquering and conquest was frequently used among Norwegian missionaries. As previously indicated, John Tosh asserts that empire was a projection of masculinity and 'national virility' in British national life. Furthermore, in the popular imagination of the empire, Tosh finds an increasing validation of ruthless violence during the period defined as New Imperialism (1870–1914). The empire had been acquired by the use of force, and force was necessary to continue the extension of the frontiers. Moreover, the empire was widely perceived to be in danger.[66] The Norwegian missionaries in south-east Africa did not represent any imperial power; they saw themselves as representatives of the 'Kingdom of God'. They still shared the imperialist understanding of one's own work as a service 'at the frontier of Christian civilisation'. Although the missionaries never participated in colonial military warfare, they did in some cases welcome colonial conquest of 'heathen monarchies', as was the case during the Anglo-Zulu war of 1879.[67] Discursively, a language of expansion, conquering and conquest was increasingly used in the last decades of the nineteenth century.

The young missionary Lars Martin Titlestad, who arrived at the Ungoye mission station in Zululand in 1893, was optimistic regarding the evangelising task in his first reports: 'The heathens in this area are like soft, well-prepared clay and it should be relatively easy to mould or print the image of Christ in them.'[68] A year later, disappointed by people's indifference to the Christian message, he started to define missionary service as 'a fight against Heathendom'.[69] He referred to the word of Paul the Apostle in Ephesians 6, 12: 'Our struggle is not against flesh and blood, but against the rulers, against the authorities, against the powers of this dark world and against the spiritual forces of the evil in the heavenly realms.' In the mission discourse, it was the 'heathen world' that should be won for the king Jesus, and this warfare forged a mobilisation of crusaders. Missionaries who died while they were in service were often described as heroic soldiers who fell in the midst of battle.[70]

Yet there was another fight going on as well. We have already seen that, from the days of Schreuder, confessionalism was a central aspect of the NMS missionaries' subjectivities. The missionaries saw themselves as representatives of Lutheran Christianity, and their aim was to establish Lutheran congregations and an Evangelical-Lutheran Zulu Church. The following examples of missionary memories from their days at the mission school show young men's eagerness to demonstrate a Lutheran identity. They furthermore reveal how this identity was strengthened by defining 'other' confessions as enemies to conquer. In a biographical text on Christian Oftebro, his peer Marcus Dahle remembered how Oftebro physically attacked a Mormon pastor during an outdoor ceremony of baptism in a Stavanger bay.[71] Ole Stavem shared a narrative about his peers lighting a fire and burning books written by a Catholic priest. The books originally belonged to one of the students, who sold them because he needed the money.[72] These narratives may illustrate hasty actions of young men, but they nevertheless reveal an attitude of regarding 'other' confessions as the enemy of Lutheran Christianity.

The Lutheran identity was definitely an essential part of the NMS missionary masculinity, and it was more clearly expressed when challenged by other expanding religious movements. In the case of the NMS in south-east Africa, the reactions of both missionaries and the Home Board when encountering new trends of non-denominational Christianity have already been described herein. In general, the tendency was for a stronger Lutheran mobilisation from the late 1880s. As displayed, a process of unification among Lutheran missions in Natal and Zululand started in 1889, and a Scandinavian Evangelical-Lutheran Church was established by the NMS in Durban in 1890. On a discursive level, in addition, the mobilisation on behalf of Lutheranism is recognisable, and two kinds of gendered metaphors were frequently used: the metaphor of 'faithful sons' and the metaphor of 'heroic soldiers'. As previously discussed, Yvonne Maria Werner and Olaf Blaschke put forth hypotheses of a religious re-masculinisation in the wake of the re-confessionalisation of European societies and churches in the 1830–1960 period. In his research on Protestant and Catholic churches in Germany, Blaschke finds processes of re-masculinisation to be latent in the last part of the nineteenth century, but open and more manifest from the early twentieth century.[73]

The faithful-son metaphor was related to both a national and a confessional identity. On 10 November 1883, on the 400th anniversary of the birth of the German church reformer Martin Luther, NMS missionaries initiated a celebration of Luther at Eshowe. 18 Norwegians, both men and women, participated in what was estimated to be the first Luther anniversary in Zululand.[74] Ole Stavem delivered the main lecture. Stavem claimed that Luther was a man chosen by God to, first, purify the Gospel and, second, to prepare for new movements in the development of churches and nations. His theology had inspired 'mature, independent and powerful' enterprises among the Germanic peoples – Germans, Scandinavians and Britons – in their home nations as well as in 'the heathen world'. The Germanic peoples were unfortunately, despite their 'brave freedom-loving minds and powerful innovative spirit', slaves to 'the legalist church of Rome'. Finally, in the fifteenth century, through divine intervention, something happened. God did not send his son Jesus Christ a second time; rather, He sent Martin Luther. Luther's mission was to put the redemption of Jesus in the right perspective: being Christians was not to be slaves, but 'to be Sons'. Stavem concluded that Luther's movement liberated spiritual life in all the Germanic nations and in the long run was a precondition for the modern missionary movement.[75]

Historian Alexander Maurits claims in his research on the masculinity of leading theologians within the mid-nineteenth-century Church of Sweden, related to the so-called Lund High Church Movement, that the movement's exemplary heroes – among them Martin Luther – were historical constructs shaped in the intersection of ecclesiology, historiography, nationalism and gender.[76] In Stavem's speech we can trace a similar link between Lutheranism and Norwegian nationalism. Besides being the first pastor of the Scandinavian Lutheran Church in Durban, he was also the first chairman of 'The Norwegian Society' established in Durban in 1896.[77] As a retired missionary back in Norway, Stavem had the opportunity to greet the congregation in Durban on its 50th anniversary in 1930. 'What was our goal?' he asks in retrospect, accentuating that by 'we' he meant the Norwegian 'brothers' with whom he used to co-operate in Durban. Stavem's unbalanced masculine perspective and his blindness of the many Norwegian women actively partaking in the church life are astonishing.[78] He continues with gendered metaphors: 'We were far away from our fatherland. But we had not left the Norwegian church. We still wanted to belong to this church. She was our mother and should remain our mother.' As faithful sons, they aimed to gather all Norwegians in Durban in a Norwegian congregation stabilised on the foundation of the Lutheran confession. Stavem claimed that their hard work was not motivated by a critical view of other denominations, although they were convinced that the Lutheran faith and confession in a special way corresponded with the Word of God: 'We know that our fathers by this faith and confession lived happy lives and thereby went home to God. Should not we do all we could for the defence and continuation of our kind of Worship?'[79]

Meanwhile, the heroic-soldier metaphor was used to describe the Norwegian missionaries' defence of Lutheranism as well as the struggle against its 'enemies'. As noted, 'heathendom' was a well-known enemy, but there were others as well. At the Luther anniversary in Zululand in 1883, the young and newly arrived NMS missionary Ole Zephanias Norgaard used military terms when he asserted in his speech that the most dangerous enemy of the Evangelical-Lutheran Church currently in Norway was 'the disbelief'. This enemy could be compared with 'the dark enemy' Luther himself had to fight – namely, 'the Roman pope church'.

A central battle on behalf of Lutheranism in south-east Africa took place in 1890. While the NMS missionaries were still waiting for the Home Board's final decision regarding the Lutheran church establishment in Durban, they discussed how they should temporarily serve the immigrants in Durban. Stavem proposed that they refrain from preaching in the Baptist-dominated Scandinavian Chapel. The majority of the missionaries supported Stavem's proposal, and Titlestad did not gain much support when he expressed that he would preach wherever he was invited, Catholic churches not excepted. Martinius Borgen, on the other hand, was applauded when he asserted that he no longer wished to be associated with the Scandinavian Chapel, where 're-baptism' occurred and 'non-Lutheran' theology was taught; it was about time to 'raise the pure Lutheran flag'.[80] The Home Board eventually commissioned Stavem for the post as pastor of the Lutheran congregation in Durban. Stavem followed Borgen's advice and enthusiastically showed the 'true colours' of the confession. After some months he reported home that the Baptists were unsatisfied with his appearance; they had obviously hoped for non-interference from the NMS side: 'Fortunately they were mistaken! This mix of Baptism and diverse arts of salvation that went on in the Scandinavian Chapel was something of a representation of Norwegian Christians. Recently these people have rented out their locations to the British Salvation Army. Same seeks the same.'[81]

While Norwegian missionaries and immigrants in the 1880s and 1890s mobilised to defend Lutheran Christianity in south-east Africa, a Nordic Evangelical-Lutheran mission conference was arranged in Kristiania in July 1889.[82] Similar conferences had been arranged in Malmö in 1863 and in Göteborg in 1885, and they can, as historian Ruth Hemstad has pointed out, be regarded as part of a second rise in the cultural movement of 'Scandinavianism'.[83] Everyone interested in the Scandinavian mission was welcomed to participate, on the condition that the person was a Lutheran and was member of a national church (*Landskirke*). The NMS Secretary Dahle, who was one of the speakers at the conference, reported that 600 men participated, including 200 visitors from Sweden and Denmark. He felt it encouraging that so many 'serious and prominent men' took part in 'the fight for the extensiveness of the Kingdom of God'.[84] As a result of the conference, the *Nordic Mission Handbook* was released.[85] In addition, the *Nordic Journal of Mission* (*Nordisk*

Missionstidsskrift) followed in the wake of the Kristiania conference; Dahle was one of the initiators of the journal launched in 1890.[86] The journal's aim was to present biographies of Nordic missionaries, historical articles, missiological discussions and actual mission literature. Whereas previous popular mission magazines had appealed to mission supporters, both men and women, at a grass-roots level, the new journal had a theological approach suitable for the leading mission men.

According to the reports from the conference debates, several of the debaters emphasised that the current Lutheran world mission faced three enemies: secularism, the Catholic Church and the reformed 'sects'. Regarding the latter, the case of the FEAM missionaries, who in 1889 prepared for their departure to Zululand, was on several occasions used as an example of 'zealotry' and 'incompetence' within this kind of evangelical missionary work. C. Strömberg, a Swede and previous missionary in the Basel Missionary Society, dealt with current mission statistics in his speech. According to Strömberg's statistics, there were 209 million Catholics and 138 million Protestants in the world. Although the Catholics still had a dominant position in the Christian world mission, the Protestants had expanded extensively during the last century. Strömberg was certain that the future belonged to the Protestants and that the Scandinavian Lutheran churches had a special part to play. The Scandinavian nations were no colonising powers, and they 'owned wonderful spiritual richness', which they were obliged to share with the 'heathen world'. In Strömberg's opinion, the Nordic missionaries as part of the 'Mission Army of Warfare' should be the front ranks in the advancements of Protestantism.[87] In an article in the first volume of the *Nordic Journal of Mission*, Strömberg asserted that the variety within Protestantism had many benefits. The different denominational, national churches were like different 'army divisions', each having its own trademarks, special tasks, strengths and abilities in the 'mission army'.[88]

As David Tjeder has shown, the concept of character was central in nineteenth-century middle-class masculinity discourses.[89] Thus, it is illuminating that Strömberg compares mission without confession to a man without character.[90] Scandinavian Lutheran mission leaders in the 1890s, as well as Lutheran missionaries in the mission field, considered faithfulness to a church confession, and likewise strong confessional identity, as masculine deeds. These men saw no nuances between interdenominational attitudes and non-confessional standpoints; to be non-confessional was the same as being spineless, indecisive and cowardly, not showing one's 'true colours'. The male representatives of the new interdenominational faith missions were regarded as sentimental, irrational, unskilled, immature zealots – namely, as effeminate and unmanly men.[91] It was therefore a manly deed to dissociate from these weird men and their non-Lutheran spirituality. Stavem, who was known to be a solid Lutheran man, sharply criticised the 'zealotry and sentimentality' of the FEAM missionaries and could not bear their 'shallow guitar-playing' and 'nerve-shaking obtrusiveness'.[92] Likewise, Lars Dahle saw it as his duty to fight non-Lutheran tendencies in the milieus that propagated Hudson Taylor's China mission in Norway. An example is his hard treatment of the China missionary Næstegaard, who was humiliated in front of a large audience. No wonder that the 'spiritual' but 'weak' Karl Larsen Titlestad, struggling with confessional doubts and having a close fellowship with re-baptised men like Witt and Wettergren, was called home from the mission field and the front line.

Conclusion

From the pioneer days in the 1840s, confessionalism was a central aspect of the NMS missionaries' identities. The missionaries saw themselves as representatives of Lutheran Christianity, and their aim was to establish Lutheran congregations and an Evangelical-Lutheran Church in Zululand. Olav Guttorm Myklebust claims that the NMS arose in the decennium – the 1840s – that more than any else marks the victory of confessionalism in the international Protestant missionary movement. This assertion corresponds with Olaf Blaschkes' theory of a 'second confessional era' in Europe from 1830 to 1960. Norwegian missionaries strengthened their Lutheran identity towards the end of the century. Confronted with new non-denominational religious trends in the 1880s and 1890s (i.e. international faith missions and Independent African Churches – trends that threatened the Lutheran church-building process both among Scandinavian immigrants and Zulu Christians), the NMS missionaries in the field mobilised on behalf of Lutheranism. Interestingly, the same tendency occurred among mission leaders at home, who mobilised through pan-Nordic Evangelical-Lutheran mission conferences and publications. The enemies of what was understood to be a Lutheran World Mission were no longer paganism alone, but also a growing secularism in the home countries, Catholic world missions and ultimately a great variety of upcoming revivalist, interdenominational faith missions. This case of a confessional mobilisation in the Norwegian missionary movement can be understood as an example of re-confessionalisation among Christian men.

Yvonne Maria Werner and Olaf Blaschke, among others,[93] have launched the theory of a religious re-masculinisation in the wake of the tendency for re-confessionalisation. It is relevant to ask whether the frequent use of a gendered language and gendered metaphors in the Norwegian missionary movement, representing the missionaries partly as faithful sons attending to their Lutheran heritage and partly as heroic soldiers struggling for a global Lutheran influence, can be seen as examples of this alleged process of re-masculinisation. The current research has further revealed that, in the hegemonic Lutheran mission discourse in Scandinavia, male missionaries attracted to non-denominational religious movements were portrayed as unskilled, emotional, unstable and weird – namely, as unmanly men. In the historical writings of Scandinavian missions in South Africa, men like Karl Larsen Titlestad, Otto Witt and Paul Peter Wettergren have been marginalised and the religious courses they followed regarded as dead ends. However, in light of the twentieth century's enormous growth of non-confessional Independent African Churches on the one hand and faith-oriented non-denominational missions and Pentecostal missions on the other, the religious paths and life stories of these men should be taken more seriously.

5

Norwegian Missionary Masculinity and 'Other' Zulu Masculinity

Introduction

In 1893, Baleni kaNdlela Mthimkhulu was ordained as the first Zulu pastor in the Norwegian Lutheran Zulu Church. He should be regarded as a pioneer for other reasons as well. After the highly celebrated baptism of the first convert in the NMS on 6 June 1858, the young woman Mathenjwase kaNondumo Shange, Mthimkhulu was among the first group of male converts baptised. This second baptism ceremony in NMS history took place on 14 July 1859 at the Umphumulo mission station and was conducted by Hans P. S. Schreuder.[1] When Baleni kaNdlela Mthimkhulu became a Christian, he wished to be called Simon Ndlela, or simply Simon, by which he is known in the NMS records.[2] Ndlela settled at the Umphumulo mission station, where he later married a Christian woman and established his own homestead. He continued to work under the supervision of station manager Tobias Udland and received some basic education in reading, writing and religion. In the early 1870s, Ndlela started assisting in the mission school as a teacher, becoming one of the first native teachers in the Norwegian mission schools.[3] Furthermore, as a result of Ndlela's evangelistic outreach, the first outstation was established in the NMS in 1875. According to Udland, the people at 'Simon's place' were eager 'to listen and learn', and they had decided to build their own chapel.[4] Ndlela was also the first Zulu evangelist put in charge of a Norwegian mission station. While missionary Petter Gottfred Nilsen was on furlough in Norway, Ndlela was appointed temporary manager of the Eotimati mission station.[5]

Olav Guttorm Myklebust asserts in his centennial history of the NMS's Zulu mission that two events were of great importance during the nineteenth century.[6] One was the 1858 baptism of the first convert; the other was the 1893 ordination of the first Zulu pastor. While the first event has made a definite impression on the NMS's organisational memory,[7] the second has not received the same attention. To be fair, the NMS's first ordination in Zululand after more than 40 years of missionary work paled in comparison to the 34 pastors ordained in the NMS's Malagasy mission in the same year. The latter was announced in the mission magazine under the heading 'A wonderful ordination', and the editor, Lars Dahle, informed Norwegian mission supporters that after a mere 26 years of missionary work in Madagascar, already 56 Malagasy pastors were in active church service.[8] The founders of the NMS were ideologically influenced by the 'three-self' theory (see Chapter 2). The goal of the mission work was to establish native churches that would become 'self-supporting, self-governing and self-propagating', and part of the mission strategy was to 'train African converts as pastors and national assistants'.[9] Given the background of this mission theory, it is relevant to ask why it took so long for NMS missionaries in Zululand to fulfil the original objective of recruiting, educating and ordaining indigenous church personnel in practice.

The recruitment of Zulu teachers, evangelists and pastors was largely a gendered project as the future leaders of the Zulu church had to be men according to contemporary theological thinking and practice. In this chapter I will examine the relationship between Norwegian and Zulu men in the NMS. Mrinalini Sinha found that English colonists in India in the late nineteenth century constructed their own masculinity by describing 'other' Indians, especially men from the Indian higher classes, as effeminate.[10] Did Norwegian missionaries construct own masculinity by making references to 'other' Zulu masculinity? We have already discussed that masculine 'countertypes' could be effective as contrasts to strengthen normative ideals of masculinity. In the three previous chapters of this book I have examined how a missionary masculinity was constructed within the community of Norwegian men in the NMS, concentrating on internal processes in the Norwegian mission and demonstrating that – although notions of the ideal missionary masculinity were contested – certain ideas became more influential and culturally hegemonic. The practical social consequences for missionary men who differed from, or opposed, the hegemonic missionary masculinity ideal could be severe, as we have seen. What practical social implications did discursive constitutions of masculinity have for different groups of men in the Norwegian–Zulu encounter?

According to Robert Morrell, Connell's theory of hegemonic masculinity, which integrates issues of power and politics, has influenced recent South African gender research.[11] The gendered idea of rival masculinities, claims to power and finally the importance of class and race have appealed to researchers working in regions of complex and mixed-gender regimes and identities. In nineteenth-century South African history, a range of masculinities can be identified and defined. The idea of a 'patchwork quilt of patriarchies' was introduced by Belinda Bozzoli in 1983, who suggested the co-existence of many patriarchies in nineteenth-century South Africa.[12] Cherryl Walker found it useful to reduce the various forms of patriarchies to two dominant systems: 'the one broadly characteristic of the pre-capitalist Bantu-speaking societies of the region, the other of the colonial states established by the European settlers'.[13] Morrell lists white colonial masculinities (British, Boer, etc.), African rural masculinities and black (multi-ethnic) urban masculinities to be the three main groups. White supremacy in South African history suggests that white ruling-class masculinity was hegemonic. However, according to Morrell, colonialism never destroyed traditional African masculinities. It continued as a 'collective gender identity' amongst African men, reflecting a pre-colonial past and the gender regimes of those institutions which remained relatively intact. Accelerated urbanisation and industrialisation processes created an urban proletariat and a black masculinity, which was homogeneous in the sense of its opposition to white masculinity.[14]

This chapter, which asks how a Norwegian masculinity was constructed in relation to 'other' Zulu masculinity, will first analyse NMS missionaries' perceptions of the Zulu male and Zulu masculinity as represented in mission literature. It will then, second, present and discuss the gendered mission strategies of the NMS in terms of winning Zulu men for the Christian faith. Third, it will examine the case of Baleni kaNdlela Mthimkhulu's ordination in 1893. However, out of necessity, I will in this chapter also examine some of the events and processes preceding the dismissal of the very same pastor ten years later. The case of Baleni kaNdlela Mthimkhulu has not been scrutinised thoroughly by previous historians. It nevertheless reveals that, although Zulu men were converted to Christianity, recruited as church personnel, and eventually ordained, they were still not treated as missionaries' equal co-workers. Regarding the fact that both groups of men were ordained as Evangelical-Lutheran pastors, and according to Lutheran church order there existed at least in theory an equal 'brotherly' relationship between them, this case of inequality between groups of men should be examined from a masculinity perspective.

The ambivalent understanding of the Zulu man

The NMS was the first missionary society in Norway. A Norwegian audience showed a growing interest in their compatriots' endeavours in south-eastern Africa, with mission magazines, books and pamphlets experiencing increased circulation from the mid-nineteenth century. Several books describing the NMS mission enterprise among the Zulus were published. In 1865, the pastor Halfdan E. Sommerfelt was engaged by the NMS to write a first historical account.[15] Sommerfelt's primary sources were the missionaries' reports and letters printed in the *NMT*. However, for the descriptions of African geographical, cultural, religious and political conditions, he relied on British and German sources, mainly books by missionaries, explorers and military officers.[16] In 1915, Ole Stavem wrote a history of the NMS's 70 years of missionary work among the Zulus, and Olav Guttorm Myklebust's centenary book was published in 1949.[17] In response to a growing enthusiasm for mission among youths participating in mission study groups in the first decades of the twentieth century, Norwegian missionaries in Zululand produced several mission study books.[18]

During the 84-year period between Sommerfelt's 1865 book and Myklebust's 1949 book, Norwegian mission literature accounts of Zulu geography, population, history, religion, culture and sociology share surprising similarities. All literature mentioned had a section where 'the Zulu' were introduced. However, *the Zulu* was a gendered idiom. In fact it was *the male Zulu* – the Zulu Man – who was discussed. Pronouns like *he*, *him* or *his* were used, as in Myklebust's description from 1949: 'As an African the Zulu is in many ways the antithesis of the European. He is neither a man of will nor a man of thought.'[19] Statements like 'The Zulus were warriors and despised all kinds of work'[20] or 'courage and manliness are the qualities they most admire'[21] seem to imply that the authors had the Zulu man, and not the Zulu woman, in mind. The life conditions of Zulu women as 'suppressed victims' were, nevertheless, frequently portrayed by Norwegian missionaries, something we will return to. However, the main discussions about the Zulu in the Norwegian mission literature were discussions about the Zulu man, while women's issues were described in separate sections.

How was the Zulu man represented in the NMS's literature? He was above all described as healthy and strong, with a sturdy physique and an appealing appearance: 'The average Zulu is tall, and his muscular, well-proportioned athletic body is a masterpiece in bronze, which only the great Creator could have achieved.'[22] In Norwegian mission material, we actually find an obsession with the physical attributes of 'the Zulu race'. Writers praised the anatomy and physiques of the 'Kaffir race' or 'Bantu race' (*Nguni*) in general, and the Zulus in particular. Compared to 'the short, sluggish, yellow-brown Hottentot' or 'the pygmy, bestial Bushmen', Sommerfelt claimed that 'the tall, beautiful and stalwart Kaffir', with his 'open, manly attitude and free, bold walk', were on a much higher racial level.[23] Most of the Norwegian writers described the nature and climate of Zululand as extraordinarily healthy, something that had influenced the development of the race.[24] Perceptions of the Zulus as superior among the African races continued to flourish in the Norwegian mission literature. Myklebust asserted in 1949 that the Zulu owned extraordinary 'abilities and possibilities'; not only in a physiological way, but also on a psychological and cultural level, the Zulus 'stand out' among Africans.[25]

The origin of the Zulu people was of great concern to Norwegian missionaries. Sommerfelt presented a theory of the Zulu's Jewish origin, descending from Abraham's son Ishmael;[26] in this he was probably influenced by the thoughts of British and American missionaries.[27] Nils Astrup, a missionary in Schreuder's mission, journeyed on foot as far north as the Limpopo river, conducting linguistic and ethnographic studies. While he studied the extension of Zulu language and Zulu customs in inner Africa, he simultaneously hoped to learn more about the origin of the Zulus. Astrup was preoccupied with Old Testament prophesies concerning Africa. He envisioned converted Zulus bringing the Christian gospel to 'blood kinsmen' in the interior of Africa – 'the heart of Africa'. According to Astrup, the Zulu people were, just like the Jewish people, a chosen people, and in several books Astrup presented his vision to Norwegian supporters.[28] Ole Stavem was also occupied with the origin of 'the Bantus', discussing various theories in his 1915 book.[29] Stavem spent some of his early missionary days in the 1870s, while stationed at Umbonambi, on ethnographic studies. Through conversations with elders he collected traditional fairy tales and myths, in which he searched for 'the moral, religious and intellectual heritage' of the Zulu people.[30] Underlying the Norwegian missionaries' obsession with Zulu origin was the hypothesis of a superior past, a glorious era that had unfortunately been followed by centuries of 'heathen' influence, ultimately dulling and degrading the Zulu people.

The Zulu man's inner qualities were also discussed in the Norwegian mission literature. While Stavem spoke of 'the national character' of the Zulu people, Myklebust discussed the 'the national mentality' some decades later. However, representations were quite ambivalent, and it is tempting to cite the post-colonial theorist Homi K. Bhabha when he points to ambivalence as typical for the object of colonial discourse – 'that "otherness" which is at once an object of desire and derision, an articulation of difference contained within the fantasy of origin and identity'.[31] Ambivalence was particularly evident in the representations of the Zulu warrior. Detailed descriptions of the warrior's national costume, his spear and his shield were given, and illustrations and photos of young Zulu warriors were printed in the mission magazines and books.[32] The brave and proud 'warrior spirit' of the Zulu man was praised, and his loyalty, dedication and love for his king and nation were admired. At the same time the Zulu warrior was represented as a cruel and bloodthirsty savage. In Norwegian mission literature, as in other colonial texts, there were numerous references to King Shaka as well as his impressive army construction and his conquest of neighbouring tribes.[33] Shaka was simultaneously portrayed as both murderer and monster.[34] According to historian John Laband, such ambivalence in Western images of the Zulu warrior continues today, in the twenty-first century, to entertain 'a counter-image of the noble, courageous tribal warrior, paradoxically admirable in his very savagery'.[35]

As Stavem formulated it, there was a relationship between geographical and natural surroundings and the Zulu national character, or *Volkgeist*.[36] The abundant natural conditions, such as the fertile soil and a warm, healthy climate, had never forced the Zulus to work hard to make a good harvest. Neither was there any need for hard efforts to produce clothes for protection against cold weather. As a result, 'laziness and idleness' had become essential features in the national character of the Zulu people. Stavem further pointed to the fact that Africans were surrounded by wild animals and that they had been forced to develop strategies to fight them. This could explain their strong bodies, 'raw power' and 'savage courage'. He admitted that the Zulu's well-known 'brave warrior spirit' was a good thing, but one should not forget that the same spirit also implied that the Zulus acted as 'bloodthirsty, cruel, robbery desirous and sly warriors'. Stavem concluded that 'laziness' and 'savage braveness' were the main traits of the Zulu national character, which unfortunately illustrated the 'weaknesses' of the same character, even if this could be related to natural and geographical conditions. He emphasised that, although the Zulus were still on a 'low level' in terms of development, they did not lack possibilities; yet their rich potentials were still not fulfilled.

According to George Mosse's theory, ideal masculinity is often created as bulwarks against 'other' stereotypes of masculinities claimed to lack masculinity and thus described as countertypes or contrasts. Missionaries' ideas and descriptions of the Zulu man were well articulated, clear and distinct, which Mosse asserts is also typical when describing counter-types. Implicit in NMS missionaries' perceptions of the Zulus as being on a 'low' level was an understanding of their own European race on a 'higher' level in terms of development. In Myklebust's 1949 text, the Zulu male was represented as 'the antithesis' of the European male. He was neither a man of will or thought, but a man ruled by his emotions – namely, by affects, instincts and impulses.[37] After serving as an NMS missionary in South Africa from 1931, Myklebust returned to Norway in 1939, where he was assigned to a research position at the Norwegian School of Theology in Oslo. In the following years he published a number of scientific articles discussing the political, religious and cultural aspects of Africans and their societies.[38]

Church historian Odd Magne Bakke has analysed Myklebust's representations of Africans.[39] Bakke challenges Torstein Jørgensen, who in his research on nineteenth-century Norwegian missionaries tends to clear them from the racist attitudes of their contemporary colonist agents.[40] Bakke finds that, although Myklebust, who served as a missionary in the 1930s, rejected biological and essentialist theories of race, he still reproduced and confirmed traditional colonial stereotypes of Africans' 'otherness'. The primary characteristic of the African mentality is what Myklebust describes as 'an explosive character', not far from Stavem's concept of 'wild braveness'. Africans are ruled by their emotions at the cost of logical and critical thinking, which Myklebust concludes serves as the fundamental difference between black and white men. This emotional trait of Africans' mentality explains their nonchalant philosophy of life, their lack of perseverance and long-term planning, and their inability to distinguish between reality and fantasy: 'We often call them big children,' Myklebust continues.[41] Even if Myklebust regarded the Africans' 'otherness' as due to culture, not to nature, Bakke claims that his 'essentializing' of culture had practically the same deterministic effect as essentialist theories of race.

Could men like the Zulus, ruled by their emotions and their explosive character, act like responsible and respectable leaders in the Lutheran church-building process in South Africa? Stavem and Myklebust, as well as others, never formulated such a question, but their assertions of Zulu mentality and masculinity both reflected and reproduced the common understanding among NMS missionaries regarding the potential of future Zulu church leaders. As we will see in our examination of the case of Simon Ndlela, Zulu church leaders were regarded and treated as young men with great potential, but as their inner emotions were still uncontrolled, they had not yet reached the level of mature manhood. For a while, even ordained Zulu pastors were regarded and treated as the missionaries' subordinates. The necessary power and means to lead and manage the church as the missionaries' co-equals could not yet be shared with the Zulus.

In this discussion it is important to distinguish between the white missionaries' paternalistic son discourses and the white settlers' boy discourses. According to Robert Morrell, the whites' frequent use of the term *boy* to refer to black men 'captured a condescension, a refusal to acknowledge the possibility of growth and the achievement of manhood'.[42] When confronted with white settlers' attitudes towards African men, which according to Morrell involved 'emasculation', the NMS missionaries defended the Christian Zulu man as a well-gifted man with great potential. In 1894, Stavem – who was then the NMS superintendent – became involved in an official dispute with Scandinavian immigrants in Durban. Some of the immigrants had written articles in Norwegian newspapers, as well as in Durban newspapers, accusing the 'Mission Kaffirs' of being the laziest, worst and most immoral men among the Zulu men. The NMS was further criticised for producing Christian men who were useless as servants and employees. Stavem conducted extensive research among 'prominent men' in Durban before he disproved the settlers' accusations in several articles. He claimed that the Christian Zulu men who came to Durban from the Norwegian mission stations were respectable men of high morals. NMS missionaries believed that Christian Zulu men, through the transforming and 'civilising' effects of Christianity, over time could reach the same societal and cultural level as themselves.[43]

How to Christianise the Zulu man: gendered mission strategies in the NMS

A feminised Lutheran Zulu Church?

The first convert in the Norwegian Zulu mission, Mathenjwase kaNondumo Shange, was a woman. In the years to come, it would be regarded as a remarkable trait of the mission work among the Zulus that more women than men responded to the Christian gospel and that the number of female converts outnumbered male converts. Norwegian missionaries in south-eastern Africa considered the large proportion of women in their congregations as an exception in the NMS, differing from the reality experienced by their colleagues in Madagascar and China.[44] Hanna Mellemsether found that the issue of female surplus in the congregations to a certain extent influenced missionaries' discussions about a first church constitution in 1914. Although it was proposed that 'men and boys' should exclusively have the right to vote in church matters, a majority of the missionaries advocated women's democratic rights. Some years later, NMS missionary Peder Andreas Strømme suggested that women become eligible for positions in the parish councils. He argued that it was hard to find enough available men to form a council; yet there were many reliable, competent Christian women in the Zulu congregations. However, missionaries who supported an increased influence of women in the church organisation, both for pragmatic reasons (the shortage of men) and by referring to universal female democratic rights, were in the minority. When the 1914 constitution of the Norwegian Lutheran Zulu Church was reviewed in 1929, and the church drew up its first formal organisational rules, women were still not able to hold any offices in the church, not even at the parish level.[45]

The shortage of Christian men was not a problem specific to the NMS. South African historian Deborah Gaitskell claims that 'laments at the depletion of male membership became a constant refrain from many rural churches', and she refers to the example of Transkei Anglican missionaries, who were concerned by the disproportionate numbers of women and girls as opposed to men and boys (3,361: 982) who had been confirmed in their diocese in 1931.[46] Two factors were singled out by Norwegian missionaries when explaining the shortage of men in the congregations.[47] The first was the stronghold of Zulu 'traditional' values and societal organisation, which were in a particular way seen to favour men's interests. The second was the fast-developing system of migrant labour from the late nineteenth century. In fact, in 1910 an estimated 80 per cent of adult males in Zululand entered migrancy to support their rural families.[48] The discussion will return to both factors, but first it will present the NMS's thinking and practice regarding the Zulu woman.

Mellemsether finds that NMS missionaries sketched a gloomy picture of Zulu women's traditional life.[49] Women were by category deprived of dignity and power, existing merely as a commodity in a masculine marketplace of 'bride trade'. After marriage they were obliged to serve their polygamous husbands as 'slaves'. The Norwegian mission magazines included numerous narratives of Zulu women who escaped oppressive patriarchal relationships – from forced marriages, from violent fathers or brothers, and from neglect and abandonment by their husbands. Thus, the NMS incorporated a general picture of Western missionaries' representations of the conditions of Zulu women.[50] It also resembles a general tendency in the nineteenth-century international missionary movement where women living in non-Christian societies were understood as 'repressed victims'.[51] Although historians continue to discuss to what extent women in pre-colonial societies were oppressed,[52] some suggest that the gloomy representations by the missionaries aimed to call forth assistance and solidarity among Western believers, particularly calling for the solidarity of female mission supporters.[53]

The NMS did not have an explicit gendered mission strategy when it started its work among the Zulus, but it soon developed a practice similar to that of other missions active in the region. Young boys and girls who came to the mission station were put to work in the missionary home, being more or less integrated into the household. Sheila Meintjes, in her analysis of gender relations in the Christian community at the Edendale mission station in Natal, speaks of 'an apprenticeship in Christian family life'.[54] Boys were trained in outdoor work on the mission farms while girls were trained in domestic skills like cooking, cleaning, childcare, sewing, ironing and gardening. According to Heather Hughes in her study of the Inanda seminary, the first mission institution to offer higher education for African women in Natal, missionaries soon became conscious of the fact that training converted men for Christian roles would produce 'only half of what was required to propagate a stable Christian community'.[55] It became precarious to mould female converts into Christian wives and mothers, and they had to be prepared for the same kinds of roles as those played by the missionary wives. Eventually NMS missionaries, including the missionary wives, also came to perceive the need for a more institutional female training to replace the apprenticeship system. Thus, in 1902, the NMS established a 'Girls' Home' at the Eshowe mission station.[56] Girls from seven to 15 years old were boarded at the institution under the patronage of a single female missionary. They attended day school in the morning and spent the afternoons doing domestic work and 'industrious activities'. In 1922, a 'Girls' Industrial School' was established at Eshowe, with the aim of training pious and industrious Christian housewives.[57]

In the mission schools, girls and boys had from the very start been offered elementary education on an equal level. In 1902, by referring to the progress of other missions in the sector of women's education, NMS missionaries discussed the possible establishment of a 'girls' higher education'.[58] There was an urgent need for qualified teachers in the mission schools; such an institution could provide the NMS with sufficient native female teachers. The plan did not become reality in 1902. Instead, the NMS's missionary conference decided in 1909 to accept female students at their teachers' training school at Umphumulo.[59] However, teaching was the only accessible employment for Zulu women within the NMS during the period under investigation. Gaitskell's statement, in her discussion on women and Christianity in South Africa, that Victorian Christianity offered a 'contradictory package' to African women – 'a way of escape from some of the constraints of pre-Christian society and yet a firm incorporation into the domesticity and patriarchy of Christian family life' – covers the experience of women in the Norwegian Lutheran Zulu Church as well.[60]

Troublesome traditional Zulu masculinity

In a mission study book entitled *Our Zulu Mission*, published by the NMS in 1921, the missionary Hans Kristian Leisegang Jr portrayed the 'obstacles' that for years had 'restrained the progress of the gospel among the Zulus'.[61] The terms *Zulu* and *man* are used interchangeably by Leisegang, who is actually discussing the problem of Christianisation of the traditionally oriented Zulu man. The first obstacle is, according to Leisegang, 'the national pride' as the Zulus were still dreaming of an independent Zulu state and reinstatement of their royal heirs. The second obstacle is the polygamous family system. The third obstacle is loyalty to the tribe, the elders and the chief. Leisegang wrote his text in the context of white settler domination and African subordination in a politically united South African Union. Nevertheless, he brought in the same issues as his predecessors had during the pre-colonised, independent Zulu monarchy when they described Zulu men's resistance towards Christianity.

The NMS missionaries landing in Zululand in the 1850s soon realised that their Christian message brought them into conflict with local beliefs, customs and political order. According to Jarle Simensen and his group of researchers, they were 'overwhelmed by the distance to the local culture' and condemned traditional religion, culture and social arrangements, labelling them as 'heathenism'. What features of the local culture were understood as irreconcilable with Christian belief and practice? Religious beliefs in 'witchcraft' and 'sorcery' were regarded by the missionaries as the chief characteristics of heathen religion. In addition, 'ancestor beliefs' and 'the cult of the king' conflicted with the Old Testament's first commandment and were defined as 'idolatry'. The strong sense of kinship and collective unity – 'the worldly love of relatives' – was also regarded as sinful and understood as a contrast to the

Christian virtues of 'individual freedom' and 'individual development'. The missionaries further found it hard to accept Zulu marriage arrangements and sexual morality. Polygamy was seen as a sign of both sexual and material greediness, and the traditional *lobola/ilobolo*, or 'bride price'/'bride wealth', was interpreted as an indication that Zulu women were considered to be objects for sale and purchase. The military regiment system, which delayed the time for entering into marriage and 'forced celibacy' on young Zulu men, was hard to accept for the missionaries. Moreover, the custom of non-penetrative sexual play before marriage, *hlobonga*, was characterised as 'unnatural sin' and condemned. Finally, for teetotalist Norwegian missionaries, both 'beer drinking' and 'hemp smoking' conflicted with Christian lifestyle ideals. Simensen and his team found that NMS missionaries' definitions of sin comprised most Zulu social arrangements. Consequently, missionaries frequently used characteristics to describe the average Zulu man – 'fatalism, laziness, mendacity, unreliability, begging and drunkenness' – suggesting that the traditional Zulu man was an awfully sinful man.[62]

Among historians it is a well-established fact that the majority of the Nguni people living in south-east Africa in the nineteenth century rejected or even resisted the message of the Western missionaries.

Figure 5.1 From a Christian wedding in Malabatini church. Western and Zulu traditional clothes and costumes symbolise conflicting masculinity ideals

Source: Mission Archives, School of Mission and Theology, Stavanger.

Norman Etherington, in his classic study of African Christian communities in Natal, Pondoland and Zululand from 1835 to 1880, found it peculiar that although this region was an extremely popular mission field among Western missions, the 'host of Christian soldiers won so few recruits'.[63] Missionaries' apprehension of the traditional Zulu patriarchal system as the major opponent in their evangelising efforts nevertheless seems plausible. Gaitskell found that common obstacles to male church membership among anti-Christian chiefs were 'indigenous ideas of manliness associated with war and fighting, the herding activities of boys (which prevented them from attending Christian schools), and the strictures against polygamy'.[64] She asks whether it was less threatening to African communities to lose their women, as opposed to their men, to Christianity. Did 'women's relative powerlessness' make them more open to conversion? Female conversion may have posed a threat to domestic paternal control, but male conversion constituted a greater political and military threat to the chiefdoms.

The fall of the independent Zulu kingdom in 1879 and its subsequent upheavals, followed by a series of agricultural disasters in the 1880s and 1890s, were, according to Simensen, met by the NMS missionaries with a somewhat surprising 'unfeeling harshness'.[65] The majority of the missionaries observed the 'degrading', 'humiliation' and 'punishment' that the Zulus experienced through the destruction of their economic basis with satisfaction.[66] What Simensen calls the missionaries' 'humiliation thesis' may not be restricted to political conditions alone. The missionaries found that the traditional Zulu world-view and traditional Zulu life as an entity were irreconcilable with Christianity. Zulu patriarchal systems in particular were targeted, while Zulu women were regarded as 'innocent victims'. A humiliation of the traditional Zulu man was necessary if a new Christian Zulu man were to emerge.

Ideal Christian masculinity

In a book that presented the NMS's missionary work among the Zulus, missionary Peder Aage Rødseth wrote a subchapter entitled 'The Christian Home'.[67] 'When Jesus enters a home', he started, 'the domestic life will totally change – also in the outward.' The first step is to abolish 'nudity' so that the Christian Zulu will start to wear Western clothes. The second step is a change in housing conditions. To the Christian, a traditional Zulu hut would be 'too miserable'; rather, he will build an upright, square house with several rooms, doors, windows, a chimney and furniture. The third step is a change in traditional internal work relations. The Christian man 'will not be satisfied by watching his wife work alone in the field and he will purchase a plough and a couple of oxen to plough with'. Other outward and visible signs of a Christian family life included, according to Rødseth, the daily family devotions with Scripture reading, singing and praying. Finally, he mentioned Christian parents' efforts in sending their children to school.

Rødseth's portrait of Zulu Christian family life in 1932 discloses a remarkable continuity in the missionaries' visions of the ideal Christian masculinity. Even at a time when the majority of South African black men, including Lutheran Zulu men, were migrant workers spending most of their time in the industrial cities of Durban and Johannesburg, or in the mining districts of Kimberly and Witwatersrand, Rødseth's ideal of a Christian Zulu man remained that of a rural farming family man. This ideal had survived since the mid-nineteenth century, when Christian Zulu men and women – the *amakholwa* (believers) – lived as farmers in small settlements on American and British mission reserves in Natal.[68] As discussed in Chapter 2, the mission reserves became enclaves where an emerging middle class of African landowners found agricultural and service opportunities within the colonial capitalist economy. The success of the industrious and engineering 'self-making' *amakholwa* men inspired some of the NMS missionaries to try to produce the same type of Christian men at their own mission stations. However, their Lutheran heritage urged them to give priority to Christian preaching and education above 'civilising' activities and, as discussed in Chapter 3, balancing between these two aspects of mission work – 'the Word or the Plough' – was a constant theme of discussion among NMS missionaries in the 1880s. An industrial school was established at the Eshowe mission station in 1887, but this project never became a success, and the school was closed in 1905.[69] NMS missionaries did not wholeheartedly follow the British and American example of encouraging Zulu Christian men to embrace agrarian and commercial enterprises. Still they shared the ideal of the Christian Zulu man as an independent and industrious farmer, living in an upright, square brick house in monogamous matrimony, wearing shirts and trousers, ploughing his field, and selling his surplus agrarian products at the nearby market. Etherington claims that nineteenth-century missionary theory accorded a special place to self-sufficient agriculture and village life, 'perversely idealizing a way of life that was already disappearing in Europe'.[70]

Even if Zulu men left their African homesteads, moved to the mission land and started their new lives as *amakholwa*, reverting back to traditional Zulu life was not unusual among the first converts. As surprising as it might seem, the NMS missionaries were never reluctant to report unsuccessful conversion stories, and the mission magazines provide numerous narratives of Christian Zulus who, because of sins committed or their backslide to 'heathen lifestyle', were excluded from the congregations.[71] Most of the 'reversion stories' were actually stories about men. For instance, in 1873, missionary Jan Kielland informed *NMT* readers that he had expelled all the male members of his congregation and ordered them to move away from the mission station area.[72]

A fascinating story of conversion and reversion is the story of Moses, reconstructed by Torstein Jørgensen.[73] Moses became quite famous in Norway since he was the first African student at the NMS mission school, living in Stavanger from 1866 to 1869. Zibokjana Ka Gudu was baptised in 1859, taking the name Moses. Since he was eight years old, Moses had been in Oftebro's apprenticeship. He was praised by the missionaries as an intelligent and well-gifted young man. When Prince Cetshwayo asked Oftebro to teach him the art of reading in 1859, Moses was put in charge of the task.[74] Moses' relation to the prince gradually became closer, a factor that seems to have worried the missionaries even before he was sent to Norway. When he returned to Zululand in 1869, he was stationed under the supervision of Schreuder at the Entumeni mission station, working as an assistant and a schoolteacher. He simultaneously took up his old friendship with the prince. However, it was ultimately a complicated and quite risky affair to be loyal to two lords. When Moses was accused of extra-marital affairs, he was outlawed by the prince and declared a 'wizard, whoremaster and outcast'; in 1872 he was also expelled by Schreuder from the Entumeni mission station. 'The fall of Moses' was an enormous disappointment to the missionaries as well as the mission supporters in Norway and was described in detail in the *NMT*.[75] After Moses' deportation from Zululand he found employment as an inspector at a sugar mill in Natal. According to Oftebro, who maintained contact with Moses, he did very well in Natal and planned to buy his own land.[76] Moses was still 'reading his Norwegian books', he held evening school for illiterate workers at the mill and every Sunday he invited them to devotions in his home. According to Oftebro, several of the people under his influence were at this time attending nearby mission stations preparing for baptism. Moses eventually disappeared from the NMS annals, but he sent a last written message to 'the congregation across the sea', assuring them that he was not 'lost': 'I am working here at the mill. God is also here. He has not hindered me to labour but afforded me with suitable work.'[77]

To a Norwegian audience the narratives of Moses and other Zulu men were presented as narratives of conversion and reversion, of a continuous

Figure 5.2   Zibokjana Ka Gudu, or Moses, which was his Christian name, was a student at the NMS's mission school in Stavanger, Norway, 1866–69

Source: Mission Archives, School of Mission and Theology, Stavanger.

Photographer: B. Norland.

fight between Christianity and 'heathendom'. When these men were expelled from the mission stations, it was explained by their backsliding into traditional life. But according to the men's own statements, retold by the missionaries, they did not go back to old customs, but continued to live as Christian believers. In one way it was impossible for them to move back to Zululand: they had provoked Zulu authorities, and a physical return could be dangerous. But it also seems likely that, during their encounter with the Christian religion and Western missionaries, they had evolved a new identity as *amakholwa* men. The issue of conversion, what Etherington in a recent article calls 'the perpetually vexing of identifying and verifying religious conversion in mission history',[78] is complex and beyond the scope of the current study.[79] Yet – and again referring to Etherington – since the missionaries themselves had little difficulty in identifying outward signs of an inward 'heathenism', it should follow that 'adopting new signs and customs might be taken as legitimate evidence of conversion'. Etherington discusses the written and symbolic material texts (the word, the custom, the picture, the song) introduced by the missionaries, texts that were quickly adopted by the new Christians, and he suggests that historians should take these outward signs of conversion more seriously.

Dangerous urban black masculinity

In Leisegang Jr's previously mentioned book *Our Zulu Mission* (1921), he listed what he perceives to be 'obstacles' to the progress of the gospel among the Zulus. In addition to the three obstacles referring to traditional Zulu societal organisation, a fourth obstacle is 'bad influence' from the colonisers and 'those who represent civilisation'.[80] This influence was, according to Leisegang, particularly strong in the cities and the mining districts: when a Zulu man left the countryside and the strong control of the tribe and the chief to move to the urban centres, he felt like a 'free man' and therefore 'indulges in new forms of immorality, which further demoralises him'. In 1932, Rødseth wrote that Zulu men in the urban centres met immoral lifestyles and 'debaucheries' they did not even know existed, where whites and blacks were mingling in a 'wild nightlife' and in a 'flood of ungodliness and savagery'.[81]

The fear of the moral dangers of urban life was common among missionaries in Natal and Zululand as well as among the first generations of *amakholwa*, who regarded themselves as rural farmers, and not as 'rickshaw pullers and dockworkers in Durban, or miners in Johannesburg'.[82] Lutheran missions operating in South Africa were, according to Georg Scriba and Gunnar Lislerud, particularly slow to adapt to the challenges of modernisation, urbanisation and the proletarisation of the black classes, and they persistently hailed the pre-modern lifestyle.[83] When the NMS established its first urban enterprise in Durban in 1890, as discussed in Chapter 4, it was primarily a response to Scandinavian immigrants' call for a Lutheran pastor in the city. Meanwhile, a mission was started among the rapidly growing black male migrant population working on the docks and living temporarily in wretched barracks. Yet the NMS's Home Board expected the missionary stationed in Durban to give priority to the latter group.[84] Mission work among this group was, according to the Home Board, promising for three reasons. First, the migrant workers had left their homesteads and were no longer under the influence of traditional customs and rituals or the clans' social expectations. Second, if the migrant workers converted to Christianity during their stay in Durban, they could influence family and relatives upon their return to their rural homesteads.

Third, it would be of importance to have a Norwegian Lutheran representation in the growing commercial centre. When Zulu Christians from the rural Norwegian mission congregations moved to Durban, it would be a pity if they were 'lost' to other denominations.

City life could be 'dangerous' for reasons beyond immorality. Durban, which housed a quickly increasing proletarian African population that historians have called 'an urban apartheid laboratory', saw the growth of black mobilisation and organised resistance from the 1920s.[85] In addition to the development of trade unions and radical militant political organisations, there was also an awakening of Zulu ethnic nationalism. The NMS's outstanding Zulu pastor Petros Lamula, who had been stationed in Durban since his ordination in 1915, became engaged in the political and cultural liberation movements of the city. According to Paul la Hausse de Lalouvière's biography, Lamula was a co-operative movement ideologue, a pioneering Zulu historian, an architect of the first Inkatha organisation, and leader of the radical African National Congress (ANC) in Natal.[86] The NMS missionaries watched Lamula's activities and enterprises with growing scepticism.[87] The Lutheran theology of 'the two realms' urged the church's men to concentrate on the religious sphere, not the profane. According to the missionary instruction, pastors were not permitted to engage in political activities. The NMS missionary conference of 1926 decided to relocate Lamula from Durban to Eshowe. They hoped that, by putting him under the control of a Norwegian missionary at a rural mission station, he would withdraw from political activities and be 'neutralised'. Lamula protested the proposal, broke with the NMS, and established a separate church – the United Native National Church of Christ.

The case of Simon Ndlela

As discussed thus far, the representations of the Zulu man in NMS source materials were quite ambivalent. On the one hand, the Zulu man was regarded as superior among African 'races', a physically and mentally well-gifted man with great potential. On the other hand, he was portrayed as childish and immature, a man unable to control his emotions. This section will examine the background to the ordination of Simon Ndlela in 1893 as well as the events preceding his dismissal ten years later. The alternate and arbitrary treatment of this first Zulu pastor in the Norwegian Zulu church reveals how this ambivalence regarding Zulu masculinity on a discursive level had practical implications for an individual man's life. According to missionary discourse and practice, even if a Zulu man became a Christian, or a Lutheran pastor, he would still be marked by an inherent Zulu 'national character'. As one NMS missionary expressed it during a discussion about Simon Ndlela: 'We must remember that even though he wears pastoral robes, he's still a Kaffir.'[88]

Recruitment of Zulu men to mission work

The NMS's first outstation in Zululand was established by Simon Ndlela in 1875. As the number of mission stations managed by NMS missionaries had been more or less constant since the mid-1880s,[89] it was the growth in outstations that characterised the period after 1880. The number of outstations increased to 29 in 1890, 49 in 1900, 109 in 1920 and 124 in 1939.[90] The number of converts also increased considerably after 1880. By the time of the 1879 Anglo-Zulu war, the Norwegian mission had approximately 300 Zulu converts. In 1890, church memberships had increased to 1,000. Post-1890 church growth continued, reaching 5,000 in 1900, 8,000 in 1920, 14,000 in 1930 and 20,000 by 1939.[91] Statistics of the NMS's Zulu mission confirms Peggy Brock's assertion that any discussion of mission and colonialism that ignores the armies of non-European evangelists 'grossly misrepresents the grass-roots dynamics of Christianization'.[92] Brock finds it to be a general tendency in modern mission history that local agents 'very soon' outnumbered foreign-born missionaries. In addition, in the case of the NMS in South Africa, although the number of missionaries remained stable or decreased,[93] the number of Zulu evangelists and teachers continued to grow. According to mission statistics, eight native evangelists/teachers were employed in 1885,[94] increasing to 34 in 1890, 40 in 1900 and 76 in 1910. After 1915, reporting was more accurate and distinctions were made between Zulu pastors, employed/ voluntary evangelists and teachers with governmental certification/ non-certificated teachers.

Norwegian and Zulu personnel in the Norwegian Lutheran Zulu Church, 1915–30

	Missionary pastors	Female missionary workers	Zulu pastors	Paid evangelists	Unpaid evangelists	Teachers with certificate	Teachers without certificate
1915	16	4	7	77	36	17	36
1920	13	5	10	91	24	20	79
1925	9	5	13	106	29	37	78
1930	12	7	11	118	115	83	62

From the early 1880s, a recurring issue of discussion at the NMS missionary conference was how to give the Zulu church personnel a proper education.[95] In 1881, it was decided to establish a Catechist school at Eshowe, and Ole Stavem was asked to be the school's principal.[96] Four students finished the course in 1884,[97] but in the same year it was decided to close the school due to the low enrolment.[98] In 1893, another attempt was made when Edward Michael Ingebrektsen was installed as principal of a new teachers' school at Umphumulo.[99] The Norwegian mission still lacked a proper theological education for its evangelists and pastor candidates; however, when the missionary conference of 1905 finally agreed to establish one, the Home Board did not sanction the proposal.[100] In 1912, the Cooperating Lutheran Missions (CLM) in Natal was established as a joint venture between the NMS, the Church of Sweden Mission (CSM) and the Berlin Missionary Society (BMS). Although this was primarily an effort to establish a joint Evangelical-Lutheran Zulu Church in Zululand, the immediate result of CLM was to provide an extensive financial and administrative co-operative among three educational institutions: the theological seminary at Oscarsberg (CSM), the evangelist school at Emmaus (BMS) and the teachers' college at Umphumulo (NMS). From 1912 onward, the NMS sent its evangelists to Emmaus and its pastoral candidates to Oscarsberg. Yet, as was the case in Madagascar from 1871, the NMS in South Africa never established its own theological institution.

According to the first constitution of the Norwegian Lutheran Zulu Church in 1914, the missionary pastor functioned as manager of the mission station as well as vicar of the district's outstations and preaching places. Zulu teachers and evangelists took care of daily teaching in the mission schools as well as the outstation's Bible teaching, prayer meetings, evangelistic campaigns and Sunday worship. According to Lutheran church order, the ministerial acts of baptism and Holy Communion, plus the conducting of church weddings and funerals, had to be ministered by ordained pastors. Against this background, it is worth asking why the numbers of ordained indigenous pastors did not cope with church growth. In his examination of the first decades of the Norwegian Zulu mission (i.e. 1850–73), Torstein Jørgensen explains the slow progress in recruiting Zulu church personnel as related to the Norwegian background, where the standards of ecclesiastical ordination were high.[101] He finds a second explanation in the slow progress of the mission work. Thus, the problem of recruiting indigenous church personnel was partly explained by the limited number of converts and partly by the quality of the converts in terms of their educational level and inner qualities and character.

After 1880, as we have seen, these explanations are no longer plausible. In the NMS's mission in Madagascar, theological education had been offered since 1871, and the first ordination of a Malagasy pastor occurred in 1883. The high standards of ecclesiastical ordination in Norway obviously did not hinder the missionaries to ordain pastors in Madagascar. Moreover, after 1880, there was a remarkable church growth in the NMS's Zulu mission. The number of converts, outstations, and native evangelists and teachers increased considerably. The only numbers in the mission statistics that did not increase were those of the ordained Zulu pastors. After the first ordination of Simon Ndlela in 1893, another 20 years passed before two more pastors – Jakob Nzuza and Metheu Mbuyazi – were ordained in 1913. By that time Ndlela had passed away. It was a watershed moment when an additional five pastors – Petros Lamula, Philip Langeni, Elias Msomi, Salathiel Msweli and Josaya Semes – were ordained in 1915. They all belonged to the first class of 'Norwegian Zulu pastors' educated at the Oscarsberg Lutheran Theological Seminary. The slow growth of ordained pastors in the Norwegian Lutheran church was noticeable in subsequent decades, with ten pastors being ordained in 1920, 13 in 1925 and 11 in 1930.

It took longer than expected for NMS missionaries to the Zulus to fulfil their original objective of recruiting, educating and ordaining indigenous church personnel. However, it should be noted that other mission societies operating in south-east Africa during this same period were likewise reluctant to ordain indigenous Zulu clergy.[102] Tiyo Soga was the first South African to be ordained (into the Presbyterian Church), which occurred in Glasgow, Scotland, in 1856. In Natal, the Methodists made the first step towards an African clergy by receiving Clement Johns as a minister on trial in 1867. Between 1870 and 1871, five Zulus were ordained by the American Zulu mission (short term for American Board of Commissioners for Foreign Missions), with the Anglicans ordaining their first two indigenous priests in 1871. According to historian Richard Elphick, the Anglicans and Methodists far outpaced the Presbyterians and Congregationalists in ordaining indigenous South African clergy during the nineteenth century. The Lutheran, Moravian and Dutch Reformed missions, on the other hand, lagged far behind American and British mission societies in terms of the pace of ordaining indigenous clergy. In 1911, the ratio of Western missionaries to ordained Africans was 5.4 to 1 (221 to 41) in British missions; 7.2 to 1 (143 to 20) in American missions; 22.5 to 1 (518 to 23) in Lutheran and Moravian (German and Scandinavian) missions; and 225 to 1 (225 to 1) in Dutch Reformed missions.[103] The ordination of indigenous clergy in mission churches encouraged a small group of black professional churchmen to expect equal treatment from their white colleagues. However, their expectations were not met and, from the 1890s onwards, numerous Ethiopian separatist churches were founded by African clergy and evangelists – many of whom were the mission societies' most trusted and admired men.[104]

The ordination of Simon Ndlela in 1893

After the NMS missionaries started to ordain Malagasy pastors from 1883, the Home Board pushed for a similar development in its oldest mission in Zululand. This confirms the observation made by several historians that, when the ordination of black pastors commenced, it was only undertaken on explicit orders from home.[105] In 1884, NMS missionaries in south-east Africa were asked to discuss an expansion of itinerant evangelisation and outstation activities as well as the increased use of Christian Zulus as evangelists and teachers.[106] When the NMS's Secretary Ole Gjerløw inspected the mission field in 1888, he requested an immediate ordination of indigenous pastors, and there seemed to be a common understanding that Simon Ndlela was an actual candidate for ministerial service.[107]

Figure 5.3 The ordination of the first Zulu pastor in the NMS, Simon Ndlela (Baleni kaNdlela Mthimkhulu), in 1893

Source: Mission Archives, School of Mission and Theology, Stavanger.

The issue of Ndlela's ordination was discussed at the NMS's missionary conference in 1889, but it was agreed to postpone any decision in the matter.[108] Ndlela had recently been appointed temporary manager of the Eotimati mission station while missionary Petter Gottfred Nilsen was on furlough in Norway. Since this was the first time a Zulu evangelist had been put in charge of a central mission station, the missionaries found this to be a good test of Ndlela's leadership abilities. At the following conference in 1890, Superintendent Ole Stavem reported that he had inspected the Eotimati mission station and found everything to be in good order.[109] Stavem was pleased with Ndlela's preaching, which he found to be both 'awakening and encouraging'. In the discussion that followed Stavem's report, several of the missionaries emphasised that the 'time was ripe' for a first Zulu pastor to be ordained: 'We have longed for this day,' proclaimed Ole Zephanias Norgaard. He recommended Simon Ndlela, 'who for years has served his people with faithfulness, diligence and zeal'. While others worried that ordinations of black pastors would imply 'heavy responsibilities' for them as white missionaries, Norgaard responded by saying they were too reluctant and anxious. He referred to Madagascar, where NMS missionaries used available human resources. Martinius Borgen, who had some missionary experience in Madagascar, supported Norgaard. Borgen stated that, even if Malagasy pastors' level of knowledge was 'far higher' than in Ndlela's case, the Zulu evangelist could beat them in 'character'. The missionaries continued to discuss whether it was necessary for the candidate to receive a formal theological education prior to ordination, but concluded that this should not be a restriction. They asked the superintendent to do the necessary preparations for Ndlela's ordination.

The Home Board approved the conference decision of 1890; yet when the missionaries assembled the following year, Ndlela's ordination had still not occurred. Stavem explained the postponement as a need to assess 'in what condition he hands over Eotimati' upon the return of missionary Nilsen, as well as 'how he separates from the position he now for a while has had'.[110] Yet Stavem also reported to his colleagues that he had engaged in discussions with Ndlela regarding a future transfer. According to the latter's own wishes, Stavem had negotiated with British officials in Zululand as well as with local chiefs. They had found a new place for him at Emamba, an area with a high population density on the Zululand side of the Tugela river. Simon was free to stay on three acres of land as long as the British government permitted it.

In 1892, when the missionaries again met for their annual conference, Norgaard confronted Stavem with the question about when

Ndlela's ordination should take place.[111] The majority of the mission-aries supported Norgaard in his suggestion of an ordination as fast as possible and stated that Ndlela's ordination was of great importance for the church. Gundvall Gundersen, the manager at the Eshowe station, reported that he had inspected Ndlela's place and found the evange-list himself, his preaching place and his district to be not only in good order, but in fact 'very promising'. Nilsen, who had by now returned to Eotimati from his furlough, confirmed that Ndlela had looked after his station in a good manner. Stavem responded that 'Simon was a good Christian man' but 'unstable'. As superintendent he still had not gained enough 'courage' to ordain Ndlela and give him an 'independent posi-tion'. Stavem feared he planned to bring his adult sons over to Zululand and that he envisioned becoming 'a Big Man' over there.

Despite Stavem's concerns, the conference agreed on a resolution stating that Ndlela should be ordained 'as fast as possible', that a school-house should be built at his place and that his monthly salary should be £3 (£36 per annum).[112] To compare, the annual salary for a male NMS missionary with a family was £150. 'As fast as possible' turned out to be yet another year and, as already noted, the ordination occurred at the missionary conference at Empangeni in 1893. It is significant that this ground-breaking event in the history of the NMS's Zulu mission was not mentioned in the superintendent's annual report of 1893.[113] What Stavem did mention, though, was the fact that Ndlela had great success at his new outstation and by Christmas had baptised 14 people.

The suspension of Simon Ndlela in 1903

In 1903, the NMS missionary conference decided to suspend from service its only indigenous pastor, Simon Ndlela.[114] Sven Eriksen was the lone vote against Ndlela's suspension. The strongest supporters of Ndlela's ordination in the early 1890s were absent from the NMS in 1903: Gundersen died in 1902, and Norgaard was himself suspended from missionary service in 1902 because of private mortgage problems. What was the background to this surprising decision, which never became officially known in the mission circles in Norway?[115]

Before presenting the events and processes preceding Ndlela's dismissal in 1903, it is important to point out that indigenous clergy in most mission organisations in Natal and Zululand, which were integrated into the Colony of Natal in 1898, were exposed to the government's stricter attitude against African evangelists and pastors caused by the rise of the Independent African Churches since the mid-1890s.[116] In 1895, an act was passed to regulate the use of mission reserves; furthermore, the Mission Reserves Act of 1903 enabled the Natal Native Trust to take over the administration of the reserves. In particular, black pastors in the American Zulu mission were subject to the government's growing suspicions as an increasing number of them had been entrusted with their own mission stations and congregations since the turn of the century. From 1903 onwards they were refused official marriage licences and were not allowed to preach in the mission reserves.[117]

At the NMS missionary conference in 1902, Ndlela had been invited to take part in a discussion about the future of Emamba. He had 'been forced' away from Emamba 'because of hunger', according to his testimony.[118] Fortunately, he found a new place to live, at Esamungu, from where he applied to the NMS for permission to build a chapel. He expressed his concern for the congregation at Emamba, stating that they should be taken care of. 'If God provides me strength, I can try to reach them from my new place,' he stated, but added that some help from the mission would also be necessary. Ndlela voiced 'some complaints', including that his books were old and worn, and he could not afford to buy new ones. He also needed a baptismal plate at his new outstation.

After Ndlela left the meeting, the missionaries continued to discuss his case. The decision to keep Emamba as a Norwegian outstation was easy enough. However, during the negotiations, the newly elected superintendent Hans Christian Leisegang and Nils Aage Rødseth, the new station manager at the Eshowe mission station (the one responsible for Ndlela's outstations), both claimed they found several aspects of the Zulu pastor's ministerial service appalling. First, he had applied for a wage increase of £60 per annum instead of the current £32, an application Leisegang described as 'meaningless'. Second, he lacked proper writing abilities and could not keep the church's ministerial books in order. Finally, he had conducted 'scandalous' marriage ceremonies, including one between a white woman and a black man. Leisegang did not keep secret his opinion that Ndlela's ordination was a mistake: 'He should never have been ordained, he is not mature enough.' Leisegang's proposal of restrictions upon Ndlela's ministerial services and responsibilities was accepted by the conference participants. Such restrictions included that his catechumens at Esamungu should be introduced to the station manager at Eshowe two weeks before the baptism ceremony. In addition, marriage ceremonies at Emamba and Esamungu should be conducted by the missionary at Eshowe, who should also conduct ministerial acts such as Holy Communion and baptism at Emamba. During the discussions in 1902, some dissident voices were heard. Gundersen declared that it was 'not nice' of them 'to take so much from Simon'. In addition, Nils Braatvedt feared that Ndlela could become 'discouraged and hard'.

At the following missionary conference in 1903, Superintendent Leisegang raised the issue of suspending Ndlela from pastoral service in the NMS, asking Rødseth to explain the background to his proposal.[119] According to Rødseth, there had been some conflict between him and Ndlela regarding the responsibilities of the Emamba outstation, misunderstandings he had thought were settled. Thus, he had been surprised when he read an anonymous article in 'the natives' newspaper',[120] in which the specific conflicts between Rødseth and Ndlela were publicly displayed, with serious accusations raised against the former (i.e. that he was greedy, and that he was disloyal to senior missionaries). Rødseth immediately confronted Ndlela with the article, asking whether he had written it. Ndlela first denied knowing anything about the issue, but when Rødseth pushed him to deny that the article described the relation between them, Ndlela could not invalidate that. Ndlela thereafter wrote a letter of apology, which Rødseth personally brought to the newspaper's editor and which was printed. According to Rødseth, Ndlela later sent two additional letters of apology.

In the discussion that followed Rødseth's accounts, a common understanding emerged of Ndlela as the guilty party, the one who had committed sins. According to Rødseth, Ndlela had shown severe insubordination. He had written an insulting newspaper article, and he had lied to his superior. However, it was difficult for the missionaries to agree about a proper punishment.[121] The NMS Secretary Lars Dahle, who was on an inspection trip to the mission fields of Madagascar and South Africa, participated at the conference of 1903. After listening to the missionaries' discussions, he formulated a proposal for the suspension of Ndlela from pastoral service in the NMS. Dahle's proposal was finally accepted by the majority of the missionaries. Out of consideration for Ndlela's age (about 70), his long and faithful service to the mission, and his lack of other income, the NMS decided to continue to pay him a monthly contribution of £1.

Surprisingly, the question of Simon's restoration became a topic of discussion at subsequent conferences.[122] The conference of 1905 eventually determined that Ndlela – because of his 'continuous humble mind', his age and his 'good work' – should be reinstated in his previous position as pastor in the Norwegian mission, with the restrictions in his ministry passed in 1902.[123] The Home Board, in its comments on the termination of the Ndlela case, remarked that it still had doubts about the Zulu pastor's 'inner conversion' and had only reluctantly approved the missionaries' wish to restore him. The NMS could therefore not accept that Ndlela would receive his previous wage as an indigenous pastor. An evangelist's salary of £2 per month was determined to be 'more than equivalent'.[124]

Ndlela continued his service for the NMS at the outstation of Esamungu.[125] He was obviously a humble man. Despite the arbitrary and humiliating treatment he received from his Norwegian employers, he was known for preaching a message of love in which Africans were encouraged 'to appreciate God's love in sending the white missionaries from across the sea to preach the gospel among black people'.[126] He died in 1910 after a long and faithful service in the Norwegian Zulu church.

Conclusion

This chapter has examined the relationship between Norwegian men and Zulu men in the NMS. Through an examination of discursive representations of the Zulu man in the mission magazines and in the mission literature, the NMS's Christianisation practices towards Zulu men, and finally the case of the ordination of Simon Ndlela, the first Zulu pastor in the NMS, the discussion asked how a Norwegian missionary masculinity was constructed in relation to 'other' Zulu masculinity. Masculinity is, as discussed in Chapter 1, often created as a bulwark against several stereotypes that lack masculinity – namely, the countertypes. The countertypes, or the 'unmanly men', are needed as contrasts, as opposites, to strengthen the normative ideal of manliness. In the NMS discourse, we find that the Zulu man was predominantly represented as an antithesis of the European man. The Zulu was claimed to be neither a man of will nor a man of thought, but a man ruled by his emotions. Yet the missionaries' understanding of the Zulu man was ambiguous and reflected common colonial discourses of the Zulus as 'noble savages'. Zulu men, Christian men and male clergy in particular were from one point of view regarded as well-gifted men with rich potential. On the other hand, they were regarded as unstable, emotional and childish men who had not yet reached the level of mature manhood and, therefore, were not yet qualified for the responsibilities of church leadership. The mid-1800s idealistic ideas of a Christian brotherhood between Norwegian and Zulu groups of clergy men in the NMS had, by the turn of the century, been abandoned by the missionaries. Instead, an ideology of a father–son relationship between the white missionary and the black pastor, where the latter was understood to be a youth who had not yet reached the level of manhood, dominated. Paternalistic and racist discourses that justified a reluctance to distribute church power and influence to a rapidly growing group of male Zulu church personnel came to the surface, particularly in the 1920s, when facing processes of independence in the Lutheran Zulu Church, as thoroughly examined by Mellemsether.[127]

One may ask whether the original plan to recruit and educate Christian Zulu men for pastoral service – men who were to become the missionaries' co-workers and join a pastoral brotherhood – was ever practised. Did not the Norwegian missionaries, as most Western missionaries, from the very start act in a paternalistic way towards their newly converted Christian Zulu brothers? Can we speak of abandoned ideals if the ideals were never realised? Perhaps we can if by ideals we mean aspirations and expectations, and I will give some examples to illustrate. In the first decades of missionary activity in Zululand the missionaries had considerable aspirations for their newly converted Christian men. Zibokjana Ka Gudu, or Moses as he is known in the Norwegian sources, was sent to the NMS missionary training school in Stavanger in 1866, where he studied theology as Ole Stavem's classmate.[128] No other Christian Zulu came to succeed him and, as we have seen, the NMS in South Africa never established a theological training seminar. During the celebrations following the first ceremony of baptism at the Empangeni mission station in 1859, the three male Zulu converts enjoyed dinner together with the Norwegian missionary staff and were personally waited on by the station manager, Ommund Oftebro, and Superintendent Hans Paludan Smith Schreuder.[129] Several decades later, Zulu pastor Petrus Lamula accused NMS missionaries of racist attitudes towards their African co-workers. One concrete example was, according to Lamula, the practice of separate meals during church conferences.[130] White missionaries and Zulu pastors ate at separate places, and they were served different food. Some of the NMS missionaries in the early twentieth century were themselves aware of the previous equality ideology. When the issue of the suspension of Zulu pastor Simon Ndlela was discussed at the missionary conference of 1903, Leisegang and Rødseth accused their predecessors of making Ndlela believe that he was 'one of us'. Rødseth claimed that, in particular, the late Gundersen (who had died in 1902) gave Simon this impression. However, Rødseth argued that Gundersen should be excused, as the idea of equality and brotherhood was 'the dominant opinion among the missionaries at that time'.[131]

6
Missionary Masculinity versus Missionary Femininity

Introduction

Martinius Borgen, a missionary to Madagascar since 1867, was relocated to the NMS's Zulu mission in 1885, where he was commissioned as principal of the school for missionary children at Umphumulo. Since his wife, Martha Nikoline Hirsch Borgen, had also been an experienced teacher and housekeeper in charge of a boys' boarding school at Antananarivo from 1873 to 1882, the couple was regarded as very competent for their new assignment. Soon after their takeover, the Borgens suggested considerable reforms of the school's curriculum as well as of the boarding arrangements.[1] They advocated a modern boarding-school system with a professional staff responsible for the diverse sections of the institution (education, cleaning, laundry, cooking, accounts, gardening, etc.). Their points of view provoked the missionary community, who still preferred the family-like structure of the institution, with the principal and his wife acting as the children's substitute parents. Martinius Borgen furthermore provoked his colleagues when he presented several proposals related to the school case, written and signed by his wife, at the missionary conference in 1886. His colleagues refused to discuss Mrs Borgen's proposals, and Mr Borgen had to remove her name from the documents and substitute his own.

The conference participants discussed the school issues for ten days without reaching any agreement.[2] To continue the discussions, an extraordinary conference was assembled in February 1887. Mrs Borgen was this time invited to take part in the negotiations, although it was emphasised that a woman's admittance to the missionary conference should not be regarded as 'future precedence'. After comprehensive pressure, the couple eventually agreed to abandon their proposals for school reform, and they signed a contract in which they promised to submit to all conference decisions.[3] Martinius Borgen was obviously surprised by his colleagues' harsh treatment of his wife's suggested school reforms. In a letter he stated that, if they were only willing to relate to the male principal of the school and not to the principal's wife, who actually did a considerable job at the institution, she was in theory free from all responsibilities. Consequently, the mission had to recruit other female personnel to assist at the school. According to Borgen, 'the principal's wife is not per definition obliged to act as bookkeeper, housekeeper and housemaid'.[4]

The Norwegian Zulu mission was never a clean-cut masculine project. Since the pioneer days, both men and women had participated in the mission enterprise. Certainly, the NMS's first two representatives in south-east Africa in 1844, Hans P. S. Schreuder and his assistant E. E. Thommesen, were men. However, in the second group of missionaries sent from Norway in 1849 there was also a woman: Martha Larsen, the wife of missionary candidate Lars Larsen. A woman married to a missionary was labelled as a missionary wife (*Missionærhustru*). Unmarried women who were employed by the NMS from 1870 were defined as female missionary workers (*kvindelige Missionsarbeidere*). From 1844 to 1930, 56 men and 76 women were labourers in the NMS in south-east Africa. Among the women listed, 51 were missionary wives while 25 were female missionary workers (three of the female missionary workers eventually became missionary wives). By the late nineteenth century, women outnumbered men in the Norwegian mission, which was also the case in most Western missions. The modern missionary movement engaged Protestant as well as Catholic women on a large scale in the United States, Britain and former British colonies, such as Canada and Australia, continental Europe and the Nordic countries. Women played central roles in the home countries as supportive fund-raisers as well as missionary agents – as wives, teachers, nurses and nuns – in parts of the world defined as non-Christian.[5]

This chapter will examine the relationship between missionary men and missionary women in the NMS. How was a missionary masculinity constructed in relation to one of its 'others' – namely, the missionary femininity? Raewyn Connell asserts that the concept of masculinity is inherently relational: masculinity does not exist except in contrast with femininity.[6] Furthermore, masculinity is a 'place in gender relations' and should not be studied in isolation from its gendered social context. As Connell claims, 'No masculinity arises except in a system of gender relations.'[7] But while Connell tend to presuppose a general male suppression of women in any society or social group, Øystein Gullvåg Holter argues that we should distinguish between gender as a system of meaning and patriarchy as a structure of power and then examine the changing connections between them. A patriarchal structure, which he defines as 'the general character of the oppression of women and the linked oppression of non-privileged men within a given society and culture', should be distinguished from a gender system, which is a 'partially independent and dynamic framework of meaning'. A gender system is not simply an echo of the structures of inequality or patriarchy. It develops its own dynamics, sometimes acting on its own, often with tension and conflict-filled relations to patriarchal structures.[8]

The NMS in South Africa was definitely a patriarchal system; in the period examined herein, gender equality was out of the question. Missionary women, as well as Zulu men and Zulu women in the Norwegian mission church, were subordinate to the structural leadership and cultural hegemony of white male missionary pastors. Karin Sarja, in her study of late nineteenth-century missionary women in the Church of Sweden Mission in Zululand and Natal, a case that in fact resembles the Norwegian case, finds that women were subordinated to three levels of patriarchal structure: the central mission management in Sweden; the missionary conference in the field; and the male missionary managing the mission station.[9] However, within the structures of patriarchy in the NMS, considerable changes took place in terms of gender inequality/ equality. Line Nyhagen Predelli, in her intersectional study of gender, race and class in the NMS in Madagascar and Norway 1880–1910, speaks of 'contested patriarchy' and 'contested gender regimes'.[10]

This chapter is organised into three sections that discuss the gendered relationship between missionary men and three categories of missionary women in the NMS's Zulu mission: the missionary wife, the female missionary worker and the professional female missionary. The discussion concerns how missionary masculinity was constructed in relation to – in contrast, conflict and coherence – missionary femininity as well as how missionary masculinity was influenced by changes in the internal gender system of the NMS. As previously stated, the NMS in South Africa during the period scrutinised was a patriarchal system, and women's positions and privileges – at least until 1924, when female missionary workers were given the right to speak and vote at the missionary conferences – were defined and settled by men. In the missionary men's discussions on missionary women and their work, three questions were of importance, although not always explicitly expressed: Should she operate within the direct or the indirect mission work (for a discussion of the terms, see Chapter 3)? Should her relationship to the NMS as employer be of a formal or an informal kind? Should she manage an independent mission work, or should she be subordinated to, or dependent on, male mission management?

The missionary and his wife

The issue of missionaries' marriages

During the first 14 years of his missionary career, Schreuder was an unmarried man. We have already seen how his ascetic, self-denying lifestyle and his many heroic achievements as a pioneer were praised by mission supporters in Norway. Having no family to care for, he could therefore dedicate himself wholeheartedly to the mission work. Yet by the mid-1850s, the majority of the missionary staff consisted of married men. Young married couples in the mission field naturally resulted in the births of missionary children. Ingeborg Hovland has revealed how issues like pregnancies and childbirths in the first missionary families caused serious internal conflicts among colleagues.[11] In 1956, Schreuder's ideas on 'the advantages and disadvantages of the presence of missionary families in Protestant mission' were expressed in an article in the *NMT*.[12] Schreuder admitted that he preferred missionary men to follow Paul the apostle's advice to remain unmarried. However, if a missionary found it impossible to live in celibacy, he should be prepared to make 'the greatest sacrifices' in terms of family life; here Schreuder referred to the care for and upbringing of children. The discussion will return to the issue of missionary children in Chapter 8; in the following it will focus on missionaries' marriages.

In 1858, Schreuder himself entered into marriage.[13] That his negative attitude towards missionaries' marriages had softened over the years became obvious in a speech held in 1867 at the wedding ceremony of the first two missionary couples in the NMS's Madagascar mission. According to Schreuder, the mission could not instruct any missionary to enter matrimony. On the other hand, a missionary was permitted to marry and, if he did, the NMS was responsible for the spiritual and physical needs of his family. However, the mission could not expect the missionary wife to do any mission work. Her primary task was to care for her family. Nevertheless, if she voluntarily engaged in mission work, this should be regarded as extraordinary, and the NMS should receive her efforts with gratefulness. What the mission could expect from the missionary couple as a joint contribution, though, was their representation of the ideal Christian family life among the indigenous people they

Figure 6.1   The pioneer missionary Hans Paludan Smith Schreuder (1817–82)
married Jakobine Emilie Adelheid Løwenthal (1814–78) in 1858

Source: Mission Archives, School of Mission and Theology, Stavanger.

Photographer: H.P. Thykien.

were evangelising. Finally, Schreuder emphasised that the married male missionary was to take extra care not to let his married position be a hindrance to his mission work. A 'mission marriage' (*Missionsægteskab*) contained a conflict between the notion of marriage as a private matter and the notion of duties towards the mission. Schreuder referred to Paul's words about the married man's concerns for 'the affairs of this world' and how he should please his wife, as contrasted to an unmarried man's dedication to 'the Lord's affairs' (1. Corinthians 7: 32–34).

Although Schreuder in the pioneer days of the NMS maintained the idea of celibacy as an ideal condition for male missionaries, his wedding speech from 1867 revealed more positive attitudes towards marriage and domestic life. His view was based on Lutheran orthodoxy, which held a hegemonic position in Scandinavian religious life from roughly 1600 to 1850. Martin Luther's conceptualisation included three hierarchies – or 'orders' – within a Christian society: the household (*oeconomia*), with the housefather as the head; the state (*politia*), where the princes and magistrates exercised secular authority; and the church, (*ecclesia*) where the clergy exercised spiritual authority. In such a patriarchal societal structure, a woman's main task or *vocation*, to use Luther's terminology, was to live and act within the household as a spouse, mother and house-wife. Married life was also presented to men as a vocation. Marriage was seen as a holy institution instituted by God, and the marriage contract was binding until death. The household was the fundamental unit of any ordered Christian society and, in addition to its basic functions of production and reproduction, marriage represented the imparting of morals to both family and society at large. Marriage was further regarded as an effective way to regulate both male and female sexuality.[14]

Although Schreuder accepted a missionary's vocation as housefather to love and care for his family, he was highly aware of the particular conflict between the 'affairs of the world' and 'the Lord's affairs'. Family life belonged to the former whereas missionary life belonged to the latter. According to Schreuder, these two could not possibly be juxtaposed, and considerations for the mission work had to be given priority over considerations for the family, an issue that will be further discussed in Chapter 8. Missionaries' marriages were not without controversy in the nineteenth-century mission discourse. In 1875, a translated version of a speech delivered by the British Baptist missionary Dr Landel was printed in the *NMT*.[15] Landel criticised the common practice in Protestant missions of allowing missionaries to marry. He called for more missionaries willing to follow Paul's example: 'self-denying, heroic men', 'free from all family ties' and ready to renounce 'the comforts of domestic life'.

Lars Dahle, who at this time was serving as a married missionary in Madagascar, responded negatively to the views expressed in Landel's article. In an 1876 article in the *NMT*, Dahle presented a thorough defence of missionaries' marriages.[16] Not only was a missionary allowed to enter marriage, both according to the Word of God and the Lutheran church order, but a missionary – at least one working in Madagascar – ought to be married, in Dahle's opinion. First, a missionary should be married for the sake of his physical health. He needed someone to take care of domestic tasks such as cooking, cleaning, laundry and nursing in case of sickness. As a single man, it was impossible to employ female Malagasy maids without risking rumours about sexual improprieties. Second, a single missionary was in constant danger of becoming 'spiritually devastated' at a remote mission station. He needed a friend, a conversation partner and a fellow Christian; a missionary wife could fulfil these needs. Third, it benefited the mission if the missionary was married as he could then freely teach and supervise the female part of the congregation. In addition, the missionary wife, by activating her female skills and virtues, could have a significant impact on local women. Like Schreuder, Dahle stressed the importance of the missionary couple's demonstration of the ideal Christian domestic life in 'heathen' surroundings.

Dahle concluded in his article that 'a Christian wife is neither redundant nor a restraining person for the missionary and his work, quite the reverse, she is an incredible blessing for both'. The unmarried male missionary, on the other hand, was what Dahle labelled 'an eremite missionary' and 'a very unfortunate man', both in private and professional terms.[17] The official discussion on missionaries' marriages faded out after Dahle's weighty arguments. In the Norwegian mission the ideal missionary man was expected to be a married man; in contrast to Catholic missions, the married status became an inevitable ingredient in Lutheran missionary masculinity ideals.[18] The historians Patricia Grimshaw and Peter Sherlock find the same development in most Protestant missions: 'The perceived need of male missionaries for companionship and domestic support, together with underlying fears of sexual misconduct, quickly made a wife a necessary asset.'[19] The overwhelming majority of the male missionaries serving in the NMS's Zulu mission in the 1844–1930 period were married.[20] Even Schreuder gave up the single life and eventually asked friends in Norway to provide him with a suitable female companion. He experienced great support from his wife, Jakobine Emilie Adelheid Løwenthal, who apparently became his closest and most loyal friend.[21]

According to Line Nyhagen Predelli, the NMS preferred its missionaries to be married, but courts, engagements, marriages and sexualities were nevertheless regulated and controlled.[22] A missionary's selection of a suitable bride was of considerable interest to the mission and could not be reduced to a simple matter of love between two individuals. The submission of applications for engagement and marriage was required, and permission depended on the satisfactory provision of extensive information about the prospective bride and her suitability for mission life. As a general rule, a missionary had to be stationed in the field for two years before he was allowed to marry.[23] In 1918, the two-year rule was renounced after some pressure from missionaries in Madagascar, and engaged missionary couples were allowed to depart together for the mission field. However, they were stationed at separate places while studying the local language, and marriage could only take place after a year. During the school days in Stavanger, the missionary candidates were definitely not permitted to enter into marriage, and a softening-up of these regulations came only in the 1970s. Predelli states that interracial marriages were not accepted in the NMS until the 1970s.

Male missionaries in the NMS tended to benefit from social betterment not only through theological seminary education at the mission school, but also through marriage. As discussed in Chapter 2, the majority of the nineteenth-century Norwegian missionaries were recruited from rural families where their fathers worked as farmers, tenants, artisans or petty traders. In comparison, the majority of the missionary women – both married and single – came from middle-class or upper-class backgrounds.[24] For example, Lars Dahle, himself the son of a smallholding farmer, married Ella Svendsen, the daughter of Sven E. Svendsen, an influential merchant and contractor in Stavanger's commercial, cultural and religious life. When examining the educational background of the missionary women in Madagascar, Predelli found the average level of education to be higher than the norm for Norwegian women at the time.[25] The missionary wives in the NMS's mission fields thus represented important resources in terms of education and class.

The missionary wife: wife or missionary?

As demonstrated, attitudes towards the female presence in the mission field changed remarkably during the first three decades of the Norwegian enterprise in south-east Africa. To Schreuder, in the pioneering phase, women in the mission field were tantamount to 'problems' like childbearing and child-rearing, and he consequently preferred celibacy. However, women in the sense of missionary wives were quite soon regarded as resources in the mission. In accordance with Lutheran household ideology, a missionary wife cared for the physical well-being of the missionary pastor. She was also the male missionary's closest soul-mate and co-worker. Missionary femininity was accepted and appreciated as supporting and complementing missionary masculinity.

The place of a missionary wife was, according to the male leadership, restricted to the missionary household. Her primary task was to serve her husband and family in respect of sexualities, childbearing, child-rearing, cooking, cleaning, sewing, gardening, and keeping poultry and cattle. However, as part of a widely accepted mission strategy in Natal and Zululand, as discussed in Chapter 5, she also 'adopted' the many young Zulus who attended the mission station and became integrated into the missionary household as apprentices. Daily devotions, religious education and reading/writing/arithmetic lessons were blended with practical training, and the missionary wives actively participated in these tasks. When a Christian congregation was established at the mission station, often founded on the Zulu 'girls and boys' who had been raised in the missionary household, the missionary wife continued to invite Christian and non-Christian women to needlework classes in her home and to women's groups in the church. The idea of the 'Christian Home', which according to mission historian Dana Robert was a 'cornerstone' of Anglo-American mission thought and practice,[26] was also central in the Norwegian mission. The main task of a missionary wife was to maintain an ideal Christian family life in the mission field. However, the Christian homemaking project was further a part of a gendered mission strategy, in which the missionary wives in particular were in charge of converting indigenous women and children to Christianity and transforming indigenous domestic life into what was understood as Christian family life. In this sense, the missionary wife actively took part in missionary work, without challenging Lutheran household ideology. She could be both a wife and a missionary.

According to Grimshaw and Sherlock, numerous case studies demonstrate that the missionary wives from the earliest days of the missionary enterprise believed that they were called to enter the mission field 'by the same evangelical imperatives that prompted men'.[27] In the case of the NMS's mission in Madagascar, historians have brought up several examples of missionary wives with strong commitments to their commissions.[28] What about the missionary wives in Zululand? Ingeborg Hovland asserts that the first baptism in the NMS's Zulu mission in 1858 was probably the result of the evangelising work of a missionary wife and a Zulu assistant, and she finds it surprising that this fact is never remarked upon in the official histories of the NMS.[29] The young woman, Mathenjwase kaNondumo Shange, received her baptism from Schreuder, who on the occasion visited Umphumulo mission station in order to minister the act. This ground-breaking event is usually represented in the Norwegian mission discourse as 'the first harvest' of Schreuder's 14 years of hard missionary work in Zululand. However, Shange had in fact been in the apprenticeship of Martha and Lars Larsen for four years preceding her baptism. She was trained in domestic skills by Mrs. Larsen, and since the latter also ran a daily reading class for the young Zulus in their service, Shange may also have received religious education from her. The Zulu assistant to whom Hovland refers was Umbijane, a young Christian man employed as a 'wagon driver' at the Umphumulo mission station who simultaneously assisted the missionary in evening prayers and Sunday morning classes. The day after her baptism, Shange was married to Umbijane. Martha Larsen died in 1890 after 41 years of uninterrupted service in the mission field, following her husband to the grave just a few months after his death. She was praised in the NMS's official obituary as a missionary wife who had 'a strong interest in Mission' and who 'actively took part in her husband's work'.[30] Ole S. Steenberg, the missionary who sat by her deathbed and also ministered her funeral, reported that 'she more than any other woman learned to know the natives and discovered a good method to promote the Lord's work among them'.[31]

The missionary wives in the NMS's mission in south-east Africa followed in the paths of Martha Larsen and participated in the mission enterprise, with the missionary household as a starting point. When female mission supporters in Norway established their own magazine in 1884, missionary wives in Zululand were among the first contributors of articles. Inga Karoline Eriksen at the Umbonambi mission station described in 1884 the training of nine young girls in domestic work, a needlework class, the women's group, her home visits in the neighbourhood, her nursing services and her visits together with her husband to the outstation mission schools.[32] Marie Steenberg wrote in a lively way in 1887 about her daily needlework classes at Imfule mission station and her work as a teacher in the mission school. She also expressed how she was often 'deeply sorrowful' for not being able to do more of 'the real mission work'.[33] Rannveig Naustvoll investigated the daily lives of the Norwegian women living and working at the NMS mission stations in Zululand and Natal in the 1900–25 period. She concludes that the missionary wives were expected to work, and they did work a lot. In these first decades of the twentieth century, most of their labour was related to the needs of their families, to the expanded missionary households and to the congregations assembled at the central mission station.[34]

This chapter began with the case of Martha Nikoline and Martinius Borgen and their conflict with the male missionary community. The Borgen case is interesting because it challenged the mission's gender system. Martha Nikoline Borgen was first and foremost regarded as the wife of the missionary Borgen. The missionary wives were not directly employed or commissioned by the NMS, and they were not paid separate wages.[35] They were not considered to be missionaries in a formal sense and therefore not regarded as members of the missionary conferences. The missionary wives did not conduct any independent mission work; their service was always related to the positions of their husbands. The NMS's Home Board had rightfully referred to Mrs Borgen's professional experience as a teacher and housekeeper when her husband was appointed to a new position in the Zulu mission. Likewise, both the Home Board and the missionaries expected her to take considerable responsibility for the well-being and education of the missionary

Figure 6.2   Nils Torbjørnsen Braatvedt (1847–1943) and his wife Severine Lisabeth Braatvedt (1847–1929) had 49 years of married missionary life

Source: Mission Archives, School of Mission and Theology, Stavanger.

children. The trouble started when she wished to have some influence on how this task should be conducted, and the trouble continued when her husband questioned a wife's obligation to obediently support the duties related to her husband's work. Markus Dahle, one of the missionaries, was shocked by Mr and Mrs Borgen's attitudes and behaviour in this case as 'every missionary wife is supposed to assist her husband's work in the best way'.[36]

The Borgen case further illustrated how a missionary wife was considered an indispensable resource in the mission work as her husband's closest co-worker and supporter. The expanded missionary household was regarded as the starting point for all missionary activity, and the first congregations were founded on these households. The missionary husbands and wives were expected to complement one another in the labour and to regard the mission station and mission congregation as a common project despite the husbands' obvious leadership as head of both the household and the congregation. The wives' services were basically related to the indirect sector of the mission enterprise, and the widespread mission strategy of making Christian homes was regarded as their particular responsibility. Nevertheless, the work of the missionary wives, which also included religious teaching of women and children, challenged the traditionally strict distinctions between the direct and indirect mission work. After the death of his wife, Severine Lisabeth, in 1929, Nils Braatvedt wrote an obituary in which he memorialised their 49 years of married missionary life. According to Braatvedt, his wife was just as dedicated to the direct mission work as he was himself, a work that 'she always carried out with love and faithfulness'.[37] He obviously regarded their missionary service as husband and wife as a joint life work.[38]

Female assistance in missionary households

As we have seen, the missionary wife was expected to manage the missionary household and support and complement the work of her husband. However, the conditions in the mission field could severely strain the gendered division of labour between husband and wife thought to be appropriate in contemporary Western societies.[39] Men occasionally spent their days taking care of sick wives and infant children; in addition, women sometimes left the domestic realm for more public activities. In 1887, NMS missionary wife Marie Steenberg reported that it had become her task to do the necessary outstationary business trips with the ox wagon, something she found interesting as she met lots of people, saw new places and learned a lot.[40] Nils Braatvedt admitted that his wife gradually took over several of the duties that naturally belonged to the station manager's responsibility.[41] In other cases, especially during childbirths and post-natal periods, a husband had to act as midwife, nurse, child-minder and housekeeper. The missionary Karl Larsen Titlestad excused himself in a letter to the Home Board in 1871, stating that due to his wife's recent confinement and weak condition as well as his three minor sons' illness, he had not been able to carry out much direct mission work.[42]

Titlestad requested that the NMS pay the travel expenses for his wife's elder sister, who was willing to come from Norway to assist them. Marthe Haaland arrived in 1872 and stayed with the Titlestad family for four years before moving to the Mahlabatini mission station in 1876 to assist missionary Gundvall Gundersen, whose wife had recently died in childbirth.[43] The following year she became Gundersen's new wife and the stepmother to his three minor children. Marthe Haaland was only one of several Norwegian women who departed for Zululand to provide female assistance in the missionary households.[44] These women were often related to the missionary or his wife either by kinship or friendship. In the absence of sisters and mothers, they supported the missionary wives in their domestic work and relieved the male missionaries from labour related to childcare, nursing and housekeeping. They had no formal relationship to the NMS; since they were often invisible in the mission archives, they were also invisible in the mission histories. However, the women were committed Christians, often with a particular calling to serve in foreign missions.[45] As was the case with Marthe Haaland, several of them eventually became missionary wives.

The previously mentioned Martha Nikoline Hirsch became the first woman contracting for a defined mission service in the NMS and is regarded as the first female missionary worker in the organisation's history.[46] She was a well-educated pastor's daughter engaged as a governess in the home of a senior state official. However, as she felt herself called to missionary service abroad, she contacted – through the help of friends in a mission association in Trondheim – the NMS's Home Board in 1869, actually the same year as Norwegian women were legally permitted to teach in governmental schools. Hirsch offered her teaching services as a response to explicit needs in the mission field. According to a report from the Zulu missionary conference in 1868, made officially through the mission magazine, the missionaries were searching for a female teacher to educate their children.[47] Hirsch's application was accepted by the Home Board, and she was commissioned as a governess

Figure 6.3   There was a growing need for female assistance in the missionary families. Hans Christian Martin Gottfried Leisegang (1838–1914) together with his wife Agnethe Torvalla Forseth Leisegang (1851–1933), their children and domestic servants

Source: Mission Archives, School of Mission and Theology, Stavanger.

Photographer: B. Kisch.

for the missionary children in Zululand. However, upon arriving at the Entumeni mission station in 1870, she received new orders, as Bishop Schreuder no longer saw the need for a female teacher in Zululand. She was instead asked to go to the newly established mission field in Madagascar.[48] After arriving in Antananarivo, she started a school for Malagasy women. In 1871, Hirsch married Martinius Borgen, thus stepping back from the formal position as female missionary worker.

Although Hirsch's career as a female missionary worker was short, her recruitment was nevertheless a response to explicit needs for female assistance in the missionary households, often clearly expressed by the male missionaries themselves. This new policy of recruiting women was merely a formalisation and institutionalisation of the already accepted practice of recruiting unmarried women to serve in missionary households on a voluntary basis. The first female missionary workers in the

NMS were on formal contracts. However, they were not recruited to any independent mission work or to direct, or 'real', mission work. They did not have their own dwellings, but lived together with missionary families.[49] Their salaries were about one-third of that of their male colleagues. Although the annual allowance of female missionary workers in Zululand in 1882 was decided to be £40 plus £20 for expenses for board and lodging, a married male missionary earned £150 and an unmarried male missionary £140.[50] The missionary femininity of the female missionary workers was, as with the missionary wives, expected to be lived out within the domestic sphere of the missionary household, supporting and complementing the male missionary. As Schreuder eventually had to accept the presence of missionary wives in the mission field, the presence of female assistance within the missionary households was thus accepted and formalised by the male mission leaders from 1870.

Yet for the women involved, this gendered arrangement had its distinct restrictions. Karin Sarja, in her detailed study of 36 missionary women in the Church of Sweden Mission in Natal and Zululand, finds that unmarried women contested the mission's expectation of them as merely female assistance in the missionary families.[51] We find examples of the same in the NMS. The issue of a professional midwife in the mission field was discussed at the missionary conferences in south-east Africa on several occasions,[52] and in 1881 the midwife and deaconess Ingeborg Ellingsdatter Jordal was employed by the NMS and sent to Zululand to serve in the missionary families. In 1885, Jordal became engaged to a Norwegian settler at Eshowe. However, she did not intend to resign from the NMS, wishing to continue her service and promising to do the best to not let the mission 'suffer any loss' by her new marital status. Jordal's application for continued service was sent to the Home Board, but the superintendent, Ommund Oftebro, also asked the missionaries to comment on the case.[53] A minority of four supported Jordal's request while a majority of seven rejected it. One of them, Karl Larsen Titlestad, declared that 'it appears like an impossibility to fulfil the vocation as midwife and deaconess within the missionary families as a married woman'. The Home Board shared the majority opinion,[54] and Jordal had to resign from mission service to marry Hans Olsen in 1886.

A second gendered conflict evolved in 1884, when the teacher at the school for missionary children, Elsebeth Kahrs, sent a proposal to the missionary conference asking for permission to establish a school for Zulu children in the district of the Umphumulo mission station. She intended to finance the construction of the school building through her own means, and Ellen Sofie Bertelsen, a deaconess and widow from the Madagascar mission temporarily serving in Zululand, was interested in joining her.[55] Kahrs' application provoked a lot of discussion at the missionary conference, where a majority rejected it and urged her to continue the service at the school for missionary children. It was argued that she was physically and mentally weak, that it was dangerous for single women to live in rural areas, and that she needed male inspection. Sven Eriksen added that the thought of her starting a mission work 'on her own' was 'frightful'. Nevertheless, Kahrs did not give up the idea of the school and in 1884 sent a new letter of application directly to the Home Board in Stavanger.[56] The Home Board permitted her in fact to start some education in the district. However, she was not allowed to raise any school building and was ordered to live at the Umphumulo mission station under the supervision of the male station manager.[57] Kahrs' mission project was never realised. In 1885 she married the maritime trader Nils Nilsen in Durban. Mrs Bertelsen went back to Madagascar in 1886 and married the widower missionary Reinert Larsen. In the nineteenth-century Norwegian Zulu mission, there was no tolerance for women's independent missionary initiatives and enterprises.

The challenge of professional missionary femininity

By the early twentieth century it had become evident that the NMS was also affected by the international female mission programme of 'Women's Work for Women'. With nineteenth-century assumptions that men and women occupied different roles in society, this gendered mission philosophy emphasised that it took women to reach other women and their children with the Gospel. The theory was based on middle-class Western assumptions that Western women needed to help liberate their sisters around the world by reaching them in their homes, teaching them to read, and providing medical care for their bodies. Conversion to Christianity not only provided eternal salvation for women, but it also raised their self-worth and improved their position in what was understood to be oppressive, patriarchal societies.[58] In Norway, the women's missionary movement formulated its programme in a similar way: 'Women helping women' (*Kvinder hjælper Kvinder*).[59] Resourceful and creative female mission leaders such as Bolette Gjør, Henny Dons and Marie Sinding established female mission networks, organisations and institutions, and recruited female missionaries. They edited women's mission magazines, wrote women's mission books, and imported and implemented the central concepts and ideologies of the international women's missionary movement into a Norwegian context.[60]

How did the international women's missionary movement influence the NMS's organisation in south-east Africa? What was the male reaction to this international feminisation of the mission forces, both in terms of a surplus of women among the missionary recruits and a feminised mission philosophy – what Dana Robert calls 'The Mission of Motherhood'?[61] What was the missionary men's response to the new missionary femininity that emerged – namely, that of the professional female missionary?[62] In 1887, the NMS's general assembly accepted the use of women in direct mission work as deaconesses and 'Bible women'. In 1904, women were granted the right to vote at the NMS's general assemblies in Norway. The same year, after an initiative from Madagascar missionaries, female missionary workers were given the right to participate and vote at the missionary conferences on issues concerning 'their own work'. In 1910 they were accepted as full members of the missionary conferences in China and Madagascar.[63] To clarify, unmarried female missionary workers were integrated into the conference fellowship, while missionary wives were not given the right to speak or vote at missionary conferences in the NMS until 1973.[64] Against this background, it is astounding that the male missionary community in South Africa did not grant female missionary workers democratic rights until 1924.[65] Furthermore, it is surprising that the Home Board never pushed the missionaries in South Africa to put into effect the democratic rights women had achieved in the other mission fields of the NMS.[66] The men in the Norwegian Zulu mission were reluctant to integrate women into their all-male missionary community and unenthusiastic in their response to the international movements of female missionary enterprises. Nevertheless, they accepted female missionary workers as equal members of the missionary conference in 1924. The following sections will take a closer look at their response to the challenge of professional missionary femininity.

Female evangelists

In 1887, the NMS's Home Board, after negotiations with the regional conferences, decided to open up access for women to direct mission work as deaconesses and Bible women. The news was celebrated by Bolette Gjør, the editor of the NMS's women's mission magazine, as an acceptance of Christian women's divine calling 'to serve the Lord among the heathens'.[67] However, the response from the missionaries in south-east Africa was reluctant, and they found the decision to be irrelevant to the Zulu mission. They saw no need for deaconesses or Bible women; rather, just 'a couple of ladies' to teach in the mission schools and arrange women's needlework classes could perhaps be useful.[68] Ten years later, in 1898, once again the question of female assistance in direct mission work was discussed at the missionary conference.[69] This time it was referred to the extensive use of female missionaries by the NMS in Madagascar as well as by Swedish and American mission organisations operating in Natal and Zululand, which all seemed to be successful arrangements. The conference decided to offer a position as 'missionary woman' (*Missionskvinde*) at the Eshowe mission station to Therese Victoria Aagaard, who had served as private governess in a missionary family since 1896. Aagaard, who had previously refused an offer to manage the school for the missionary children by referring to her missionary calling to serve 'the heathens',[70] accepted the request this time.

Aagaard continued her work in the NMS until 1910. In Henny Don's history of the female mission movement in Norway, Aagaard is remembered as the first 'independent' female missionary in the NMS's Zulu mission.[71] Aagaard was an enthusiastic writer and provided female fund-raisers and supporters at home with regular reports from her varied missionary work at different mission stations.[72] However, her relation to both the male missionary community in South Africa and to the Home Board was conflicted. Aagaard's formal relation to the NMS and her work and placement in the mission field were ongoing issues of discussion both at the missionary conferences and in negotiations between the Home Board and the local missionary community.[73] In 1910, Aagaard left the NMS in what was understood as her disapproval of a conference decision to relocate her from Mahlabatini to the Imfule mission station. 'She is leaving us now, and then we are finished with her' was how Superintendent Ole Stavem informed Lars Dahle in Stavanger about her resignation.[74] Aagaard was immediately engaged as a missionary in the Church of Sweden Mission and served at the Ceza mission station until 1922.

The use of women as evangelistic missionaries was never regarded as a real option by male NMS missionaries in south-east Africa. Evangelisation and pastoral work was understood as the realm of male spiritual authority. With the exception of Sofie Kyvik, who managed the Ungoye mission station from 1919 to 1921 while the congregation was waiting for a new male pastor to arrive, there are no examples of women in similar positions in the first half of the twentieth century. Even this temporary arrangement caused a lot of discussion among the missionary men. Some found Kyvik to be physically weak and mentally unstable – 'a melancholic character'. Others warned against placing a single white lady alone 'in the wilderness'.[75] It is obvious that Scandinavian Baptist and Holiness Missions operating in Natal and Zululand, where female missionaries worked as both preachers and church founders, had a less restrictive practice in this regard than the Lutherans.[76]

Female missionary teachers

The enterprises of female missionaries in the field of education were to a greater extent tolerated by the missionary men in the NMS. Missionary women's success in the field of education was closely related to the Christian homemaking programme, which was originally the responsibility of the missionary wives. In south-east Africa, missions like the American Zulu Mission and the Church of Sweden Mission established boarding institutions for Zulu girls in the last decades of the nineteenth century that were managed by single female missionaries.[77] In the NMS, the missionary wives continued to educate and train the girls in domestic skills, as expressed by Inga Eriksen in 1901: 'We have no boarding schools to put them in, so we have to run the institution ourselves.'[78] Stavem also asserted in 1915 that the Norwegian mission in reality had many 'girls' homes which didn't cost the mission a penny, as the missionary families paid the costs themselves'.[79] Eventually the male NMS missionaries, not only the missionary wives, also came to perceive the need for a more institutional female training to replace the apprenticeship system.

In 1902, the missionary conference decided to establish a Girls' Home at the Eshowe mission station, a plan that was realised in 1905.[80] Andrea Sofie Paus Kyvik was commissioned to establish and develop the institution. She was a teacher by profession, but had also been educated at the Women's School of Mission in Kristiania, a school established in 1901 by female mission leaders in Norway. This school further financed Kyvik's residence for study purposes at the Inanda Girls' Seminary in Natal, run by the American Zulu Mission. Kyvik was regarded by female mission leaders in Norway as their representative, and she wrote regular reports in the women's magazine about her work at the girls' home.[81]

In 1916, the Native Teachers' Conference in the Co-operating Lutheran Missions suggested that the NMS develop professional industrial education for girls. At the missionary conference that same year, plans were worked out for a Girls' Industrial School.[82] Six years later, in 1922, the plans were finally fulfilled, and an institution was established at Eshowe with an overall aim to 'lift up the Zulu Woman and Zulu family life' by training pious and industrious Christian housewives in housekeeping, handicraft, gardening, hygiene and health.[83] Emilie Larsen, whose salary was paid by the Female Teachers' Missionary Association (Lærerindenes

Missionsforbund) in Norway, held the position as matron from 1923 until 1941.[84] Starting in 1925, Larsen was accompanied by the teacher Margarete Skavang, who was then released from her work at the home for missionary children in Durban. In the following years these women developed programmes and plans, raised funds, negotiated with South African governmental officials, and actively participated whenever the issue of the girls' institutions was discussed at the missionary conferences.[85] In 1929, the Girls' Home and the Girls' Industrial School were merged, and new and modern buildings with a dormitory, classrooms, living rooms and school kitchen were constructed, partly financed by governmental funds.[86]

In the mission schools, girls and boys had from the very start been offered elementary education on an equal level. In 1902, by referring to the progress other missions had made in the sector of women's education, NMS missionaries discussed the possible establishment of 'girls' higher education'.[87] There was an urgent need for qualified teachers in the mission schools, and such an institution could provide the mission with sufficient native female teachers. The plan did not become reality in 1902. Instead, the missionary conference decided in 1909 to accept female students at their training school for teachers at Umphumulo. They agreed to seek a 'cultivated and educated lady' to teach and to serve as matron at the girls' dormitory.[88] Even the Home Board accepted that this position was 'of such importance' that the matron's salary should be £60, not the £45 regular annual salary for a female missionary worker.[89] By January 1912, 32 young men and 14 women were enrolled at the college, whose staff consisted of two male and two female teachers.[90]

The educational work of the female teachers Kyvik, Larsen and Skavang, and the institutions they successfully established and managed, convinced their male colleagues of women's abilities and capacity to participate in independent missionary enterprises. The missionary men, who were mostly theologians, realised that these women possessed professional skills that were sorely needed in the Norwegian mission. The missionary men's acceptance of female missionary workers' democratic rights in 1924, and the inclusion of this group of women into the all-male association of the missionary conference, can thus be interpreted as the breakthrough of a new idea of a professional partnership between men and women in the mission. In the gender system of the NMS in South Africa, we definitely see a development towards increasing gender equality in the first decades of the twentieth century. Yet the system was simultaneously marked by gender inequality, as women were not permitted to choose freely between missionary professions. They were still excluded from the discipline of theology and the profession of evangelist/pastor.

Female medical missionaries

Another sector of the NMS's Zulu mission in which professional female missionaries were the leading agents was health. Ever since the sudden interruption of Christian Oftebro's career as a medical missionary in 1888 (see Chapter 3), no physicians had been sent by the NMS to South Africa. The missionaries had occasionally brought up the issue,[91] as both the mission fields in Madagascar and China were well equipped with physicians, nurses, deaconesses and deacons, and the construction of health institutions had been an area of priority. In 1921, the issue of a medical mission in Zululand was again raised at the missionary conference, and during the 1920s this became an ongoing theme of negotiation between the conference and the Home Board.[92] While it was discussed whether the mission should recruit a female or male physician, where a possible hospital should be situated and how extensive its services should be, two missionary nurses went unnoticed in their establishment of tiny hospitals at the Ekombe and Mahlabatini mission stations. The medical mission in Zululand was, in its first three decades, run entirely by professional missionary nurses. Only after the 1950s did the NMS equip its mission hospitals in South Africa with physicians, who then happened to be men.[93]

Elida Ulltveit-Moe was supposed to go to Madagascar as a missionary nurse but, due to medical reasons, was transferred to South Africa in 1922. Since there were no hospitals in the NMS's mission in South Africa, the missionary conference appointed her to assist in the congregational work at the Ekombe mission station.[94] She arrived at Ekombe in December 1922, where she soon offered her medical services. The first equipment she purchased was a horse to take her to patient visits in the neighbouring homesteads.[95] Patients started to approach the mission station to receive medical care. In 1924 she opened a hospital. A storeroom functioned as the dispensary and two traditional Zulu huts were raised for the inpatients, who slept on straw mats.[96] Ulltveit-Moe's efforts were very much supported by the missionary couple with whom she lived, Peter Andreas R. Strømme and his wife Kirsten. Mrs Strømme was a nurse herself, while Mr Strømme, in addition to his theological education, had been trained as a deacon, actually a male nurse, at the Norwegian Deacons' Home.[97] The activities quickly expanded, and in 1926 the hospital was visited by 3,200 patients.[98] By this time Ulltveit-Moe was mentally and physically exhausted, and female colleagues wrote

Figure 6.4   The missionary nurse Martha Palm (1886–1965) established a hospital at Malabatini mission station in 1925

Source: Mission Archives, School of Mission and Theology, Stavanger.

letters to the newly established Female Nurses' Missionary Association (Sykepleierskenes Missionring – SMR) in Norway, begging it to recruit and financially support a missionary nurse in Zululand. The SMR answered the Zulu missionaries' prayers, sending Borghild Magnussen as its first representative to the mission field, an event that in the history of the SMR has been described as a milestone.[99] The interest in Ulltveit-Moe's medical mission among supporters in Norway was growing, and she raised considerable funds for the purpose of a proper hospital at Ekombe. With the Home Board's blessing – though not their grants – a tiny hospital building with five rooms was erected in 1929.[100]

Martha Palm started a similar hospital at the Malabatini mission station in October 1925.[101] She originally came to South Africa in 1920 to work as a housekeeper at the home for missionary children in Durban, but in 1923 she applied for an opportunity to serve in a medical mission. Her application was accepted, although no financial support for her new medical mission project was granted. As was the case at Ekombe, money was raised among supporters in Norway in addition to the Scandinavian settler milieu in Durban. Palm was also supported and encouraged by the missionary couple serving at Mahlabatini, Marie and Johan Kjelvei. She received her first patients in an old stable at the mission station, and a children's room in Kjelvei's house functioned as the dispensary. Quite soon she was able to build a first simple hospital building containing three rooms: one served as an admission room, kitchen and dispensary; a second was for inpatients; and a third room was for Palm herself. A year later she raised a new building for inpatients and also two traditional Zulu huts for accompanying family members. To a great extent the hospital functioned as a maternity ward. In 1927, Palm reported that she had received 2,049 patients in her polyclinic and helped 78 mothers with their deliveries.

By 1930, the central management of the NMS had accepted the medical mission as a new and important sector of work in the Zulu mission. When General Secretary Einar Amdahl inspected the mission field of South Africa in 1929, the issue of the medical mission was thoroughly discussed with the male and female missionaries.[102] Upon returning home, he presented a theological legitimisation of the effort by explaining why hospital work in South Africa was to be regarded as important mission work. First, the love of Christ urges the mission to practise the deeds of love. Second, it paves the way for the Gospel to 'huts and hearts' that would otherwise be closed. Third, the power of the 'witch doctors' was challenged and in many cases broken, which Amdahl asserts was of great importance for the evangelising task. The Zulu people had 'a strong fear' of evil spirits and supernatural enemies, something which bound them to the traditional diviners and healers who were supposed to help in cases of sickness and health problems. Through the Christian nursing and medical care, people's faith and trust in the traditional religion were challenged, Amdahl concluded.

How missionary femininity affected missionary masculinity

By the mid-1920s, the professional female missionary in the form of a teacher or nurse had been accepted by the male missionary community of the NMS in South Africa. Ulltveit-Moe admitted that, upon first arriving in the mission field, she had been met with a lot of scepticism towards female missionaries. However, after some years, the situation changed and in 1925 she reported that her work was highly supported by male colleagues.[103] Einar Amdahl asserted that Ulltveit-Moe's transfer from Madagascar to Zululand should be regarded as 'the work of God'.[104] Her missionary colleague Nils M. S. Follesøe had a similar divine explanation: 'Sister Elida started the nursing work in our mission. No one asked her to come, but the Lord himself sent her.'[105]

This new attitude towards missionary femininity actually affected the missionary masculinity discourses in several ways. First, the missionary men realised that their gendered relationship to women was not restricted exclusively to their roles as superiors. In professional settings they could act as women's equal partners. Certainly, they continued to claim a housefather's superior role as head of his wife and family and, in the direct mission work, preaching and pastoral work were still regarded as men's divine responsibilities, meaning women thus had to submit to men's spiritual leadership. However, in the indirect mission work and in the fields of teaching and nursing in particular, women were accepted as matrons and managers, and matters concerning these institutions and this work were discussed and negotiated between men and women in professional partnership.

Second, the missionary men started to speak of their dispensability. We have already seen that the notion of a missionary in the NMS context was identical to the notion of a male pastor. The Norwegian Lutheran mission enterprise had thus been dependent on a staff of ordained male pastors since the pioneer days. The early 1920s started with a financial crisis in the NMS; consequently, the Home Board was reluctant to recruit new missionary pastors for mission work in South Africa. This situation caused a lot of frustration in the missionary community. However, some of the male missionaries saw how the current economic crisis created opportunities to openly discuss a reorganisation of the missionary resources. In a speech given at the missionary conference in 1923, Strømme envisioned a new recruitment policy in the NMS's Zulu mission. He asked for more female missionaries – teachers, nurses and church workers – and fewer traditional missionary pastors. As an alternative to the present situation of 12 male pastors in the field, he suggested a future team of six male and six female missionaries. Strømme's speech provoked much discussion. Ole Aadnesgaard expressed that he was 'deeply hurt' by the hints that there was no future need for male missionary pastors. Lars Martin Titlestad, on the other hand, stated that they should not be 'so afraid' of receiving more missionary women at the expense of missionary men. The conference finally agreed to ask for more female missionaries, which also provided a cheap solution to the recruitment crisis.[106]

Third, as the work of the professional female missionaries in the field of health and education gradually became increasingly respected, and as female missionaries in 1924 became accepted as members of the missionary conference, it simultaneously resulted in an expanded understanding of the nature of mission work. Both the education and health sectors, the traditional responsibilities of female missionaries, were to a greater extent accepted as real mission work and defined as direct mission work. These processes were, of course, of great importance to the women involved, but also affected missionary men's subjectivities. From merely being the servants of the Word, the male missionaries broadened their scope and accepted social work as part of their commission. Thus, the development of the NMS in South Africa reflected international trends in Western mission organisations from the 1920s, which meant both a wider acceptance of social work as mission work and an integration of the many female missionary enterprises into the mainline confessional, missionary organisations.[107]

Strømme, educated as both a deacon and pastor, had for years missed a focus on diaconias in the mission work; he ultimately became an outstanding defender of Ulltveit-Moe's and Palm's medical missions. During a discussion in 1924, he proclaimed that he never regretted becoming a missionary, but he regretted not becoming a medical missionary.[108] The 1888 dismissal of medical missionary Christian Oftebro was, according to Strømme, 'an unhealed wound in our mission', and the NMS had, with its long-lasting neglect of the medical mission in Zululand, 'an old debt to pay'.[109] Strømme regarded the NMS's strong focus on evangelisation and congregational work and its neglect of social service to be signs of a mission in unbalance. However, the persistent work of the professional female missionary and the influential mission theory of the women's missionary movement had helped restore the whole. Missionary femininity did more than complement missionary masculinity; it healed and restored the mission as an entity.

Conclusion

This chapter has examined the relationship between missionary masculinity and missionary femininity, including how missionary men related to three categories of missionary women: missionary wives, female missionary workers and professional female missionaries. The missionary wives had no formal relationship to the NMS as an employer, but they were nevertheless regarded as necessary assets in the mission. The wives were supposed to serve their husbands within the missionary household and thus support what was regarded as the direct, or real, mission work in an indirect way. Meanwhile, the programme of creating Christian homes in non-Christian communities was regarded as essential indirect, or civilising, mission work. The employment of female missionary workers in the NMS from 1870 provided the formalisation of an already widespread practice of recruiting unmarried women for female assistance in the missionary households. The female missionary workers certainly had a formal employment in the mission, but as their labour was strictly restricted to the missionary households and the supervision of the male missionary housefather, they had no independent position and conducted no independent mission work. In the early twentieth century the international programme of Women's Work for Women also reached the shores of South Africa. Professional female missionaries in the form of nurses and teachers gradually gained acceptance for their mission theory and mission practice among the male missionary community, and from 1924 they were integrated as full members of the missionary conference.

The acceptance of the professional female missionary affected the internal gender system of the NMS in South Africa. It also affected missionary masculinity discourses. First, male missionaries accepted women as equal partners in specific professional settings, and the unconditional general rule of male supremacy was contested. Second, male missionaries realised their own dispensability when accepting that the mission enterprise was no longer dependent on a group of ordained male pastors. Third, as the traditional missionary work of women in the fields of education and health was accepted to a greater extent as real mission work, the missionary men simultaneously found that that their soul-saving activities had been prioritised on behalf of the healing of bodies. Missionary femininity was thus regarded as more than a complement to missionary masculinity; the mission theory and practice of the female missionaries had in fact healed and restored, and consequently consolidated, the mission as an entity.

This examination of the relationship between missionary masculinity and missionary femininity in the NMS's Zulu mission is an example of changed gender relations within a patriarchal system. A certain group of missionary women – namely, unmarried professionals – experienced a greater extent of gender equality in the period examined. It would therefore be an oversimplification to follow Connell and state that hegemonic missionary masculinity as a general rule suppresses missionary femininity. Holter's assertion of gender as a system of meaning makes sense in the case of the NMS's Zulu mission. As long as a missionary was defined as an ordained pastor and real mission work was defined as evangelising, preaching and congregational work – all offices and appointments that according to Lutheran orthodox theology excluded women – missionary men continued to be the missionary women's superiors. An expanded definition of the terms, stemming in part from missionary women's mission theory and practice, thus resulted in changed gender relations in terms of equality. However, this did not mean that a general notion of equality emerged between men and women in the mission. In the period scrutinised, the Lutheran theology of men as head of the households did not lose its grip, nor did the doctrine of men as spiritual leaders and supervisors of the congregations.

Part II

Missionary Masculinity between Professionalism and Privacy

7
Missionary Men

Introduction

The profession of a missionary was to preach the Christian Gospel in areas of the world regarded as non-Christian in order to convert and baptise non-believers in the Christian faith. A missionary should moreover consolidate the expansion of Western Christianity by establishing indigenous congregations and churches and recruiting and educating indigenous church personnel. The professional work of a missionary was understood as God-related work – as service in 'the Kingdom of God'. A combination of human abilities/ambitions and subordination to a divine cause, of 'hardness' in human matters and 'softness' in spiritual matters, characterised missionary ideals. But to what extent should a missionary man rely on his own strengths and abilities in his missionary work, and how much help should he expect to receive from the God he trusts in? How much is his profession to be regarded as the work of God and how much 'the work of man'?

Religious faith was essential to the NMS missionaries. Their religious world-view significantly affected their male subjectivities and male social practices. The Swedish historian Inger Hammar claims that Western historians tend to pursue 'religion-blind' research when conducting gender studies. She finds that, although religious discourses were central to the female emancipation movement in nineteenth-century Sweden, this dimension is generally overlooked.[1] Roald Berg, a Norwegian historian, asserts that social history scholars tend to underestimate religious belief as a causal factor in societal change. Although the effects of the modern Christian mission as a close associate of Western imperialism have been thoroughly examined and discussed by historians, Berg asserts that the motivations for mission – particularly religious motivations – have not attracted the same interest. He claims that missionaries' faith in God should be integrated in the analysis of missions, and that the actors' religious emotions and experiences should be taken seriously.[2]

This chapter examines how missionary masculinity was constructed within the context of the individual man, taking the religious dimension into consideration. The focus here is on the missionary man – namely, the man and his relation to the profession. How did his personality and his personal life influence his professional life, and how were his personality and personal life affected by his professional life? The missionary lives and missionary subjectivities of three generations of missionaries, Karl Larsen Titlestad (1832–1924), Lars Martin Titlestad (1867–1941) and Karl Michael Titlestad (1898–1930), are analysed in order to answer the questions. First, their biographies will be presented, demonstrating that the missionaries' social conditions changed considerably during the historical time span under scrutiny. The conditions also changed remarkably in terms of education and actual work. Second, the central concept of the divine missionary calling will be discussed. The Titlestad men's perceptions of male missionary service, and how their personal experiences in the missionary service may have influenced their masculine subjectivity, will then be explored. Finally, the discussion will examine how missionaries constructed a Christian masculinity in the era of modernity.

The Titlestad men across three generations

Karl L. Titlestad was born on 7 November 1832 on a farm called Titlestad at Fana, south of Bergen.[3] His parents, Lars Carlsen and Marthe Nielsdatter, had ten children, but only four of them reached adulthood. Like most children who grew up in rural areas in mid-nineteenth- century Norway, Karl learned basic theoretical and practical skills at home. After turning seven, he attended the village school, where education was offered for six to eight weeks every year by an itinerant teacher.[4] After church confirmation, he continued to work at his parents' farm for some years, until eventually it was handed over to his elder sister and her husband. At the age of 19, he moved to Bergen and entered into apprenticeship with a shoemaker. City life did not please him, however, and he returned to the countryside and the work of a farmhand. For a period he also served as a postal worker. Although lacking secondary education, in 1857 he was appointed as an itinerant teacher in his home district.[5] In 1859 Karl applied for admission to the NMS's mission school. His social and educational background was typical of the group of young men who sought a career as missionaries in nineteenth-century Norway (Chapter 2). Karl was one of 12 young men accepted from 27 applicants, becoming a student in the school's 'First Class' from 1859 to 1864.[6] He was also among the first group of missionary pastors who, on 11 November 1864, were ordained according to the rituals of the Evangelical-Lutheran Church of Norway in the venerable Cathedral of Stavanger. Moreover, Karl belonged to the first band of missionaries who were passengers on the mission ship *Elieser* when it departed from Stavanger in February 1865. In front of a jam-packed church, the candidates were prayed for and blessed in the Sunday morning service. Several farewell parties were arranged, and hundreds of mission friends assembled to get a last glimpse of the newly graduated missionaries.[7]

Karl lived and laboured at the mission station of Nhlazatsche in North-Western Zululand from 1865 to 1869. In 1869 he was ordered by Bishop Schreuder to establish a mission station in the district of the Zulu chief Sihayo, but the following year he had to give up the settlement and look for a better place on the east side of the Umzinyathi River.[8] Karl continued his mission work at Umzinyathi for the next eight years. When the political situation in Zululand grew tense in the late 1870s, however, the NMS missionary conference decided in March 1878 that all missionaries should leave Zululand and find shelter in Natal.[9] The Titlestad family left Umzinyathi in April, and for the next nine months they lived partly in their ox wagon and partly as guests at Swedish, German and Norwegian mission stations in Natal. At the end of the Anglo-Zulu war in July 1879, Karl started preparations for his return, and in September he went on an inspection trip to Umzinyathi.[10] Owing to the new political conditions in post-war Zululand, Karl 'lost' his station at Umzinyathi. His previous chief Sihayo was ordered by the British to leave the district, and Hlubi, the chief of a Sotho group, was awarded the chiefdom.[11] As a majority of Hlubi's people were already Anglicans, he therefore hesitated to let missionaries from other denominations work in his chiefdom; consequently, Karl was refused entry to Umzinyathi. The mission land was eventually handed over to the Anglican mission, which established the St Augustine mission station on the ruins of the Norwegian settlement.[12] In 1880 – and for the third time in his missionary career – Karl set out to search for a proper place to establish a mission station. In the district of Nkandla he established the Ekombe mission station, where he remained until returning to Norway in 1891. At the age of 60, Karl acted as the NMS's itinerant emissary in Norway. From 1891 to 1909, he travelled throughout the country; after his retirement he continued his voluntary work for the mission.[13] Karl Larsen Titlestad died on 10 December 1924 in Drammen.

Lars Martin Titlestad was the oldest son of Karl and Karen Titlestad. Born on 25 June 1867 at the Nhlazatsche mission station, he was home-schooled by his parents before moving to the NMS's boarding school for missionary children at Umphumulo when he was 13 years old. After graduating from elementary school in 1885, he returned to his parents' home at Ekombe, where he assisted in the mission work. He started to prepare for theological studies in Norway, and his parents engaged a private tutor to teach him Latin, German, English and geometry.[14] In 1887 he was accepted as a student of 'the Sixth Class' at the mission school in Stavanger.[15] He completed the last exams in June 1892 and was ordained together with his peers on 13 July in St Peter's Church in Stavanger. The event which Secretary Lars Dahle called 'the great ordina-tion day' took place while the NMS was celebrating its fiftieth anniver-sary.[16] Forty Church of Norway pastors participated in the ordination ceremony of the 13 young missionary pastors. Lars Martin was commis-sioned as a station manager of the Ungoye mission station in 1893. In 1895 he was transferred to the Ekombe mission station, the previous station of his father. Lars Martin stayed at the Ekombe mission station for 23 years. The first period lasted from 1895 to 1904, and after two years of vacation in Norway, he spent another period at Ekombe from 1906 to 1920. In 1920 he was re-stationed at Eshowe, where he worked as station manager until 1925. During the same period, he also func-tioned as the NMS's superintendent in South Africa. After two years of vacation in Norway (1925–27), he was relocated to Durban. At the age of 70, Titlestad applied for retirement. He moved to Eshowe in 1938, where he died on 23 April 1941.

Karl Michael Titlestad, son of Margaretha and Lars Martin Titlestad, was born at the Ekombe mission station on 12 December 1898. As a boy he attended British primary schools in Durban while he boarded at the NMS's home for missionary children. At the age of 13 he moved to Norway for educational reasons. He completed his middle school exams at Kongsgaard School in Stavanger and high school exams at Kristelig Gymnasium in Kristiania.[17] In 1917 he started his theological studies at the Norwegian School of Theology in Kristiania. As a missionary's son and a prospective missionary pastor, Karl Michael was granted an annual stipend from the NMS. The mission supported secondary and higher education for the children of their missionaries, and children with academic ambitions and abilities were also granted loans. Karl Michael, unlike his father and grandfather, preferred the School of

Theology in Kristiania to the NMS's mission school in Stavanger, partly for practical reasons, as the NMS did not plan to accept new students until 1918. Both Lars Dahle and his parents back in Zululand, however, recommended the school in the capital,[18] where Karl Michael could obtain the university degree *candidatus theologiae*, which would qualify him for clerical service in the Church of Norway. This latter aspect was obviously important for NMS missionaries when they advised their sons on educational issues.[19]

Karl Michael graduated as a theologian candidate in the spring semester of 1923. In the autumn semester he completed his practical theologian exams and was ordained on 16 December. He departed for South Africa soon after his ordination and arrived in Durban in January 1924. The following year, Karl Michael studied for the Higher Diploma of Education at the University of Pietermaritzburg. In January 1925, at only 26 years old, became Principal of the Lutheran Teachers' Training College at Umphumulo. Karl Michael died unexpectedly on 20 May 1930, when he was 31 years old. There had been an outbreak of typhoid fever among the students at Umphumulo, and he was infected. He was taken to hospital in Durban, but died three weeks later.

The missionary calling

In 1859 Karl Larsen Titlestad applied for admission to the NMS's mission school in Stavanger. When the mission advertised for young, male, missionary candidates, it was stated that special emphasis would be placed on 'the truth and depth' of the candidate's faith, 'the sincerity of his devotion to the Lutheran confession' and finally 'his particular calling to missionary service'.[20] The mission leadership believed that religious motivation was decisive for admission to the school and later missionary service. We have already seen that young Norwegian men could have many reasons for seeking a missionary career. A majority of the applicants were already 'on the move' both geographically and socially and thus part of the comprehensive demographic and socio-economic changes of the time (see Chapter 2).[21] Yet the actors themselves strongly emphasised 'the calling' or 'the vocation' (in Norwegian *Kallet*) as the central factor of motivation. The idea of a particular calling to missionary service is, according to Ingeborg Hovland, 'one of the most important driving forces' in the history of the Norwegian mission.[22] Hovland, who conducted an anthropological inquiry into the nature of faith in the NMS, nevertheless found it surprising that the important concept of 'calling' is usually not mentioned, let alone discussed, in literature in the field of the anthropology of mission. She moreover finds a general tendency among social science researchers to avoid studies on the nature of religious faith, particularly the faith of Western Christians.[23] Theologians and scientists of religion, however, have widely discussed the importance of the subjective missionary calling in the modern missionary movement.[24]

The three Titlestad men all had an experience of a personal call to mission, but both their description of it and their response to it differed. In his letter of application to the mission school, Karl Larsen Titlestad described in detail the spiritual journey that ultimately led to an acceptance of his experience of God's calling. His early adult years had been filled with restlessness and religious ponderings. Although his parents had raised him in the Christian faith and had provided a

Figure 7.1 Karl Larsen Titlestad (1832–1924), first row in the middle, with peers and teachers at the NMS's mission school in Stavanger. He was a student at the school from 1859 till 1864

Source: Mission Archives, School of Mission and Theology, Stavanger.

strict moral upbringing, as a teenager he felt drawn towards 'the vanity of the world', and he started to play the violin at local dance events. This caused him a lot of guilt and sorrow, however, and after some years he abandoned his musical interest. At the age of 20, Karl saw a deadly disease attack several of his fellow workers, resulting in the religious conversion of some of them. He then realised 'the truth' of the biblical words of 'the small gate and narrow road' that was supposed to 'lead to life' (Matthew 7: 13–14). Unfortunately, he found himself to be on 'the broad road' that led to destruction, and in the years to come his despair at standing outside God's grace and salvation resulted in a long-term condition of depression, anxiety and finally physical breakdown. He was no longer able to work and had to return to his parents' home, where he was confined to bed for days at a time.[25] One midwinter morning in 1856, while he was driving dairy products to the town market for sale, suddenly – according to his own account – he saw lightning in the sky. He had a lively vision of the suffering of Christ on the cross, 'with the blood streaming from his side', and finally 'believed in his heart' that Christ had died for his sins. He stopped the horse, jumped off the wagon, fell down on his knees, cried with 'tears of joy and thankfulness', and praised God. He then made the following promise: 'Dear Lord, send me wherever you will, even to the heathen, if I can only be your witness.'[26]

Karl's description of his own religious development follows a stereotypical pattern of religious conversion. According to the historian Bjørg Seland, radical conversion experiences were more or less standard in pietistic, revivalist milieus in nineteenth-century Norway.[27] Gynnild and Simensen also find that most of the young men who contacted the NMS referred to similar experiences: a pious Christian upbringing, an initial crisis that occurred immediately after confirmation when they moved on from the naïve belief of their childhood, a second crisis that occurred when they were approximately 18 to 20 years old and they experienced a desperate awareness of guilt and sin, and finally a conversion experience that resulted in a renewed belief in Jesus Christ.[28] The calling to become a missionary was frequently released through the conversion experience. Karl's narrative of conversion from a life as a sinful man, a nobody, to a life as God's servant, a somebody, expressed how low his confidence was in his own suitability for missionary service and how strong his trust was in God's arming and preparation of his servant. This humble, modest, and guarded attitude was, as discussed in Chapter 3, not highly esteemed in contemporary masculinity discourses that asked for strong, bold, and confident men.

The religious experience of conversion and calling was obviously a story often told by Karl L. Titlestad, both in sermons and personal testimonies, but also in family settings.[29] Like his father, Lars Martin Titlestad could also refer to a personal missionary calling. According to family narratives, the experience occurred during a hunting party at Ekombe in which he and his brothers participated with Zulu friends. An accident occurred, and a man was fatally stabbed by a spear. 'Where am I going?', the dying man screamed in terror. The Titlestad brothers were greatly affected by the sight. They realised that unless someone told the Zulus about the reality of eternal life through Jesus Christ, their friends would all experience eternal perdition. Lars Martin and his brother Lauritz felt that God had called them to go to Norway to prepare for missionary service in Zululand.[30] Lars Martin's approach to the missionary calling was different from his father's approach. It was not related to his own experience of conversion, but rather to an acknowledgement of others' unconverted condition. He apparently felt that there was a job to do. God had called him to serve, and he responded positively, turning out to be a man of action. This kind of response to God's calling was more in accordance with late nineteenth-century masculinity ideals that preferred vigorous, energetic and active men.

Karl Michael Titlestad also experienced a subjective missionary calling:

> Already as a boy I had this certain missionary calling, which later took root and grew without any doubt or insecurity. Driven by this calling I went alone to Norway as a 13-year-old boy, with the purpose of being educated as a missionary.[31]

Karl Michael overheard a conversation in which his mother urged his older brother, who also happened to be the oldest son, to become a missionary and continue the work of his father and grandfather.[32] Her words made a deep impression on Karl Michael, who felt that God had called him, the second oldest son, to take up the work of his forefathers. His mother Margaretha Titlestad described in an article in the *NMT* how astonished she was when her 12-year-old son confided in her 'the secret' of the missionary calling.[33] She had asked him why he so much wanted to go to Norway for missionary service. His answer was as follows: 'Mamma, Jesus has done so much for me. I have asked him to help me to do something for him in return, and now I believe he wants me to become a missionary.' Karl Michael left his family and went to Norway, where he stayed at the NMS's home for missionary children in

Stavanger while completing his middle school examinations. He later recalled these as being the most difficult years of his life. In the challenging time of transition between childhood and manhood, he felt lonely, with no close family members or friends to support him. Yet in religious terms this difficult period was decisive; 'because my mind turned inwards and upwards to God'.[34]

In 1923 Karl Michael Titlestad graduated as a theologian candidate with the best marks in his class. The management of the School of Theology offered him a scholarship and a position as Research Fellow in Old Testament Studies. He found it very difficult to make a decision. On the one hand, he wanted the job. He believed that working as a professor and teacher of future generations of Norwegian pastors was an important and responsible task. On the other hand, he had prepared for missionary service for years. The NMS's General Secretary Einar Amdahl, obviously surprised by the School of Theology's attempt to recruit a promising missionary candidate, nevertheless encouraged Karl Michael seriously to consider the offer. Titlestad's case was discussed at the NMS Home Board meeting, and the Board concluded that Titlestad himself – 'you, and you only'– had to make the final choice between missionary work and scientific theological work. Amdahl hesitated to give any advice other than 'to consider seriously what work God has called you to do'.[35] Eventually Titlestad made his final choice:

> But after much considerations and prayers, it is still clear for me that the mission has my heart, and that God has called me to this service. I have never really wavered in my conviction about this. The mission is for me the most important and most adorable work in the Lord's vineyard.[36]

The case of Karl Michael Titlestad is yet another example of a masculine response to the missionary calling. It is characterised by a stirring sense of duty. Already as a boy he had felt an obligation to continue the work of his grandfather and father. He was obviously a talented and skilful man, and as we have seen he was offered an attractive academic position. Yet his conviction of a divine calling to a particular missionary service was strong, and he wished to be faithful to what he regarded as the object of his life. Whereas his grandfather had regarded himself as a 'nobody' who could be used as a humble servant in mission only with God's help, and his father was more God's labourer willing to act and respond to his Master's command, Karl Michael was the noble professional ready to sacrifice his own career and secular success in order to follow the divine missionary calling.

The missionary service

Construction of missionary masculinity within the individual man was also coloured by his personal experiences of missionary service. The three Titlestad men served in different eras of the NMS's Zulu mission, where the external working conditions changed considerably. In addition the differences between the three men on an individual level, and external social, economic and political conditions, also influenced their perceptions of their missionary service. Karl L. Titlestad's perception of service was coloured by his 'humble servant' approach. His many accounts of work in the field highlight his low confidence in his own abilities and he did not hesitate to report his failures and lack of results. He started his missionary career at the mission station of Nhlazatsche, established in North-Western Zululand in 1862 by Lars and Martha Larsen. Karl was supposed to study the Zulu language under Larsen's tutorship and simultaneously provide itinerant preaching in the surrounding districts. In private letters written in the first years of service at Nhlazatsche, he praises his seniors as wonderful missionary models in both a religious and a practical sense.[37] After some time, however, he expresses growing frustration at not having his 'own' station.[38] He believed that having two ordained missionary pastors at the same tiny mission station was a misuse of resources, as 'one can manage the work alone without difficulty, while the other feels redundant'.[39]

When the opportunity for independent mission work arose, it turned out to be a less glamorous project than expected. In 1869 Karl L. Titlestad was ordered by Bishop Schreuder to search for appropriate land for a new mission.[40] He felt insecure and 'too inexperienced and incompetent to alone and make a decision like this on my own'.[41] Eventually he decided to build a temporary house of sticks and straw while waiting for the bishop's inspection of the area. He called the settlement 'Ekutembeni', a Zulu word meaning 'in hope', as he was waiting and hoping for progress in his work in terms of Zulu converts. In March 1870 he reported the establishment of daily devotions and day school for his teenage male servants, or 'boys', as he called them. Every week Sunday service was held, but no one apart from his family and servants attended.[42] During the week he visited the surrounding districts to evangelise and invite people to the mission station but had to report disappointedly that 'although I have travelled a lot, still no one comes to this place to listen to the Word of God'.[43] In addition, he was losing control of his servants, who were 'running around in the farms' and participating in 'beer-drinking parties'. Karl was frustrated, impatient and eager to construct more solid houses for his family, as their health was deteriorating, but he was still waiting for the bishop's inspection.[44]

Figure 7.2   Karl Larsen Titlestad (1832–1924) worked as a missionary in Zululand for 26 years. At the age of 60 he started a second career as itinerant emissary serving the NMS in Norway

Source: Mission Archives, School of Mission and Theology, Stavanger.

Photographer: Louise Engene.

Schreuder, in fact, never visited the Ekutembeni mission station. Instead he ordered Karl L. Titlestad to give up the settlement and look for a better place east of the Umzinyathi River. Karl eventually found a good and fertile place with rich grassland for his cattle and plenty of fresh drinking water. As the area was also densely populated, he had great expectations of the new mission.[45] Karl served at Umzinyathi for the next eight years, but could seldom report progress in evangelistic work. 'Will I ever be able to report a heathen's conversion at this station?,' he asked in 1874.[46] The following year, 21-year-old Umpukeni, his servant for the last five years, finally received baptism and was given the Christian name Joseph. Unfortunately, the following year Karl had to report Joseph's 'total relapse into heathendom'.[47] From the mid-1870s, Karl L. Titlestad often asked whether the mission work at Umzinyathi should be terminated. He felt sick and exhausted but also frustrated about spending his strength and power in vain. He admitted to having been 'a miserable servant of the Lord' and presumed that other missionaries would have done a better job.[48] Owing to the political conditions in Zululand, he was forced to leave the station in 1878 and, as we saw, it was later 'lost' to Anglican missionaries. Despite the difficulties he experienced in the mission work, he was persistent in his wish to return. During a confrontation with the new chief of the district, Hlubi, Titlestad was asked if he had built the houses at the mission station himself. According to his own account, he gave the following answer: 'Yes, these hands have built them, and these feet stamped the dirt floor, together with some natives. We have laboured, suffered and cried a lot at this place, and now we want to continue our work.'[49]

Titlestad's loss of Umzinyathi was irrevocable, and at the missionary conference in March 1880 he announced that he was ready to take up new mission work in Zululand.[50] For a third time he set out to search for an appropriate place at which to establish a mission station. When a site was elected at Ekombe, he sat down alone and sang the well-known Norwegian psalm 'In the name of Jesus, all our work shall be done' ('I Jesu Navn Skal al vor Gjerning ske'). With this act he inaugurated the place and his future work.[51] He felt 'weak and incapable' at the thought of the new commission, but put his trust in 'the power of God's help and support'.[52] Four years later, Karl L. Titlestad, in an article in the newly established women's mission magazine, presented a history of the Norwegian mission in Zululand, including his own personal history. In the text, entitled 'A Clearing Work in Zululand', he described himself as a pioneer in an area where the Word of God was unknown. By this time he was a mature man who could see the project of his life in retrospect and had a more harmonious missionary identity than before. There had been years of 'darkness' in the NMS Zulu mission, he explained, escalating with the Anglo-Zulu war of 1879 when the missionaries left their stations and the Christian congregations were scattered. The missionaries had waited patiently for 'the storm to calm down'. He described how in 1880 he started work at Ekombe by clearing a road to the station, chopped down trees and constructed the first simple station buildings. That first year no one came to listen to the Word of God, in the second year a young boy started preparation for baptism, in the third year the number of catechumens expanded and in 1884 church attendance had increased to 50 people.[53]

When Karl Larsen Titlestad – after 20 years of 'struggle and trials' – finally experienced some progress in the work, his missionary service was interrupted. As we saw in Chapter 5, he was called home because of his admission of doubts about central Lutheran dogma. The Home Board did not permit him to return to Zululand, but instead offered him a position as itinerant emissary in Norway. Titlestad accepted the offer on condition that his son, Lars Martin, should be appointed new station manager at Ekombe.[54] Both the Home Board and the missionary conference agreed,[55] and Lars Martin admitted to being 'happy and grateful to return to the old station of my father and the happy memories of my childhood'.[56] Karl obviously wished to see his son follow in his footsteps and continue his labour in Zululand. Through service for the NMS in Norway, he could indirectly support his son's work at Ekombe. Although father and son were separated, they stood together in service, and Karl found encouragement in this thought. According to Titlestad's biographer Anders Olsen, what he cherished most of all as an old man were letters from Zululand: 'How happy he was when he received news from the mission work in Zululand, where he had invested the power and strength of his youth and manhood. The face of the old patriarch was shining.'[57] Although he never himself experienced success in his mission service in terms of converts, he had the pleasure of being succeeded by his son. As an old man he had accepted his own part in the mission drama of Zululand – that of the clearer, who prepared the way for other (in his opinion certainly more talented) missionaries.

In sharp contradiction to his father's low self-esteem and distrust of his own abilities, the confident missionary candidate Lars Martin Titlestad could not wait to get started. In December 1892 he applied to the NMS's Home Board for permission to depart for Zululand as quickly as possible: 'I really want to come out and start the work I feel ready to take over.'[58] His first account of the work at the Ungoye mission station had an optimistic touch. After six months of missionary service in Zululand, he concluded that 'the heathen in this area are like soft, well-prepared clay and it should be relatively easy to mould or print the image of Christ in them'.[59] Although he found quite soon that converting the Zulus to Christianity was a harder task than he had first expected, and although he promised to be more prudent when officially expressing personal hopes and visions,[60] his accounts, articles and letters continued to be characterised by optimism, high spirits and courage.

The church in the mission district of Ekombe experienced remarkable growth during Lars Martin's era.[61] When Lars Martin and his family celebrated Christmas before their home leave in 1904, 500 Zulus attended the service and 41 were baptised.[62] Another landmark was the inauguration of a new church in 1914 after several years of planning and fundraising.[63] A tenth of the money had been raised by the church members, and after another four years the congregation was free of debt.[64] When Lars Martin left Ekombe in 1920, he could report 1 141 church members and 156 baptisms in 1919. The station had 16 satellite stations and eight preaching places. Altogether 30 Zulu pastors, evangelists, and teachers were working under the supervision of the station manager. The church

Figure 7.3   Lars Martin Titlestad (1867–1941) was born in Zululand and served as a missionary in South Africa for 45 years. Here together with his wife Margaretha Thompsen Titlestad (1865–1953) and their daughter Svanhild Titlestad Farrell

Source: Mission Archives, School of Mission and Theology, Stavanger.

Photographer: Selmer Norland & Co.

members financed one-third of the congregation's budget. There were 488 children in 20 mission schools, seven of which received governmental grants. 'We never had a better year at Ekombe,' Lars Martin stated in his annual report, regarding this as the peak of his missionary career.[65]

Lars Martin emphasised mission progress and expansion not only in his own district but also in the NMS's Zulu mission in general. He first raised the issue of possible missionary activity in the three northern magistrates of Zululand in 1916, receiving the missionary conference's agreement to further investigations.[66] In 1917 he set out on several expeditions to the north.[67] Titlestad gained much support from his missionary colleagues when suggesting a Lutheran evangelistic outreach in these areas, and a tiny outstation managed by a Zulu evangelist was established. The NMS's Home Board, however, was reluctant to accept the ideas of expansion.[68] A persistent Lars Martin nevertheless continued to present his visions in the mission magazines. In a 1922 article he reported from two recent tours. The first trip was to the north of Zululand, where the mission still struggled to 'get a foothold'. The second trip was to Ekombe, where 'the worst fight against the darkness and heathendom is over, and the light of victory fills our heart with hope and thankfulness'. Lars Martin reminded himself and his readers that the recent success of the Christian church at Ekombe was the result of a lot of 'struggle and hard work'. A middle-aged Lars Martin proclaimed that, if he had been a young man, he would have asked to be sent to the north of Zululand. He felt certain that 25 years of hard work and struggle there would certainly lead to victory.[69] Lars Martin believed that the hard missionary work of a man, and likewise, a masculine persistent struggle towards 'heathendom', would more or less by a law of nature lead to victories in the mission field. God's working men and God's soldiers in the fight for His kingdom needed a progressive approach to missionary service.

On some occasions, but not very often, Lars Martin expressed frustration with being a Zulu missionary, 'the black sheep' in the NMS, as he once stated in a letter to Lars Dahle.[70] As optimism and enthusiasm characterised his personality, however, he apparently regarded it as his lot to defend, promote and market the Zulu mission in the NMS milieus in Norway. He was a productive writer and published articles, essays and poems in the mission magazines every year. His articles often had titles like 'Good news from Zulu'[71] or 'Patches of Light from Zulu'.[72] During a vacation in Norway from 1925 to 1927, he spent some time on mission studies in general and on the history of the NMS's Zulu mission in particular. He concluded that there were reasons to be optimistic as the Zulu mission was growing in terms of church members, congregations, indigenous clergy and the financial 'self-reliance' project. 'Cheer up, our Zulu mission', was how he ended his presentation in the *NMT*.[73] Lars Martin often referred to Jesus' parable of the talents (Matthew 25: 14–28) when comparing the Zulu missionary to the servant, who was entrusted by his Lord with 'the one talent'. Whereas missionaries to 'the intelligent and industrious people' of Madagascar had been given two talents, and missionaries to 'the culture nation' of China five, the missionaries to the 'slow and stubborn' Zulus had received merely one, he claimed, and he interpreted the 'talent' to be a missionary's 'material' in the sense of its being an ethnic group.[74] The biblical term 'talent' could have another interpretation as well, meaning the servant's talents in terms of personal abilities and qualities. Lars Martin aimed to be a man who fully utilised his own personal talents as well as those entrusted to him in the 'Zulu material'. In his opinion, God needed missionary men rich in initiative and action, not men characterised by passivism and pessimism.

Karl Michael Titlestad definitely shared his father's activist approach to missionary service but whereas his father's service in the Kingdom of God was the service of the blue-collar worker, Karl Michael was more of a white-collar worker who advocated professionalism and perfectionism in the mission enterprise. The decision of a 13-year-old boy to leave his family in Zululand and prepare for missionary service in Norway revealed a systematic, purpose-driven approach to service. In order to prepare for his missionary service, he combined academic studies with practical voluntary Christian youth work. He was a member of the Kristiania YMCA and had leadership responsibilities in youth and children's groups. At some point he also worked as a paid assistant secretary in the regional YMCA.[75] During summer vacations he served as secretary at the YMCA's 'Soldiers' home' at Trandum. In 1918, the Norwegian YMCA was responsible for the management of 24 soldiers' homes at military camps.[76] The soldiers' homes usually offered library services and a teetotal cafeteria, and the soldiers' secretary was responsible for devotions and Bible study classes as well as cultural and social activities.[77]

Karl Michael was also engaged in volunteer movements that aimed to strengthen students' theoretical and theological approach to mission. A close connection existed between the YMCA movement in the United States and the establishment of the Student Volunteer Movement for Foreign Missions (SVM). The memorable Mount Hermon Summer Conference, which was originally a Bible study meeting for college students sponsored by the YMCA, saw the birth of the highly influential SVM. By the end of the conference, 100 students had signed a missionary pledge, and the watchword 'The Evangelization of the World in this Generation' was launched.[78] The movement became a world movement, and in 1896 a Norwegian branch was established in Kristiania. When the Nordic Student Volunteer Mission Association ('Nordens Akademiska Frivilligas Missionsförbund') celebrated its twenty-fifth anniversary in Uppsala in 1921, Karl Michael was on the organising committee; he also wrote an essay for the anniversary book.[79] As a 19-year-old student, Karl Michael strongly recommended that young Christians should participate in mission study circles. First, the study circle could function like 'a holy community' and strengthen one's spiritual life, he stated. Second, the mission studies helped youths realise God's grace towards humankind as well as their responsibility to remedy 'the sufferings of the heathen'. Finally, mission studies increased one's knowledge about 'the Evangelisation of the World' and 'The Decisive Hour of Christian Mission'.[80] Karl Michael's terminology displayed his spiritual affinity with the international mission study movement related to the SVM, which launched a journal in 1893, providing outlines for mission study circles and encouraging the circles to create mission libraries.[81] The first mission study book in use in Norway was a translated version of the American student and mission leader John R. Mott's 1910 book *The Decisive Hour of Christian Mission*,[82] which was launched at the first mission summer school arranged in Norway in 1911.[83]

The NMS management had great expectations of Karl Michael, and he was praised for his combination of 'spiritual gifts' and 'practical abilities'.[84] When Karl Michael took a vacation from the theological studies in 1919 to visit his family in Zululand after seven years of separation, he convinced the NMS that the journey was part of his 'practical preparation for missionary service', and the NMS supported it financially.[85] Even before he was formally accepted as an NMS missionary in May 1923,[86] he was commissioned as Principal of Umphumulo Teachers' Training College.[87] In the years before his departure, he frequently negotiated with the NMS's superintendent in the field, who happened to be his father, and the General Secretary Einar Amdahl about practical matters regarding his future missionary service.[88] The responsibilities put on the young newcomer's shoulders were considerable, and after some weeks of work he admitted in a letter to Amdahl that it would have been preferable if he had more experience of practical fieldwork.[89] The Teachers' Training College at Umphumulo accepted students from four co-operating Lutheran missions as well as from other denominations. A three-year teachers' course and a two-year preparation course were offered; the institution also ran an elementary school where the students engaged

Figure 7.4 Lutheran Teachers' Training College at Umphumulo, where Karl Michael Titlestad (1898–1930) served as Principal

Source: Mission Archives, School of Mission and Theology, Stavanger.

in their teaching practicum. Swedish, English, Norwegian and Zulu personnel from different backgrounds worked together at the college, which in itself was a challenge. Despite his young age and lack of work experience, Karl Michael did meet everyone's expectations during the five years he managed the college.[90] The number of students increased from 80 to 160, and the government's financial support increased from £900 to £2,000 annually.[91] He made plans for the modernisation and renovation of the school buildings and succeeded in raising the necessary funds for his many projects.[92]

The sudden death of the young and promising missionary Karl Michael Titlestad naturally came as a shock to his family, friends and colleagues, but also to a broader community of church leaders, political leaders, and governmental officers.[93] J. E. Norenius, the Church of Sweden missionary and chairman of the Cooperating Lutheran Mission's executive board, gave a memorial speech at Titlestad's funeral. He probably spoke on behalf of many when he asked: 'Lord, why this? Why just him? Why just now?' According to Norenius, Titlestad was in the 'blooming vigour of manhood', he was still at the beginning of a promising missionary carrier, and he was a man full of plans and visions: 'In him we saw a

future leader of Lutheran mission in South Africa', Norenius stated.[94]
His father, Lars Martin Titlestad, felt the 'double grief' of losing both a
dear son and an able missionary colleague. Only hours after the death
of his son, he sent a report to the NMS's Home Board, revealing his
feelings: why should the Lord take away his young son and a much-
needed servant in the mission field? Simultaneously, he indicated that
although God's thoughts and plans were impossible for a man to understand, they were always the best. The father's description of his son's
deathbed further reflected the same dual state of despair and trust in
God. Although extremely weak, Karl Michael had revealed a strong will
to continue to live and, at the same time, a readiness to meet death:

> I asked Karl today: 'Are you really going to leave us?' 'No', he answered,
> 'I'll be all right.' 'But you'll go home to Jesus', we said. 'Yes', he said,
> 'it's all right.' He could not say any more. 'Wipe me, wipe me', he
> whispered. He did not want to leave us, but still he should go home
> to heaven.[95]

The missionary character: missionary or man?

In Chapter 3 we referred to research demonstrating that, towards the
end of the nineteenth century, notions of Christian values and qualities
no longer corresponded with what was regarded as prevailing masculinity. Christian values could actually be understood as contradictions
of hegemonic masculinity. In contrast to masculine values of activity
and action, Christian virtues were regarded as passive. In contrast to
values of rationality and sense, Christian virtues such as tenderness and
compassion were understood as sentimental and emotional and thus
female. Anna Prestjan has introduced a model of two types of strategies
for Christian manliness. In the first type, qualities and values perceived
to be masculine are added to the Christian character: 'a Christian, *but to
that*, a man'. In the other type of strategy, a prevailing ideal of masculinity and Christian virtues are united at the same time as the latter are
masculinised and described as true manly virtues. Christian qualities,
ideals and values are recoded into correspondence with secular masculinity: 'a Christian, and *therefore* a man'.[96]

   If we apply Prestjan's model to the case of the three Titlestad men,
we find that Karl L. Titlestad, in both his self-presentations and others'
representations of him, was described first and foremost as a protagonist
for Christian values and virtues like love, gentleness, modesty, piety,
patience and obedience. In the obituary written by former colleagues, he

was praised for his 'gentleness' (*saktmodighet*), 'patience' (*taamodighet*) and 'modesty' (*beskjedenhet*).[97] According to the authors, 'he condemned no one, but believed in everyone's good intentions, and he always met those who got lost with mild and kind words'.[98] Unpublished minutes from missionary conference discussions show a silent and discreet Titlestad, and his many unpublished letters indicate a prudent man who avoided direct confrontations and hard discussions, and was sensitive to his colleagues' reactions and feelings. To present some examples, after Schreuder's breach with the NMS in 1873, Titlestad wrote him a personal letter of thanks, in which he emphasised that he still regarded Schreuder as a 'dear brother'. The letter was obviously appreciated by the receiver, and Titlestad's personal relationship to Schreuder continued to be good.[99] When Christian Oftebro was barred from further missionary service by the Home Board representative Ole Gjerløw during the 1888 missionary conference, Titlestad was the only one among the missionaries who publicly gave Oftebro words of thanks and proclaimed their brotherly love.[100]

Karl L. Titlestad was a humble and modest missionary. His social background was humble, and he may have lacked self-confidence – a fact often commented upon by his colleagues.[101] One also wonders if his experience of radical conversion in his youth marked him for life: he found relief in the religious conviction that God had saved him when he was depressed and suicidal, and by 'God's grace alone' he had been elected to become a servant in the mission field. Although he belonged to the first group of low-class, non-academic missionary candidates who received priestly ordination in the Church of Norway, thereby experiencing a remarkable social upgrading, he voluntarily went through a social down-grading by the end of his career. We saw in Chapter 4 that Titlestad became influenced by revivalist, denominational movements and developed doubts about central dogma in the Lutheran confession. In a letter to his superiors he suggested refraining from priestly offices and positions in order to serve simply as an evangelist.[102] When he was called home, he met the order with piety and obedience: 'In your wish for me to come home, I can see the Lord's will for me, and I will follow this calling as fast as possible, if only God grants me life and health.'[103] In the years he spent as an itinerant emissary in Norway he always travelled third-class and was known to be 'the cheapest emissary' the mission had ever had in its service. On ferries and boats one would find him sitting 'on a sack or a case' outside among the cargo; at night he slept on a bench or the floor.[104]

Towards the end of Titlestad's missionary service at Ekombe, however, a slight change in his self-presentations emerged. In his texts, which were usually manifestations of his own weakness and insufficiency, he did on a few occasions present himself as a physically strong and hard-working pioneer. Interestingly, it is this latter perspective of Titlestad's missionary character that is accentuated in his sons' and successors' representations of him. Peter Andreas Strømme, one of his successors at the Ekombe mission station, claimed that he stood in 'the holy tradition of Titlestad'.[105] It was Titlestad who in the pioneer days had 'cleared the way' and constructed the station: 'Oh, how he had to work!' Titlestad worked 'with the shovel, the trowel and the hammer in the one hand and the Holy Book in the other'. In Strømme's opinion, Titlestad was an ideal missionary man: 'God, give us more of the kind of steel with which that man was built.' Although Karl Larsen Titlestad, as well as other pioneers, usually regretted and excused the enormous amount of time spent on construction work, his successors emphasised the importance of this work and praised the muscular, physical and practical side of Titlestad's missionary character. To refer to Prestjan's model, qualities primarily regarded as masculine were added to his Christian character. A missionary man is of course a Christian, but he is also a real man.

As discussed in Chapter 3, the latter half of the nineteenth century witnessed cultural and political movements, first and foremost in Great Britain and the USA, which aimed to counteract the separation of Christian spiritual life from temporal life. One example was Muscular Christianity, proclaiming a way to combine robust, physical strength with Christian ethics. Another example was the Social Christianity movement, which advocated the duty of the church to engage in social challenges. Recent scholarship has interpreted these movements as reactions to the image of religion as unmanly and feminised, and as efforts to find spiritual dimensions in what were regarded as typical and traditional male activities. Lars Martin Titlestad, unlike his father, never tried to apologise for the many hours and the considerable strength and energy expended on practical construction and reparation work – quite the contrary. He was apparently proud of his craftsman's work, which not only saved the mission from a lot of expense, but also illustrated his ability to engage in hard physical work.[106] For him, the concepts of indirect and direct mission work were intimately connected. To a lesser extent than the previous generation of missionaries he distinguished between the spiritual and temporal world, between the needs of the body and the needs of the soul.

Most male and female missionaries in Zululand spent considerable time learning dentistry, elementary medical care and small-scale surgery. As this part of the missionary work was considered to be indirect mission work and subordinate to the preaching of the Word, however, it was seldom reported. Yet Lars Martin Titlestad accentuated this part of his service with great enthusiasm.[107] Moreover, in the discussions of a medical mission in Zululand in the 1920s (see Chapter 7), Lars Martin and Strømme were the main male supporters of the mission hospital projects.[108] Lars Martin also engaged with social issues and wished to shed light on the material and physical sufferings of the Zulu people, particularly underprivileged groups like the elderly, orphans and disabled. He appealed to potential Norwegian donors through the mission magazines and established a 'Fund for the physically distressed in Zululand'.[109]

In theory and practice, Lars Martin propagated ideas central to the Muscular Christianity movement, thereby striving to combine a Christian character with contemporary masculinity ideals. His peers, however, remembered him first and foremost as a warm, loving and friendly man, just like his father. After his death, two obituaries were printed in the *NMT*,[110] and a eulogy given at the missionary conference in 1942.[111] What characterised him as a person, according to his colleagues, were his 'friendly and bright personality' and his 'warm heart'. He was 'peaceful', 'companionable', 'mild' and 'generous'. He was a 'zealous' missionary, always eager and enthusiastic about his mission work. His fluency in the Zulu language was also emphasised, as were his good relations with the Zulus: 'he was loved by the blacks', 'he was close to the natives' and 'to the natives he was like a father'. The character of Lars Martin was described in terms of the traditional Christian deeds of love, friendliness, generosity, mildness and peacefulness.

Lars Martin Titlestad was regarded as a warm, zealous missionary who was liked and loved by everyone. Yet he never gained enough support and trust among his colleagues to be elected as their leader. There were obviously traits in his personality that collided with what were regarded as mission leader qualities. In 1920, when the superintendent Hans Kristian Leisegang went on furlough, the NMS's Home Board commissioned Lars Martin to be his substitute. At the missionary conference two years later, an ordinary election of superintendent was arranged. To Lars Martin's surprise, he was not elected – neither as superintendent nor vice-superintendent – and he felt that he lacked the trust of his colleagues.[112] While Lars Martin was on furlough in Norway, the 1927 missionary conference elected Peder Aage Rødseth as its new superintendent, an office he kept until 1937.[113] The conference also decided to relocate Lars Martin to Durban, and to place Rødseth at Eshowe.[114] Both decisions came as a great surprise and disappointment to Lars Martin, who felt that he had 'lost' both his position and his home.[115]

The obituary written after the death of Peder Aage Rødseth in 1945 differed significantly from Lars Martin's obituary. Rødseth was described as a 'big and powerful man' and a 'man of a chief's character'. He was moreover represented as intelligent and well informed, a man with heavy responsibilities in the mission, in the Zulu church and in the Cooperating Lutheran Missions. His foremost leadership qualities were 'outstanding clear-sightedness', 'critical sense' and 'his ability to seek the truth'.[116] Comparing such representations with those of Lars Martin, we see distinct differences emerge. Lars Martin was a good missionary, he was a warm and zealous servant of God among the Zulus, and he was a friendly and loving type. Lars Martin was a 'man of heart', and his characteristics belonged to the category of 'soft' Christian virtues. Rødseth, on the other hand, was 'a man of thought' whose qualities corresponded with 'hard' ideals of modern masculinity. 'Hardness' in human matters and 'softness' in spiritual matters characterised ideal missionary masculinity, and both 'soft' Christian virtues and 'hard' masculine values were appreciated in missionary men. Yet when a mission leader needed to be elected, a missionary man of Rødseth's character was regarded as being better equipped to handle the task.

Karl Michael Titlestad was elected a mission leader by the NMS before his actual departure. His sudden death came as a shock to the mission management as he had already been seen as a future Lutheran church leader in South Africa. What kind of missionary man was Karl Michael? According to a friend, he was 'the embodied missionary ideal': 'You will be missed as the faithful and good friend, as the intelligent and talented theologian, as the ardent labourer in the Kingdom of God, and as the powerful and enthusiastic missionary.'[117] He was described as a man who used his extraordinary talents – practical as well as intellectual – in the service of a higher religious purpose. He belonged to a new generation of white-collar professional missionaries who adopted a scientific approach to their commitment in the mission and applied business-like managerial skills to their practical mission work. He lived a disciplined, well-planned and well-organised life in the Lord's service, and his life as well as his work was purpose-based. He had confidence in his own manly abilities and skills and ardently desired a successful outcome to his work. Still, the ideal was to be a follower of Christ and God's servant. In the case of Karl Michael, we find an example of Prestjan's second strategy. In both his self-presentations and others' representations of him, modern ideals of masculinity and Christian deeds were united. As a Christian, Karl Michael was obedient to God, and faithful to God's calling, which were interpreted as signs of manly persistence, steadiness and self-confidence. As a godly man he sacrificed his many talents and skills in God's service, a manly sign of courage, boldness, strength and selflessness. As a follower of Christ he loved 'the heathen', his warm heart was burning for the salvation of every man and woman, suggesting masculine energy, enthusiasm and spirituality.

Conclusion

This chapter has examined how missionary masculinity was constructed in the lives of three individual men. The discussion focused on the three Titlestad men's perceptions of their own missionary calling and missionary service as well as how they regarded themselves as Christian missionary men in the era of modernity. Karl Larsen Titlestad understood himself as a humble servant of the Lord, completely dependent on God's equipping and God's guidance. Although his missionary service was characterised by difficulties and lack of success, he gradually started to look at himself as a pioneer, a man preparing the way for others. His son Lars Martin was confident in his own abilities and optimistic about his own ability. In his missionary service his self-understanding was more about being God's blue-collar working man, always prepared and willing to work hard. Karl Michael represented a new generation of white-collar missionary workers, professional and perfectionist in their approach to the mission enterprise. He was a man regarded as extraordinarily talented, and his missionary service was also a sign of obedience to God's calling, as he obviously sacrificed attractive career opportunities in order to serve him.

The examination of these three generations of Titlestad missionary subjectivities highlights certain changes over time. As a result of higher education and societal upgrading, confidence in their abilities and skills increased significantly during the generations. The presentation of self as the Lord's weak and humble servant, as was the case of Karl Larsen, or as a man competent and ready to work hard, as in Lars Martin's case, or as a man willing to sacrifice his prospects in the Lord's service, as was the case of Karl Michael, could also be the result of changing mission discourses, however. From 1870 to 1930, international Christian movements emerged that aimed to counteract the separation of the Christian spiritual life from temporal life. Recent scholarship has interpreted these movements as reactions to the image of religion as unmanly and feminised, and as efforts to find spiritual dimensions in what were regarded as typical and traditional male activities. Indeed, in the case of the Titlestad missionary subjectivities, over the years we find more harmony between notions of the temporal and the spiritual, between indirect and direct mission work, between the needs of the body and the needs of the soul, and between being a man and being a Christian. Whereas Karl Larsen Titlestad was portrayed first and foremost as representing Christian deeds and the virtues of self-denial and world-denial, Lars Martin Titlestad advocated missionary men's chance to combine traditional Christian values and qualities with modern masculinity ideals. Karl Michael Titlestad was the optimal example of a man in whom modern ideals of masculinity and Christian deeds were united.

8
Family Men

Introduction

In addition to work and all-male associations, the home or the family is an area where masculinity is constructed.[1] Like the concept of masculinity, 'home' and 'family' are social constructions that make sense only in terms of historically and culturally specific shared understandings. Nevertheless, boys and men 'come from' and 'have' families. In Western tradition, boys are generally expected to reject their mothers and leave their families in order to achieve manhood, but to become respectable men they are also expected to return to family life after a time to create and lead families of their own. Yet modern Western notions of masculinity, according to the social scientists Michele Adams and Scott Coltrane, have 'much less to do with everyday life in domestic settings than they do with accomplishments in extra-familial arenas such as business, sports, or politics'.[2] The ideal of separate spheres that emerged during the Victorian age advocated that men and women were part of diverse social worlds: men inhabited the public sphere and women the private sphere. Adams and Coltrane assert that throughout the twentieth century the putatively separate public and private spheres continued to reflect and reproduce gender differences and perpetuate gender equality. They claim that the ideal of separate spheres explains modern Western men's difficulties in 'being in' their families and their resistance to being closely connected with the domestic.

In pre-modern Lutheran orthodox theology, by contrast, which had a hegemonic position in Norwegian religious life from roughly 1600 to 1850, married family life was represented as every Christian man's divine vocation. In addition, male priests' family responsibilities were expressed in positive terms in Lutheran discourses, and a harmony between the priests' professional and private lives was sketched: clergymen had a double vocation as the head of a household and the head of a congregation. Nevertheless, Chapter 6 highlighted that Schreuder – when discussing missionaries' family life – referred to the apostle Paul's notions of the married man's concern for 'the affairs of this world' as contrasted with the unmarried man's dedication to 'the Lord's affairs' alone (1. Corinthians 7: 32–34). Referring to the single Paul, Schreuder advocated more negative attitudes towards a missionary pastor's family life. Such attitudes had long traditions in the Christian religion and, in the Catholic Church, materialised in the practice of clergy's celibacy. According to Schreuder, the vocations of being a housefather and a missionary pastor could not possibly be juxtaposed; the mission work had to be given priority over the family.

Balancing professional obligations as a missionary pastor and private obligations as a family father was in fact an issue of frustration and confusion in the lives of the missionary men. Through a presentation of the family lives of Karl Larsen Titlestad (1832–1924), Lars Martin Titlestad (1867–1941), and Karl Michael Titlestad (1898–1930), this chapter will discuss how their private family lives influenced their professional subjectivity as well as how their private family lives were affected by their professional subjectivity. The chapter will also examine the case of the Titlestad men in the light of the theory of 'separate spheres'. The metaphor of separate spheres, which briefly refers to the idea that the private or domestic sphere of family and household belongs to women and the public sphere belongs to men, has had an enormous influence on how historians have explained gender relations in nineteenth-century industrialised societies. According to Norwegian Lutheran missionary masculinity ideals, however, the domestic sphere also seems to be a man's sphere, which will be discussed in further detail herein.

The family man Karl Larsen Titlestad

When Karl Larsen Titlestad applied for entrance to the NMS's mission school in 1859, he apologised for already being engaged to a girl from his home village, Karen Ellingsdatter Haaland. Since it had been explicitly mentioned in the recruitment advertisements, Karl was well aware of the fact that the NMS preferred missionary candidates to be free from romantic entanglements. In his letter to the Home Board, he explained that Karen was 'a true Christian girl' who had guided 'her three sisters' to religious conversion. In addition, she had already stated a willingness to follow him to 'the Heathen'. Karl's letter reveals anxiety about the whole situation. If he let Karen down, he might hurt her feelings, which was a sin. On the other hand, if his engagement to the girl prevented him from following God's calling, this was also a sin.[3] The NMS's Home Board provided a liberal treatment of his case. He was accepted as a student at the mission school without being forced to break his relationship with Karen. In 1864, when he asked for permission to marry her before departing to the mission field, the application was accepted. Because of Karl's relatively advanced age (he was 32 years old) and the long duration of the engagement, the Home Board made an exception to the rule that the fiancée of a missionary candidate should wait for two years in Norway while the prospective husband established a household in the mission field. The wedding ceremony between Karen and Karl took place at the Titlestad farm on 20 September 1864.[4]

When Karen and Karl Titlestad arrived in Durban in 1865, they followed the advice of their seniors and purchased, with the help of borrowed assets from the NMS, a tent-wagon and oxen. In 1865 the annual salary for a married missionary was £60, and a wagon and oxen amounted to about £120. Like most young missionary couples, they started their career with a considerable debt to the mission. According to their son Elias Titlestad, this debt continued to be a matter of grave concern: 'This was brought home to me by the frequent reference made by my parents in serious tone to "the debt", sometimes adding, "that must be paid first", whenever the question of spending a pound or two was deliberated.'[5] In fact, some of the missionaries encountered great difficulties in paying back their debt to the mission as well as those to private creditors. In some exceptional cases, the result was personal bankruptcy and dismissal from the missionary service.[6]

Karen and Karl Titlestad headed for the Nhlazatsche mission station in the north-western part of Zululand, where they moved into a little house with two rooms and kitchen. Although they brought groceries and other household goods from Durban, in order to be self-sufficient they ploughed and cultivated fields for vegetables and planted fruit trees. In a private letter in 1867, Karl described their blooming garden of potatoes, beans, turnips, carrots, onions, parsley, thyme, lettuce and strawberries. He also wrote of hoping to harvest oranges, lemons, peaches and grapes from their fruit trees.[7] Elias had many memories of his parents' joint engagement in agrarian work:

> We cultivated a small plot and grew whatever we could in the way of vegetables, but owing to the difficulty of getting seed in such an out of the way place, it was sometimes impossible to keep up a regular

supply. I can clearly remember how my parents planted a small field of mealies on one occasion. Father went in front along the row, chopping a hole in the ground with a long-handled roe, every two or three feet apart. Mother followed behind him dropping two or three mealies into each hole and kicking the overturned turf back into its place, to cover the seed.[8]

Karl and Karen Titlestad also kept stocks of cattle and sheep and were therefore well supplied with milk, butter and a variety of cheeses that Karen made. According to Elias, 'mealie meal porridge and good wholesome bread formed the major portion of our diet', and he added that the bread was baked in an iron pot on an open fireplace – 'in real pioneer style'. If they required fresh meat, Karl would go out and shoot some pigeons. Elias's memories of his parents' lives as farmers highlight the white settler's narrative of the heroic pioneers living on the frontier, struggling to survive under primitive conditions in the wilderness:

> Those early missionaries must have been very brave men indeed to take their lives into their hands and to venture out as they did amongst the heathen, but the palm must go to their women folk, those plucky wives who stood faithfully by their side, prepared to face bravely any circumstance that might arise.[9]

On 25 June 1867 Karen and Karl's first son, Lars Martin, was born. According to the father, the event was 'a grave but, thanks be to God, still a happy time'.[10] It is evident that Karl assisted his wife during labour, as he stated that 'our only human help' was Martha Larsen. In rural areas of Scandinavia it was common for fathers to assist during childbirth.[11] Given the lack of a chapel or church, the child was home-baptised on 30 June in a 'simple' but 'solemn' service. His wife was weak, and Karl had to remain at home permanently during this period to nurse her, even though he was supposed to do itinerant preaching. The private letters written during this period nevertheless reflect a young father's pleasure at having 'more of a family life'.[12] A second son, Lauritz, was born in March 1869. That same year, Karl was ordered by Bishop Schreuder to establish a new NMS station in Northern Zululand. The family settled in a temporary straw hut with earthen floors; after a year they had to move again. At that time, the two children were already suffering from chronic cold and croup, and Karen's health was also deteriorating.[13] Markus Dahle, a missionary colleague who visited them in 1870, was surprised to see the 'primitive' living conditions of the family. Their house was

Figure 8.1   Karl Larsen Titlestad (1832–1924) and wife Karen Haaland Titlestad (1834–1907)

Source: Mission Archives, School of Mission and Theology, Stavanger.

Photographer: Thea Nielsen.

'quite simple' and looked like 'a roof that was put on the ground'. He felt pity for them having lived like this for almost a year.[14] The house Karl built for his family at the next mission station at Umzinyathi was a wooden house thatched with straw. In 1872 he started to construct a brick house, and reported the following year that 'we are happy to live in a solid and draught-free house after several years in straw huts'.[15]

Combining the professional work as a pioneer missionary with the private responsibilities of a family father was probably very difficult indeed, especially during events such as pregnancy, childbirth and child-rearing. A third son, Elias, was born in 1871; this time Karl was alone with his wife during labour. In both private letters and official reports Karl often referred to the weak health of his wife.[16] He was frustrated by the need to spend most of the time nursing and caring for his family and admitted stagnation in the mission work. He eventually asked the NMS for permission to invite Karen's sister to come to Zululand and assist them. As previously discussed, Marthe Haaland arrived in 1872 (see Chapter 6), and her company and domestic help apparently largely accounted for Karen's recovered health.[17] A fourth son, Peder Ernst, was born in 1873, and a fifth son, Niels, in 1875. When it was time for a sixth son to be born, Marthe had moved to another mission station to assist the widower Gundvall Gundersen, whom she later married. Unluckily, the child was stillborn. Karl conducted the funeral while Karen was bedridden, and their oldest son at nine carried the coffin.[18] Karen Titlestad said several years later how difficult it was for her to move from their home at Umzinyathi, particularly because of the little grave.[19]

The Titlestad family was in limbo from April 1878 until January 1879, living partly in their ox wagon, where son number seven, Karl, was born in June 1878, and partly as guests at Swedish, German and Norwegian mission stations in Natal. This was a critical period for Karl, who seriously considered withdrawing from the mission. In a letter to the superintendent Ommund Oftebro in May 1878, he made it clear that he did not intend to return to Zululand, as 'my duties as a family man will then collide with my duties in the mission service'.[20] To prepare for a future as farming settler, he obtained a loan from a bank in Natal in January 1879 and bought the farm Bozamo, close to Umphumulo. Bad luck, or 'trials', to use Titlestad's religious vocabulary, followed the family. A fire destroyed their home and most of their private belongings in March 1879, and the family had to live temporarily in a cowshed while the house was reconstructed. Karl regretted that the missionary life had brought his wife so much pain; the fire was merely another accident 'added to the many shocking experiences she has already had'.[21]

The unstable living conditions for the Titlestad family negatively affected the children's education, which was regarded by the NMS as parents' private responsibility. Yet Karl Titlestad had already expressed worries about the lack of proper educational facilities for his two oldest sons in 1875. He had himself taught them basic skills in reading, writing and arithmetic, but he admitted that there was no regularity in the home-schooling. Furthermore, he worried about how an upbringing in a non-Christian, 'uncivilised' society was affecting his sons' moral and spiritual development. Titlestad saw it as a weakness that the mission did nothing to support missionary parents in raising and educating their children.[22] Proper schooling for the missionary children was an issue of great concern and resulted in much discussion at the NMS's missionary conferences in the 1870s, especially when it turned out that several promising missionaries had left the field to further their children's education.[23] The NMS's Home Board eventually accepted the management and financial support of educational institutions for missionary children as part of their responsibility as an employer. A boarding school was established at the Umphumulo mission station in 1877, but the outbreak of the Anglo-Zulu war in 1879 caused the temporary closure of the school, which was re-opened in August 1880.[24]

Titlestad's three oldest sons – at 13, 11 and nine – were among the first school boarders in 1880. For Karl it was a relief no longer to be responsible for his sons' education, and he sent his warmest thanks to the Home Board for the 'blessed home' the children now had at Umphumulo.[25] The NMS boarding school for missionary children had (as described in Chapter 6) the social structure of a family as one of the missionary pastors and his wife were commissioned to be the children's substitute father and mother. In addition to the schooling, the children also participated in outdoor and indoor domestic work; girls learned to clean and mend their clothes whereas boys did farming and repair work. The level and amount of education offered at the school at Umphumulo was high compared with Norwegian conditions in general, modelling the curriculum taught at urban, private middle-class schools in Norway.[26] Nils Braatvedt, the school's principal from 1880, found it challenging, however, to teach children with poor theoretical knowledge and almost no school experience. The paternal responsibility with regard to religious and moral upbringing was even more challenging, according to Braatvedt, particularly since he could find no way to control the children's 'relationships with the natives'.[27] The missionary children had been born in Zululand and had grown up with Zulu playmates. Even when they were sent to the mission's boarding institution at Umphumulo, they naturally continued to relate to the local surroundings. Braatvedt, an ordained missionary pastor with a vocation for 'real' mission work, found his role as substitute father to his colleagues' children unsatisfactory and applied for a transfer several times. The same was true of his successor, Martinius Borgen.[28] As a result, in 1891, the position of housefather disappeared and was replaced by female management.[29]

Although Karl Titlestad was glad to be relieved of the burden of educating his children so he could concentrate wholeheartedly on his profession and the establishment of a new mission station at Ekombe, Karen found the long periods of separation from her children the hardest part of the new arrangement.[30] Because of the distance the boys had only annual home-leave, although their parents occasionally visited them at school. In his memoirs, Elias Titlestad described the journeys back home as long and exciting tours through deep valleys and up steep hills on horseback. The missionary home he returned to was humble and lacked any luxury, but they were always welcomed 'by a loving mother'. According to Elias, he soon discovered that Ekombe was 'a boy's paradise'. The supposed fantasy of Western men that manhood can be tested and proved, refreshed and renewed, in untamed, rugged frontier areas[31] is visible in the adult Elias Titlestad's memoirs. In the 'wild and untamed' nature of Zululand, the Titlestad brothers could practise a range of boyish activities. Their father used to take them hunting in the forests and the veldts, 'as the country was teeming with game', and he taught them to shoot with 'his old muzzle-loading gun'. The boys learned to make their own gunpowder, they learned to interpret weather signs, and they competed in horse-riding and horse races. When they grew older and could handle guns properly they were, according to Elias, 'allowed to attend big hunts organised by the natives'.[32]

The happy days of the family staying together at Ekombe, at least once a year, came to an end in August 1891, when Karl was ordered to return to Norway and together with his wife left South Africa for good. As we have already seen, they never returned. Elias continued for a while to live at the mission station while he held diverse jobs and tried to build a career as a shop manager. When his family left, he could 'not help feeling very sad and wondering whether I should ever see all of them again'.[33] Some years later, in 1895, he married Martha Dahle, the daughter of missionary Markus Dahle, and established himself as a farmer and businessman at Ntingwe, close to the Ekombe mission station. His younger brothers Nils and Peder Ernst also established themselves as farmers, businessmen and storekeepers in Zululand. They married the sisters

Barbara Bertranda Nicolina and Lovise Borgen, missionary daughters of Martha Nikoline and Martinius Borgen. Titlestad's youngest son, Karl Johannes, was educated as a medical doctor while living with his parents in Norway, but he also returned to South Africa, where he established a district practice at Nkandhla. Over the years, Karen and Karl Titlestad became separated from all their children and grandchildren, who had established themselves as settlers in South Africa. In the family history the following sad, but appealing, narrative about Karen is told: 'It has been said that Kari "put her grandchildren to bed every evening". She had their photos on a covered table in the sitting room and at bedtime she would cover them over with the table cloth and say good night.'[34]

Karl Titlestad was still in the service of the NMS as an itinerant emissary when Karen died in 1907. Two years after the death of his wife, at the age of 76 he applied to the Home Board for permission to enter into marriage with Kristiane Sønju. The Home Board refused his application for two reasons. First, they found it inappropriate for a man of his age to re-marry, and they feared it could hurt both his and the mission's reputation. Second, the NMS was not willing to be financially responsible for a possible widow's pension. The NMS advised him instead to apply for his retirement and pension, as he would then be free to re-marry without their permission.[35] As was his custom, Karl Titlestad followed the advice of his superiors. He asked for retirement and married in 1909. According to his biographer, Anders A. Olsen, the couple were happy together, and they continued to serve the mission as volunteers until Karl died in 1924, at 92 years of age. The termination of Karl Larsen Titlestad's life-long employment in the NMS, however, is just another example of how difficult it was for a missionary man to distinguish strictly between the private and the professional in his life. He was not a free man in terms of private family affairs. As he had dedicated himself completely to the mission cause, it always took priority over private family needs.

The family man Lars Martin Titlestad

While still a student at the mission school, Lars Martin met his cousin Margaretha Thompson at a summer family gathering, and they soon became fond of each other. Born in 1865 as the seventh of 11 children to businessman Mikael Thompson and his wife Margaretha Haaland, Margaretha grew up in Bergen, had her secondary education in København and thereafter worked for four years as a secretary in the United States. The courting cousins became engaged, but were separated in December 1892 when Lars Martin departed for Zululand. Margaretha and Lars Martin were married at the Eshowe mission station in 1894 and soon moved to Ungoye, where he was already commissioned as a station manager. After six months, in early 1895, they moved to Ekombe. In the following years, they had five children – three sons and two daughters: Frithjof in 1895, Svanhild in 1897, Karl Michael in 1898, Gundvald Martin in 1900 and Helene Margaretha in 1903. Unlike his father, Lars Martin could call on a professional midwife, employed by the NMS and situated at Eshowe, to assist his wife during labour.[36]

In contrast to the roaming life of his parents, Lars Martin lived a stable family life at the Ekombe mission station for more or less 25 years (with the exception of a vacation in Norway from 1904 to 1906). The gendered roles in the missionary household were clear. The missionary was the head of the household, the manager of the mission station land and the pastor of the congregation. The missionary wife was the housemother of her own family as well as of the household community of apprentices, servants, evangelists and teachers, all of whom lived at the mission station. As commonly expressed in the mission discourse, the missionary couple were also 'the father and mother' of the Zulu congregation. Margaretha and Lars Martin shared religious dedication to their service. Margaretha, when describing the mission work at Ekombe, always spoke of 'our mission', 'our congregation' and 'our Christians'.[37] Yet she often apologised for her tiny contribution to direct mission work, especially when the children were small.[38] When the children reached the age of six, they moved out of the missionary home and were sent to the NMS's boarding institution for missionary children. While their own children were taken care of by mission-approved substitute parents, Margaretha and Lars Martin continued to provide paternal and maternal love and guidance for numerous Zulu 'boys and girls' in apprenticeship as well as for the many new Christians converted as a result of their work – 'their spiritual children'.

Lars Martin and Margaretha were both talented writers, and mission supporters in Norway were often presented with vivid coverage from their domestic life in Zululand. For instance, in 1897 Lars Martin metaphorically 'invited' the readers of the *NMT* into their home, and the readers were guided from room to room and presented with interior decorations and furnishings, ultimately leading to the porch for an outlook on the landscape.[39] In the article he described their family meals, their family devotions and their leisure time at home. The Titlestad husband and wife were both musicians, and on 'lonely evenings' they entertained each other with guitar and organ. According to Karina Hestad Skeie, in her study of the nineteenth century Norwegian missionary home in inland Madagascar, the construction of missionary homes was partly an attempt to create 'an ordered, clean Norwegian world inside the house', a world that also needed to be protected from the 'dirty and dangerous Malagasy world outside'.[40] Sidenvall also points to how the Swedish missionaries in China strove to construct middle-class Western homes in foreign places.[41] The missionary home was like a 'castle', protecting the missionary family from bad 'heathen' influence, but it was also like 'a lighthouse in the darkness', an outstanding example of the ideal Christian family life. In the missionary discourse, a Christian home was usually identical to a Western bourgeois home, which was reflected in the family values and the gender system as well as in the exterior and interior of the house.

The Titlestad couple had a romantic literary style, and neither of them hesitated to express the love and affection they felt for one another. Margaretha called a journey with her husband to a missionary conference a 'honeymoon', 'because we are always on "honeymoon" when we are out together, and we always enjoy life'.[42] To write openly about love and romantic emotions between a husband and wife was uncommon in the missionary context. Margaretha's texts were also unusual in the sense that she openly expressed feelings of loneliness, grief, and depression.[43] For example, she described how she felt when she nearly lost her husband to enteric fever in 1901 and she and her young children were removed from their home because of the danger of infection:

> O, how my heart felt anguished and repressed by the thought of being left alone with the children. If I only could have thrown myself in the arms of one of my beloved at home and cried out, so that my tormented heart could have some room to breathe.[44]

In both official and unofficial sources Lars Martin described his marriage to Margaretha as a very happy one. During periods of serious sickness, she had been his 'human help and salvation', as she continuously loved him, and prayed for his recovery.[45] Like the high-spirited and cheerful person she was, she 'coloured' his 'grey, everyday life'. She was loving and caring, tender and affectionate. She was an ideal housemother who cared for her children and inspired her husband to 'manly courage and endurance in difficult times'. In Lars Martin's speech at Margaretha's sixtieth birthday, the metaphor of the wife as an angel is evident. This concept acquired its feminine and largely domestic associations in the Victorian period, which historian John Tosh defines as 'the climax of domesticity':[46]

She fills the empty rooms with merry talk and laughter, and over home and labour she lowers a banner of peace. The crown of the creation, God's little angel who stretches out her wings and by her voice blesses the home – that is a true woman. And that is how Margaretha has been.[47]

The Titlestad couple also stood out among their colleagues in the sense that they published articles in the mission magazines where they proudly presented their children as successful settlers in South Africa. Their oldest son Frithjof was educated as an agronomist and worked for three years at the Lutheran Teachers' Training College at Umphumulo before purchasing a farm and establishing a business. He married the British Norah Jansen Birkett. Svanhild, the oldest daughter, married the British businessman John Thomas Farrell. Their third son, Gundvald, was educated as a teacher and worked as a government inspector of schools before gaining an educational position at the Teachers' Training

Figure 8.2   Lars Martin Titlestad (1867–1941) and Margaretha Thompsen Titlestad (1865–1953) with children, in-laws and grandchildren

Source: Mission Archives, School of Mission and Theology, Stavanger.

College. He married the Scottish teacher Jessie Doreen Ferguson. Their youngest daughter, Helene Margaretha, married Odmund Christian Oftebro, the grandson of the late missionary Ommund Oftebro. In addition, Lars Martin and Margaretha's second son Karl Michael was, as already known, educated as a missionary pastor and in NMS service from 1925.[48] Lars Martin and Margaretha's 'family-writings' were ridiculed by their colleagues.[49] It was claimed that other missionaries might equally well have published accounts of the successful careers of their children but wisely refrained from doing so.

We have already seen that the issue of proper educational facilities for missionary children was extensively discussed in the missionary community. The Norwegian school for missionary children at Umphumulo was closed in 1897, and a home for the children, who subsequently enrolled in British schools, was established in Durban.[50] Superintendent Ole Stavem explained the rationale of the missionary conference decision: 'The children who grow up here belong to this nation. And British schools will best prepare them for the struggle for life under British conditions.'[51] Hanna Mellemsether, who studied the relationship between Norwegian missionary families and Scandinavian and British settler milieus, finds that the NMS families were successful in their integration into the white middle classes of Natal. Among the NMS missionaries who served in South Africa until World War II, the great majority established themselves in the country after retirement. This was usually because their children and grandchildren had settled in the country. Mellemsether finds that many missionary parents invested considerable amounts in the education of their children. This was regarded as a kind of insurance, and several of them were also economically dependent on their children after retirement from the mission.[52] According to the South African historian Robert Morrell, education was an integral part of the 'social engineering' in colonial settings. The children enrolled in white settler schools soon distanced themselves from the African community in which they grew up, and they gradually developed new networks in the settler communities. Morell claims that the boys' schools, particularly the boarding schools, were 'cradles of masculinity' as they were 'complicit in constructing male dominance and hegemonic masculinity within the colonial order'. At the school, networks were established, hierarchies developed, and 'boys were toughened into men'.[53] It became a common pattern among white settlers who lived in rural areas of Natal to send their children to white boarding schools. Their children needed to be separated from 'heathen' and 'uncivilised' surroundings and integrated in the white ruling classes of the colony. We will return to this issue in Chapter 9.

Lars Martin Titlestad was proud of being a father who could offer his children good education and a promising future in the young nation of South Africa. Compared with missionaries in other countries, he found himself to be in a privileged situation.[54] This was pointed out by others as well, especially by missionaries in Madagascar who had to send their children to Norway for education.[55] Nevertheless, for the children of missionary parents, the arrangement was challenging. The children born and raised at the rural mission stations in Zululand moved to Durban when they reached the age of six and were taken care of by unmarried female missionaries. Twice a year they visited their parents. The transition from the home of their childhood to a boarding institution, and likewise to a British school system in the colony's private and public schools, could in fact be difficult.[56] When Margaretha packed her family's belongings after 26 years at Ekombe, she discovered the letters her children wrote while living at the home in Durban. She shared some extracts with the readers of the NMS women's magazine:

> Dear mum and dad! I miss you, and I cry when I go to sleep every night. We pray that God will protect you.
>
> Dear Mum and Dad! We are all well here at the Home, but the children at school are not kind to us, because we cannot speak English very well, and then we miss home. We know that you pray for us.[57]

The family man Karl Michael Titlestad

As discussed in the previous chapter, as a boy Karl Michael Titlestad told his mother that he wished to follow in the missionary footsteps of his grandfather and father and intended to move to Norway in order to receive the necessary education. When Karl Michael bade his family farewell for seven years, his mother gave him a Bible and a poem written to him personally:

> **Goodbye**
> Three things I ask of you before we part
> One little corner for me in your heart
> One thought of me in every passing day
> One little prayer for me where'er you pray
> And so good bye – dear Karl! Yet Love's chain
> Will hold us fast until we meet again
> For over all the leagues of land and sea
> My thoughts will pass to you, and yours to me[58]

When just 13 years old, he travelled alone to the boarding institution of Solbakken ('Sunny Hill') in Stavanger, the NMS's Norwegian home for missionary children.[59] He stayed at the institution for two years while finishing secondary school. The vast majority of the boarders at Solbakken were children of missionaries in Madagascar.[60] An NMS boarding school for missionary children had been established in Antananarivo in 1881, but the missionary conference decided in 1887 to move the institution to Norway. Missionary parents in Madagascar preferred a boarding arrangement for their children in Norway for several reasons. First, they wished to offer proper education and prepare them for adulthood in Norway. While missionary parents in South Africa eventually concluded that their children had better prospective in the colony and thereby sent them to British schools in Durban, missionary parents in Madagascar saw no similar possibilities in their host country. Second, there were medical reasons for sending the children to Norway. In Madagascar, most missionary families experienced the death of one or several children caused by 'tropical diseases'. In addition, physicians regarded as experts in tropical medicine advised parents to keep their children out of 'tropical' areas for longer periods, as these areas could negatively affect their physical, mental and intellectual development. Finally, it was further recommended to remove children from non-Christian and 'uncivilised' surroundings by the time they reached school age. As a main rule, missionary children were sent to Solbakken at the age of seven, but there are many examples of even younger children who were left at the institution when their parents departed for Madagascar. The periods of separation could last from eight to 12 years, and by the time of family reunion the children were in many cases regarded as adults and had already left Solbakken.[61]

The NMS's decision to establish a boarding institution for missionary children in Norway was definitely influenced by the practice of other Western missions. In 1856 Schreuder suggested that Norwegian missionaries should send their children home as soon as possible.[62] The first missionary child in the history of the NMS, Christian Gunhildus Oftebro, was consequently sent to relatives in Norway at the age of 13.[63] European missionary organisations had already established boarding institutions for missionary children in the home countries. Generally speaking, Moravian missionaries sent their children to a boarding institution in Kleinwelke between the ages of five and six.[64] The German Basel and Barmen missions ran similar institutions for missionary children.[65] The NMS missionaries in Madagascar were in contact with missionaries representing the London Missionary Society, an organisation that had run a home for missionary daughters in England since 1838 and a similar home for missionary sons since 1842.[66]

Historian of the British Empire Elizabeth Buettner has examined what she calls 'Empire Families' – the families of civil servants, military personnel and private entrepreneurs who served and laboured in the British colony of India during the 1850–1950 period.[67] She claims that the common practice in these families of sending their children back to the metropolis collided with the Victorian cult of domesticity. What characterised these families was 'the temporary death of nuclear family life'. The children grew up as 'orphans of Empire', lacking a family. Buettner introduces the term *discourse of family sacrifice* and finds that contemporary essays, family letters and fiction literature were characterised by this discourse. The discourse of family sacrifice further legitimised and justified the continued colonial rule in India. The significant human sacrifices demanded of the imperial servants illustrated the sincerity of

Figure 8.3   Norwegian missionary children at the NMS's boarding institution in Durban

Source: Mission Archives, School of Mission and Theology, Stavanger.

Photographer: The Greyville Studio.

their dedication: 'The price of empire paid by families is offered as proof of selflessness as opposed to self-interest.'[68]

The widespread practice in European missions of sending missionary children to boarding schools, either in the colony or in the metropolis, makes it appropriate to speak of this group of children as 'Orphans of Mission'. The famous missionary David Livingstone introduced the term himself when he was said to have proclaimed that 'nothing but the conviction that the step will lead to the glory of Christ would make me orphanise my children'.[69] Karl Michael Titlestad may be regarded as an 'orphan of mission' when, as a six-year-old boy, he was sent to the NMS's boarding school in Durban, but the situation was slightly different when he himself chose to leave his family for schooling in Norway. Although this was somewhat early, as boys mostly left their parents by the end of adolescence, in a certain sense he merely fulfilled the general expectation that boys would leave their mother and family in order to achieve manhood. According to Adams and Coltrane, in the interim between being banished from and returning to family life, 'boys-becoming-men' are often subjected to a higher level of initiation into manhood involving 'male bonding and solidification of the collective practice of masculinity'.[70] In the case of Karl Michael, as discussed in the previous chapter, in addition to academic studies at an all-male theological faculty, he was engaged in voluntary, male-dominated movements such as the YMCA, the Student Volunteer Movement for Foreign Mission and the soldiers' mission movement.

Karl Michael also fulfilled the goal of establishing his own family. He met his future wife, Signe Brekke, at Trandum soldiers' home, where she was the housekeeper and he the YMCA soldiers' secretary. When they were planning a life together in mission, he was the one responsible for all correspondence with their employer NMS. Even issues concerning Signe's preparations for missionary service were taken care of by her fiancé.[71] In 1921 Karl Michael sent an application to the NMS asking them to finance Signe's travel expenses in relation to a stay he had organised for her in England. A future missionary wife should be prepared for life in the British colony, he wrote, as 'the mission stations in Natal are social centres for British colonists; farmers, storekeepers and so on'. Signe was hosted by a Christian family in Manchester and worked as a housekeeper while studying and practising the English language.[72] From 1922 to 1923, Signe was a student at the NMS's Women's Missionary School in Oslo. She was inaugurated as a missionary on 19 June 1923 and departed in July for South Africa, six months earlier than her fiancé. The NMS's Home Board wanted her to study the Zulu language and get accustomed to South African living conditions before marriage. The decision came as a surprise to Signe and Karl Michael, who had planned to arrange a wedding in Norway. Yet, as already discussed, the missionary candidates in the NMS did not have the freedom to decide when to marry. According to Karl Michael, they nevertheless soon got used to the thought of a temporary separation and regarded the Home Board decision as 'the will of God'.[73]

Their wedding was celebrated on 23 January 1924 in the church at the Eshowe mission station. The wedding ceremony was, according to Karl Michael's report, an 'evocative celebration'. His father Lars Martin officiated, and his oldest brother led the bride to the altar.[74] The couple established their first home in Pietermaritzburg, where Karl Michael studied for the Higher Diploma of Education. They rented a small apartment with two rooms, a kitchen and bathroom. 'We prefer to keep the house ourselves without domestic servants, and we are very happy', Karl Michael informed the NMS General Secretary Einar Amdahl.[75] A year later, their daughter Thora-Margaretha was born. Whereas his grandfather acted as midwife during the birth of his children and his father went on horseback to collect one, Karl Michael's child was born at a hospital. The first month after delivery, Signe stayed with her parents-in-law at Eshowe while Karl Michael started his new position as Principal of Umphumulo Teacher's Training College.[76] In their short missionary family life, Karl Michael was the professional missionary and Signe was in charge of their home. As was the case with all missionary homes, however, it was not strictly private. Their home functioned as a guest-house and residence for visiting missionaries and governmental officers. Signe, who was a professional housekeeper with experience as a matron of soldiers' homes in Norway, created a 'beautiful home' according to her proud husband: 'Signe is so clever and industrious, and she keeps everything clean, neat and tasteful.'[77] As discussed in Chapter 7, Karl Michael was an extraordinarily skilful and hardworking man, and in the five years he managed the college at Umphumulo, he reported good results in terms of organisational development, increased budgets and reformed school buildings. A hardworking missionary husband forged a hardworking missionary wife and, according to the accounts of their daughter, they were very busy.[78] In 1929, however, Karl Michael informed Amdahl that Signe had health problems and had regular 'seizures of fainting and shivering'.[79] The shock she felt when her husband became seriously ill and unexpectedly died of typhoid fever in 1930 resulted in a miscarriage and a stillborn baby boy. She saw no other alternative than to return to Norway and to her own folk.[80]

The missionary home: a man's place

The metaphor 'separate spheres' has had an enormous influence on how historians have explained gender relations in nineteenth-century industrialised societies. The private or domestic sphere of the family and household belonged to women and the public sphere belonged to men.[81] Processes of industrialisation and a growing market economy had altered the traditional business of the household – be it farming, craft production, or shopkeeping – which was often independent of the labour of wife, children, apprentices and servants. In the modern family economy, business and industrial production were separated from the household, and men became the significant producers and breadwinners outside the home, in the public sphere. Women continued to stay at home, but merely as reproducers. A 'cult of domesticity' evolved, and women became central as mothers and homebuilders, but also as protectors and producers of moral and religious values.

Recent scholarship has challenged the separate sphere theory. On one hand, there are many examples of nineteenth-century female wage labourers and entrepreneurs participating in family businesses and industrial production. Moreover, middle-class women participated in the public sphere as agents in philanthropy and mission and propagandists for moral causes.[82] On the other hand, historians in the field of men's history claim that men's role in the private domestic sphere was considerable, although compared with their public activities their domestic activities are underexplored. John Tosh, in his study of masculinity and the middle-class home in Victorian England, and Shawn Johansen, in a study of American middle-class fatherhood in early industrialised America, both claim that the nineteenth-century 'cult of domesticity' was in fact created by and highly valued by British and American men.[83] In addition, Scandinavian researchers like Tomas Berglund and Jørgen Lorentzen have, in recent works, asked if continuity more than change characterised Nordic men's relation to their homes and families in the transition from pre-modern to modern society.[84] Lorentzen claims that, in the case of Norway, the 1850–1920 period involved the considerable presence and authority of the father in the domestic sphere. The deterioration of his role and position at home started later.

The theory of gendered separate spheres has also influenced scholars' analyses of gendered practices in missionary families. Karina Hestad Skeie, in her examination of the importance of the house to nineteenth-century NMS missionaries in Madagascar, found the missionary's dwelling to be a materialistic manifestation of the mission's presence and determination to stay in the country. According to Skeie, however, clear boundaries existed within the missionary's home – namely, 'the inside', which was the domain of the missionary wife, and the 'outside', which was the sphere where the male missionary operated and where the 'real' mission work took place. According to Skeie, whereas the male missionary often left his home for evangelistic tours and inspection trips to satellite stations, the missionary wife 'held the fort' in the relatively safe, clean and ordered world of the mission station.[85]

The current study of missionary family life in the NMS's South Africa mission from a man's perspective has resulted in somewhat different conclusions from Skeie's. First, the father's influence, as well as his labour, in the missionary home was considerable in the first decades of the Norwegian mission enterprise. Given the lack of female relatives, he occasionally acted as midwife, child-minder, housekeeper and nurse. He was also responsible for his children's schooling. When the NMS started to employ female missionary workers as midwives, deaconesses and teachers to assist in missionary families, the husband was gradually relieved of domestic labour. Moreover, when the NMS established institutions for missionary children, he was also relieved of the educational task. Second, the missionary wives in south-east Africa operated within the domestic sphere; ideologically, their vocation was regarded as 'inside' the household (see Chapter 6). Yet the NMS's Zulu mission provides many examples of missionary couples always travelling together on inspection trips, evangelistic tours and business trips.[86] Moreover, there are several examples of missionary wives as the ones in charge of outstationary business activities while their husbands 'held the fort' at the mission stations.[87]

Third, Skeie's assertion of the missionaries' sharp distinctions between spaces – and, further, of mission stations constructed as a 'Christian and civilised island in a heathen ocean' – is also valid in the case of the NMS's Zulu mission. The idea of the mission station land as 'Christian space' to be captured and inhabited is an essential point in Ingeborg Hovland's study of the Norwegian mission stations in Natal and Zululand between 1850 and 1890.[88] A division between a mission station's 'inside' and 'outside' clearly existed, but how gendered were these separate spheres? Was the missionary wife alone in charge of the inside, as Skeie tends to claim in the case of Madagascar? Was the missionary home as well as the internal conditions in the missionary household and at the mission station of no interest to missionary men? We have seen that Christian homemaking became fundamental in the Norwegian mission strategy, and the missionary wife thus became a necessary asset in the mission work. Yet this does not mean that the missionary wives alone were responsible for building Christian homes while the missionary men alone took care of the building of congregations. The male missionary was the head of the missionary family, but he was also the head of the expanded missionary household of servants and apprentices (the 'boys and girls'), of teachers and evangelists, and of landholders and tenants, all living together on mission station land. The male missionary was further 'the spiritual father' of the Christian congregation.

The male missionary was to a certain extent a pre-modern housefather, and the domestic sphere was indeed his sphere and his realm. In the case of the Norwegian missionaries, it is important to remember their socio-economic background. Most were raised in rural families, where the husband, wife, children, apprentices and servants all lived under the same roof and participated in the family's rural production. This was an economic system that prevailed in rural Norway until the mid-twentieth century. Despite the male missionaries' own non-privileged background, by becoming clergy they achieved a social upgrade. Among Norwegian clergy, as Tosh has also stated in the case of England,[89] the separation of work from home was not applicable in the nineteenth century. The clergy conducted church business from their home, where they prepared their sermons and received their parishioners. A priest's household in nineteenth-century Norway consisted – in addition to the priest's wife and children – of relatives, governesses and servants. Considerable areas of farming land belonged to the priest's farm (*Prestegården*), and he was its landlord as well as the manager of its many labourers (and in some cases smallholders). The home of the priest was further regarded as a centre of cultural and social activities in rural Norway.

The missionary man was a pre-modern housefather, but simultaneously a modern professional breadwinner employed in a modern missionary enterprise. His private family life was, on the one hand, regarded as an important tool in the mission work, whereas on the other hand it belonged to 'the affairs of the World' and should be subordinate to 'the Lord's affairs'. The male missionary was expected to give priority to his tasks as an employee of NMS, even if this seriously affected his family. In most Western mission organisations, the practice of sending missionary children to boarding schools in the home country or in the host country developed. The missions established institutions to function as substitute homes for missionary children. Historians have accentuated the widespread gendered mission strategy of constructing Christian homes on the borders of civilisation, but very few have commented on the fact that the missionaries' own children disappeared from their parental homes. Scholars in the field of gender and mission have apparently failed to see the irony in the fact that when the Victorian 'cult of domesticity' and gender systems were exported to the colonies by the missionaries, the children of missionary parents grew up as 'orphans of mission'.[90]

Conclusion

The current study of three generations of Titlestad men as family men has demonstrated how their private family life influenced their professional subjectivity. The often-cited 'separate sphere' theory is problematic when we look at practical missionary family life from a masculinity perspective. The domestic sphere was in fact also a man's sphere. The mission case study examined in the current work thus supports recent results in the field of men's history, which claim that men's role in the domestic sphere was greater than previously thought. First, the father's influence, as well as his labour, in the missionary home was considerable in the first decades of the Norwegian mission enterprise. Given the lack of female relatives, he occasionally acted as midwife, child-minder, housekeeper and nurse. He was also responsible for his children's schooling. Second, although the mission strategy of Christian homemaking was fundamental and the missionary wife was thus regarded as a necessary asset in the mission work, this does not mean that the missionary home and mission station area were the domain of the wives alone – quite the reverse. The male missionary was the head of the missionary family as well as the head of the expanded missionary household of servants and apprentices, teachers and evangelists, all living together on mission station land. To a certain extent we can say that the missionary man lived a pre-modern family life; his home was both an arena for private reproduction and professional production in terms of Christian issues.

Furthermore, the study of the Titlestad men as family men displayed how their private family lives were affected by their professional subjectivity. It is a paradox that in the efforts to export the concept of Western Christian homes to non-Christian areas of the world, the lack of a nuclear family life came to characterise the missionaries' own privacy. The missionary wife and husband were regarded as ideal Christian parents. They were regarded as the father and mother of their congregations but their own children were sent away as 'orphans of missions' to boarding institutions. Missionaries were expected to prioritise the cause of the mission, not private and familial emotions and wishes. On the other hand, the working fellowship between husband and wife often strengthened the emotional bonds between them and their mutual dependence. The 'loss' of their own children could also create strong, emotional paternal/maternal relationships between the missionary 'father and mother' and their spiritual 'children' at the mission station or in the congregation. The NMS missionaries in colonial South Africa were, however, not alone in sending their children away to boarding institutions. The Norwegian missionary children were raised in British schools and institutions for white children that toughened them and prepared them for a life as privileged white minority settlers, which will be further discussed in the next chapter.

9
Men in the World

Introduction

For a full understanding of the masculinity construction of the Norwegian missionaries to the Zulus, it is necessary to move from local and regional levels and think globally. Raewyn Connell claims that locally situated lives are (and were) 'powerfully influenced by geopolitical struggles, Western imperial expansion and colonial empires, global markets, multinational corporations, labour migration, and transnational media'.[1] She furthermore claims that the structure of gender relations in transnational and global arenas does not simply mirror patterns found in local arenas. The interaction of many local gender orders multiplies the forms of masculinities present in a global context. Connell speaks of 'globalizing masculinities' – patterns of masculinities that are standardised across localities'.[2]

According to Robert Morell, race, class, geographical conditions and other factors constitutive of gender identities have left nineteenth- and twentieth-century South Africa with a 'highly complex mix of gender regimes and identities'. Until recently South Africa was 'a man's country' because power was exercised publicly and politically by men. Colonialism created new 'white masculinities', like Afrikaner settler masculinity and British imperial masculinity. Nevertheless, the history of white supremacy suggests that white ruling-class masculinity was hegemonic. In the South African Union, established in 1910, white men were 'predominantly employers, law-makers, decision-makers, heads-of-household and posses-sors of bank-accounts'. Although traditional African masculinities were altered by colonialism, often by military means, it was never destroyed, Morell claims. It continued as a 'collective gender identity' among African men, reflecting a pre-colonial past and the gender regimes of those institutions which remained relatively intact. Although African masculinity continued to be influential in the rural black reserves ruled by African chiefs, accelerated urbanisation and the creation of a black proletariat saw the awakening of a black masculinity that was no longer tied to the countryside, to chiefs or to the homestead. This black masculinity was homogeneous in its opposition to white masculinity.[3]

To this 'patchwork quilt of patriarchies', to borrow Belinda Bozzoli's expression,[4] a group of Norwegian men arrived. The all-male association is, in addition to work and family, a third area in which masculinity is constructed.[5] I have already examined how missionary masculinity was constructed in the homosocial, all-male community of missionaries. What about male encounters in the 'temporal' world outside the church and mission? The missionary had a life to live and a role to play as a male citizen in south-east African societies. In fact, his everyday life was lived far away from the community of other Norwegian missionaries. He could be regarded by men outside the NMS as a stranger and immigrant or settler and colonist. He could be regarded as an expert in linguistics, medicine, agriculture and civil engineering or as a diviner and magician. He could be regarded as a superior employer and chief or a subordinate employee and servant.

In this chapter I will examine the missionary as a male civil citizen in the social and political context of south-east Africa. How did his private life in the sense of being a citizen influence his professional subjectivity, and how was his private life as a citizen affected by his professional life and work? Although this starting point is the biographies of Karl Larsen Titlestad (1832–1924), Lars Martin Titlestad (1867–1941) and Karl Michael Titlestad (1898–1930), these men are not regarded as isolated cases but rather as examples of Norwegian missionaries. The first section focuses on the Titlestad men as white men in Zululand. The second section investigates the Titlestad men's relation to the white settler community in the colony of Natal, exploring whether they contributed to creating a particular Norwegian settler masculinity. Finally, the NMS men's attempt to represent Christian ideals of manliness in south-east Africa, advocating the Lutheran concept of the 'the Two Kingdoms' or 'the Two Realms', namely the temporal and the spiritual, and New Testament idea of Christ's followers being 'in the world' but not 'of the world' (John 17: 11, 16), will be discussed.

White men in Zululand

The chief's subordinates

Karl Larsen Titlestad arrived at the Nhlazatsche mission station in Zululand in 1865, at a time that Per Hernæs calls the NMS missionaries' 'national phase', as Schreuder had chosen a strategy of co-operating and negotiating with the political elite of Zululand.[6] The purchase of the Umphumulo Mission Reserve in 1850 meant that the NMS was already established in the British colony of Natal. From 1851 to 1869, however, the Zulu King Mpande ka Senzangakhona allowed six Norwegian mission stations to be established in Zululand: at Empangeni (1851), Entumeni (1852), Mahlabatini (1860), Eshowe (1861), Nhlazatsche (1862) and Imfule (1865). A critical situation occurred in 1869 when Prince Cetshwayo ka Mpande expelled a German missionary from Zululand. In the same year, Schreuder was nevertheless permitted to establish three new mission stations at Umbonambi (1869), Umizinyati (1870) and Kwahlabisa (1871). According to Schreuder, the Prince claimed that the Norwegians were in a privileged position compared with other missions: 'We Norwegians were quite different as we were the first and as such belonged to the Zulu people.'[7]

This was the background to Schreuder's order to Karl Larsen Titlestad in 1869 to search for appropriate mission land in the chiefdom of Sihayo. Titlestad eventually settled on the east side of the Umzinyathi River. In the following nine years, he was subordinate to Chief Sihayo, a position he in fact found challenging. At the first meeting between the two men, Sihayo expressed (according to Titlestad's accounts) that he would like the missionary to live on a hill close to his chiefly homestead:

> And then, he said, I should plough for him, let him borrow my wagon whenever he wished, and build him the same kind of houses that the teachers [NMS missionaries] had built for the king at Emathlabatini. I should bring him timber from Ikude, and provide him with candles, sugar, coffee, flour and medicines.[8]

The two men were frequently in contact, and according to Titlestad, the chief spoke 'a mixed' language of Zulu, Dutch and English when communicating with foreigners.[9] Sihayo claimed that he had a 'white heart'; he loved 'the white man's things' and expected Titlestad to be 'his white man' and Titlestad's things to be 'his things'. Despite Titlestad's resolve to offer no services other than religious education, he did in reality work a lot at Sihayo's homestead. In 1877, he reported being called upon two or three times a week and having performed much 'tiresome' labour for the chief.[10] He was apparently regarded as the chief's subordinate handyman and servant, a role he found uncomfortable.

The Lutheran concept of the 'the Two Kingdoms' or 'the Two Realms' – namely, the temporal and the spiritual – implied that the missionaries had to accept their role as subordinates of secular authorities. This theological principle was ambiguous, however. The presumption was that the two acted as a team, with the 'secular sword' working in the cause of Christianity. Yet what if the secular authority was clearly anti-Christian? How should a man live a life as 'civil citizen' in a regime regarded as 'uncivilised'? The political conditions grew tense in Zululand in the late 1870s. Sihayo became involved in a conflict with a neighbouring chief, something that sparked Cetshwayo's anger, and he had to flee for protection. According to Titlestad, Sihayo forced the missionary to give him one of the mission houses to store his private goods. Sihayo aggressively claimed his chiefly rights to the mission station land and, in September 1877, he started to construct a dwelling close to the walls of Titlestad's house.[11] As previously mentioned, the Titlestad family fled from Umzinyathi on 12 April 1878 after the NMS missionaries at their conference in March agreed to effectuate evacuation from Zululand. Titlestad's report on the incident is marked by a feeling of relief. He wrote that, during the last months at Umzinyathi, he and his family had constantly been troubled by Chief Sihayo and his people. Their things, crops and cattle were stolen, they were teased and shot at with guns, and he had seriously felt that their lives were in danger. Titlestad claimed that Chief Sihayo had no respect for him or his family, his private property or his mission station.[12] It was a common perception in the missionary community that Titlestad's last months at Umzinyathi among the 'plundering savages' of Sihayo's people were 'hard school' and that he and his family suffered more than any other of the Norwegian missionaries in the pre-war turbulence.[13] The men Titlestad described as his 'worst tormentors', the sons of Sihayo, were actually involved in several conflicts on the border between Natal and Zululand and, according to Jeff Guy, their incursion into the colony provided the British with one of the pretexts for invasion in 1879.[14]

Per Hernæs defines the 1873–79 period, the last years of the independent Zulu kingdom, as the NMS missionaries' 'imperialistic phase'. The missionaries 'threw off the secular master they had acquired when they built their stations in the land of the Zulu King' and alternatively welcomed the British colonial power.[15] The fall of the independent Zulu kingdom in 1879 and its subsequent upheavals, followed by a series of agricultural disasters in the 1880s and 1890s, were according to Jarle Simensen met by the NMS missionaries with a somewhat surprising 'unfeeling harshness'. Simensen speaks of the missionaries' 'humiliation thesis', as a majority of them observed with satisfaction the 'degradation', 'humiliation' and 'punishment' that the Zulus experienced through the destruction of their political independence and economic base.[16] Karl

Titlestad was also convinced that war was inevitable. His statement in 1879 provides an example of the attitudes described by Simensen:

> This is the best we can wish for the Zulus, since as an independent people they will never stop destroying each other, and in the pride of their independence they build barricades against both civilisation and Christianity. We hope that the time of humiliation is awaiting them, and that after this period they will be more susceptible to the Gospel.[17]

Simensen asks if the Norwegians' 'humiliation thesis' could be related to their pietistic view of conversion, whereby distress, crisis and humiliation were regarded as 'positive' factors that could create an awareness of sin and thus lead to salvation.[18] As discussed in Chapter 5 the missionaries regarded the humiliation of the traditional Zulu man necessary if a new Christian Zulu man were to emerge. In the case of Titlestad, we can further speculate as to whether 'primitive' feelings of hate and revenge influenced his attitudes.[19] He had for years been humiliated and treated like a slave by a Zulu chief; he had been threatened and teased and had feared for his life as well as that of his family. After nine years of frustration under the rule of a secular master, he felt relieved to be free, and he also felt some pleasure in learning that his previous tormentors had lost their power, positions and land. Titlestad had no other choice than to accept his subordinate position under a Zulu chief, but like the rest of the missionaries he welcomed the new rulers.

Colonial landholders

The NMS missionaries, who had welcomed the British invasion of Zululand, were soon disappointed by the colonial system of indirect rule. Zululand was to be governed by 13 chiefs under the guidance of a British resident. In Titlestad's previous mission district, Hlubi, a leader of the Sotho group, Tlokoa, was awarded the chiefdom previously held by Sihayo, who was ordered to leave the land.[20] Titlestad 'lost' the mission station of Umzinyathi under the new political conditions, but the white Chief John Dunn, who was awarded the largest chieftainship in Zululand, offered him Ekombe in Nkandhla district as compensation.[21] The lifespan of the 1879 'settlement' was brief, lasting barely four years, as in 1883 a new division of Zululand took place. The chiefdoms of John Dunn and the other chiefs in Southern Zululand were regarded as Reserved Territory under the protection and active control of the British Resident Commissioner. King Cetshwayo was reinstated as the chief in the central district of Zululand and Chief Zibhebhu in the northern territory. A civil war broke out, which eventually resulted in the British annexation of all of Zululand in May 1887. In 1898, the effective administrative control of Zululand was transferred from the metropolitan authorities in London to the self-governing colony of Natal, which had gained its independence in 1893.

The question of the NMS's right to land in Zululand, as well as the boundary lines of the Norwegian mission land, became a frustrating issue of concern for the mission and the missionaries during these rapidly changing political conditions. The NMS missionaries believed that they had legal rights to the land originally allotted to them by the Zulu kings. By the turn of the century, however, the situation felt insecure, and the new colony rulers from 1898 were regarded as unstable and unpredictable as the old Zulu regime.[22] What really alarmed the Norwegian missionaries was the intrusion of white farmers into 'their' mission districts, leaving the mission stations as islands in white settlements. Superintendent Ole Stavem gave high priority to the task of securing the land deemed to be mission property and gaining official recognition of its borders.[23] The NMS owned title deeds for three of the mission stations,[24] but otherwise lacked legal documents authorising their land rights. In 1898, Ole Stavem sent a thorough report to the new colonial authorities in Pietermaritzburg, explaining the background and history of all the Norwegian mission stations in Zululand and Natal, claiming legal rights to the land.[25] The land question was also a central theme of discussion during Secretary Lars Dahle's inspection tour in 1903.[26] Stavem in his 1898 report had asked for 4,000 acres of land per mission station and a double set of title deeds, one transferring to the NMS a glebe of 500 acres and the other securing 'each native congregation' 3,500 acres of land. Dahle, however, advised the missionaries to be more modest in their claims, claiming that 500 acres per station was sufficient.

Karl Larsen Titlestad believed that the boundary lines of the Ekombe mission station were fixed after a visit from British Resident Commissioner John W. Shepstone in 1883.[27] After the administration of Zululand was transferred to the Colony of Natal, however, Superintendent Stavem had difficulties getting official acceptance of the previous survey.[28] A joint imperial and colonial Zululand Lands Delimitation Commission operated from 1902 until 1904. The land was measured, and the government first parcelled out lands for white farmers, then 'locations' for the indigenous people and land for black townships, and finally land for the 'mission farms'.[29] When the districts of Zululand were offered for sale to white settlers from 1904 to 1906, the Ekombe mission station received merely 200 acres of the much larger area that had originally been donated by John Dunn and later surveyed by John W. Shepstone.[30] This frustrated Lars Martin Titlestad, who took over his father's station in 1895, and for a while he considered buying the private farm land bordering the mission station. Titlestad wished to buy the farm as a private person, but needed the Home Board's permission since 'by principle, a missionary is not allowed to buy land'.[31] Titlestad got the Home Board's permission, although the transaction was never realised.[32] In their response, the Home Board expressed scepticism about 'the NMS as farm owner'. At Umphumulo, Imfule, and Nhlazatsche, for which the NMS owned title deeds, the missionaries were responsible for collecting taxes from Zulu families settling on the mission land as tenant farmers. This was a practice disliked by the Home Board, who feared the missionaries' 'strong master relationship with their tenants and believers'. That being so, it seems paradoxical that the Home Board saw no danger in the prospective mixing of professional and private interests and positions in Titlestad's case. 'We trust him', they stated, and they believed Titlestad could perfectly well combine 'business sense' with 'an intense interest for his real work as a missionary'.[33]

The missionaries fought for the NMS's right to land in Zululand. This was not a struggle for private property, but could nevertheless be understood as foreign white colonisation of land. The impression of white colonisation was further strengthened by the fact that the sons and daughters of the missionaries, who definitely had private interests in land accumulation, settled in areas close to the Norwegian mission stations. Elias Titlestad stated in his memoirs that 'ours was the first European family to come and settle permanently in this district'.[34] Then, he continued, came the magistrate, 'who was the first to collect tax in the district from the natives'; in the case of Ekombe, the magistrate also happened to be the missionary son Martin Oftebro. The traders, sawyers and gold-diggers came on the heels of the Titlestad missionary family, according to Elias's narrative. After Karl Larsen Titlestad returned to Norway in 1891, three of his sons continued to live in Nkandhla district, where they were successful traders, farmers and businessmen. When the districts of Zululand were sold off to white settlers after 1904, the Titlestad brothers all had the opportunity to buy land.[35] No wonder that the Titlestad name at Ekombe and in other districts of Nkandhla until recently held connotations of white colonialism. Themba Khathi, a pastor in the Evangelical Lutheran Church of South Africa who originated from Ekombe, was interviewed in the 1990s about his experiences as a black clergyman during the apartheid era. As a representative of black people living at Ekombe, he regarded the Titlestad missionary men both as Christian evangelists and as greedy purchasers of land:

> The whites enjoyed apartheid, they liked it. In fact they were bene-fiting from it. Let me take an example. Originally I come from Ekombe. Ekombe is a mission station with some land…These people, at least some of them, did not come only for the gospel, they also came for land. This is why I am saying they were benefiting. Their sons got land and bought farms. They were owning those farms. Following the apartheid laws, the people were moved from these places and put on barren land. All the fertile lands were taken by the missionaries next to the church. I think that the poverty that we are experiencing now is the result of apartheid…[36]

'Friends of the Zulus'

Lars Martin Titlestad was born in Zululand. He spoke the Zulu language fluently and was familiar with the cultural traditions. His colleagues portrayed him as a 'friend of the Zulus', saying 'he was like one of them'.[37] When Lars Martin was commissioned as a mission station manager at Ekombe in 1895, he felt it was like coming home to the 'paradise of his childhood'.[38] As discussed in Chapter 8, the young Titlestad brothers living at the boarding school in Natal were delighted every time they could return to Zululand and their parents' home. Ekombe was described in their memoirs as 'a boy's paradise'. In the 'wild and untamed' nature of Zululand they could practise boyish activities like hunting and horse-riding, and they learned how to interpret weather signs and secret signs of nature. In the late nineteenth and early twentieth centuries, the popular masculine stereotype of the frontiersman – the hunter, the pioneer, the explorer, the missionary – as representative of 'true manli-ness' inspired voluntary movements among boys and young men like the scouting movement.[39]

Lars Martin Titlestad's discussions on traditional Zulu culture and religion were actually characterised by a respect and tolerance unusual in contemporary Norwegian mission discourse. In an article in *NMT* in 1904, he referred to the fact that Westerners often described 'the Zulus' (the term 'the Zulu' in colonial discourses was a gendered term usually referring to the male population – see Chapter 5) as 'sluggish, dull, conservative and stubborn'.[40] He, on the other hand, emphasised that the Zulus were 'clever and brave', a people skilled at 'thinking and reasoning'. Titlestad asserted that human beings in general had much in common, and he saw similarities between 'superstitions' in the civilised world, for instance spiritism, and the cult of ancestor spirits in Africa. He hesitated to reject the sincerity of the Zulu religious worldview: 'I think that in our eagerness to wipe out superstition, we should be careful not to harass and deny the forces of nature that we really don't know.'[41]

The Titlestad brothers were all proud of their upbringing 'under the Zulu kings', which was the title of the memoirs of Elias Titlestad. Yet their many references to an exotic upbringing in the land of the proud and brave Zulu warriors resemble a common obsession among the settlers of Natal with the glorious past of the Zulu kingdom. They furthermore resemble colonisers' tendencies to distinguish between 'more manly' and 'less manly' masculinities among their subjects.[42] The Titlestad brothers actually had good relations with the Zulu royalties. Nils Titlestad visited King Dinizulu during his exile at St Helena in 1897.[43] When the king died in 1914, the NMS's missionary conference sent Lars Martin Titlestad to offer condolences to Dinizulu's sons Salomon and David.[44] Titlestad sympathised with the national feelings of the Zulu people: 'That the people have strong feelings for their royalty is merely national and natural. The national feeling is no sin, but to harass and trample on other people's national feelings – that is a sin.'[45]

In the case of Lars Martin Titlestad, his sympathy with Zulu nationalism can partly explain his opposition to the NMS's treatment of the political activist and Lutheran pastor Petros Lamula. Titlestad was particularly critical of the uncompromising attitude of Peder Aa. Rødseth. From a nationalistic perspective, Titlestad accepted Lamula's campaign to raise the political and cultural consciousness of the suppressed Zulu people.[46] There were also personal reasons for his support of Petros Lamula and his brother Filemon Lamula, who both broke with the Norwegian Lutheran church in 1926 and established the separatist United National Church of Christ. The Lamula brothers had attended the mission school at Ekombe, they had been baptised by Titlestad, and Filemon Lamula had for years been his most trusted evangelist.[47] Titlestad was proud of the intelligent, hardworking Lamula brothers and felt they were like sons. He argued that the missionary community should guide Petros Lamula and treat him in a mild, fatherly way. Lamula should be regarded as a rebellious teenager who in time would reach maturity and manhood. We have already discussed the missionaries' common understanding of the Zulu pastors as 'immature sons', a perception that in fact implied the continued subordination of black pastors under white missionary leadership. Titlestad's attitude towards Lamula – tolerant and loving but still paternalistic – obviously frustrated Lamula, who revealed ambiguous feelings of love and hate towards his 'father'.[48]

In the world of early twentieth-century South Africa, a huge social gap existed between white and black men. In the Norwegian Lutheran Zulu church, the contradictions surfaced in the 1920s, when several Zulu pastors left the NMS and established independent churches. The issue of race caused a lot of discussion between the NMS's Home Board and the missionary community in South Africa. The Home Board accused the missionaries of revealing racist attitudes towards their Zulu 'brothers'. The missionaries were further criticised for tight bonds to the white settler milieus.[49] Lars Martin Titlestad responded to the critique as follows: 'We and our families cannot extend our social contact with the natives without hurting both ourselves and them.'[50] He claimed that the missionaries, as white civil citizens in a British colony, had to consider the reputation of their families. The wedding of his son Karl Michael to Signe Brekke in 1924 actually illustrated the social gap between the white missionaries and their black congregation. The wedding was celebrated in the church at the Eshowe mission station. According to Karl's accounts, 'our Norwegian friends and family' sat in the upper part of the church while 'the natives sat further down in the church'. Also the wedding party was celebrated in segregated parties. The missionaries and their relatives had dinner at the missionary home, and a cow was slaughtered for the natives to eat outside.[51]

The family history of the Titlestad men displays a growing social segregation between the Norwegians and the Zulus. In pre-colonised Zululand, the Titlestad family lived physically close to Zulu converts at the mission station and had much social contact, whether they liked it or not, with their Zulu neighbours. Owing to the white colonisation of Zululand, which took place later than in the case of Natal, the missionaries were gradually integrated into white settler communities. It is a paradox that, as the social segregation increased, so did the respect and admiration of 'tribal', patriarchal Zulu traditions and culture. In the case of the Titlestad men, their exotic upbringing 'under the Zulu kings' was used as a mark of masculine robustness and strength.

Norwegian men in a British colony

As immigrants and foreigners in south-east African societies, the Norwegian missionaries often expressed feelings of loneliness. The annual missionary conferences were social highlights where they enjoyed the community of 'brothers' of the same ethnic and cultural background as themselves, speaking the same Norwegian language. For a missionary who lived in remote areas, this could be the only chance to meet countrymen. In 1873, Karl Larsen Titlestad reported from the Umzinjathi mission station that during the last six months he had conducted the ministerial act of Eucharist only once, and then with his wife and sister-in-law as the only attendants. He had waited in vain for any of the Norwegian Lutheran 'brothers' to come and assist, so that he himself could participate in the Holy Communion.[52] Albeit Norwegian visitors were rare, the Titlestad family usually received many guests at the mission station. In 1875, Karl registered 41 'white visitors' and 50 'black visitors' in his journal, most staying overnight.[53] The station was situated close to a busy cart road, and he used to leave his work to chat with passers-by. At Ekombe, he continued the practice of meeting and greeting travellers. According to his son Elias, Karl had the Zulu nickname '*Umnqandi wezindwendwe eziya Ensingabantu*', which meant 'he who waylays the strings of travellers going to Ensingabantu'.[54]

Karl L. Titlestad also had many acquaintances among white settlers in his district; however, this private side of the missionary's daily life was usually not recounted in reports to the Home Board. Yet references to construction work, agriculture, trading and negotiations with the Zulu, British and Boer government officers all reveal that the Norwegian missionaries were part of an international, inter-professional and inter-confessional community of white settlers in Natal and Zululand. Lars and Martha Larsen at the Nhlazatsche mission station were known for their isolation from the Norwegian community. They did not partici-pate in the missionary conferences for long periods. Indeed, when Ommund Oftebro visited his old peer in 1890, the two men had not seen each other since the Anglo-Zulu war.[55] Even if Larsen was isolated from the Norwegian community, his mission station functioned as an inn for travelling white people, and they received lots of visitors of many nationalities.[56] The northern part of Zululand, where the Nhlazatsche mission station was situated, was occupied in 1885 by the Boers as the 'New Republic', and Larsen was surrounded by Afrikaner farmers.[57] He apparently developed friendly and peaceful relations with the new white neighbours, as many attended both his and his wife's funeral in 1890.[58]

Robert W. Connell asserts that colonial conquest was primarily carried out by segregated groups of men: soldiers, sailors, traders and adminis-trators. Moreover, it is likely that the men drawn from the metropolis towards colonisation were the more 'rootless'. The process of conquest in itself could produce frontier masculinities with an unusual level of violence and egocentric individualism.[59] In several articles, Lars Martin Titlestad presented narratives of 'lost' white male settlers whom he had helped in both physical and spiritual matters.[60] His travel reports reveal a thorough knowledge of white farmers and settlers in many parts of Zululand, and he apparently had many acquaintances among Afrikaners, Germans, Swedes, Britons and Americans.[61] When he returned to Ekombe and Zululand in 1906 after his two-year furlough in Norway, he discovered that a dozen white farmers – most of them single men – had bought land in the areas close to the mission station.[62] As there was no Anglican church nearby, Titlestad started to arrange monthly Sunday services in English. Central members in the English-speaking congregation were his three brothers, who all lived nearby. In 1911 Titlestad reported that between 20 and 40 whites attended the English services at Ekombe and that the group had made considerable donations to the congregation. He admitted that it was challenging to address congregations of white settlers of diverse confessional backgrounds: 'Here are rigid high-church Anglicans, Presbyterians, Methodists, Dutch Reformed people and German and Norwegian Lutherans. God has in any case blessed our meetings, and in a remote mountain village even the lion and the lamb can eat grass together.'[63]

In his wife's opinion, however, both the Norwegian and the feminine elements in the settler milieu at Ekombe were too weak, and she complained in a private letter in 1908: 'Oh, if only our white neighbours could have been Norwegians, how wonderful that would have been.'[64] When Margaretha and Lars Martin Titlestad were relocated to Eshowe in 1920, and later to Durban in 1927, there were plenty of Norwegians with whom to socialise and celebrate Norwegian Lutheran services. Hanna Mellemsether speaks of 'missionary settlers' in an essay in which she claims that the NMS employees were among the first Norwegian settlers in Natal and Zululand, and that Norwegian immigrant communities evolved in the wake of missionary activity. What distinguished the missionaries in this region, in contrast to missionaries to Madagascar and China – at least until the mid-twentieth century – was the fact that most of them never returned to Norway, but rather continued to live in South Africa after retirement. The sons and daughters of the missionaries in South Africa married other Norwegians or English-speaking settlers. They often married within the missionary community. Mellemsether finds the Titlestad family an interesting example of the latter. For four generations, this family was connected with the following Norwegian missionary families in South Africa: Leisegang, Braatvedt, Dahle, Eriksen, Borgen, Oftebro, Gundersen and Aadnesgaard.[65]

When Norwegian missionaries settled with their families in Zululand and Natal, they were part of the broad European colonisation of south-east Africa, and they were quite aware of it. In several articles in the mission magazines, Lars Martin Titlestad informed readers about the 'Norwegian Homes' in Zululand. He thought it would be interesting for Norwegian readers to learn how 'the Norwegian tribe' was dispersing throughout the world and also in South Africa.[66] According to Titlestad, like good old Abraham, who left his home at God's command to go to a foreign land and a foreign people, the pioneer missionaries did the same. They had no private fortune for their children to inherit, but through the support of the mission they had provided them with a proper education. Titlestad believed that, just as the Lord never forgot Abraham, blessing both him and his descendants, 'He now blesses the missionary children and grandchildren'. Not only were the missionary families blessed themselves, but the country of South Africa was also blessed by the new generations of Norwegian settlers: 'It is a wonderful side of our mission work, that so many good Norwegian homes are established in the world's new countries.' Titlestad thought the contribution of the Norwegian race in South Africa valuable, as there were much 'energy and power' in the Norwegians, who had always been a travelling people. The Norwegians were few in the world, but had 'the power of salt' and an ability to make themselves known wherever they went. He claimed that the Norwegian tribe could bring 'new and fresh forces' to other races.[67]

There was a consciousness about the close link between Norwegian mission and Norwegian colonialism in immigrant milieus in South Africa. Ernst Hallen, pastor in the Norwegian Seaman's Mission, who served the Norwegian settler congregation in Durban from 1922, stated the following in 1929: 'Whereas most nations first send colonists to foreign countries, and let the missionaries follow in their footsteps, Norwegians do it in an opposite way. First they send the missionaries, and then follow the colonists.'[68] In Hallen's opinion, the Norwegian case was preferable. The Norwegian missionaries in Zululand had won the love and respect of the natives, which in turn had benefited the Norwegian colonists in South Africa, he claimed. Mellemsether's study demonstrates that Norwegian settlers, missionaries, and farmers and businessmen actually supported one another. Missionary sons were recruited to jobs in Norwegians' business establishments. Missionaries recruited Zulu labourers to Norwegian commercial enterprises.[69] An outstanding example is the business of Norwegian-based whaling companies, which expanded into the Durban area in early 1900. Dag Ingemar Børresen has documented that hundreds of Zulu labourers working under harsh conditions in the factories and ships of the whaling industry, and also at the Norwegian whale station in New Fortuna Bay in South Georgia, were recruited mostly from Durban, Nkandhla and Eshowe, areas where the missionary factor was strong. A central entrepreneur in the whaling industry, Abraham Larsen, was married to the daughter of NMS missionary Sven Eriksen. His companion Jacob Egeland, who also served as the Norwegian consul in Durban, had a central position in the Norwegian Lutheran church in Durban.[70]

As we already have seen, the Titlestad brothers established themselves as businessmen, traders and farmers in Zululand. Other missionary children had prominent positions in the colonial 'native' administration and education. The children of Siver Marthin Samuelsen, a missionary assistant of Schreuder who eventually left the NMS to serve in the Anglican mission, all held influential positions. Samuel Olaf Samuelson served for many years as the Undersecretary of the Native Affairs Department. Levine Henrietta Samuelson was a teacher in Zulu schools and an authority on Zulu language, history and folklore. Robert Charles Samuelson published ethnographical studies on Zulu history and culture; as an educated lawyer, he was part of the defence team at Prince Dinizulu's trial in Greytown (1908–09).[71] Meanwhile, of Nils Braatvedt's five children, three sons became magistrates and a daughter married a British magistrate.[72] Peder Aa. Rødseth had one son who served as a magistrate and another as a major in Pietermaritzburg.[73] The integration of the descendants of the Norwegian missionaries into the white ruling class of Natal was a success story, which Peter H. Rodseth summarised as follows: 'Many of the children and grandchildren of these hardy, hardworking Christian and honest people have made a great contribution towards building South Africa. They have become true and loyal citizens of our country.'[74] In other words, the descendants of the missionaries became loyal supporters of the white ruling regime of South Africa.

Although the Norwegian immigrants were integrated into the British-dominated settler communities, they continued to emphasise and remember their Norwegian heritage. We have seen that the Norwegian Lutheran church, established in Durban in 1890, had a central position in the milieu (see Chapter 4). There also existed, however, a Norwegian association, a Norwegian hall, and a Norwegian weekly newspaper called *Fram* (*Fram* was the name of a ship used by Norwegian polar explorers from 1893 to 1912 and thus symbolised Norwegian progress and expansion in polar areas). The missionary children living at the

NMS's home in Durban attended the weekly 'Norwegian school' in the Norwegian church, where education was offered in the Norwegian language and in Lutheran Christianity. The children at the home were considered to be faithful church attendants, and Norwegian Sunday school and mission groups were also arranged at the home.[75] Church services held in the Norwegian language and with an Evangelical-Lutheran liturgy were central in all national celebrations among the Norwegian settlers, such as the annual celebration of the national day on 17 May and special occasions like the grand centennial celebration of the Norwegian constitution in 1914.[76] Lars Martin Titlestad's last article in the *NMT* before his retirement from missionary service, and actually his last greeting to Norwegian mission supporters, was called 'Home in Durban'. Although he was born in Zululand, his family had always regarded Norway as 'home', he explained: 'When we are out in the mission field we tend to say "home in Norway".' But, he admitted, things had changed over the years, especially after his own children and grandchildren had made their home in the new country of South Africa. As an old man, Durban was now his home. He praised the Norwegian church in Durban and gave his thanks to the NMS and the Seamen's Mission, who had created an alternative 'Norwegian Home' for immigrants in South Africa.[77]

Norwegian nationalism bloomed in the first decades after 1905, as the newborn nation struggled to establish its neutral political position among influential nations like Great Britain and Russia, and further expand its commercial interests and imperialistic aspirations in the world's polar areas.[78] The expanding colony of Norwegians in Durban symbolised the young nation's commercial success in the sense of its being the world's leading nation in the whaling industry. It further represented a centre for imperialistic interests in the southern arctic areas.[79] Norwegian missionaries contributed considerably to establishing and nurturing the Norwegian settler community in south-east Africa. Moreover, they contributed ideologically to a discourse of Norwegian settler masculinity. The writings of Lars Martin Titlestad reflected a view of Norwegians as men who, from the time of the Vikings, had been 'fresh and free' travellers on global oceans. The Norwegians consisted of strong fishermen and whale hunters, brave polar explorers, and persevering missionaries. From a global perspective, Norwegian men were few, but of a particularly strong and healthy blend, Titlestad asserted. In his opinion, the extensiveness of the Norwegian tribe in a young nation like South Africa would help to renew and refresh the white population as an entity.[80]

Missionary men: in the world, but not of the world

Lars Martin Titlestad once described himself as a 'frontier guard', partly because of the site of his mission station on a long, narrow piece of land between white farms and black locations and partly because as a Christian missionary he was supposed to 'neutralise' the tense relations between white and white, white and black, and black and black.[81] The metaphor of the mission station as a fort in a war zone, and likewise the missionary as a soldier struggling against 'heathendom', was familiar in the mission discourse, but the situation was referred to as a 'spiritual fight' that went on in the spiritual realm. In the temporal realm, 'in the man's world', the missionaries preferred to see themselves as 'men-in-between', as non-commercial and non-political men and thereby neutral actors in worldly matters. It makes sense to refer to the biblical words of 'living in the world', but still not being 'of the world' (John 17: 11, 16). Their Lutheran concept of 'the Two Realms' was also part of their ideological heritage. The missionaries tended to let this ideological-religious foundation guide their attitudes in political and ideological issues as well as their social practice. First, they strove to live like 'born again' Christian men among secularised settler men. Second, as Norwegian men they saw themselves as representatives of a politically neutral, non-imperialistic Norwegian masculinity in a world of imperial masculinities. Third, owing to their perceived roles as men-in between as well as the Lutheran ideology of the two kingdoms, they constructed an identity as 'negotiating men' in the growing conflicts between white oppressors and the black oppressed. The crucial question, however, is whether their position as neutral men in between was a real alternative in the segregated society of South Africa characterised by inequality in terms of race, class, and gender.

Regarding the first, as missionary men they saw it as the ideal to – in both words and deeds – to live like 'born again' Christian men among secularised settler men. Rhonda A. Semple found in her research on British missionary masculinity that missionaries for the most part did not participate in the type of homosocial 'clubs' so important to masculine imperial identity. This contributed to a position of marginal masculinity, a position on the fringes of imperial all-male societies.[82] In the case of Christian Oftebro, we saw that his alleged worldly lifestyle was deemed to be problematic and was among the factors that eventually resulted in the NMS's dismissal of him. He had interests in gold-mining companies; he had many British officers, magistrates and farmers among his acquaintances; and he attended gentlemen's social parties and clubs.

His close connection with the settler milieus and his alleged profane interests were seen as irreconcilable with the ideal missionary masculinity. The NMS missionaries aimed for good relations with colonial authorities – in other words, the white ruling settler class – but it should obviously be balanced.

Lars Martin Titlestad arranged monthly English services for his white neighbours at Ekombe, who in many cases were single men. He saw it as his task to protect and nurture the religious life of men who could otherwise easily become secularised. A much-discussed theme in the mission discourse was the immoral and secular white settler: the drinker, the fornicator and the swindler. His condition was regarded as worse than the 'heathen's', because he was raised in the Christian faith and was supposed to know better. In the missionaries' opinion, these men represented the dark, negative side of civilisation that unfortunately also had a bad influence on African men. There was another prospective and terrifying scenario attached to the secular settler man as well. In non-civilised, non-Christian lands, there was always a potential risk of a man 'going native' and being absorbed into 'heathendom'. John Dunn, the settler and hunter of Scottish origin who lived a life as a polygamist Zulu chief, was regarded as an extreme example of such a 'white heathen'.[83]

Some of the missionaries' close bonds with the settler milieus, even if the settlers were born-again Christians and teetotallers, were regarded as problematic by other missionaries. The settler brothers of Lars Martin Titlestad were principal members of the English-speaking congregation at Ekombe, and they supported the Norwegian Zulu mission with their offerings. They also supported each other financially in private. For instance, when Lars Martin became ill from enteric fever in 1901 and later in 1907, his brothers paid the hospital bills when the NMS refused to.[84] The missionary community actually found the tight bonds between Lars Martin Titlestad and his settler brothers to be problematic. In a letter to Lars Dahle in 1901, Stavem stated that he would have preferred to relocate Titlestad in order 'to get him away from his clever businessmen brothers'.[85] Titlestad's 'family writings' in Norwegian mission magazines also caused irritation among his colleagues (see Chapter 8). When Titlestad held the position of superintendent from 1920 to 1925, on several occasions the missionaries accused him of mixing private family and professional interests. For instance, in 1921, when he launched the idea of a medical mission in Zululand, he suggested that the NMS should buy the hospital and medical practice of his younger brother Karl Titlestad at Nkandhla.[86] Although Titlestad claimed that his mission interest had priority over his brother's business,[87] the NMS never bought the hospital of his younger brother. A majority of the missionaries thought Lars Martin lacked judgement in failing to make clear enough distinctions between his role as a mission leader and his private interests and contacts in the settler milieus.[88]

Second, as Norwegian men the NMS missionaries perceived themselves as representatives of a politically neutral, non-imperialistic Norwegian masculinity among powerful imperial and colonial masculinities. Arne Gunnar Carlsson observed that Norwegian men participated as soldiers in the South African war (1899–1902), on both the British and the Boer sides.[89] Generally speaking, Norwegians living in the colonies of Natal and Cape were British-friendly, whereas Norwegians living in the free states of Transvaal and Orange were Boer-friendly. The NMS missionaries were mostly British-friendly, according to Carlsson. In 1899, the mission stations at Nhlazatsche and Mahlabatini were evacuated when Boer troops approached the area.[90] At the Ekombe mission station, Lars Martin Titlestad was first visited by British troops, who accused him of providing the Boers with intelligence. Later on, Boer troops arrived in the area and plundered the stores and other possessions of white British settlers, leaving the mission station undisturbed. Titlestad was praised by Superintendent Stavem for his manly courage in staying calm, 'holding the fort', and for his faith and trust in God during difficult times.[91] Stavem, reporting from the South African war, levelled severe criticism against both parties. What should be blamed for the terrible situation? British imperialism or Boer 'South-Africanism'? According to Stavem, Christians should interpret the war in a deeper, religious sense. How had European Christian nations behaved in Africa? Had they not been greedy? Had they not stolen land and property from the Africans? Cold-blooded white men had cruelly killed Africans. The war between the two so-called Christian nations, 'white against white, Europeans against European', was a divine punishment, according to Stavem: 'The injustice done towards defenceless heathens in Africa is now being punished. The blood of the defenceless has been crying to the Almighty, and the cry has been heard. The punishment came upon the performer of injustice.'[92]

Stavem was persistent in maintaining a critical distance from colonial authorities and British settler milieus. We have already seen his struggle for the NMS's right to mission land. After Scandinavian settlers in Durban accused the missionaries of producing 'Mission-Kaffirs' of bad quality, he ran an official campaign to defend the Norwegian mission's capacity to recruit and educate industrious and trustworthy Christian Zulu men (see Chapter 5). On political questions, he urged the Norwegian Christian missionaries to remain neutral. On the other hand, he was a warm supporter of Norwegian nationalism and Lutheran Christianity, and he prioritised his efforts to defend this confession in Durban, as we saw in Chapter 4. The Norwegian church in Durban was established by Stavem. In the growing Norwegian settler milieus of both Durban and Eshowe, the Lutheran congregations served by the NMS missionaries had central positions.

Third, the Norwegian missionaries' position on the periphery of white settler masculinity, while still profiting from the white patriarchal rule in the colony of Natal, and their position close to the Zulus among whom they lived and worked, created a identity as 'negotiators' in the growing conflicts between the white oppressors and the black oppressed. Stavem was not alone in his sharp critique of the white man's treatment of the black man in Africa. The Zulu uprising in 1906, remembered as the Bambatha rebellion, was provoked by colonial authorities' imposition of a poll tax on people already suffering from the material and social consequences of colonialism. The resistance was put down with uncompromising violence.[93] Hernæs claims that, during the rebellion, the NMS missionaries, on the one hand, preached a message of obedience to the colonial authorities but, on the other hand, criticised the brutality of the pacification campaign.[94] Lars Berge, in his examination of Swedish missionaries and African Christians during the Bambatha rebellion, finds that Swedish missionaries were far less critical of the colonial government than their Norwegian colleagues. He explains this by referring to the different views on nation and nationalism in the two countries at the time owing to Norway's dissolution of its political union with Sweden in 1905.[95]

In the case of the Titlestad men, a striking contrast exists between the missionary Lars Martin's version of the Bambatha rebellion and his settler brother Elias's. In the missionary account we find a critical view of the authorities' devastation of Zulu property and the slaughter of Zulu men as well as compassion for the many widows and fatherless children in the Nkandhla area.[96] He is further impressed by the rebels' 'civilised' behaviour towards the missionaries and the mission stations, an attitude he in fact shares with other NMS missionaries.[97] His brother Elias, on the other hand, in retrospect proudly recounted his duties as sergeant in the Zululand Mounted Rifles and in military intelligence, paving the way for the government's final massacre at Mome.[98] After the Bambatha rebellion, Elias was decorated with the Distinguished Conduct Medal. In the trial of Zulu Prince Dinizulu kaCetshwayo in 1908, he participated as a witness for the prosecution. Interestingly, another Norwegian missionary son, the lawyer R. C. Samuelson, was part of the Prince's defence team.[99]

When the 'issue of race' and 'the race problem' were discussed in Norwegian mission literature, the missionaries tended to present themselves as neutral commentators. The whites' unjust treatments of the blacks – in political, social and economical terms – were frequently referred to.[100] In addition, the official policy of segregation was occasionally criticised. Olav Guttorm Myklebust, who was a missionary in the 1930s, stated that segregation was 'a utopia' and that the black and white races were independent of each other, not least because of the capitalist economy.[101] Yet the missionaries defended white political rule. In 1932, Laurits Aadnesgaard claimed that 'the natives' low level of development' made social equality impossible.[102] Furthermore, Myklebust asserted that the blacks had never asked for 'political and social equality'; indeed, they were not even interested in higher wages. What they asked for, he believed, was 'respect for their human worth and dignity'. In the tense situation between blacks and whites in South Africa, he saw only one possible path for missionaries to follow: 'the path of the Gospel, of love and cooperation'.[103] The missionary should primarily preach the message of 'the Law and Gospel', and thereafter show solidarity with the suppressed blacks. Myklebust admitted that this middle course was controversial – perceived as radical by European settlers and as reactionary by the natives.

According to the NMS's missionary instruction, the missionaries were not allowed to participate in political parties and political activities. This partly explains their opposition to the political activities of Zulu pastors and evangelists, most visibly in the case of Petros Lamula in 1926.[104] Yet the Lutheran theology of 'the Two Realms' also explains their resistance to political actions, as loyalty towards any secular regime was expected by Lutheran church leaders. Against this background, it is interesting that the middle course advocated by the missionaries in South Africa was criticised by the NMS leadership in Norway. The huge social gap between white and black men in South Africa, which was also reflected in the church organisation, in which the black pastors were subordinated to the leadership of the white pastors, worried the mission management in Norway. The missionaries in South Africa were harshly criticised for not treating their Zulu 'brothers' as equals. The Home Board furthermore feared that the missionaries' close relations to the white privileged classes paralysed their ability to make ethical reflections on a Christian foundation. When NMS General Secretary Einar Amdahl visited South Africa in 1929, these issues were thoroughly discussed with the missionaries.[105]

Missionaries' self-understanding as 'neutral men-in-between' was in fact an impossible position. As Norwegian men, they were profiting from the white patriarchal rule of South Africa. Their close family bonds with the white ruling establishment, as well as their broad network among farmers and landholders, businessmen and factory owners, magistrates, and native administrators, made them representative of white hegemonic masculinity, whether they were aware of it or not. Berit Hagen Agøy, who examined the NMS missionaries' attitudes towards the apartheid regime from 1948, finds that albeit the missionaries theologically and ideologically condemned the apartheid ideology, their official protest was ambiguous, as it was not followed by political action.[106] Georg Scriba and Gunnar Lislerud assert that Lutheran missions in general were slow to adapt to the new conditions of twentieth-century South Africa and the challenges of modernisation and urbanisation, and the proletarianism of the black classes. They were furthermore slow to challenge apartheid politics and less prepared than Anglo-American missions to grapple with questions of structural justice and national politics. The Lutherans usually protested against any emphasis on social issues and politics.[107]

Some Lutheran missionaries were nevertheless open to the new idea of 'Social Christianity', which according to Richard Elphick peaked in early twentieth-century pre-apartheid South Africa. Protestant missionaries in alliance with Africans and white liberal Christian settlers crafted a Christian response to the social and cultural crises inflicted on Africans by rural impoverishment, urbanisation and racially discriminatory policies enacted by the all-white parliament.[108] Karl Michael Titlestad, at the missionary conference of 1929, gave a lecture called 'A historical, social and religious analysis of the native South African of today (the Zulu in particular)'.[109] The speech was profound and scholarly in style, with many references to mission histories, ethnographies, books by mission theologians, missionaries and African church leaders, and reports from international and South African church and mission conferences. It started by describing the mentality and religion of 'the Zulus', discussing 'the race issue' and the many conflicts between blacks and whites in South Africa. Yet what distinguished the speech from ordinary Norwegian Lutheran mission discourse was the many references to influential leaders of the 'Social Christianity' movement in South Africa. In his speech Titlestad also referred to central themes of discussion at the recent International Missionary Council in Jerusalem in 1928.[110] The theme of the Christian religion's relationship with 'Non-Christian systems of thought and life' had obviously fascinated him, as he referred to Christianity as a means to 'fulfil and complete other religions and faiths' without 'destroying' them. Titlestad also emphasised other important themes of discussion at the Jerusalem conference, such as the relationship between older and younger churches and between mission and church. He envisioned a self-critical Norwegian mission in South Africa, a mission willing to examine its own traditional missionary methods while being anxious at the same time to let the representatives of the young Zulu church influence and mark the church's future.

To Karl Michael Titlestad it came as a great disappointment that his lecture met with silence from the other missionaries. In a private letter to Einar Amdahl, who as previously mentioned participated in the missionary conference in 1929, he admitted that no one had commented or responded to his ideas. He feared that his colleagues were all 'untouched' and that his comprehensive preparations had been in vain.[111] Amdahl, however, was impressed by the ideas of the young Titlestad.[112] In the lecture he himself gave at the missionary conference, his many references to the Jerusalem conference (in which he had actually participated) revealed the considerable influence of new trends in international missiology.[113] Amdahl shared Titlestad's desire for radical changes in the relations between mission and church and for radical thinking in terms of missionary methods. He was, however, a lot more sceptical than Titlestad regarding the influence of the Anglo-American 'Social Gospel' movement as well as certain mission theologians' positive approaches towards other religions.[114]

Conclusion

In the 'patchwork quilt of patriarchies' in nineteenth- and twentieth-century south-east Africa, a group of Norwegian Lutheran missionary men arrived. They conducted their profession as missionaries, but they also lived their private lives as civil citizens. In a country that has been characterised as 'a man's world', the missionaries constructed their subjectivities as 'men in the world' but not 'of the world'. By representing what was regarded as an alternative masculinity, they saw themselves as 'neutral men-in-between'. First, they wished to live as 'born again' Christian men among secularised settler men. Second, as Norwegian men they saw themselves as representatives of a neutral, non-imperialistic Norwegian masculinity among imperial masculinities. Third, as missionary men living in the periphery of white settler masculinity, but still profiting from the white patriarchal rule in the colony of Natal and living and working in close proximity to the Zulus, they constructed subjectivities as 'negotiators' in the growing conflicts between the white oppressors and the black oppressed.

The Norwegian missionary men who represented modern ideals of democracy and equality, and also were influenced by the nationalism in their homeland, naturally sympathised with political and national movements aiming to liberate the Zulus from oppressive white rulers. Yet as Lutheran missionaries they could not allow themselves to participate in any political activities; neither could they permit the Zulu pastors to do so. The Norwegian missionaries liked to see themselves as neutral mediators between men of a different class, nation and race. As good Lutheran Christians, they accepted their positions 'in the world' and strove to have good relations with the authorities. But they were not 'of the world', and profane and worldly matters should not be their main focus. Karl Michael Titlestad, encountering the many challenges of a race-segregated society and church in the 1920s, searched for inspiration and ideas among non-Lutheran theologians and church leaders. He asked for radical changes in missionary ideology and methodology as well as for more 'social Christianity'. In his own missionary community, however, he was alone in these attempts, as the majority of the Norwegian missionaries in South Africa continued to stress the Lutheran dogma of the two kingdoms.

The missionaries' self-understanding as neutral men-in-between was in fact an impossible position. As Norwegian men they were profiting from the white patriarchal rule of South Africa. Their close family bonds with the white ruling establishment, as well as their broad network among farmers and landholders, businessmen and factory owners, magistrates, and native administrators, made them representative of white hegemonic masculinity.

Concluding Remarks

Missionary masculinity between self-making and self-denial

Michael S. Kimmel argues that the masculine ideal of the self-made man was born in Western industrialised societies in the early nineteenth century.[1] Men were now free to create their own destinies, to find their own ways and to rise as high as they could. Erik Sidenvall, in a study of Swedish low-class missionaries to China in the late nineteenth century, asks if religious activism in terms of missionary service could in fact be understood as a road to male self-making: these humble missionaries 'made' it in the religious world.[2] The current study of Norwegian Lutheran missionaries to the Zulus supports Sidenvall's assertion. The nineteenth-century missionary masculinity ideals were actually related to modern, middle-class notions of masculinity, particularly the concept of male self-making. The Norwegian missionaries were mostly rural men who lacked resources in terms of class; however, through their missionary education and career, they ended up as respected and championed seniors. Their background was humble, but they possessed other valued masculine qualities. Missions, like all overseas expansions, depended on manpower and on the supply of men of a certain type. To survive in the 'pagan wilderness' and to be able to construct Christian communities on the 'frontiers of civilisation', the missionary men had to be physically strong, tough and robust; they had to be handymen who could manage a variety of crafts; and they had to be self-reliant men who were rich in initiative and energy.

Yet at the same time, the missionaries were Christian men. As pastors they were – to borrow Anna Prestjan's wording – 'the Christian man personified'.[3] The missionaries had been trained in a range of virtues that were regarded as Christian, such as world-denial, self-denial, modesty, patience and calmness. Moreover, the Lutheran theology restricted their engagement to the spiritual realm (i.e. the church) while forbidding them from becoming extensively involved in secular projects. The combination of masculine 'self-making' and Christian 'self-denial' could in fact be challenging for modern men. Towards the end of the nineteenth century, notions of Christian values no longer corresponded with what were regarded as prevailing masculinity ideals. Christian virtues were regarded as sentimental, emotional, weak and passive, making Christian virtues seem feminine and unmanly.

In the mission discourse, however, Christian virtues and modern masculinity ideals were not regarded as incompatible. 'Self-making' and 'self-denial', which at first glance look like opposites, continued to be the core elements of missionary masculinity. Yet every missionary had to strive to find the right balance between the two; consequently, 'self-control' was also needed. Learning to master one's passions and develop a strong and sturdy character was a central idea in modern masculinities, as demonstrated by David Tjeder.[4] Perhaps the difference between the secular man and the Christian man was that, whereas the former strove to achieve control over himself and the world around himself by himself, the latter continued the Christian tradition of daily exercises in self-denial, self-reform and self-control through the help of what was believed to be a divine force outside himself. The missionary pioneer Hans Paludan Smith Schreuder continued to be a missionary hero even after he left the NMS. Physically he was extraordinarily strong; he was described as a man of character and a man of willpower and energy. He was strong and independent, but he was also a man of faith, a man obedient to and dependent on God. This combination of human abilities/ambitions – and subordination to a divine cause, of 'hardness' in human matters and 'softness' in spiritual matters – was central in missionary masculinity.

The missionaries believed in God – a fact so obvious that scholars still tend to overlook it, according to Roald Berg.[5] The famous mission psalm of 1912, *Din Rikssak, Jesus, være skal min største herlighet*, is often described as 'the anthem of the Norwegian mission'.[6] The psalm, which is still used in the twenty-first century, was an obligatory part of the programme at mission-related services, meetings, conferences and camps, especially at farewell and welcome arrangements for missionaries. The title of the song in English means 'the cause of your Kingdom, Jesus, is my greatest glory'. In the text the author expresses gratitude for the divine missionary calling. Although he feels unworthy, the friendship and love of Jesus have empowered him and made him strong, and he is ready to participate in the army of Jesus and serve as a soldier in his realm. The author asks Jesus to provide him with 'the tender mind of a saviour', make him 'strong and warm', teach him 'to carry the sufferings and shame of the world with love' and 'to be patient, strong and faithful until death'. The metaphor of the missionary as a 'tender and loving soldier' may seem contradictory. It refers to values regarded as masculine: being strong, dutiful, persistent and bold. At the same time it refers to the Christian values of love, tenderness, humility and patience. Ideal missionary masculinity contains both 'hard' and 'soft' ideals, as an ideal missionary is both 'strong' and 'warm'. Yet the central point is that both his strength and his love are gifts continuously poured out by God. God both empowers and softens man.

Missionary masculinity between professionalism and privacy

The male NMS missionaries were employees in a private, modern missionary enterprise. They signed a contract, received an annual salary and were obliged to report regularly from their work in the field to the headquarters at home. The male missionary was in this sense a modern, professional breadwinner in an enterprise with global interests. In the missionary family, the husband was the one in the office and the wife was in charge of the domestic tasks in the private sphere. Historians who have studied nineteenth-century missionary families from a gender perspective tend to claim that the ideal of 'separate spheres' that emerged during the Victorian age characterised the cultural values and gendered social organisation of these families. According to the theory of separate spheres, men and women were part of diverse social worlds in which men inhabited the public sphere and women the private sphere. Missionary families were the chief exporters of Western bourgeois family values in a transnational arena, as they advocated these values in the non-Western, 'non-Christian' regions of the world in which they lived and worked.

This study confirms that missionary men and missionary women intended to export Western gendered ideals to the mission field. Mission theories of feminine Christian homemaking and masculine Church self-making systematised against the background of missionary experience and practice while influencing strategy and long-term objectivities, characterised the Norwegian Zulu mission. By looking at the practical family life of the male missionaries, this work has however questioned the validity of the separate sphere theory. It has further questioned the validity of the distinction between public and private spheres in male missionaries' lives.

In the case of the late nineteenth- and early twentieth-century NMS male missionaries, it is in fact impossible to distinguish between their private and professional lives as missionaries. As young men they were like 'sons' adopted into the household community at the mission school in Stavanger, where they were educated, nurtured and shaped as missionary pastors-to-be. Their inner spiritual life and their outward conduct were scrutinised and controlled by teachers, pastors, mission secretaries and lay friends. Like 'spiritual sons' of the Norwegian Lutheran church, they were sent to the mission fields. The NMS preferred their representatives abroad to be married men, and courting, engagement, and marriage were thus regulated and controlled by the mission, which also educated and raised their children. Once the missionaries eventually settled as family men in the mission field, their dwellings and farming fields were the property of the mission. The missionary home consisting of a housefather and a housemother was the starting-point of all missionary activity, and building Christian homes in 'the heathen world' was a prioritised mission strategy. The missionary home had the structure of a pre-industrial household in which family members, relatives, apprentices and servants lived under the same roof, all under the guidance and protection of the housefather. As much farmland belonged to the mission station, and converted indigenous families often settled on 'the mission farm' as tenant farmers, the missionary also played the role of landlord. Finally, as pastor of the congregation, the missionary acted as soul-winner, counsellor and superintendent in religious matters.

To refer to the Lutheran concept of the three hierarchies within a Christian society, the missionary in fact exercised paternal authority as a housefather, secular authority as an employer and landlord, and spiritual authority as a clergy. A male missionary's private and domestic life was therefore integrated into his professional missionary life. In other words, it was expected that the male missionary would dedicate himself 100 per cent, body and soul, to the cause of the mission. He should give all sectors of his life, including the private sector, over to work for the kingdom of God, which was materialised in the organisation of the NMS.

The missionary man was a pre-modern housefather, but simultaneously a modern, professional breadwinner employed in a modern missionary enterprise. His private family life was, on the one hand, regarded as an important tool in the mission work and, on the other hand, belonged to 'the affairs of the World' and should be subordinated to 'the Lord's affairs'. The male missionary was expected to prioritise his tasks as an NMS employee, even if this seriously affected his family. Indeed, in most Western mission organisations, the practice of sending missionary children to boarding schools in the home country, or in the host country, developed. The missions established institutions to function as substitute homes for the missionary children. It is ironic that, in the efforts to export the concept of Western Christian homes to non-Christian areas of the world, the lack of nuclear family life came to characterise the missionaries' own privacy. The missionary wife and husband were regarded as ideal Christian parents, but their own children were sent away as 'orphans of missions' to boarding institutions. Meanwhile, the joint working fellowship between husband and wife often strengthened the emotional bonds between them and their dependence on each other. The 'loss' of their own children could also create strong emotional paternal/maternal relationships between the missionary 'father and mother' and their spiritual 'children' at the mission station or in the congregation.

Missionary masculinity between powerlessness and power

Claes Ekenstam's theoretical model of manliness–unmanliness paves the way for a process-oriented and flexible understanding of masculinity.[7] The model further helps to offer an in-depth understanding of what emotional and personal costs certain masculinity ideals have for individuals and groups of men. Masculine identity, or subjectivity, is a complex concept. David Tjeder points out that the fear of demasculinisation, of stooping to unmanliness, works as an internal guardian against improper behaviour in every single man. Not even the 'manly man' can be sure of his manliness; he continuously has to prove and be confirmed of his value as man.[8] The current study on how missionary masculinity was constructed on homosocial relations among men, as well as individual men, has revealed that much was expected of the missionary man. He should be strong and independent, innovative and persistent, spiritual and warm. He should convert and baptise, construct churches and guide congregations. He should make the mission the highest priority, sacrificing himself and his family to the higher cause of the mission. These high expectations were articulated by the mission management, the mission supporters at home and the missionary community. Moreover, the high expectations were developed within the missionary man himself. This study has revealed that not all men lived up to the standard; they failed and they fell. The personal costs of missionary unmanliness in some cases meant catastrophe and death.

Missionary unmanliness meant powerlessness. Yet, on the other hand, missionary manliness, or proper missionary masculinity, meant powerfulness. The missionary men were originally men of humble social background. Through their engagement in the missionary enterprise they were empowered, moving from being 'nobody' to being 'somebody'. The male self-making spirit of the Norwegian mission movement created missionaries favouring a democratic system that distributed power equally among them. That being so, it is a paradox that missionary masculinity in the NMS, although characterised by internal social equality among men, was simultaneously grounded on the exclusion of others from equal opportunities. In the nineteenth-century NMS, democracy was the privilege of missionary men – not women – exclusively. Moreover, it was the privilege of Norwegian men, as African church personnel (evangelists, teachers, and pastors) were excluded from the mission's decision-making bodies. Not all groups of Norwegian male missionaries possessed the privilege of democratic rights, however. Craftsmen and artisans defined as assistant missionaries were never included in the decision-making community of the missionary conference. Only male missionary pastors were perceived to be real missionaries.

Norwegian missionary masculinity was constructed on both a local and a national level as well as in a transnational, or global, scene. Against the backdrop of African masculinities, settler masculinities and imperial masculinities in south-east African societies, the complexity of Norwegian missionary male subjectivities was further increased. In the pre-colonial period Norwegian missionary men were the subordinates of powerful Zulu kings and chiefs, and feelings of vulnerability and powerlessness were prevalent. As later subordinates of British imperial rule and British-dominated settler rule, they joined other Norwegian expatriate men in their efforts to construct a Norwegian minority settler masculinity in south-east Africa. As Norwegian men, they were nevertheless profiting from the white patriarchal rule of South Africa. Their close family bonds with the white ruling establishment, as well as their broad network among wealthy farmers and landholders, businessmen and factory owners, magistrates and colonial administrators, made them representative of white hegemonic masculinity, whether they were aware of it or not.

Raewyn Connell's model encourages the analysis of the plurality of masculinities in a social group, a society, or even globally; likewise, the hierarchy of masculinities is extremely relevant when missionary masculinity is analysed in a global context.[9] Norwegian missionaries, who landed in Zululand in the 1840s, took part in a transnational gendered missionary project to save and empower detribalised and marginalised African men. In theory and practice, they intended to shape self-making African men just like themselves and establish self-supporting, self-governing and self-propagating churches. In the era of Western colonial conquests of south-east African societies, however, missionary masculinity was also constructed in relation to 'other' African masculinities. In the Norwegian mission discourse, as in most colonial discourses, Zulu masculinity was represented as the opposite of and the counter-type of ideal masculinity. Zulu men were regarded from one perspective as strong, brave and well-gifted men with rich potential. From another perspective, they were regarded as unstable, emotional and childish men who had not yet reached the level of mature manhood and, therefore, were not yet qualified for the responsibilities of church leadership. Paternalistic and racist masculinity discourses justified the reluctance to distribute church power and church influence to a rapidly growing group of male Zulu church personnel. Original ideas of 'Christian brotherhood' between Norwegian and Zulu male pastors were eventually abandoned by the NMS missionaries in south-east Africa. Thus, in the context of late nineteenth- and early twentieth-century South Africa, Norwegian missionary masculinity meant power, not powerlessness.

Appendix: NMS Missionaries in South Africa, 1844–1930

Missionary Pastors

Name	Birth/ death	Period of missionary service in South Africa	Education/profession, missionary service
Berge, Lars	1851–1934	1880–98	Mission school 1874–79. Ordained in 1880. Stationed at Nhlazatsche 1880–84, 1888–90, Eshowe 1885–87, Imfule 1893–95, Umphumulo 1895–98.
Borgen, Martin Fredrik Nikolai (son of missionary Martinius Borgen)	1874–1953	1910–46	Studied theology at Eshowe. Ordained in 1910. Stationed at Umbonambi 1911–13, Empangeni 1913–16, Nhlazatsche 1916–25, Isinyambusi 1928–46.
Borgen, Martinius	1834–1915	1885–1901	Mission school 1859–64. Ordained in 1864. NMS missionary in Madagascar 1867–82. Stationed at Umphumulo 1885–91, Nhlazatsche 1891–99, Mahlabatini 1899–1901.
Bovim, Gunerius	1868–1945	1902–22	Cand. theol. 1901, University of Oslo. Ordained in 1902. Stationed at Umphumulo 1902–03, Eotimati 1903–04, Umbonambi 1904–09, Isinyambusi 1909–15, Durban 1915–22.
Braatvedt, Nils Torbjørnsen	1847–1943	1880–1916	Teacher seminary 1866. Mission school 1874–79. Ordained in 1880. Stationed at Umphumulo 1880–87, Mahlabatini 1887–91, Ekombe 1891–95, Ungoye 1895–1916.

Continued

Name	Birth/ death	Period of missionary service in South Africa	Education/profession, missionary service
Dahle, Markus	1838–1915	1865–1908	Mission school 1859–64. Ordained in 1864. Stationed at Imfule 1865–74, Empangeni 1874–85, Isinyambusi 1886–1908.
Dahle, Peder Joakim Blessing (son of missionary Markus Dahle)	1877–1948	1908–22	Cand. theol. 1903, University of Oslo. Ordained in 1904. Stationed at Eotimati 1908–10, Umphumulo 1911–13, Eshowe 1913–15, Kangelani 1915–22.
Dahle, Sivert (son of missionary Markus Dahle)	1873–1944	1897–1956	Mission school 1892–96. Ordained in 1897. Stationed at Imfule 1898–1902, Mahlabatini 1902–09, Eotimati 1911–23, Umphumulo 1923–29, 1930–38, Durban 1938–44.
Eriksen, Sven	1854–1925	1880–1921	Mission school 1874–79. Ordained in 1880. Stationed at Umbonambi 1880–92, 1894–1902, Eotimati 1902–03, Durban 1903–21.
Follesøe, Nils Martin Severin Jakobsen	1894–1963	1922–61	Mission school 1915–21. Ordained in 1921. Stationed at Kangelani 1923–26, Eotimati 1926–29, Umphumulo 1929–30, Ungoye 1932–61.
Frøise, Yngvar	1901–74	1926–68	Mission school 1921–24. Ordained in 1924. Stationed at Isinyambusi 1927, Imfule 1927–30, Ungoye 1930–32, Ekombe 1932–43, Empangeni 1936–51, Eshowe 1951–63.
Fykse, Sjur Sjursen	1895–1966	1934–38	Mission school 1915–21. Ordained in 1921. NMS missionary in Madagascar 1922–33. Stationed at Eshowe 1934–37, Kangelani 1937–38.
Gundersen, Gundvall	1835–1902	1865–1902	Mission school 1859–64. Ordained in 1864. Stationed at Entumeni 1865–68, Mahlabatini 1868–69, Umbonambi 1869–73, Entumeni 1873, Eshowe 1873–74, Mahlabatini 1874–78, Ungoye 1881–93, Eshowe 1893–98, 1900–02, Durban 1902.

Continued

Name	Birth/ death	Period of missionary service in South Africa	Education/profession, missionary service
Haldorsen, Martinius Caspari	1902–?	1928–1969	Mission school 1921–27. Ordained in 1927. Stationed at Eshowe 1928–30, Empangeni/Umbonambi 1930–36, Kangelani 1938–42, Mahlabatini 1942–49, 1951–53, Imfule 1953–60, Eshowe 1960–69.
Ingebrektsen, Edward Michael (son of missionary Erik Ingebrektsen)	1866–1956	1893–1905	Cand. theol. 1891, University of Oslo. Ordained in 1892. Stationed at Umphumulo 1893–1905.
Kielland, Jan Olaus	1833–98	1863–1874	Cand. theol. 1858, University of Oslo. Ordained in 1862. Stationed at Empangeni 1863–74.
Kjelvei, Johan	1879–1962	1909–44	Mission school 1903–08. Ordained in 1908. Stationed at Eotimati 1910–11, Imfule 1911–13, Mahlabatini 1913–21, 1922–33, Imfule 1930–31, Eotimati 1934–38, Eshowe 1938–44.
Larsen, Lars	1812–90	1849–90	Mission school 1843–48. Ordained in 1860. Stationed at Uitkomst 1849–51, Umphumulo 1851–60, Entumeni 1860–62, Empangeni 1862–63, Nhlazatsche 1863–90.
Leisegang, Hans Christian Martin Gottfried	1838–1914	1865–1911	Mission school 1859–64. Ordained in 1864. Stationed at Mahlabatini 1865–73, Umphumulo 1873–74, 1875–95, 1899–1911.
Leisegang, Hans Kristian (son of missionary Hans Chr. Leisegang)	1876–1947	1902–20	Cand. theol. 1900, University of Oslo. Ordained in 1902. Stationed at Umbonambi 1902–04, Umphumulo 1904–20.
Leisegang, Theodor Martin (son of missionary Hans Chr. Leisegang)	1882–1948	1910–48	Studied theology at Eshowe 1908–10. Ordained in 1910. Stationed at Mahlabatini 1910–12, 1934–37, Umphumulo 1912–25, 1930–34, 1938–48, Empangeni 1926–30.

Continued

Name	Birth/ death	Period of missionary service in South Africa	Education/profession, missionary service
Nerø, Johannes Charles	1886–1963	1915–46	Mission school 1909–14. Ordained in 1915. Stationed at Umbonambi 1915–16, Empangeni 1916–25, Kangelani 1926–36, 1945–46, Mahlabatini 1939–41.
Nilsen, Petter Gottfred	1836–1906	1865–1906	Mission school 1859–64. Ordained in 1880. Stationed at Empangeni 1865–69, Nhlazatsche 1869–72, Entumeni 1872–74, Eshowe 1874–77, Umphumulo 1879–86, Eotimati 1886–89, 1891–1902, 1904–06.
Norgaard, Ole Zephanias	1855–1929	1880–99 (Independent missionary 1902–09. In Church of Norway Mission 1909–21)	Mission school 1874–1879. Ordained in 1880. Stationed at Eshowe 1880–86, Empangeni 1886–99.
Oftebro, Ommund Christiansen	1820–193	1849–93	Mission school 1843–48. Ordained in 1860. Stationed at Umphumulo 1850–54, Empangeni 1854–61, Eshowe 1861–93.
Rødseth, Peder Aage	1869–1945	1893–1939	Mission school 1887–92. Ordained in 1892. Stationed at Patane 1894–98, Eshowe 1898–1905, 1907–20, 1926–30, 1933–38, Oscarsberg 1920–24.
Schreuder, Hans Paludan Smith	1817–82	1844–73 Left the NMS and established Church of Norway Mission in 1873.	Cand. theol. 1841, University of Oslo. Ordained in 1843. Natal 1844–49. Stationed at Uitkomst 1849, Umphumulo 1850, Empangeni 1851–52, Entumeni 1852–73, Untunjambili 1873–82.
Solberg, Sigurd Tesli	1879–1962	1910–50	Mission school 1903–08. Ordained in 1908. NMS missionary in Madagascar 1908–10. Stationed at Umphumulo 1910–12, Eshowe 1912–13, 1929–39, Imfule 1913–20, Isinyambusi 1920–23, Ungoye 1946–49.

Continued

Name	Birth/ death	Period of missionary service in South Africa	Education/profession, missionary service
Stavem, Ole Olsen	1841–1932	1869–1912	Printer. Mission school 1864–69. Ordained in 1869. Stationed at Entumeni 1869–71, Kwahlabisa 1871–72, Umbonambi 1872–82, Eshowe 1882–90, 1905–12, Durban 1890–1902.
Steenberg, Ole Sigbjørnsen	1834–1906	1865–1906	Mission school 1859–64. Ordained in 1880. Stationed at Umphumulo 1865–80, Imfule 1880–91, 1902–06, Mahlabatini 1891–1900.
Strømme, Peter Andreas Robertsen	1874–1961	1903–35	Educated a deacon 1897. Mission school 1897–1902. Ordained in 1903. Stationed at Ekombe 1904–06, 1920–26, Empangeni 1906–13, Isinyambusi 1915–20, Nhlazatsche 1928–32, Eotimati 1932–35.
Titlestad, Karl Larsen	1832–1924	1865–91	Mission school 1859–64. Ordained in 1864. Stationed at Nhlazatsche 1865–69, Ekutembeni 1869–70, Umzinyathi 1870–79, Ekombe 1880–91.
Titlestad, Karl Michael (son of missionary Lars Martin Titlestad)	1898–1930	1924–30	Cand. theol. 1923, School of Theology in Oslo. Ordained in 1923. Stationed at Umphumulo 1925–30.
Titlestad, Lars Martin (son of missionary Karl L. Titlestad)	1867–1941	1893–1938	Mission school 1887–92. Ordained in 1892. Stationed at Ungoye 1893–95, Ekombe 1895–1904, 1906–20, Eshowe 1920–25, Durban 1827–38.
Tvedt, John Mikal	1871–1910	1897–1909	Teacher seminary 1891. Mission school 1892–96. Ordained in 1897. Stationed at Durban/Eshowe 1897–99, Empangeni 1899–1905, Eshowe 1905–06, Eotimati 1906–08.
Udland, Tobias Finkelsen	1819–75	1849–75	Hatter. Mission school 1843–48. Ordained in 1860. Stationed at Uitkomst 1849, Umphumulo 1850, 1855–75, Empangeni 1851–55.

Continued

Name	Birth/ death	Period of missionary service in South Africa	Education/profession, missionary service
Wettergren, Paul Peter	1835–89	1861–70	Cand. theol. 1860, University of Oslo. Ordained in 1861. Stationed at Nhlazatsche 1862–63, Mahlabatini 1863–68, Entumeni 1868–70.
Aadnesgaard, Laurits O. (brother of missionary O. Aadnesgaard)	1882–1957	1915–52	Carpenter. Mission school 1909–14. Ordained in 1915. Stationed at Ekombe 1915–18, 1926–32, 1934–52, Umbonambi 1919–21, Imfule 1921–25, Eshowe 1925–28.
Aadnesgaard, Otto Alfred (brother of missionary L. Aadnesgaard)	1876–1956	1909–47	Carpenter. Mission school 1903–08. Ordained in 1908. Stationed at Nhlazatsche 1909–16, Ungoye 1916–19, 1921–30, Eshowe 1931–34, Imfule 1934–47.

Medical Missionary

Name	Birth/ death	Period of missionary service in South Africa	Education/profession, missionary service
Oftebro, Christian	1842–88	1865–68 1876–88	Assistant missionary at Eshowe 1865–68. Mission school 1868–73. Medical education in Edinburgh 1873–76. Stationed at Eshowe 1876–77, Mahabatini 1877–79, 1881–84, Eshowe 1884–88.

Assistant Missionaries

Name	Birth/ death	Period of missionary service in South Africa	Education/profession, missionary service
Borgen, Thomas Conrad Hirsch (son of missionary Martinius Borgen)	1872–?	1893–95	Teacher at the NMS industrial school at Eshowe. Settler in Zululand.
Carlsen, Georg Fredrik	1834–?	1860–68	Mason. Stationed at Mahlabatini 1860–68. Colonist at Eshowe 1868–71. Entered an Anglican Mission in 1871.
Gjerager, Nils Davidsen	1854–1935	1880–89	Carpenter. Teacher at the NMS industrial school at Eshowe 1888–89.
Ingebrektsen, Erik Robert	1828–1912	1860–71	Carpenter. Stationed at Empangeni 1860–61, Eshowe 1861–63, Nhlazatsche 1863–65, Imfule 1865–68, Entumeni 1868–71. Farmer in Natal from 1871.
Kyllingstad, Johannes Larsen	1829–1890	1863–78	Teacher seminary 1852. Stationed at Entumeni/Eshowe 1863–74, Imfule 1874–78. Emigrated to the United States in 1881 where he had a career as Lutheran pastor and teacher in theology.
Loftheim, Tallak	?	1889–94	Teacher at the NMS industrial school at Eshowe. Settler in Zululand.
Meberg, David Johannes	1865–?	1888–93	Mason and carpenter. Teacher at the NMS industrial school at Eshowe.
Nilsen, Daniel	1928–?	1860–67	Carpenter. Stationed at Entumeni 1860–62, Empangeni 1862–67. Farmer in Natal from 1867.
Olsen, Johan	1826–?	1854–62	Carpenter. Stationed at Umphumulo 1854–55, 1858–62, Entumeni 1855–58, Nhlazatsche 1862.

Continued

Name	Birth/ death	Period of missionary service in South Africa	Education/profession, missionary service
Samuelsen, Siver Marthin	1828–1916	1854–55 1863	Carpenter. Stationed at Entumeni/Empangeni 1854–55. Entered an Anglican Mission in 1857, was ordained as a deacon in 1861 and a priest in 1871.
Skaar, Knud Ellingsen	1837–?	1869–1878	Mission school 1864–68. Stationed at Mahlabatini 1869–77, Imfule 1877–78. Emigrated to the United States in 1878.
Steenberg, Ole Gabriel (son of missionary Ole S. Steenberg)	1874–?	1895	Mason. Teacher at the NMS industrial school at Eshowe.
Thommesen, E.E.	1819–?	1844–1847	Veterinarian. Natal 1844–47.
Thorsen, Thor Christian	1833–1912	1860–1865 1875	Machinist. Stationed at Entumeni/Mahlabatini 1860–65. Colonist in Durban from 1875.
Tjomsland, Ole Olsen	1836–1905	1859–72	Carpenter. Mission school 1864–68. Stationed at Entumeni 1859–64, 1869–72. Emigrated to the United States were he became an ordained pastor in the Lutheran Augustana-Synod.
Tønnesen, Arnt	1827–?	1854–57	Carpenter and teacher. Stationed Entumeni. Entered an Anglican Mission in 1857.

Missionary Wives

Name	Birth/ death	Period of missionary service in South Africa	Education/profession, missionary service
Berge, Louise Amalie Lunøe	1856–1946	1882–98	Stationed at Inhlazatshe 1882–84, 1888–90, Eshowe 1885–87, Imfule 1893–95, Umphumulo 1895–98.

Continued

Name	Birth/ death	Period of missionary service in South Africa	Education/profession, missionary service
Borgen, Laura Norgaard (daughter of missionary Ole Norgaard)	1887–1966	1911–46	Stationed at Umbonambi 1911–13, Empangeni 1913–16, Nhlazatsche 1916–25, Isinyambusi 1928–46.
Borgen, Martha Nikoline Hirsch	1843–1918	1885–1901	Governess. The first female missionary worker in the NMS, recruited in 1870. In NMS-service in Madagascar 1870–82. Stationed at Umphumulo 1885–91, Nhlazatsche 1891–99, Mahlabatini 1899–1901.
Bovim, Anna Sofie Gohn	1868–1928	1902–22	Stationed at Umphumulo 1902–03, Eotimati 1903–04, Umbonambi 1904–09, Isinyambusi 1909–15, Durban 1915–22.
Braatvedt, Severine Lisabeth Pedersdatter	1847–1929	1880–1916	Stationed at Umphumulo 1880–87, Mahlabatini 1887–91, Ekombe 1891–95, Ungoye 1895–1916.
Carlsen, Johanne Olsdatter Fedt	1832–?	1860–71	Midwife. Stationed at Mahlabatini 1860–68, Eshowe 1868–71.
Dahle, Anna Elisabeth Ekstrøm	1873–1970	1900–44	Teacher. Stationed at Mahlabatini 1900–09, Eotimati 1911–23, Umphumulo 1923–29, 1903–38, Durban 1938–44.
Dahle, Annie Marie Hagemann	1894–?	1917–22	Stationed at Kangelani 1917–22.
Dahle, Bertha Sivertsen	1834–1910	1867–1908	Stationed at Imfule 1867–74, Empangeni 1874–85, Isinyambusi 1886–1908.
Eriksen, Inga Karoline Bertelsen	1857–1940	1882–1925	Stationed at Umbonambi 1882–92, 1894–1902, Eotimati 1902–03, Durban 1903–25.
Follesøe, Emma Racine Eriksen	1893–1959	1922–59	Women's mission school 1921. Stationed at Kangelani 1923–26, Eotimati 1926–29, Umphumulo 1929–30, Ungoye 1932–59.

Continued

Name	Birth/ death	Period of missionary service in South Africa	Education/profession, missionary service
Frøise, Gunvor Margareta Dahle (daughter of missionary Sivert Dahle)	1910–?	1930–?	Women's mission school 1929. Stationed at Ungoye 1930–32, Ekombe 1932–43, Empangeni 1936–51, Eshowe 1951–63.
Fykse, Anna Elida Ulltveit-Moe	1890–?	1922–29 1934–38	Nurse. Established and managed Ekombe mission hospital 1922–29. Married to NMS-missionary in Madagascar Sjur Sjursen Fykse in 1930. After three years of service in Madagascar transferred to South Africa in 1934 and stationed at Eshowe 1834–37 and Kangelani 1837–38.
Gjerager, Gudveig Josefsdatter Bjørgo	1848–1939	1876–89	Female missionary worker in Church of Norway Mission by Schreuder at Untunjambili 1876–80 and Umphumulo 1880–83. Stationed at Eshowe 1883–89 after marrying NMS assistant missionary Nils D. Gjerager.
Gundersen, Joachime Blessing	1832–76	1866–76	Stationed at Entumeni 1866–68, Mahlabatini 1868–69, 1874–76, Umbonambi 1869–73, Eshowe 1873–74.
Gundersen, Marthe Haaland	1830–1922	1877–1902	Stationed at Mahlabatini 1877–78, Ungoye 1881–93, Eshowe 1893–98, 1900–02, Durban 1902.
Haldorsen, Gudrun Heng	1902–?	1929–69	Nurse. Stationed at Eshowe 1929–30, Empangeni/ Umbonambi 1930–36, Kangelani 1938–42, Mahlabatini 1942–49, 1951–53, Imfule 1953–60, Eshowe 1960–69.
Ingebrektsen, Anna Cathrine Elye	1823–92	1860–71	Housekeeper in Schreuder's house at Entumeni 1860–61. Stationed at Empangeni 1861–61, Eshowe 1861–63, Nhlazatsche 1863–65, Imfule 1865–68, Entumeni 1868–71.

Continued

Name	Birth/ death	Period of missionary service in South Africa	Education/profession, missionary service
Ingebrektsen, Laura Aleksandra Jenssen	1868–?	1893–1904	Stationed at Umphumulo 1893–1904.
Kielland, Anna Olsen Aarre	1842–1913	1863–74	Stationed at Empangeni 1863–74.
Kjelvei, Marie Espedal	1883–1971	1910–44	Stationed at Eotimati 1910–11, Imfule 1911–13, 1930–31, Mahlabatini 1913–21, 1922–33, Eotimati 1934–38, Eshowe 1938–44.
Kyllingstad, Anne Marthea Hansen	1839–1925	1863–79	Stationed at Entumeni/Eshowe 1863–74, Imfule 1874–79.
Larsen, Marthe Thomsen	1809–90	1849–90	Teacher. Stationed at Uitkomst 1849–51, Umphumulo 1851–60, Entumeni 1860–62, Empangeni 1862–63, Nhlazatsche 1863–90.
Leisegang, Agnethe Torvalla Forseth	1851–1933	1875–1911	Stationed at Umphumulo 1875–95, 1904–11.
Leisegang, Kirsten Theresia Eriksen (daughter of missionary Sven Eriksen)	1889–1976	1911–48	Stationed at Mahlabatini 1911–12, 1934–37, Umphumulo 1912–25, 1930–34, 1938–48, Empangeni 1926–30.
Leisegang, Kristiane Marie Lieungh	1879–1950	1902–20	Stationed at Umbonambi 1902–04, Umphumulo 1904–08, 1911–20.
Loftheim, Helene	?	1889–94	Stationed at Eshowe 1889–94.
Meberg, Mathilde Sophie Berntsdatter Frøyland	1868–?	1888–93	Stationed at Eshowe 1888–93.
Nerø, Gustava Elise Pauline Kvalsvik	1883–1961	1916–46	Nurse. Stationed at Umbonambi 1915–16, Empangeni 1916–25, Kangelani 1926–36, 1945–46, Mahlabatini 1939–41.
Nilsen, Caroline Paulsen	1835–?	1860–67	Stationed at Entumeni 1860–62, Empangeni 1862–67.

Continued

Name	Birth/ death	Period of missionary service in South Africa	Education/profession, missionary service
Nilsen, Marthe Reime	1843–1927	1867–1906	Stationed at Empangeni 1867–69, Nhlazatsche 1869–72, Entumeni 1872–74, Eshowe 1874–77, Umphumulo 1879–86, Eotimati 1886–89, 1891–1902, 1904–06.
Norgaard, Laura Sofie Aas	1859–1932	1882–99	Stationed at Eshowe 1880–86, Empangeni 1886–99.
Oftebro, Guri Hogstad	1816–1899	1853–93	Stationed at Umphumulo 1853–54, Empangeni 1854–61, Eshowe 1861–93.
Oftebro, Johanne Guri Mathea Oftebro (daughter of missionary Ommund Oftebro)	1855–1917	1881–88	Stationed at Mahlabatini 1881–84, Eshowe 1884–88.
Olsen, Elise Antinsdatter	?	1854–1862	Stationed at Umphumulo 1854–55, 1858–62, Entumeni 1855–58, Nhlazatsche 1862.
Rødseth, Marit Sødahl	1885–?	1915–39	Nurse. Women's mission school 1912–13. In NMS-service in Madagascar 1914. Transferred to South Africa in 1915 due to medical reasons. At the girls' home at Eshowe 1917–18. Married to missionary Peder Aa. Rødseth in 1918. Stationed at Eshowe 1918–20, 1926–30, 1933–38, Oscarsberg 1920–24.
Rødseth, Ragnhild Hærem	1872–1917	1894–1917	Stationed at Patane 1894–98, Eshowe 1898–1905, 1907–17.
Samuelsen, Thorine Olsdatter	?	1854–55	Stationed at Entumeni/ Empangeni 1854–55.
Schreuder, Jakobine Emilie Adelheid	1814–1878	1858–1878	Teacher. Stationed at Entumeni 1858–73, Untunjambili 1873–78.

Continued

Name	Birth/ death	Period of missionary service in South Africa	Education/profession, missionary service
Schreuder, Johanne Margrethe Vedeler	1835–98	1866–95	Teacher. Came to South Africa to assist in Hans P. S. Schreuder's house at Entumeni. Married to Schreuder in 1879. Stationed at Untunjambili 1873–95.
Skaar, Marie Hægge	?	1871–78	Stationed at Mahlabatini 1871–77, Imfule 1877–78.
Solberg, Edle Landmark	1881–1970	1912–50	Stationed at Eshowe 1912–13, 1929–39, Imfule 1913–20, Isinyambusi 1920–23, Ungoye 1946–49.
Stavem, Tea Ditmarine Dreyer	1842–1919	1871–1912	Stationed at Kwahlabisa 1871–72, Umbonambi 1872–82, Eshowe 1882–90, 1905–12, Durban 1890–1902.
Steenberg, Birgitte Marie Abrahamsen	1834–98	1867–98	Stationed at Umphumulo 1867–80, Imfule 1880–91, Mahlabatini 1891–98.
Strømme, Kirsten Raaen	1874–1932	1905–32	Stationed at Ekombe 1905–06, 1920–26, Empangeni 1906–13, Isinyambusi 1915–20, Nhlazatsche 1928–32.
Titlestad, Karen Ellingsdatter Haaland	1834–1907	1865–91	Stationed at Nhlazatsche 1865–69, Ekutembeni 1869–70, Umzinyathi 1870–79, Ekombe 1880–91.
Titlestad, Margaretha Thompsen	1865–1953	1894–1938	Stationed at Ungoye 1894–95, Ekombe 1895–1904, 1906–1920, Eshowe 1920–25, Durban 1827–38.
Titlestad, Signe Kristine Brekke	1896–?	1924–30	Women's mission school 1922–24. Stationed at Umphumulo 1925–1930.
Tjomsland, Anna Margrete Bergstrøm	?	1859–64 1869–72	Stationed at Entumeni 1859–64, 1869–72.

Continued

Name	Birth/death	Period of missionary service in South Africa	Education/profession, missionary service
Tvedt, Dorthea Emilie Nerø	1882–1969	1903–46	Stationed at Empangeni 1903–05, Eshowe 1905–06, Eotimati 1906–08. After the death of her husband in 1910 employed by the NMS as a female missionary worker. Managed the girls' home at Eshowe 1913–21, 1923–32; the mission work among women in Kangelani 1934–35; the home for missionary children in Durban 1935–46.
Udland, Guri Messing	1818–1888	1853–88	Stationed at Empangeni 1853–55, Umphumulo 1855–75.
Wettergren, Wenche von der Lippe Knudsen	1835–68	1865–68	Stationed at Mahlabatini 1865–68.
Aadnesgaard, Anna Helene Grefstad	1879–1952	1910–47	Midwife. Stationed at Nhlazatsche 1910–16, Ungoye 1916–19, 1921–30, Eshowe 1931–34, Imfule 1934–47.
Aadnesgaard, Jenny Anette Amalie Nuland Grefstad	1885–1973	1920–52	Stationed at Umbonambi 1920–21, Imfule 1921–25, Eshowe 1925–28, Ekombe 1926–32, 1934–52.

Female Missionary Workers

Name	Birth/death	Period of missionary service in South Africa	Education/profession, missionary service
Andresen, Ragna Kristine	1888–?	1911–1919	Housekeeper at the home for missionary children in Durban 1911–19.

Continued

Name	Birth/ death	Period of missionary service in South Africa	Education/profession, missionary service
Bertelsen, Ellen Sofie Olsen	1882–1934	1883–86	Deaconess. Married to NMS missionary in Madagascar, Elling Andreas Bertelsen, who died in 1883. Served as a female missionary worker in South Africa until she married missionary and widower Reinert Larsen and returned to Madagascar in 1886.
Engh, Martine	1841–1918	1885–87	Assistant at the school for missionary children at Umphumulo. Married to Thor Thorsen (farmer, previous assistant missionary) in 1887.
Fergstad, Inga	1855–1911	1888–1911	Teacher at the school for missionary children at Umphumulo 1888–91, matron at the same school 1891–96. Matron at the home for missionary children in Durban 1901–11.
Gilje, Bertha	1889–?	1925–62	Teacher. Women's mission school 1922–24. Teacher and matron at the girls' division of Umphumulo teachers' training college 1925–44. Teacher at KwaMondi bible school 1948–56. Served at Ekombe mission hospital 1958–62.
Grung, Jenny Marie	1856–93	1888–90	Housekeeper at the school for missionary children at Umpumulo. Married to Sivert Olsen (merchant) in Natal 1890.
Jorddal, Ingeborg Ellingsdatter	1845–1941	1881–86	Deaconess and midwife. Served in the missionary families. Married to Hans Olsen (farmer) in Natal 1886.
Kahrs, Elsebeth	1841–1908	1880–84	Teacher at the school for missionary children at Umphumulo. Married to Nils Nilsen (maritime trader) in Durban 1885.
Knudsen, Berthe Christine	1858–1944	1885–1911 1919–23	Housekeeper at the school for missionary children at Umphumulo 1885–97 and at the home for missionary children in Durban 1898–1911. Managed a needlework school at Ungoye mission station 1919–21; the girl's home at Eshowe 1922–23.

Continued

Name	Birth/ death	Period of missionary service in South Africa	Education/profession, missionary service
Kure, Oline Elise Stenersen	1881–1935	1916–19 1926–35	Midwife. Matron at the home for missionary children in Durban 1916–19, 1926–35.
Kyvik, Andrea Sofie Paust	1868–1925-	1904–23	Teacher. Women's mission school 1903–04. Established and managed the girls' home at Eshowe 1905–13. Matron at the girls' department of Umphumulo teachers' training college 1915–16, 1917–18. Managed Ungoye mission station 1919–21; the girls' industrial school at Eshowe 1922–23.
Larsen, Anna Emilie	1887–1967	1923–47	Teacher. Women's mission school 1922. Managed the girl's industrial school at Eshowe 1924–1941; the girls' home at Eshowe 1941–47.
Magnussen, Borghild Nora Betzy	1899–?	1929–1946	Nurse and midwife. Women's mission school 1927. Ekombe mission hospital 1929–35, 1939–40. Umphumulo mission hospital 1935–36, 1940–46.
Nærø, Bertha	1890–?	1906–30	Teacher (South African certificate). The mission school at Eotimati mission station 1906–08; Umphumulo teachers' training college 1910–13. Served at Ekombe mission hospital 1926–30.
Oftebro, Berte Marie Tobiasdatter	1855–99	1882–90	Teacher. At the mission school at Eshowe mission station and the school for missionary children. Married to Gustav Hojem (carpenter) in 1890. Established "Hojem's Foundation" to support industrious and talented Zulu girls.
Olsen, Elvine	1872–1967	1911–16	Teacher. Matron at the home for missionary children in Durban 1911–16. Matron at the Women's mission school in Oslo 1921–31.

Continued

Name	Birth/ death	Period of missionary service in South Africa	Education/profession, missionary service
Palm, Martha	1886–1965	1920–47	Nurse. Housekeeper at the home for missionary children in Durban 1920–25. Established and managed Nkonjeni mission hospital at Mahlabatini 1925–1929, 1930–38, 1939–47.
Pedersen, Gunhild	1866–1927	1890–99	Midwife serving in the missionary families and at Eshowe mission station 1890–99. Married to Martin Oftebro (farmer and magistrate) in 1899.
Samuelsen, Else Salmine	1870–1940	1893–1900	Teacher at the school for missionary children at Umphumulo 1893–97 and at the home for missionary children in Durban 1898–1900. Married to Petro Bøe (photographer) in Durban 1900.
Skavang, Margarethe	1882–1944	1920–39	Teacher. Matron at the home for missionary children in Durban 1920–25. Teacher at the girl's industrial school at Eshowe 1925–29, 1931–39.
Svenningsen, Helene	1860–?	1885–87	Teacher at the school for missionary children at Umphumulo. Married to Mr Aswell (plantation owner) in Natal 1887.
Sødahl, Marit	1885–?	1915–1939	Nurse. Women's mission school 1912–13. In NMS-service in Madagascar 1914. Transferred to South Africa in 1915 due to medical reasons. At the girls' home at Eshowe 1917–18. Married to missionary Peder Aa. Rødseth in 1918. Stationed at Eshowe 1918–20, 1926–30, 1933–38, Oscarsberg 1920–24.

Continued

Name	Birth/ death	Period of missionary service in South Africa	Education/profession, missionary service
Tvedt, Dorthea Emilie Nerø	1882–1969	1903–46	Married to NMS-missionary John Mikal Tvedt i 1903 and stationed at Empangeni 1903–05, Eshowe 1905–06, Eotimati 1906–08. After her husband's death in 1910, employed by the NMS as a female missionary worker. Managed the girls' home at Eshowe 1913–21, 1923–32; the mission work among women in Kangelani 1934–35; the home for missionary children in Durban 1935–46.
Ulltveit-Moe, Anna Elida	1890–?	1922–29 1934–38	Nurse. Established and managed Ekombe mission hospital 1922–29. Married to NMS-missionary in Madagascar Sjur Sjursen Fykse in 1930. After three years of service in Madagascar transferred to South Africa in 1934 and stationed at Eshowe 1834–37 and Kangelani 1837–38.
Aagaard, Therese Victoria	1860–1939	(1896–99) 1899–1910	Teacher. Engaged as a private teacher for Sven Eriksen's children at Umbonambi 1896–99. Employed by the NMS in 1899. Teacher at the mission school in Eshowe 1899–1909. Manager at Mahlabatini mission station 1909–10. Served in Church of Sweden Mission at Ceza mission station 1910–22.

Notes

1   Introduction: Missionaries and Masculinities

1. A range of terms is used to describe the 'Zulu' people (e.g. amaZulu, isiZulu-speaking Africans, iziZulu speakers and so forth), and there is a disagreement over what defines a Zulu person and Zulu polity. For a broad presentation and discussion of the issue of 'Zulu-ness', see Benedict Carton, John Laband and Jabulani Sithole, eds, *Zulu Identities: Being Zulu, Past and Present* (Scottsville: University of KwaZulu-Natal Press, 2008).

2. The NMS missionaries called the regions they worked in 'mission fields' and their dwellings 'mission stations'. They adopted a terminology already in use by other mission organisations which in turn was borrowed from a military-colonial context. See Karina Hestad Skeie, *Building God's Kingdom in Highland Madagascar: Norwegian Lutheran Missionaries in Vakinankaratra and Betsileo 1866–1903* (dissertation for the degree of Dr Art, University of Oslo, 2005), 98–99.

3. Norman Etherington, *Preachers Peasants and Politics in Southeast Africa, 1835–1880: African Christian Communities in Natal, Pondoland and Zululand* (London: Royal Historical Society, 1978), 24–46.

4. The British Captain Allan Francis Gardiner was, although laic, the first missionary to introduce Christianity to Zululand. The American Board of Commissioners for Foreign Mission established mission stations in Zululand as early as 1836, but by 1840 the missionaries were forced to leave the area. The Anglican missionary Francis Owen was allowed by King Dingane to establish a station close to the royal homestead. He did, however, leave Zululand after four months, shocked by being an eyewitness of the King's murder of Piet Retief and a company of 70 Boers in 1838. See Norman Etherington, 'Kingdoms of This World and the Next: Christian Beginnings among the Zulu and Swazi', in *Christianity in South Africa: A Political, Social and Cultural History*, ed. Richard Elphick and Rodney Davenport (Oxford: James Curry, 1997), 89–106.

5. Jeff Guy, *The Heretic: A Study of the Life of John William Colenso: 1814–1883* (Johannesburg: Ravan Press, 1983).

6. Jeff Guy, *The Destruction of the Zulu Kingdom: The Civil War in Zululand, 1879–1884* (Pietermaritzburg: University of Natal Press, 1994).

7. Endre Sønstabø, *Fortropper for europeisk imperialisme: Norske misjonærer i Zululand 1850–1880* (unpublished MA thesis, University of Trondheim, 1973); Thomas M. Børhaug, *Imperialismens kollaboratører? En analyse av norske misjonærers holdning og rolle under den europeiske etableringsfase i Zululand 1873–1890* (unpublished MA thesis, University of Trondheim, 1976); Per O. Hernæs, *Norsk misjon og sosial endring: Norske misjonærer i Zululand/Natal 1887–1906* (unpublished MA thesis, University of Trondheim, 1978).

8. Vidar Gynnild, *Norske misjonærer på 1800-tallet: Geografisk, sosial og religiøs bakgrunn* (unpublished MA thesis, University of Trondheim, 1981).

9. Jarle Simensen, ed., *Norwegian Missions in African History, Vol. 1: South Africa 1845–1906* (Oslo: Norwegian University Press, 1986).

10. Jarle Simensen, 'Norsk misjonsforskning: Faser i utviklingen av historiske studier', *Norsk tidsskrift for misjonsvitenskap* 61, no. 4 (2007).

11. Torstein Jørgensen, *Contact and Conflict: Norwegian Missionaries, the Zulu Kingdom, and the Gospel: 1850–1873* (Oslo: Solum, 1990).

12. Hanna Mellemsether, *Misjonærer, settlersamfunn og afrikansk opposisjon: Striden om selvstendiggjøring i den norske Zulukirken, Sør-Afrika ca. 1920–1930* (dissertation for the degree of Dr Art, University of Trondheim, 2001).

13. Frederick Hale, *The History of Norwegian Missionaries and Immigrants in South Africa* (doctoral thesis, University of South Africa, 1986).

14. Jørgensen, *Contact and Conflict*, 78.

15. Simensen, *Norwegian Missions in African History*, 15; Roald Berg, 'The missionary impulse in Norwegian history', *Studia Historiae Ecclesiasticae. Journal of the Church History Society of Southern Africa* 36, no. 1 (2010), 1–13.

16. Steven Maughan, '"Mighty England Do Good": The Major English Denominations and Organisation for the Support of Foreign Missions in the Nineteenth Century', in *Missionary Encounters: Sources and Issues*, ed. Robert A. Bickers and Rosemary Seton (Richmond, UK: Curzon Press, 1996), 11–37.

17. Halfdan E. Sommerfelt, *Den Norske Zulumission: Et Tilbageblik paa de første 20 Aar af det Norske Missionsselskabs Virksomhed* (Christiania: Wm. Gram, 1865), 345.

18. Per Hernæs, 'The Zulu Kingdom, Norwegian Missionaries, and British Imperialism, 1845–1879', in *Norwegian Missions in African History, Vol. 1: South Africa 1845–1906*, ed. Jarle Simensen (Oslo: Norwegian University Press, 1986), 117–136.

19. E.g. The Norwegian Mission Covenant (1884); The Norwegian Lutheran Federation for Mission in China (1891).

20. Hilde Nielssen, Inger Marie Okkenhaug, and Karina Hestad Skeie, 'Introduction', in *Protestant Missions and Local Encounters in the Nineteenth and Twentieth Centuries: Unto the Ends of the World*, ed. Hilde Nielssen, Inger Marie Okkenhaug and Karina Hestad Skeie (Leiden/Boston: Brill, 2011), 1–22.

21. Some examples: Jean Comaroff and John Comaroff, *Of Revelation and Revolution: The Dialectics of Modernity on a South African Frontier* (Chicago: University of Chicago Press, 1997); Ann Laura Stoler, *Carnal Knowledge and Imperial Power: Race and the Intimate Colonial Rule* (Berkeley, CA: University of California Press, 2002); Fredrick Cooper, *Colonialism in Question: Theory, Knowledge, History* (Berkeley, CA: University of California Press, 2005); Esme Cleall, *Missionary Discourses of Difference: Negotiating Otherness in the British Empire, 1840–1900* (Basingstoke: Palgrave Macmillan, 2012).

22. Torstein Jørgensen, 'De første 100 år', in *I tro og tjeneste: Det norske misjonsselskap 1842–1992*, ed. Torstein Jørgensen and Nils Kristian Høimyr (Stavanger: Misjonshøgskolen, 1992), 69–70.

23. An ethnographic mission exhibition launched by the NMS in 1948 toured Norway from 1948 to 1960 and was visited by 990 000 people, more than a quarter of the population at the time. This event is outside the historical period under investigation, but it nevertheless illustrates the influential position of the mission enterprise in Norwegian society. See Hilde Nielssen, 'From Norway to the Ends of the World: Missionary Contributions to Norwegian

Images of "Self" and "Other"', in *Encountering Foreign Worlds. Experiences at Home and Abroad: Proceedings from the 26th Nordic Congress of Historians*, ed. Christina Folke Ax et al. (Reykjavik: 2007).

24. Patricia Grimshaw and Peter Sherlock, 'Women and Cultural Exchanges', in *Missions and Empire*, ed. Norman Etherington (Oxford: Oxford University Press, 2005), 173–193. In their review of the last decades of research on women and mission, Grimshaw and Sherlock identify three central developments. First, American feminist historians with an interest in women and religion were the first to argue that the missionary enterprise had played a critical role in transforming the whole of society and, further, that women were central historical agents in the mission movement. Seminal works are Jane Hunter, *The Gospel of Gentility: American Women Missionaries in Turn-of-the-century China* (New Haven, CT: Yale University Press, 1984); Patricia R. Hill, *The World Their Household: The American Woman's Foreign Mission Movement and Cultural Transformation, 1870–1920* (Ann Arbor, MI: University of Michigan Press, 1985); Dana L. Robert, *American Women in Mission: A Social History of their Thought and Practice* (Macon, GA: Mercer University Press, 1997). Second, anthropologists and social historians, also in the 1980s, found missions to be interesting bases for observation and ethnographically historical studies of cultural conflicts and gender relations. Influential works in this category are Diane Langmore, *Missionary Lives: Papua, 1874–1914* (Honolulu: University of Hawai'i Press, 1989); Patricia Grimshaw, *Paths of Duty: American Missionary Wives in Nineteenth-Century Hawaii* (Honolulu: University of Hawai'i Press, 1989); Fiona Bowie, Deborah Kirkwood and Shirley Ardner, eds, *Women and Missions: Past and Present: Anthropological and Historical Perceptions* (Oxford: Berg, 1993). Third, since the late 1980s feminist scholars have responded to post-colonial critiques questioning the role of white women as agents of mission enterprises, and mission archives have been used to explore the relation between gender, race and empire. The influence of post-colonial studies can be seen in a number of recent works on women and mission: Antoinette Burton, *Burdens of History: British Feminists, Indian women, and Imperial Culture, 1865–1915* (Chapel Hill, NC: University of North Carolina Press, 1994); Jayawardena Kumari, *The White Woman's Other Burden: Western Women and South Asia during British Colonial Rule* (New York/London: Routledge, 1995); Mary Taylor Huber and Nancy Lutkehaus, *Gendered Missions: Women and Men in Missionary Discourse and Practice* (Ann Arbor, MI: University of Michigan Press, 1999); Susan Thorne, *Congregational Missions and the Making of an Imperial Culture in Nineteenth-Century England* (Stanford, CA: Stanford University Press, 1999); Myra Rutherdale, *Women and the White Man's God: Gender and Race in the Canadian Mission Field* (Vancouver: UBC Press, 2002).

25. Kristin Fjelde Tjelle, *'Kvinder hjælper Kvinder': Misjonskvinneforeningsbevegelsen i Norge 1860–1910* (unpublished MA thesis, University of Oslo, 1990).

26. Kristin Norseth, *'... at sætte sig imod vilde være som at stoppe Elven'* (unpublished MA thesis, Norwegian School of Theology, 1997); Kristin Norseth, *'La os bryte over tvert med vor stumhet!': Kvinners vei til myndighet i de kristelige organisasjonene 1842–1912* (dissertation for the degree of Dr Theol., Norwegian School of Theology, 2007).

27. Line Nyhagen Predelli, *Issues of Gender, Race and Class in the Norwegian Missionary Society in Nineteenth Century Norway and Madagascar* (Lewiston, NY: Edwin Mellen Press, 2003).

28. Inger Marie Okkenhaug, *The Quality of Heroic Living, of High Endeavour and Adventure: Anglican Mission, Women and Education in Palestine, 1888–1948* (Leiden: Brill, 2002); Inger Marie Okkenhaug, 'Herren har givet mig et rigt virkefelt: Kall, religion og arbeid blant armenere i det osmanske riket', *Historisk tidsskrift* 88, no. 1 (2009); Inger Marie Okkenhaug, 'Refugees, Relief and Restoration of a Nation: Norwegian Mission in the Armenian Republic, 1922–1925', in *Protestant Missions and Local Encounters in the Nineteenth and Twentieth Centuries: Unto the Ends of the World*, ed. Hilde Nielssen, Inger Marie Okkenhaug and Karina Hestad Skeie (Leiden/Boston: Brill, 2011). Okkenhaug was also the editor of a 2003 collection of essays discussing women and mission in a Nordic context; see Inger Marie Okkenhaug, *Gender, Race and Religion: Nordic Missions 1860–1940* (Uppsala: Swedish Institute of Missionary Research, 2003).

29. Hanna Mellemsether, *Kvinne i to verdener: En kulturhistorisk analyse av afrikamisjonæren Martha Sannes liv i perioden 1884–1901* (Trondheim: Senter for kvinneforsknings skriftserie, 1994).

30. Rannveig Naustvoll, *Kvinner i misjonen: Kvinneliv og hverdagsliv på de norske misjonsstasjonene i Natal og Zululand 1900–1925* (unpublished MA thesis, University of Trondheim, 1998).

31. Carol Summers, 'Mission Boys, Civilized Men, and Marriage: Educated African Men in the Missions of Southern Rhodesia, 1920–1945', *Journal of Religious History* 23, no. 1 (1999), 75–91; Christopher Petrusic, 'Violence as Masculinity: David Livingstone's Radical Racial Politics in the Cape Colony and the Transvaal, 1845–1852', *International History Review* 26, no. 1 (2004), 20–55; Inger Marie Okkenhaug, 'To Give the Boys Energy, Manliness, and Self-Command in Temper: The Anglican Male Ideal and St. George's School in Jerusalem, c. 1900–40', in *Gender, Religion and Change in the Middle East: Two Hundred Years of History*, ed. Inger Marie Okkenhaug and Ingvild Flaskerud (Oxford: Berg Publishers, 2005), 47–65; Anne O'Brien, 'Missionary Masculinities, the Homoerotic Gaze and the Politics of Race: Gilbert White in Northern Australia, 1885–1915', *Gender & History* 20, no. 1 (2008); Rhonda A. Semple, 'Missionary Manhood: Professionalism, Belief and Masculinity in the Nineteenth-Century British Imperial Field', *Journal of Imperial and Commonwealth History* 36, no. 3 (2008); Esme Cleall, 'Missionaries, Masculinities and War: The London Missionary Society', *South African Historical Journal* 61, no. 2 (2009); Erik Sidenvall, *The Making of Manhood among Swedish Missionaries in China and Mongolia, c. 1890–c. 1914* (Leiden/Boston: Brill, 2009).

32. Michael S. Kimmel, Jeff Hearn, and R. W. Connell, eds, *Handbook of Studies on Men & Masculinities* (Thousand Oaks, CA: Sage, 2005), 3.

33. Todd W. Reeser, *Masculinities in Theory* (Malden, MA: Wiley-Blackwell, 2010), 13.

34. A landmark article by Tim Carrigan, John Lee and Robert William Connell (subsequently known as Raewyn Connell), introduced the concept of 'hegemonic masculinity'; see Tim Carrigan, Robert William Connell and John Lee, 'Toward a New Sociology of Masculinity', *Theory and Society* 14, no. 5 (1985). Connell elaborated upon the concept of hegemonic masculinity in her books *Gender and Power* (1987) and *Masculinities* (1995). Other influential books by Connell are *The Men and the Boys* (2000) and *Gender* (2002).

35. Robert William Connell, *Masculinities*, 2nd edn (Berkeley/Los Angeles: University of California Press, 2005), 76.
36. Connell, *Masculinities*, 71–81.
37. Connell, *Masculinities*, 77.
38. Victor J. Seidler, *Unreasonable Men: Masculinity and Social Theory* (London: Routledge, 1994); Jeff Hearn, 'Is Masculinity Dead? A Critique of the Concept of Masculinity/Masculinities', in *Understanding Masculinities: Social Relations and Cultural Arenas*, ed. Mairtin Mac an Ghaill (Buckingham: Open University Press, 1996); Øystein Gullvåg Holter, *Gender, Patriarchy and Capitalism: A Social Forms Analysis* (Oslo: Work Research Institute, 1997); Marie Nordberg, 'Hegemonibegreppet och hegemonier inom mansforskingsfältet', in *Hegemoni och mansforskning*, ed. Per Folkeson, Marie Norberg and Goldina Smirtwaite (Karlstad: University of Karlstad, 2000); Claes Ekenstam, 'Mansforskningens bakgrund och framtid: Några teoretiska reflexioner', *Norma* 1, no. 1 (2006).
39. Øystein Gullvåg Holter, *Can Men Do It? Men and Gender Equality: The Nordic Experience* (Copenhagen: Nordic Council of Ministers, 2003).
40. Øystein Gullvåg Holter, 'Social Theories for Researching Men and Masculinities', in *Handbook of Studies on Men & Masculinities*, ed. Michael S. Kimmel, Jeff Hearn and R. W. Connell (Thousand Oaks, CA: Sage, 2005).
41. Robert William Connell and James W. Messerschmidt, 'Hegemonic Masculinity: Rethinking the Concept', *Gender & Society* 19, no. 6 (2005), 846.
42. Robert Morrell, *Changing Men in Southern Africa* (Pietermaritzburg: University of Natal Press, 2001), 6.
43. Robert Morrell, 'Of Boys and Men: Masculinity and Gender in Southern African Studies', *Journal of Southern African Studies* 24, no. 4 (1998): 605–630.
44. Ekenstam, 'Mansforskningens bakgrund och framtid'; Claes Ekenstam, 'Män, manlighet och omanlighet i historien', in *Män i Norden: Manlighet och modernitet 1840–1940*, ed. Claes Ekenstam and Jørgen Lorentzen (Hedemora: Gidlund, 2006); Claes Ekenstam, 'Klämda män: föreställningar om manlighet & umanlighet i det samtida Norden', in *Män i rörelse: Jämställdhet, förändring och social innovation i Norden*, ed. Øystein Gullvåg Holter (Stockholm: Gidlund, 2007). Ekenstam is furthermore editor of two anthologies discussing issues of men and masculinities: Claes Ekenstam et al., eds, *Rädd att falla: Studier i manlighet* (Stockholm: Gidlund, 1998); Claes Ekenstam, Thomas Johansson and Jari Kuosmanen, eds, *Sprickor i fasaden: Manligheter i förändring* (Hedemora: Gidlund, 2001).
45. Jonas Liliequist, 'Från niding till sprätt: En studie i det svenska omanlighetsbegreppets historia från vikingatid till sent 1700-tal', in *Manligt och umanligt i ett historisk perspektiv*, ed. Ann-Marie Berggren (Stockholm: Forskningsrådnämden, 1999), 73–95.
46. George L. Mosse, *The Image of Man: The Creation of Modern Masculinity* (New York: Oxford University Press, 1996).
47. David Tjeder, *The Power of Character: Middle-Class Masculinities, 1800–1900* (dissertation for the degree of PhD, Stockholm University, 2003).
48. Reeser, *Masculinities in Theory*, 13.
49. Refers to Ekenstam's book called *Rädd att falla*, 'the fear of falling'.
50. Jørgen Lorentzen and Wenche Mühleisen, *Kjønnsforskning: En grunnbok* (Oslo: Universitetsforlaget, 2006).

51. Yvonne Maria Werner, ed., *Kristen manlighet: Ideal och verklighet 1830–1940* (Lund: Nordic Academic Press, 2008); Yvonne Maria Werner, ed., *Christian Masculinity – a Paradox of Modernity: Men and Religion in Northern Europe in the 19th and 20th Century* (Leuven: Leuven University Press, 2011).

52. Yvonne Maria Werner, 'Kristen manlighet i teori och praxis', in *Kristen manlighet: Ideal och verklighet 1830–1940*, ed. Yvonne Maria Werner (Lund: Nordic Academic Press, 2008); Yvonne Maria Werner, 'Religious Feminisation, Confessionalism and Re-masculinisation in Western European Society 1800–1960', in *Pieties and Gender*, ed. Lene Sjørup and Hilda Rømer Christensen (Leiden: Brill, 2009).

53. Werner refers to the works of Hugh McLeod, *Secularisation in Western Europe, 1848–1914* (New York: St. Martin's Press, 2000) and Callum G. Brown, *The Death of Christian Britain: Understanding Secularisation, 1800–2000* (London: Routledge, 2001).

54. Tine Van Osselaer and Thomas Buerman, '"Feminisation" Thesis: A Survey of International Historiography and a Probing of Belgian Grounds', *Revue d'histoire ecclésiastique* 103, no. 2 (2008); Tine Van Osselaer, *The Pious Sex: Catholic Constructions of Masculinity and Femininity in Belgium c.1800–1940* (dissertation for the degree of Doctor in history, University of Leuven, 2009), 8–13.

55. Werner refers to the works of German historians Hartmun Lehmann and Olaf Blaschke: Olaf Blaschke, 'Das 19. Jahrhundert: Ein zweites konfessionelles Zeitalter?' *Geschichte und Gesellschaft. Zeitschrift für historische Sozialwissenschaft* 26, no. 1 (2000); Hartmut Lehmann, ed., *Säkularisierung, Dechristianisierung, Rechristianisierung im neuzeitlichen Europa: Bilanz und Perspektiven der Forschung* (Göttingen: Vanderhoeck & Ruprecht, 1997); Hartmut Lehmann, *Säkularisierung: Der europäische Sonderweg in Sachen Religion* (Göttingen: Wallstein, 2004).

56. Blaschke, 'Das 19. Jahrhundert: Ein zweites konfessionelles Zeitalter?'

57. Olaf Blaschke, 'Fältmarskalk Jesus Kristus: Religiös remaskulinisering i Tyskland', in *Kristen manlighet: Ideal och verklighet 1830–1940*, ed. Yvonne Maria Werner (Lund: Nordic Academic Press, 2008).

58. Gail Bederman, '"The Women Have Had Charge of the Church Long Enough": The Men and Religion Forward Movement of 1911–1912 and the Masculinization of Middle Class Protestantism', *American Quarterly* 41, no. 3 (1989); Evelyn A. Kirkley, 'Is It Manly To Be a Christian? The Debate in Victorian and Modern America', in *Redeeming Men: Religion and Masculinities*, ed. Stephen D. Boyd, M. Longwood and M. Muesse (Loisville: Westminster John Knox Press, 1996); Derek K. Hastings, 'Fears of a Feminized Church: Catholicism, Clerical Celibacy, and the Crisis of Masculinity in Wilhelmine Germany', *European History Quarterly* 38, no. 1 (2008); Tyler Carrington, 'Instilling the "Manly" Faith: Protestant Masculinity and the German *Jünglingsvereine* at the *fin de siècle*', *Journal of Men, Masculinities and Spirituality* 3, no. 2 (2009).

59. *NMT* 45, no. 1 (1889), 11.

60. Jørgensen, 'De første 100 år', 69–70.

61. John Nome, 'Det Norske Misjonsselskaps historie i norsk kirkeliv: Fra syttiårene til nåtiden', in *Det Norske Misjonsselskap 1842–1942*, ed. John Nome (Stavanger: Dreyer, 1943), 161.

62. Skeie, *Building God's Kingdom in Highland Madagascar*, 18–28. See also Karina Hestad Skeie, 'Misjonsmateriale som historisk materiale', *Norsk tidsskrift for misjonsvitenskap* 62, no. 2 (2008).

63. They continued, however, to write their reports which now were regarded as part of the employer–employee relationship and thus removed from the public sphere.

64. From 1925 to 1937 the *NMT* had a column called 'Women's Mission Work' (*Kvindernes missionsarbeide*). For youths the *NMT* had columns called 'Youth Column' (*Ungdomsspalten*) from 1925 and 'Norwegian Mission Youth' (*Norsk misjonsungdom*) from 1937.

65. Tjelle, *'Kvinder hjælper Kvinder'*, 119–131.

66. Nome, 'Det Norske Misjonsselskaps historie i norsk kirkeliv: Fra syttiårene til nåtiden', 136.

67. Michael Parker, *The Kingdom of Character: The Student Volunteer Movement for Foreign Missions (1886–1926)* (Lanham, MD/New York/Oxford: American Society of Missiology and University Press of America, 1998); Anders Tangeraas, *Ungdom og misjon* (Oslo: Norges Kristelige Ungdomsforbund, 1944).

68. Odd Kvaal Pedersen, 'Misjonslitteratur', in *Norsk Misjonsleksikon*, ed. Fridtjov Birkeli, Trygve Bjerkheim, Alfred K. Dahl, Johannes Gausdal, Halvor Hjertvik, Arnfinn Nordbø, Gunnar Rødahl, Martin Ski, Christian Tidemann Strand and Johan Straume. (Stavanger: Nomi forlag – Runa forlag, 1967).

69. Marianne Gullestad, *Picturing Pity: Pitfalls and Pleasures in Cross-Cultural Communication: Image and Word in a North Cameroon Mission* (New York/Oxford: Berghahn, 2007).

70. Marianne Gullestad, *Picturing Pity*, 21.

71. Lisbeth Mikaelsson, *Kallets ekko: Studier i misjon og selvbiografi* (Kristiansand: Høyskoleforlaget, 2003); Lisbeth Mikaelsson, '"Self" and "Other" as Biblical Representations in Mission Literature', in *Protestant Missions and Local Encounters in the Nineteenth and Twentieth Centuries: Unto the Ends of the World*, ed. Hilde Nielssen, Inger Marie Okkenhaug and Karina Hestad Skeie (Leiden/Boston: Brill, 2011).

72. Mikaelsson, *Kallets ekko*, 88.

73. Mikaelsson, *Kallets ekko*.

74. Felix Driver, *Geography Militant: Cultures of Exploration and Empire* (Oxford: Blackwell, 2001).

75. Nielssen, 'From Norway to the Ends of the World', 48. See also Hilde Nielssen, 'James Sibree and Lars Dahle: Norwegian and British Missionary Ethnography as a Transnational and National Activity', in *Protestant Missions and Local Encounters in the Nineteenth and Twentieth Centuries: Unto the Ends of the World*, ed. Hilde Nielssen, Inger Marie Okkenhaug and Karina Hestad Skeie (Leiden/Boston: Brill, 2011).

76. Mikaelsson, *Kallets ekko*, 251–259.

77. Aslaug Hestnes, *Fortellinger fra Midtens rike: En studie i Racin Kolnes' barne- og ungdomsbøker med særlig henblikk på misjonssyn, -motivasjon og -metoder* (unpublished thesis, School of Mission and Theology, 1987).

78. Parker, *The Kingdom of Character*, 105.

79. R. Pierce Beaver, *All Loves Excelling: American Protestant Women in World Mission* (Grand Rapids, MI: Eerdmans, 1968), 143–175; Robert, *American Women in Mission*, 260–269.

80. Kristin Fjelde Tjelle, 'Lærerinnenes Misjonsforbund gjennom 100 år', *Norsk tidsskrift for misjon* 56, no. 2 (2002), 82–83.

81. Ivar Aasen, 'Misjonssommerskolene', in *Norsk Misjonsleksikon*, ed. Fridtjov Birkeli et al. (Stavanger: Nomi forlag – Runa forlag, 1967).
82. A Danish translation of the book was used; John R. Mott, *Den afgørende Time i den kristne Mission* (København: Det Danske Missionsselskabs forlag, 1911).
83. Nome, 'Det Norske Misjonsselskaps historie i norsk kirkeliv: Fra syttiårene til nåtiden', 42.
84. Halfdan E. Sommerfelt, *Den Norske Zulumission: Et Tilbageblik paa de første 20 Aar af det Norske Missionsselskabs Virksomhed* (Christiania: Wm. Gram, 1865).
85. Lars Dahle and Simon Emanuel Jørgensen, *Festskrift til Det Norske Missionsselskabs Jubilæum i 1892* (Stavanger: Det Norske Missionsselskabs Forlag, 1892).
86. Ole Stavem, *Et bantufolk og kristendommen: Det norske missionsselskaps syttiaarige zulumission* (Stavanger: Det norske missionsselskaps forlag, 1915).
87. Olav Guttorm Myklebust, 'Sør-Afrika', in *Det Norske Misjonsselskap 1842–1942*, ed. John Nome (Stavanger: Dreyer, 1949).
88. John Nome, 'Det Norske Misjonsselskaps historie i norsk kirkeliv: Fra stiftelsestiden til Schreuders brudd', in *Det Norske Misjonsselskap 1842–1942*, ed. John Nome (Stavanger: Dreyer, 1943); Nome, 'Det Norske Misjonsselskaps historie i norsk kirkeliv'.
89. Erling Danbolt, 'Det Norske Misjonsselskaps forhistorie', *Norsk Teologisk Tidsskrift* 44, no. 1 (1943).
90. Jens Arup Seip, 'Kirkelig historieteori og kirkelig historieforskning', *Historisk tidsskrift* 34 (1944).
91. Simensen, 'Norsk misjonsforskning'. For a recent discussion on the character of 'mission history' see Tomas Sundnes Drønen, 'Misjonshistorie: fagets akademiske egenart og forhold til samfunnsvitenskapelige metoder', *Norsk tidsskrift for misjon* 63, no. 1 (2009).
92. Tomas Sundnes Drønen, *Communication and Conversion in Northern Cameroon: the Dii People and Norwegian Missionaries, 1934–60* (Leiden: Brill, 2009).
93. Nome, 'Det Norske Misjonsselskaps historie i norsk kirkeliv: Fra syttiårene til nåtiden', 13.
94. Semple, 'Missionary Manhood', 401.
95. Ibid., 379–415.
96. John Tosh, *A Man's Place: Masculinity and the Middle-Class Home in Victorian England* (New Haven, CT: Yale University Press, 1999), 2.

2   Missionary Self-Making

1. John Nome, 'Det Norske Misjonsselskaps historie i norsk kirkeliv: Fra stiftelsestiden til Schreuders brudd', in *Det Norske Misjonsselskap 1842–1942*, ed. John Nome (Stavanger: Dreyer, 1943), 288–90.
2. Olav Guttorm Myklebust, *H. P. S. Schreuder: Kirke og misjon* (Oslo: Land og kirke/Gyldendal, 1980), 61.
3. H. P. S. Schreuder, *Beretning om Missionspræst Schreuders Ordination til Biskop over den Norske Kirkes Missionsmark i Bergens domkirke den 8de juli 1866 samt Prædikener og Foredrag af Biskop Schreuder, holdte under hans Nærværelse i Hjemmet* (Stavanger: Det Norske Missionsselskabs Forlag, 1868).

4. John Nome, 'Det Norske Misjonsselskaps historie i norsk kirkeliv: Fra syttiårene til nåtiden', in *Det Norske Misjonsselskap 1842–1942*, ed. John Nome (Stavanger: Dreyer, 1943), 12–13.
5. Michael S. Kimmel, *Manhood in America: A Cultural History*, 2nd edn (New York/Oxford: Oxford University Press, 2006), 19.
6. Kimmel, *Manhood in America*, 6.
7. Erik Sidenvall, *The Making of Manhood among Swedish Missionaries in China and Mongolia, c. 1890 –c. 1914* (Leiden/Boston: Brill, 2009), 159.
8. The biography on Schreuder is based on Daniel Thrap, *Biskop H.P.S. Schreuders Liv og Virksomhed i korte Træk fremstillet* (Christiania: Nils Lunds Forlag, 1877); Nome, 'Det Norske Misjonsselskaps historie i norsk kirkeliv: Fra stiftelsestiden til Schreuders brudd'; Øystein Rakkenes, *Himmelfolket: En norsk høvding i Zululand* (Oslo: Cappelen, 2003).
9. H. P. S. Schreuder, *Nogle ord til Norges Kirke om christelig Pligt med Hensyn til Omsorg for ikke-christne Medbrødres Salighed* (Christiania: 1842).
10. Torstein Jørgensen, *Contact and Conflict: Norwegian Missionaries, the Zulu Kingdom, and the Gospel: 1850–1873* (Oslo: Solum, 1990), 78.
11. Moravian groups in Norway trace their history back to the early eighteenth century when they constituted a centre of missionary interest and initiative. Their learning was strongly evangelical in the sense of an emphasis on salvation in Jesus Christ. Moravian preaching was emotional, emphasising each individual's need of a personal religious experience of conversion. The Haugians were followers of the pietistic religious leader Hans Nielsen Hauge (1771–1824). They shared the Moravians' ideals of religious individualism and voluntary engagement. Stressing the fact that every individual was responsible of living a decent and hardworking life, the Haugian groups appeared to be more industrious and active than the Moravians.
12. Nome, 'Det Norske Misjonsselskaps historie i norsk kirkeliv: Fra stiftelsestiden til Schreuders brudd', 37.
13. Nome, 'Det Norske Misjonsselskaps historie i norsk kirkeliv: Fra stiftelsestiden til Schreuders brudd', 258–71, 303–37; Myklebust, *H. P. S. Schreuder: Kirke og misjon*, 280–333.
14. *Aktstykker til belysning af Forholdet mellom Biskop Schreuder og det Norske Missionsselskab. Fra Biskopens Ordination indtil generalforsamlingen 1873* (Stavanger: Kielland, 1876), 275.
15. Nome, 'Det Norske Misjonsselskaps historie i norsk kirkeliv: Fra stiftelsestiden til Schreuders brudd', 328.
16. See *Aktstykker til belysning af Forholdet mellom Biskop Schreuder og det Norske Missionsselskab*. That the Home Board never published the complete correspondence is proved by Olav Guttorm Myklebust in Myklebust, *H. P. S. Schreuder: Kirke og misjon*, 22–3.
17. Hanna Larsen, *Skisser fra Zululand* (Decorah, Iowa: Lutheran Publishing House, 1905), 117; Stavem, *Et bantufolk og kristendommen: Det norske missionsselskaps syttiaarige zulumission* (Stavanger: Det norske missionsselskaps forlag, 1915), 87, 98.
18. Olav Guttorm Myklebust, C. M. Doke, and Ernst Dammann, *Én var den første: Studier og tekster til forståelse av H. P. S. Schreuder* (Oslo: Land og kirke/Gyldendal, 1986), 17–20.
19. Myklebust, Doke, and Dammann, *Én var den første*, 19.

20. Olav Guttorm Myklebust, 'Sør-Afrika', in *Det Norske Misjonsselskap 1842–1942*, ed. John Nome (Stavanger: Dreyer, 1949), 73–8.

21. Myklebust, *H.P.S. Schreuder*; Myklebust, Doke, and Dammann, *En var den første*.

22. See Dahle's representation of Schreuder in Lars Dahle, '"Et smaalig og snever-synt Missionsstyre"', *Norsk Kirkeblad* (1917), 626–33; Lars Dahle, *Tilbakeblik paa mit liv – og særlig paa mit missionsliv: Første del* (Stavanger: Det Norske Missionsselskabs trykkeri, 1922), 231–67.

23. Emil Birkeli, 'Kirken og misjonsproblemet', in *Misjonshistorie* (Oslo: Selskapet til Kristelige Andagtsbøkers Utgivelse, 1935), 74–5.

24. Nome, 'Det Norske Misjonsselskaps historie i norsk kirkeliv: Fra stiftelsestiden til Schreuders brudd', 258–337.

25. Oscar Handeland, *Fram kristmenn, korsmenn! Hovedlinjer og førerskikkelser i norsk hedningemisjon* (Bergen: Lunde, 1963), 195.

26. Seip, 'Kirkelig historieteori og kirkelig historieforskning', *Historisk tidsskrift* 34 (1944), 390.

27. See for example Halfdan E. Sommerfelt, *Den Norske Zulumission: Et Tilbageblik paa de første 20 Aar af det Norske Missionsselskabs Virksomhed* (Christiania: Wm. Gram, 1865); Ludvig Kristensen Daa, 'Om den Norske Hedning-Omvendelse', *Tids-tavler* 2 (1873); Thrap, *Biskop H.P.S. Schreuders Liv og Virksomhed i korte Træk fremstillet*; D. Thrap, *Til vore 3 store Missionærers Karakteristik: Foredrag ved Missionsmødet i Skien 22. August 1903* (Skien: 1903).

28. Myklebust, *H. P. S. Schreuder: Kirke og misjon*, 280–334.

29. Schreuder's and Dahle's views of church and mission have been an issue of interest in recent theological discussions: see Terje Ellingsen, 'Lars Dahle som misjonær, teolog og kirkemann', *Norsk tidsskrift for misjon* 27, no. 3 (1973): 147–61; Svein Ragnvald Tjora, *Valg eller vigsel: En undersøkelse av Lars Dahles syn på kirkeforfatningsspørsmål med særlig henblikk på innføringen av misjonærkonferansen på Madagaskar 1877 og på diskusjonen ved århundreskiftet om den gassisk lutherske kirkes selvstendiggjøring* (Unpublished thesis in theology, School of Mission and Theology, 1985): 209–20; Thor Halvor Hovland, 'Embetssyn og dåpssyn hos Schreuder og Dahle', *Norsk tidsskrift for misjon* 56, no. 3 (2002); Thor Halvor Hovland, 'Kirkesyn og konferanse-ordning', *Norsk tidsskrift for misjon* 56, no. 3 (2002): 193–208.

30. Roald Berg, 'Misjonshistorie og samfunnsforskning', *Nytt Norsk Tidsskrift*, no. 3–4 (2009), 330.

31. For a discussion on the pietistic mission and laymen's movement in Norway from the perspective of modernity, see Bjørg Seland, *Religion på det frie marked: Folkelig pietisme og bedehuskultur* (Kristiansand: Høyskoleforlaget AS – Norwegian Academic Press, 2006), 60–3.

32. Jørgensen, *Contact and Conflict*, 83.

33. Nome, 'Det Norske Misjonsselskaps historie i norsk kirkeliv: Fra stiftelsestiden til Schreuders brudd', 185.

34. *NMT* 29, no. 4 (1874): 150–1.

35. Vidar L. Haanes, *'Hvad skal da dette blive for prester?' Presteutdannelse i spenningsfeltet mellom universitet og kirke, med vekt på modernitetens gjennombrudd i Norge* (Trondheim: Tapir, 1998), 110–23.

36. Nome, 'Det Norske Misjonsselskaps historie i norsk kirkeliv: Fra stiftelsestiden til Schreuders brudd', 191–2.

37. Reidun Høydal, *Nasjon – region – profesjon: Vestlandslæraren 1840–1940* (Oslo: Noregs forskingsråd, 1995), 37–9, 91–109.

38. Nome, 'Det Norske Misjonsselskaps historie i norsk kirkeliv: Fra stiftelsestiden til Schreuders brudd', 192. At the NMS's general assembly of 1858, 42 of the delegates were schoolteachers, 22 were pastors.
39. Jørgensen, *Contact and Conflict*, 65–72.
40. Vidar Gynnild, *Norske misjonærer på 1800-tallet: Geografisk, sosial og religiøs bakgrunn* (unpublished MA thesis, University of Trondheim, 1981).
41. Torstein Jørgensen implies that Schreuder was part of 'the intelligentsia' of the 1830s, a group regarding themselves as 'the aristocracy of spirit' who generally tended to display more conservative viewpoints than the 1814 generation. John Nome associates Schreuder with 'the stiff generation of the 1830s'.
42. Nome, 'Det Norske Misjonsselskaps historie i norsk kirkeliv: Fra stiftelsestiden til Schreuders brudd', 336–7.
43. Nome, 'Det Norske Misjonsselskaps historie i norsk kirkeliv: Fra stiftelsestiden til Schreuders brudd', 334.
44. Dahle, *Tilbakeblik paa mit liv – og særlig paa mit missionsliv: Første del*, 294.
45. Myklebust, 'Sør-Afrika', 73–8.
46. The leopard (stuffed) that attacked Schreuder in 1857 was one of the objects at the NMS's ethnographic mission exhibition called 'To the Ends of the World' which toured Norway between 1948 and 1960 and was visited by 990 000 people. The narrative of Schreuder's fight with the leopard was vividly retold by exhibition guides. See Hilde Nielsen, 'From Norway to the Ends of the World: Missionary Contributions to Norwegian Images of "Self" and "Other"', in *Encountering Foreign Worlds. Experiences at Home and Abroad: Proceedings from the 26th Nordic Congress of Historians*, ed. Christina Folke Ax, Anne Folke Henningsen, Niklas Thode Jensen, Leila Koivunen and Taina Syrjämaa (Reykjavik: 2007).
47. Stavem, *Et bantufolk og kristendommen*, 203.
48. Stavem, *Et bantufolk og kristendommen*, 195–208.
49. *NMT* 29, 3 (1874): 109.
50. *Aktstykker til belysning af Forholdet mellom Biskop Schreuder og det Norske Missionsselskab*, 182.
51. *Aktstykker til belysning af Forholdet mellom Biskop Schreuder og det Norske MissionsselskabIbid.*, 302–9.
52. Kimmel asserts that for American men the American Revolution brought a revolt of the sons against the fathers – 'the Sons of Liberty against Father England'. Being a man thus meant *not* being a boy: a man was independent, self-controlled and responsible whereas a boy was dependent, irresponsible, and lacked control. Kimmel, *Manhood in America*, 14.
53. Ole Stavem, 'Lars Dahle som missionselev', in *Fra Norges indsats i verdens-missionen: Festskrift ved Lars Dahles femtiaars-jubilæum* (Stavanger: Det norske missionsselskaps trykkeri, 1921), 10.
54. Jarle Simensen and Vidar Gynnild, 'Norwegian Missionaries in the Nineteenth Century: Organizational Background, Social and World View', in *Norwegian Missions in African History, Vol 1: South Africa 1845–1906*, ed. Jarle Simensen (Oslo: Norwegian University Press, 1986).
55. Haanes, 'Hvad skal da dette blive for prester?' 110–23.
56. Erling Danbolt, 'Det Norske Misjonsselskaps misjonærer 1842–1948', in *Det Norske Misjonsselskaps historie i hundre år*, ed. John Nome (Stavanger: Dreyer, 1948), 31–2.

57. Torstein Jørgensen, 'En liten sommerdebatt om misjon: Dikteren Alexander Kielland i diskusjon med generalsekretær Lars Dahle', *Misjon og teologi* 5/6 (1998/1999), 77–82.

58. Minutes from MC 1911, MA-MHS, 65.

59. Einar Amdahl and Otto Chr. Dahl, 'Lars Dahle', in *Norsk Misjonsleksikon*, ed. Fridtjov Birkeli et al. (Stavanger: Nomi forlag – Runa forlag, 1967).

60. Lisbeth Mikaelsson, *Kallets ekko: Studier i misjon og selvbiografi* (Kristiansand: Høyskoleforlaget, 2003), 260–9.

61. Sidenvall, *The Making of Manhood among Swedish Missionaries in China and Mongolia*, 11.

62. E. Anthony Rotundo, *American Manhood: Transformations in Masculinity from the Revolution to the Modern Era* (New York: Basic Books, 1993), 285.

63. Sidenvall, *The Making of Manhood among Swedish Missionaries in China and Mongolia*, 12.

64. E. E. Thommesen who was a trained veterinarian and blacksmith returned to Norway in 1847 and eschewed further missionary service.

65. Myklebust, 'Sør-Afrika', 24–5.

66. Norman Etherington, *Preachers, Peasants and Politics in Southeast Africa, 1835–1880: African Christian Communities in Natal, Pondoland and Zululand* (London: Royal Historical Society, 1978), 24–46; Norman Etherington, 'Kingdoms of This World and the Next: Christian Beginnings among the Zulu and Swazi', in *Christianity in South Africa: A Political, Social and Cultural History*, ed. Richard Elphick and Rodney Davenport (Oxford: James Curry, 1997).

67. Etherington, *Preachers, Peasants and Politics in Southeast Africa*, 115–34; Robert Morrell, John Wright and Sheila Meintjes, 'Colonialism and the Establishment of White Domination, 1840–1990', in *Political Economy and Identities in KwaZulu-Natal: Historical and Social Perspectives*, ed. Robert Morrell (Durban: Indicator Press, 1996), 42–5.

68. Henry Venn (1796–1873) and Rufus Anderson (1796–1880) arrived at their ideas separately, in spite of the outstanding similarities in the basic outline of the three-self theory. From the mid- to late-nineteenth century the 'three-self'-programme was the stated policy of both British and American Protestant missions. See C. Peter Williams, *The Ideal of the Self-Governing Church: A Study in Victorian Missionary Strategy* (Leiden: E. J. Brill, 1990); Paul William Harris, *Nothing but Christ: Rufus Anderson and the Ideology of Protestant Foreign Missions* (New York: Oxford University Press, 1999).

69. Dana L. Robert, ed., *Converting Colonialism: Visions and Realities in Mission History, 1706–1914* (Grand Rapids, MI: Wm. B. Eerdmans Publishing Co., 2008), 16.

70. Dana L. Robert, 'The "Christian Home" as a Cornerstone of Anglo-American Missionary Thought and Practice', in *Converting Colonialism: Visions and Realities in Mission History, 1706–1914*, ed. Dana L. Robert (Grand Rapids, MI: Wm. B. Eerdmans Publishing Co., 2008), 165. This widespread mission theory of Christian homemaking has been neglected in current studies on mission theology, Robert claims, and she asks if this is partly because it was mostly women who propagated the theory and partly because the theory is associated with the now-discredited 'civilisation' project of Western missions.

71. Robert, *Converting Colonialism*, 13.

72. Etherington, *Preachers, Peasants and Politics in Southeast Africa, 1835–1880*, 135–44.

73. Richard Elphick, 'Evangelical Missions and Racial "Equalization"', in *Converting Colonialism: Visions and Realities in Mission History, 1706–1914*, ed. Dana L. Robert (Grand Rapids, MI: Wm. B. Eerdmans Publishing Co., 2008).
74. C. Peter Williams, 'The Church Missionary Society and the Indigenous Church in the Second Half of the Nineteenth Century: The Defense and Destruction of the Venn Ideals', in *Converting Colonialism: Visions and Realities in Mission History, 1706–1914*, ed. Dana L. Robert (Grand Rapids, MI/Cambridge: Wm. B. Eerdmans Publishing Co., 2008).
75. Sigmund Edland, 'Lars Dahle og den gassisk-lutherske kyrkjas frihet og sjølvstendighet', *Norsk tidsskrift for misjon* 60, no. 2 (1982): 97–104; Sigmund Edland, 'Lars Dahle's "regime" og sjølvstendighetstrongen i den gassisk-lutherske kyrkja (1889–1902)', *Norsk tidsskrift for misjon* 60, no. 3 (1982): 171–83; Karina Hestad Skeie, *Building God's Kingdom in Highland Madagascar: Norwegian Lutheran Missionaries in Vakinankaratra and Betsileo 1866*–1903 (Dissertation for the Degree of Dr. Art, University of Oslo, 2005), 273–313
76. Kimmel, *Manhood in America*, 62.

3   Proper Missionary Masculinity

1. Ole Gjerløw, *Beretning vedkommende Sekretærens Reise til Missionsmarken i Zululand og Natal 1887–88* (Stavanger: Det Norske Missionsselskab, 1888).
2. See a copy of the resolution in Gjerløw, *Beretning vedkommende Sekretærens Reise til Missionsmarken i Zululand og Natal 1887–88*, 58–60.
3. Gjerløw, *Beretning vedkommende Sekretærens Reise til Missionsmarken i Zululand og Natal 1887–88*, 57–8.
4. Oftebro had received a letter which announced the Home Board's distrust of him and their disapproval of his re-election as superintendent; see the letter from the NMS's Home Board to Ommund Oftebro dated 2 December 1887, MA-MHS, HA/G.sekr.91/Box 165/Copy-book A. Gjerløw arranged a new election but when considering the result – Hans C. M. G. Leisegang had six votes, Stavem five – he used his authority to overrule it and proclaimed Stavem to be the new superintendent; see Gjerløw, *Beretning vedkommende Sekretærens Reise til Missionsmarken i Zululand og Natal 1887–88*, 41–3.
5. See the letter sent by the missionaries to the NMS's regional boards of 28.8.1890, MA-MHS, HA/G.sekr.91/Box 165/Outgoing letters 1887–1893.
6. Erik Sidenvall, *The Making of Manhood among Swedish Missionaries in China and Mongolia, c. 1890 – c. 1914* (Leiden/Boston: Brill, 2009), 13.
7. Yvonne Maria Werner, 'Religious Feminisation, Confessionalism and Re-masculinisation in Western European Society 1800–1960', in *Pieties and Gender*, ed. Lene Sjørup and Hilda Rømer Christensen (Leiden: Brill, 2009).
8. The following biography on Christian Oftebro is based on Markus Dahle, 'Christian Oftebro,' in *Hjem fra Kamppladsen: Livsbilleder af norske missionærer*, ed. Anders Olsen (Kristiania: Steen'ske Bogtrykkeri og Forlag, 1906); Christian Oftebro's letter of application to the NMS's mission school of 27.2.1866, in MA-MHS, HA/G.sekr.90/Box 131/Jacket 4.
9. All shipping traffic from Durban to Madagascar did pass Mauritius, which was a British colony from 1810. Sigmund Edland, *Evangelists or Envoys? The Role of British Missionaries at Turning Points in Malagasy Political History, 1820–1840. Documentary and Analysis* (PhD dissertation, School of Mission and Theology, 2006), 30–7.

10. Letter from Christian Oftebro dated 27.2.1866, in MA-MHS, HA/G.sekr.90/Box 131/Jacket 4.

11. Christian Oftebro was a student of the so-called 'third class' of 1868/69, which is renowned as a class of missionary pioneers. There were two admissions; nine out of 23 applicants were accepted in 1868, and in the following year eight out of 22 applicants were accepted. See Emil Birkeli and C. Tidemann Strand, *Kallet og veien: Det Norske Misjonsselskaps misjonsskole 1850–1959* (Stavanger: Misjonsselskapets Forlag, 1959), 40–6, 245.

12. Minutes from the NMS's Home Board meeting of 27.6.1873, Journal of Negotiations 1862–1875, MA-MHS, HA/G.sekr.10. According to the school principal, the decision was made in accordance with Christian Oftebro's own wish. Edinburgh Medical Missionary Society (EMMS) was founded in 1841 by a group of doctors. In 1852 EMMS started a scheme to train students to become medical missionaries. In 1853 a medical mission dispensary and clinic was opened. This acted as a practical training ground for student doctors, but also benefited the residents in the area. See David Hardiman, 'Introduction', in *Healing Bodies, Saving Souls: Medical Missions in Asia and Africa*, ed. David Hardiman (Amsterdam/New York: Editions Rodopi B.V., 2006),12.

13. Ommund Oftebro in *NMT* 33, no. 8 (1877): 309.

14. Ole Stavem, *The Norwegian Missionary Society: A Short Review of Its Work among the Zulus* (Stavanger: The Norwegian Missionary Society, 1918), 14.

15. Jeff Guy, *The Destruction of the Zulu Kingdom: The Civil War in Zululand, 1879–1884* (Pietermaritzburg: University of Natal Press, 1994), 29.

16. See, e.g., Ommund Oftebro in *NMT* 33, no. 8 (1877): 306–7; Christian Oftebro in *NMT* 44, no. 16 (1888): 315 and *NMT* 40, no. 5 (1884): 93–4.

17. See, e.g., Gundvall Gundersen in *NMT* 31, no. 10 (1875): 377.

18. While Mr Dickens, an acquaintance of Ommund Oftebro, stayed in England during the war, the Oftebro family looked after his farm.

19. Christian Oftebro in *NMT* 36, no. 12 (1880): 236.

20. Charles Ballard, 'From Sovereignty to Subjection: The Political Economy of Zululand 1820–1906', in *Norwegian Missions in African History, Vol 1: South Africa 1845–1906*, ed. Jarle Simensen (Oslo: Universitetsforlaget 1986).

21. Christian Oftebro in *NMT* 40, no. 5 (1884): 95–7.

22. Guy, *The Destruction of the Zulu Kingdom*, 219–20.

23. Christian Oftebro in *NMT* 40, no. 5 (1884): 99–100.

24. *NMT* 44, no. 12 (1888): 233–4.

25. Det Norske Missionsselskabs 47de Aarsberetning (Stavanger 1889), 62–9.

26. *Aktstykker til belysning af Forholdet mellom Biskop Schreuder og det Norske Missionsselskab. Fra Biskopens Ordination indtil generalforsamlingen 1873* (Stavanger: Kielland, 1876).

27. The Secretary's report was printed as a manuscript, which could explain why it was dispersed. Copies of the manuscript were available to all the delegates at the NMS's general assembly in 1888.

28. Letter from the NMS's Home Board to the missionaries in South Africa of 16.12.1889, in MA-MHS, South Africa/Box 1A/Jacket 15.

29. Lars Dahle was in fact critical of Gjerløw's treatment of the Oftebro missionaries. In the NMS's mission archive there is a copy of Gjerløw's report filled with Lars Dahle's underscorings, question marks, and critical comments. See MA-MHS, HA/G.sekr.92/Box 182/Jacket 14. It should also be mentioned that Dahle's wife was the niece of Ommund Oftebro.

30. Letter from Hans Christian Leisegang to the NMS's Home Board of 23.3.1904, MA-MHS, HA/G.sekr.93/Box 191/Jacket 9.
31. Lars Dahle and Simon Emanuel Jørgensen, *Festskrift til Det Norske Missionsselskabs Jubilæum i 1892* (Stavanger: Det Norske Missionsselskabs Forlag, 1892), 137.
32. Dahle and Jørgensen, *Festskrift til Det Norske Missionsselskabs Jubilæum i 1892*, 140.
33. Dahle, 'Christian Oftebro', 25.
34. Ole Stavem, *Et bantufolk og kristendommen: Det norske missionsselskaps syttiaarige zulumission* (Stavanger: Det norske missionsselskaps forlag, 1915), 282.
35. John Nome, 'Det Norske Misjonsselskaps historie i norsk kirkeliv: Fra syttiårene til nåtiden', in *Det Norske Misjonsselskap 1842–1942*, ed. John Nome (Stavanger: Dreyer, 1943).
36. Olav Guttorm Myklebust, 'Sør-Afrika', in *Det Norske Misjonsselskap 1842–1942*, ed. John Nome (Stavanger: Dreyer, 1949), 101–5.
37. Thomas M. Børhaug, *Imperialismens kollaboratører? En analyse av norske misjonærers holdning og rolle under den europeiske etableringsfase i Zululand 1873–1890* (unpublished MA thesis, University of Trondheim, 1976), 117–18, 198, 204. See also Myklebust's critical remarks on Børhaug's understanding of Christian Oftebro in Olav Guttorm Myklebust, 'Norsk misjon og britisk imperialisme i Syd-Afrika', *Norsk tidsskrift for misjon* 31, no. 2 (1977), 70–1.
38. Per O. Hernæs, *Norsk misjon og sosial endring: Norske misjonærer i Zululand/Natal 1887–1906* (Unpublished Ma thesis, University of Trondheim, 1978), 141–52.
39. Andrew Porter, *Religion versus empire? British Protestant Missionaries and Overseas Expansion, 1700–1914* (Manchester: Manchester University Press, 2004), 91–115.
40. Gjerløw, *Beretning vedkommende Sekretærens Reise til Missionsmarken i Zululand og Natal 1887–88*, 11.
41. Christian Oftebro and Ole Z. Norgaard on a committee proposal regarding the issue of a prospect industrial school in the NMS; see minutes of MC 1886, MA-MHS, HA/G.sekr.90/Box 35/Jacket 13.
42. Christian Oftebro in *NMT* 38, no. 9 (1882): 174.
43. See, e.g., minutes of MC 1884, issue 12, MA-MHS, HA/G.sekr.40/Box 35/ Jacket 8; MC 1885, issue 5, MA-MHS, HA/G.sekr.40/Box 35/Jacket 10.
44. Jarle Simensen, Thomas Børhaug, Per Hernæs and Endre Sønstabø, 'Christian Missions and Socio-Cultural Change in Zululand 1850–1906: Norwegian Strategy and African Response', in *Norwegian Missions in African History, Vol 1: South Africa 1845–1906*, ed. Jarle Simensen (Oslo: Norwegian University Press, 1986), 230.
45. Minutes of MC 1884, issue 12, MA-MHS, HA/G.sekr.40/Box 35/Jacket 8.
46. Minutes of MC 1881, issue 4 & 5, MA-MHS, HA/G.sekr.40/Box 34/Jacket 21; MC 1885, issue 4, MA-MHS, HA/G.sekr.40/Box 35/Jacket 10.
47. Minutes of MC 1881, MA-MHS, HA/G.sekr.40/Box 34/Jacket 21.
48. Minutes of MC 1884, MA-MHS, HA/G.sekr.40/Box 35/Jacket 8.
49. *NMT* 39, no. 10 (1883): 195.
50. See, e.g., *NMT* 42, no. 22 (1886): 432–8. Ole Stavem was on a furlough in Norway in 1885–87, and opened the discussion at the regional conference in Christiania.

51. Letter from Ole Gjerløw to Christian Oftebro of 2.12.1887, in MA-MHS, HA/G.sekr.91/Box 165/Copybook A.
52. Gjerløw, *Beretning vedkommende Sekretærens Reise til Missionsmarken i Zululand og Natal 1887–88*, 12.
53. Christian Oftebro and Ole Z. Norgaard on a committee proposal regarding a prospective industrial school in the NMS in the minutes of MC 1886, MA-MHS, HA/G.sekr.90/Box 35/Jacket 13.
54. Letters from Christian Oftebro to the NMS's Home Board of 6.3.1875 and 29.2.1876, MA-MHS, HA/G.sekr.90, Box 90/Jacket 3.
55. John McCracken, *Politics and Christianity in Malawi 1875–1940* (Cambridge: Cambridge University Press, 1977), 17–33.
56. In 1869 the NMS sent Christian D. Borchgrevink, who was both a theologian and a physician, to Madagascar. The first NMS hospital was established in Antananarivo in 1879. See Ludvig Munthe, *Venstrehandsmisjon? Misjonslegar på Madagaskar frå 1860-åra og ut hundreåret* (Oslo: Luther, 1985).
57. Esme Cleall, *Missionary Discourses of Difference: Negotiating Otherness in the British Empire, 1840–1900* (Basingstoke: Palgrave Macmillan, 2012), 85–8.
58. Michael Gelfand, *Christian Doctor and Nurse: The History of Medical Missions in South Africa from 1799–1976* (Sandton: Mariannhill Mission Press, 1984), 18.
59. Norman Etherington, 'Education and Medicine', in *Missions and Empire*, ed. Norman Etherington (Oxford: Oxford University Press, 2005), 278.
60. Hardiman, 'Introduction'.
61. See Lars Martin Titlestad's article 'The Missionary as a Doctor' in *NMT* 72, no. 4 (1916): 73–6.
62. Etherington, 'Education and Medicine', 280.
63. Norman Vance, *The Sinews of the Spirit: The Ideal of Christian Manliness in Victorian Literature and Religious Thought* (Cambridge: Cambridge University Press, 1985); J. A. Mangan and James Walvin, ed., *Manliness and Morality: Middle-class Masculinity in Britain and American 1800–1940* (Manchester: Manchester University Press, 1987); Donald E. Hall, ed., *Muscular Christianity: Embodying the Victorian Age* (Cambridge/New York/Melbourne: Cambridge University Press, 1994); Clifford Putney, *Muscular Christianity: Manhood and Sports in Protestant America 1880–1920* (Cambridge, MA: Harvard University Press, 2001).
64. The British Christian Socialist Movement was established in 1848 and the American Social Gospel Movement in the mid-1860s; see Charles Howard Hopkins, *The Rise of the Social Gospel in American Protestantism 1865–1915* (New Haven, CT: Yale University Press, 1940).
65. A copy of the 1874 'House Order' is printed in Birkeli and Tidemann Strand, *Kallet og veien*, 214–24.
66. Gjerløw, *Beretning vedkommende Sekretærens Reise til Missionsmarken i Zululand og Natal 1887–88*, 11.
67. The alleged discoveries of gold turned out however out to be minor, and Oftebro lost the money he had invested; see copy of a transcript of a letter from Ommund Oftebro to his brother Tobias Oftebro dated 5.6.1888. Torstein Oftebro's private archive.
68. See, e.g., minutes of MC 1885, issue 5, MA-MHS, HA/G.sekr.90/Box 35/Jacket 10.
69. Tobias Udland, who died in 1876, was praised for his practical skills and his ability to profit from farming activities; see *NMT* 34, no. 2 (1878): 33–4.

When his widow died childless in 1888 and left a considerable fortune to the NMS, this was regarded as exemplary and noted in *NMT* 44, no. 11 (1888), 219.

70. Letter from the NMS's Home Board to Christian Oftebro of 2 December 1887, in MA-MHS, HA/G.sekr.91/Box 165/Copy-book A.

71. Gjerløw, *Beretning vedkommende Sekretærens Reise til Missionsmarken i Zululand og Natal 1887–88*, 28.

72. *Instruks for det Norske Missionsselskabs Udsendinger,* § 13. See a copy of the 1858 revision in Halfdan E. Sommerfelt, *Den Norske Zulumission: Et Tilbageblik paa de første 20 Aar af det Norske Missionsselskabs Virksomhed* (Christiania: Wm. Gram, 1865), 349–52.

73. Per Hernæs, 'The Zulu Kingdom, Norwegian Missionaries, and British Imperialism, 1845–1879', in *Norwegian Missions in African History, Vol 1: South Africa 1845–1906*, ed. Jarle Simensen (Oslo: Norwegian University Press, 1986).

74. Gjerløw, *Beretning vedkommende Sekretærens Reise til Missionsmarken i Zululand og Natal 1887–88*, 12.

75. Gjerløw, *Beretning vedkommende Sekretærens Reise til Missionsmarken i Zululand og Natal 1887–88.*, 20.

76. Gjerløw, *Beretning vedkommende Sekretærens Reise til Missionsmarken i Zululand og Natal 1887–88*, 24–6.

77. Myklebust, 'Sør-Afrika', 103–5.

78. Jarle Simensen and Vidar Gynnild, 'Norwegian Missionaries in the Nineteenth Century: Organizational Background, Social Profile and World View', in *Norwegian Missions in African History, Vol 1: South Africa 1845–1906*, ed. Jarle Simensen (Oslo: Norwegian University Press, 1986), 35.

79. Det Norske Missionsselskabs 28de Aarsberetning (Stavanger 1870), 57–68.

80. Minutes of the NMS Home Board meeting of 25.9.1868, the Home Board's Journal of Negotiations 1862–1875, MA-MHS, HA/G.sekr.10.

81. Minutes of the NMS Home Board meeting of 12.7.1872, the Home Board's Journal of Negotiations 1862–1875, MA-MHS, HA/G.sekr.10.

82. Line Nyhagen Predelli, 'Marriage in Norwegian Missionary Practice and Discourse in Norway and Madagascar, 1880–1910', *Journal of Religion in Africa* 31, no. 1 (2001): 4–48.

83. Letter from Ole Stavem to the NMS's Home Board of 27.12.1890, MA-MHS, HA/G.sekr.90/Box 139/Jacket 3.

84. Predelli, 'Marriage in Norwegian Missionary Practice and Discourse in Norway and Madagascar, 1880–1910', 38.

85. Birkeli and Tidemann Strand, *Kallet og veien. Det Norske Misjonsselskaps misjonsskole 1850–1959*, 215. § 10 in the House Order.

86. In October 1876, a few days before his departure to South Africa, Christian Oftebro attended a Home Board meeting where he signed a contract and with a handshake confirmed his missionary vows. See minutes of the NMS's Home Board meeting of 19.10.1876, the Home Board's Journal of Negotiations 1875–1881, MA-MHS, HA/G.sekr.10.

87. Letter from the NMS's Home Board to Christian Oftebro of 2.12.1887, in MA-MHS, HA/G.sekr.91/Box 165/Copybook A.

88. Minutes of MC 1886, issues 1 and 3, MA-MHS, HA/G.sekr.40/Box 35/Jacket 13.

89. The resolution is printed in Gjerløw, *Beretning vedkommende Sekretærens Reise til Missionsmarken i Zululand og Natal 1887–88*, 58–60.
90. *Instruks for det Norske Missionsselskabs Udsendinger*, § 18.
91. Minutes of the extraordinary MC 1887, MA-MHS, HA/G.sekr.40/Box 36/ Jacket 3.
92. *Instruks for det Norske Missionsselskabs Udsendinger*, § 17.
93. Gjerløw, *Beretning vedkommende Sekretærens Reise til Missionsmarken i Zululand og Natal 1887–88*, 56–7.
94. *NMT* 43, no. 12 (1887): 228.
95. Letter from Ole Stavem to the NMS's Home Board of 30.4.1888, MA-MHS, HA/G.sekr.90/Box 138/Jacket 3.
96. Letter from Karl Larsen Titlestad to the NMS's Home Board of 30.6.1888, MA-MHS, HA/G.sekr.90/Box 138/Jacket 3.
97. Letter from Ommund Oftebro to the NMS's Home Board of 5.5.1888, MA-MHS, HA/G.sekr.90/Box 138/Jacket 3.
98. Copy of a transcribed letter by Ommund Oftebro to his brother Tobias Oftebro of 5.6.1888. Torstein Oftebro's private archive.
99. Copy of a transcribed letter by Ommund Oftebro to his brother Tobias Oftebro of 5.6.1888. Torstein Oftebro's private archive.
100. The title of this subchapter refers to Yvonne Maria Werner's research project: *Christian Manliness – a Paradox of Modernity?*
101. Vance, *The Sinews of the Spirit*, 10–17.
102. Anna Prestjan, *Präst och karl, karl och präst: Prästmanlighet i tidigt 1900-tal* (Lund: Sekel Bokförlag, 2009), 102.
103. Anna Prestjan, *Präst och karl, karl och präst*, 29–32. See also Anna Prestjan, 'The Man in the Clergyman: Swedish Priest Obituaries, 1905–1937', in *Christian Masculinity: Men and Religion in Northern Europe in the 19th and 20th Centuries*, ed. Yvonne Maria Werner (Leuven: Leuven University Press, 2011).
104. A copy of the 1874 'House Order' is printed in Birkeli and Tidemann Strand, *Kallet og veien. Det Norske Misjonsselskaps misjonsskole 1850–1959*, 214–24.
105. Gjerløw, *Beretning vedkommende Sekretærens Reise til Missionsmarken i Zululand og Natal 1887–88*, 16.
106. Gjerløw, *Beretning vedkommende Sekretærens Reise til Missionsmarken i Zululand og Natal 1887–88*, 26.
107. David Tjeder, 'Borgerlighetens sköra manlighet', in *Män i Norden: Manlighet och modernitet 1840–1940*, ed. Claes Ekenstam and Jørgen Lorentzen (Hedemora: Gidlund, 2006), 56–60.
108. David Tjeder, *The Power of Character: Middle-Class Masculinities, 1800–1900* (PhD dissertation, Stockholm University), 39–44.
109. Tjeder, *The Power of Character*, 56–63.
110. Gjerløw, *Beretning vedkommende Sekretærens Reise til Missionsmarken i Zululand og Natal 1887–88*, 1.
111. Myklebust, 'Sør-Afrika', 105.
112. John Tosh, 'Manliness, Masculinities and the New Imperialism, 1880–1900', in *Manliness and Masculinities in Nineteenth-Century Britain: Essays on Gender, Family and Empire*, ed. John Tosh (Harlow: Longman, 2005), 193.
113. Hall, ed., *Muscular Christianity*, 7.
114. Gjerløw, *Beretning vedkommende Sekretærens Reise til Missionsmarken i Zululand og Natal 1887–88*, 22–24, 28. See also letters from Ole Stavem

to the NMS's Home Board of 17.4.1888 and 28.6.1888, MA-MHS, HA/G. sekr.90/Boks 138/Jacket 3.

115. Letters from Ole Stavem to the NMS's Home Board of 2.6.1888 and 28.6.1888, MA-MHS, HA/G.sekr.90/Boks 138/Jacket 3.

116. Minutes of MC 1926, MA-MHS, 57.

117. Per Hernæs examined the NMS's Industrial School at Eshowe and found that this institution was never given priority in terms of competent personnel or capital investments; see Hernæs, *Norsk misjon og sosial endring*, 234–40.

118. See, e.g., minutes of MC 1911, MA-MHS, 19–25.

119. Munthe, *Venstrehandsmisjon? Misjonslegar på Madagaskar frå 1860-åra og ut hundreåret*; Thor Strandenæs, 'Misjonsdiakonien som kulturuttrykk i Kina: En tekst- og billeddokumentasjon fra Hunanprovinsen', in *Misjon og kultur. Festskrift til Jan-Martin Berentsen*, ed. Thor Strandenæs (Stavanger: Misjonshøgskolens forlag, 2006).

4 Confessional Missionary Masculinity

1. Anders Olsen and Ole Stavem, 'Misjonsprest Karl Titlestad. 1832–1924', *Norvegia Sacra* 5 (1925): 151.

2. Olsen and Stavem, 'Misjonsprest Karl Titlestad', 150. Gustav Adolph Lammers (1802–1878), a pastor in the Church of Norway, broke with the official church in 1856 and established an 'apostolic-Christian' congregation in Skien, his hometown. Lammers inspired the establishment of similar congregations in several parts of Norway. It is, however, incorrect to label the Lammers movement a Baptist movement. Lammers eventually returned to the official church in 1860. The first Baptist congregation in Norway was established in Skien in 1860 by the Danish seaman Fredrik L. Rymker (1819–84), see Ingunn Folkestad Breistein, *'Har staten bedre borgere?' Dissenternes kamp for religiøs frihet 1891–1969* (Trondheim: Tapir Akademisk Forlag, 2003).

3. Yvonne Maria Werner, 'Kristen manlighet i teori och praxis', in *Kristen manlighet: Ideal och verklighet 1830–1940*, ed. Yvonne Maria Werner (Lund: Nordic Academic Press, 2008); Yvonne Maria Werner, 'Religious Feminisation, Confessionalism and Re-masculinisation in Western European Society 1800–1960', in *Pieties and Gender*, ed. Lene Sjørup and Hilda Rømer Christensen (Leiden: Brill, 2009).

4. Olaf Blaschke, 'Fältmarskalk Jesus Kristus: Religiös remaskulinisering i Tyskland', in *Kristen manlighet: Ideal och verklighet 1830–1940*, ed. Yvonne Maria Werner (Lund: Nordic Academic Press, 2008).

5. Olav Guttorm Myklebust, 'Sør-Afrika', in *Det Norske Misjonsselskap 1842–1942*, ed. John Nome (Stavanger: Dreyer, 1949), 24–5.

6. Ole Stavem, *Et bantufolk og kristendommen: Det norske missionsselskaps sytti-aarige zulumission* (Stavanger: Det norske missionsselskaps forlag, 1915), 87–94.

7. Olav Guttorm Myklebust, *H. P. S. Schreuder: Kirke og misjon* (Oslo: Land og kirke/Gyldendal, 1980), 245.

8. Myklebust, 'Sør-Afrika', 28–9.

9. Norman Etherington, 'Kingdoms of This World and the Next: Christian Beginnings among the Zulu and Swazi', in *Christianity in South Africa: A*

Political, Social and Cultural History, ed. Richard Elphick and Rodney Davenport (Oxford: James Curry, 1997).

10. Norman Etherington, *Preachers Peasants and Politics in Southeast Africa, 1835–1880: African Christian Communities in Natal, Pondoland and Zululand* (London: Royal Historical Society), 4.

11. Per Hernæs, 'The Zulu Kingdom, Norwegian Missionaries, and British Imperialism, 1845–1879', in *Norwegian Missions in African History, Vol. 1: South Africa 1845–1906*, ed. Jarle Simensen (Oslo: Norwegian University Press, 1986), 117–36. This period is defined by Hernæs as the NMS missionaries' 'national phase', contrasting with a later 'imperialistic phase'.

12. Halfdan E. Sommerfelt, *Den Norske Zulumission: Et Tilbageblik paa de første 20 Aar af det Norske Missionsselskabs Virksomhed* (Christiania: Wm. Gram, 1865), 345.

13. Olav Guttorm Myklebust, 'Bekjennelsesspørsmålet og Det Norske Misjonsselskap i 1840- og 1850-årene', *Norsk tidsskrift for misjon* 13, no. 4 (1959): 237–46.

14. Olav Guttorm Myklebust, 'Bekjennelsesspørsmålet i den protestantiske misjonsbevegelsens gjennombruddstid', *Norsk tidsskrift for misjon* 13, no. 3 (1959): 148–61.

15. E.g. The London Missionary Society constituted in 1795.

16. William Carey and the Baptist Missionary Society, established in 1792, did not accent the society's confessional basis, rather vice versa.

17. Myklebust, 'Bekjennelsesspørsmålet og Det Norske Misjonsselskap i 1840- og 1850-årene'.

18. Etherington, *Preachers Peasants and Politics in Southeast Africa*, 24–46.

19. Etherington, *Preachers Peasants and Politics in Southeast Africa*, 46.

20. See, e.g., Ommund Oftebro referring to the Anglican missionary Robert Robertson in *NMT* 34, no. 19 (1878): 386–87; Ole Stavem referring to his stay at the American Board's mission station Umvoti in *NMT* 35, no. 7 (1879): 138; Karl Larsen Titlestad describing his friendly-neighbour relationship to the Swedish missionary Otto Witt in *NMT* 40, no. 18 (1884): 364–65; and Ommund Oftebro reporting from a trip he had to Pietermaritzburg where he attended services in both Dutch Reformed and Wesleyan churches in *NMT* 41, no. 40 (1885): 204–05.

21. Siver Marthin Samuelsen and Arnt Tønnesen, who both arrived in Zululand as assistant missionaries in 1854, transferred to the Society for the Propagation of the Gospel in Foreign Parts (SPG) in 1857. Georg Fredrik Carlsen started out as an assistant missionary in 1860, but left the NMS in 1868. After some years as a colonist he was employed by the SPG in 1871.

22. Lars Dahle and Simon Emanuel Jørgensen, *Festskrift til Det Norske Missionsselskabs Jubilæum i 1892* (Stavanger: Det Norske Missionsselskabs Forlag, 1892), 136; Stavem, *Et bantufolk og kristendommen*, 308–13; Myklebust, 'Sør-Afrika', 106–17.

23. Herman Schlyter, *The History of the Co-operating Lutheran Missions in Natal 1912–1951* (Durban: Lutheran Publishing House, 1953). Representatives from six Lutheran missions assembled for a first conference – The Free Evangelical Lutheran Church Conference of South Africa – at Umphumulo. Besides the NMS, the Berlin Mission Society (BMS), the Hermannsburg Mission Society (HMS), the Church of Sweden Mission (CSM), the Church of Norway Mission

by Schreuder (from 1928 American Lutheran Mission (ALM)) and the Hanover Free Church Mission (HFCM) participated.

24. Herman Schlyter, *The History of the Co-operating Lutheran Missions in Natal 1912–1951*, 59.

25. For an overview of the process, see Helge Fosseus, *Mission blir kyrka: Luthersk kyrkobilding i södra Afrika 1957–1961* (Stockholm: Verbum, 1974). ELCSA has an Episcopal organisation and consists of seven dioceses. The previous Norwegian mission church is part of the south-eastern diocese.

26. Klaus Fiedler, *The Story of Faith Missions: From Hudson Taylor to Present Day Africa* (Oxford: Regnum Books International, 1994).

27. Robert Edgar, 'New Religious Movements', in *Missions and Empire*, ed. Norman Etherington (Oxford: Oxford University Press, 2005), 216.

28. Bengt Sundkler, *Bantu Prophets in South Africa* (London: Lutterworth Press, 1948); Bengt Sundkler, *Zulu Zion and some Swazi Zionists* (London: Oxford University Press, 1976); Etherington, *Preachers Peasants and Politics in Southeast Africa*, 145–63; Erhard Kamphausen, 'Unknown Heroes: The Founding Fathers of the Ethiopian Movement in South Africa', in *The Making of an Indigenous Clergy in Southern Africa: Proceedings of the International Conference held at the University of Natal, Pietermaritzburg, 25–27 October 1994*, ed. Philippe Denis (Pietermaritzburg: Cluster Publications, 1995), 83–100; Simon Moripe, 'Indigenous Clergy in the Zion Christian Church', in *The Making of an Indigenous Clergy in Southern Africa*, ed. Philippe Denis (Pietermaritzburg: Cluster Publications, 1995), 102–7.

29. *NMT* 45, no. 2 (1889): 30–1.

30. To further inform the Norwegian mission supporters about the 'revival among the kaffirs in the colony of Natal', translated extracts from some of pastor Turnbull's mission pamphlets were printed in the *NMT* 46, no. 5 (1890): 88–92. The Dutch Reformed Church had traditionally been reluctant to do mission work among Africans and had mainly been a church for the Boer settler population. After a 'mission revival' in the 1860s, however, inspired by Andrew Murray (1828–1917), a first step was taken towards mission activity. Murray established a Missionary Institute in Wellington where both lay men and pastors were educated and equipped for service among indigenous groups. See Bengt Sundkler and Christopher Steed, *A History of the Church in Africa* (Cambridge: Cambridge University Press, 2000), 331.

31. *NMT* 45, no. 3 (1889): 44–51.

32. Lars Dahle, *Inspektionsreisen til Zulu og Madagaskar i 1903: Indberetning til Generalforsamlingen i Bergen 1904* (Stavanger: Det norske Missionsselskabs Forlag, 1904), 13–14.

33. Josaya Semes resigned from the NMS in 1925 and joined the African Congregational Church. Petros Lamula broke with the NMS in 1926 and established the United Native National Church of Christ. See Paul La Hausse de Lalouvière, *Restless Identities: Signatures of Nationalism, Zulu Ethnicity and History in the Lives of Petros Lamula (c. 1881–1948) and Lymon Maling (1889–c. 1936)* (Pietermaritzburg: University of Natal Press, 2000), 124–45.

34. The most thorough study of the FEAM is Frederick Hale, *Scandinavian Free Church Missions in Southern Africa, 1889–1960* (doctoral thesis, University of South Africa, 1988). See also Anne Folke Henningsen, '*En straalende Juvel i Frelserens Krone': Civiliseringsbestræbelser i Den Frie Østafrikanske Missions*

frelsesvirksomhed i Natal og Zululand 1889–1899 (unpublished master's thesis, Roskilde Universitetscenter, 2003). Biographical research on the FEAM female missionaries Emilie Häggberg and Martha Sanne is done by Karin Sarja, *'Ännu en syster till Afrika': Trettiosex kvinnliga missionärer i Natal och Zululand* (Uppsala: Studia Missionalia Svecana LXXXVIII, 2002), 112–45 and Hanna Mellemsether, *Kvinne i to verdener: En kulturhistorisk analyse av afrika-misjonæren Martha Sannes liv i perioden 1884–1901* (Trondheim: Senter for kvinneforsknings skriftserie, 1994).

35. Fiedler, *The Story of Faith Missions*, 11–12, 33.

36. Hale, *Scandinavian Free Church Missions in Southern Africa*, 42–58. See also Erik Sidenvall, *The Making of Manhood among Swedish Missionaries in China and Mongolia, c. 1890–c. 1914* (Leiden/Boston: Brill, 2009), 23–46.

37. The following biography on Paul Peter Wettergren is based on Hale, *Scandinavian Free Church Missions in Southern Africa*, 66–79; Frederick Hale, 'Scandinavian Urban Evangelisation in Southern Africa: The Free East Africa Mission in Durban, 1889–1999', *Swedish Missiological Themes* 86, no. 2 (1998): 227–50; Terje Solberg, '1877–1902: "Og nu staar os intet tilbage..."' in *Midt i livet: Den Evangelisk Lutherske Frikirke 1877–2002*, ed. Ole Angell, Per Eriksen, and Terje Solberg (Oslo: Norsk Luthersk Forlag, 2002).

38. Paul Peter Wettergren, *Brev til mine Venner i Anledning af min Udtrædelse af Statskirken den 27 de Marts 1877* (Risør: J.G. Fryxell, 1877).

39. The concept of *re-baptism* (*anabaptism*) is controversial and reflects huge theological and confessional controversies. In the Scandinavian countries where practically all citizens had been baptised as children, a second baptism as an adult was understood as a *re-baptism* and according to Lutheran theology strictly condemned.

40. The FEAM came to feel most affiliated with the denomination Norwegian Mission Covenant (Det Norske Missionsforbund), and the magazine *Missionæren* served for many years as an unofficial organ for this organisation. Norwegian Mission Covenant came into existence in 1884 in the wake of Franson's first campaign in Norway and regarded itself a Fransonian organisation. Hale, *Scandinavian Free Church Missions in Southern Africa*, 59–64.

41. Hale, *Scandinavian Free Church Missions in Southern Africa*, 118–27. For a history of the Church of Sweden Mission, see Tore Furberg, *Kyrka och Mission i Sverige 1868–1901: Svenska Kyrkans Missions tillkomst och första verksomhetstid* (Uppsala: Svenska Institutet för Missionsforskning, 1962).

42. This station is best known in the annals of South African military history as the site of the battle of Rorke's Drift during the Anglo-Zulu war of 1879. Otto Witt and his family escaped to Sweden in 1878 and were not present at Rorke's Drift during the battles.

43. Hale, *Scandinavian Free Church Missions in Southern Africa*, 118–27. See also Frederick Hale, *The Missionary Career and Spiritual Odyssey of Otto Witt* (doctoral thesis, University of Cape Town, 1991). Hale seems to be alone in his biographical research on this remarkable Swedish missionary.

44. Otto Witt left both South Africa and FEAM and returned to Sweden in late 1891. For a while he was employed by the Swedish Holiness Union (*Svenska Helgelseförbundet*), but from 1894 he worked as a religious freelance, with no denominational affiliation. He finally joined the Pentecostal movement. Witt died in 1923.

45. NMS missionary Gundvall Gundersen reported in *NMT* 46, no. 12 (1890): 231–34 that Olaf Wettergren had recently 're-baptised' eight adults in the Scandinavian congregation.
46. See, e.g., *NMT* 37, no. 21 (1881): 40–4, where Ommund Oftebro reported preaching in the Scandinavian congregation consisting of around 40 members. Also Ole Stavem and Lars Berge had, according to Oftebro, recently visited the congregation.
47. For a history of the Scandinavian church in Durban, see Ernst Hallen, *Nordisk Kirkeliv Under Sydkorset: Festskrift i anledning Den Norsk Lutherske Kirkes 50 Aarsjubileum i Durban 14 mars 1880–14 mars 1930* (Durban: The Mission Press, 1930); M. F. Lear, *The St. Olav Lutheran Church 1880–1980: Its Origin and History Over One Hundred Years* (Durban: Unity Publications, 1980).
48. Letter from Ole Stavem to the NMS's Home Board of 27.12.1889, in MA-MHS, HA/G.sekr.90/Box 138/Jacket 10.
49. Letter from Ole Stavem to the NMS's Home Board of 25.1.1890, in MA-MHS, HA/G.sekr.90/Box 139/Jacket 3.
50. Minutes from MC 1890, issue 8, MA-MHS, HA/G.sekr.40/Box 36/Jacket 15.
51. Letter from the NMS's Home Board of 5.5.1890, in NMS/South Africa/Box 1A/Jacket 16.
52. Letter from Ole Stavem to the NMS's Home Board of 27.12.1890, in MA-MHS, HA/G.sekr.90/Box 139/Jacket 3.
53. Letter from Ole Stavem to the NMS's Home Board of 6.3.1891, in MA-MHS. HA/G.sekr.40/Box 37/Jacket 6.
54. Letter to Karl Larsen Titlestad of 16.3.1891, in MA-MHS, HA/G.sekr.91/Box 165/Copybook A.
55. Letter from Karl Larsen Titlestad to the NMS's Home Board of 11.5.1891, MA-MHS, HA/G.sekr.90/Box 139/Jacket 10.
56. *NMT* 45, no. 12 (1889): 357–9.
57. Sidenvall, *The Making of Manhood among Swedish Missionaries in China and Mongolia*, 30–1.
58. John Nome, 'Det Norske Misjonsselskaps Historie i Norsk Kirkeliv: Fra Syttiårene til Nåtiden', in *Det Norske Misjonsselskap 1842–1942*, ed. John Nome, vol. 2 (Stavanger: Dreyer, 1943), 105–21.
59. Oscar Handeland, *Det Norske Lutherske Kinamisjonsforbund Gjennom 50 år* (Oslo: Forbundets Forlag, 1941), 35–54.
60. Handeland, *Det Norske Lutherske Kinamisjonsforbund,* 53–4.
61. *NMT* 47, no. 19 (1891): 375–7.
62. *NMT* 20, no. 3 (1865): 49–61. On the ship were Marcus Dahle, Gundvall Gundersen, Hans Christian Leisegang, Petter Nilsen, Ole Steenberg and Karl Larsen Titlestad, who were all commissioned for service in Zululand, and also the pioneer missionaries to Madagascar, John Engh and Nils Nilsen. Two women were among the travellers. Karen Titlestad was the wife of Karl Larsen Titlestad. Wencke von der Lippe Knudsen was the fiancée of Wettergren, who had served in Zululand since 1861.
63. Lovise Olsen, a sickly young woman in Bergen, initiated the building of a Norwegian mission ship. She envisioned a ship at the disposal of the NMS, crewed with proper Christian seamen, and which should be like a Norwegian home for departing and arriving missionaries. The NMS ran the ship *Elieser* from 1864 until 1884 and *Paulus* from 1885 until 1893. For a history of *Elieser*, see Edle Solberg, *I misjonærfart: Med kaptein Landmark*

og Elieser (Stavanger: Nomi, 1965); Gunnar Andreas Meling, *På tokt med Elieser: Pionermisjonærene og deres skip 1864–1884* (Stavanger: Det Norske Misjonsselskap, 1982). For a history of *Paulus*, see Gunnar Andreas Meling, *I fredens kjølvann: Misjonsskipet Paulus i storm og stille 1884–1894* (Stavanger: Det Norske Misjonsselskap, 1984).

64. *NMT* 29, no. 3 (1865): 61.
65. Nome, 'Det Norske Misjonsselskaps historie i norsk kirkeliv: Fra syttiårene til nåtiden', 38–41.
66. John Tosh, 'Manliness, Masculinities and the New Imperialism, 1880–1900', in *Manliness and Masculinities in Nineteenth-Century Britain: Essays on Gender, Family and Empire*, ed. John Tosh (Harlow: Longman, 2005), 192–214.
67. Hernæs, 'The Zulu Kingdom, Norwegian Missionaries, and British Imperialism', 136–75.
68. *NMT* 48, no. 15 (1893): 289–92.
69. *NMT* 49, no. 18 (1894): 346–50.
70. See, e.g., the poem that Arne Valen, a missionary in Madagascar, wrote after the death of his colleague Johan Christian Haslund in 1886 in *NMT* 41, no. 19 (1886): 374–76.
71. Markus Dahle, 'Christian Oftebro', in *Hjem fra Kamppladsen: Livsbilleder af Norske Missionærer*, ed. Anders Olsen (Kristiania: Steen'ske Bogtrykkeri og Forlag, 1906), 23.
72. Ole Stavem, 'Lars Dahle som missionselev', in *Fra Norges indsats i verdens-missionen: Festskrift ved Lars Dahles femtiaars-jubilæum* (Stavanger: Det norske missionsselskaps trykkeri, 1921), 11–12.
73. Olaf Blaschke, 'Fältmarskalk Jesus Kristus', 28–32.
74. *NMT* 40, no. 2 (1884): 33–40.
75. Stavem argued that the Catholic mission efforts initiated by Ignatius Loyola and the Jesuits were reactions to Luther's reformation.
76. See Alexander Maurits, 'Treståndläran och den lutherske prästmannen', in *Kristen manlighet: Ideal och verklighet 1830–1940*, ed. Yvonne Maria Werner (Lund: Nordic Academic Press, 2008); Alexander Maurits, 'The Exemplary Lives of Christian Heroes as an Historical Construct', *Journal of Men, Masculinities and Spirituality* 3, no. 1 (2009): 4–21.
77. Hallen, *Nordisk Kirkeliv Under Sydkorset*, 45–6.
78. The congregation's memorial volume from 1930 (ibid.) has many references to central church women.
79. Hallen, *Nordisk Kirkeliv Under Sydkorset*, 85–88.
80. Minutes from MC 1890, issue 8, MA-MHS, HA/G.sekr.40/Box 36/Jacket 15.
81. Letter from Ole Stavem to the NMS's Home Board of 02.10.1890, in MA-MHS, HA/G.sekr.90/Box 139/Jacket 3.
82. An open invitation to the conference was printed in *NMT* 45, no. 10 (1889): 200.
83. Ruth Hemstad, *Fra Indian Summer til nordisk vinter: Skandinavisk samarbeid, skandinavisme og unionsoppløsningen* (Oslo: Akademisk publisering, 2008), 99.
84. See *NMT* 45, no. 11 (1889): 223–24; no. 15: 296–300; no. 16: 306–12, 314–20; no. 17: 335–43.
85. Løgstrup, *Nordisk Missionshaandbog* (København: 1889).
86. *NMT* 45, no. 21 (1889): 424.
87. *NMT* 45, no. 16 (1889): 308–09.

88. C. Strömberg, 'Hednamissionens återverkan på hemlandskyrkans religiøsa lif', *Nordic Journal of Mission* 1 (1890): 97–120.
89. David Tjeder, *The Power of Character: Middle-Class Masculinities, 1800–1900* (PhD dissertation, Stockholm University, 2003).
90. Strömberg, 'Hednamissionens återverkan på hemlandskyrkans religiøsa lif', 113.
91. Sidenvall, *The Making of Manhood among Swedish Missionaries in China and Mongolia*, 8–9.
92. Myklebust, 'Sør-Afrika', 121.
93. See the recent articles: Derek K. Hastings, 'Fears of a Feminized Church: Catholicism, Clerical Celibacy, and the Crisis of Masculinity in Wilhelmine Germany', *European History Quarterly* 38, no. 1 (2008): 34–65; Tysler Carrington, 'Instilling the "Manly" Faith: Protestant Maculinity and the German *Jünglingsvereine* at the *fin de siècle*', *Journal of Men, Masculinities and Spirituality* 3, no. 2 (2009): 142–54.

5 Norwegian Missionary Masculinity and 'Other' Zulu Masculinity

1. *NMT* 14, no. 11 (1859): 186–88. Udland reported that one infant and six adults were baptised. The adults' new Christian names were 'Utomase, Usimone, Ukosi, Uvelemu, Uhendreke and Unokutemba'.
2. Prince Bongani kaShelemba Zulu, 'The Ministry of the Black People in the Lutheran Norwegian Mission Stations in Zululand and Natal from 1875 to 1963' (unpublished conference paper, University of Stellenbosch, 2009).
3. *NMT* 30, no. 6 (1875): 207–10.
4. *NMT* 30, no. 6 (1875): 241–42.
5. Minutes from MC 1889, MA-MHS, NMS/HA/G.sekr.40/Box 36/Jacket 11.
6. Olav Guttorm Myklebust, 'Sør-Afrika', in *Det Norske Misjonsselskap 1842–1942*, ed. John Nome (Stavanger: Dreyer, 1949), 114.
7. In June 2008 the 150th anniversary of this first baptism in the history of the NMS was celebrated at the present head office in Stavanger.
8. *NMT* 48, no. 15 (1893): 309–11.
9. Torstein Jørgensen, *Contact and Conflict: Norwegian Missionaries, the Zulu Kingdom, and the Gospel: 1850–1873* (Oslo: Solum, 1990), 218.
10. Mrinalini Sinha, *Colonial Masculinity: The 'Manly Englishman' and the 'Effeminate Bengali' in the Late Nineteenth Century* (Manchester and New York: Manchester University Press, 1995).
11. Robert Morrell, *Changing Men in Southern Africa* (Pietermaritzburg: University of Natal Press, 2001), 6.
12. Belinda Bozzoli, 'Marxism, Feminism and South African Studies', *Journal of Southern African Studies* 9, no. 2 (1983), 149.
13. Cherryl Walker, 'Women and Gender in Southern Africa to 1945: An Overview', in *Women and Gender in Southern Africa to 1945*, ed. Cherryl Walker (Cape Town/London: David Philip/James Currey, 1990), 1.
14. Robert Morrell, 'Of Boys and Men: Masculinity and Gender in Southern African Studies', *Journal of Southern African Studies* 24, no. 4 (1998), 616–30.

15. Halfdan E. Sommerfelt, *Den Norske Zulumission: Et Tilbageblik paa de første 20 Aar af det Norske Missionsselskabs Virksomhed* (Christiania: Wm. Gram, 1865).

16. Sommerfelt refers to Henry H. Methuen's *Life in the Wilderness or Wanderings in South Africa* (1846), Robert Moffat's *Missionary Labours and Scenes in Southern Africa* (1842) and Captein William Ross King's *Campaigning in Kaffirland or Scenes and Adventuresof the Kaffir War of 1851–2* (1853). He also refers to the German missionary Karl Wilhelm Posselt's articles in *Berliner Missionsbericht*.

17. Ole Stavem, *Et bantufolk og kristendommen: Det norske missionsselskaps syttiaarige zulumission* (Stavanger: Det norske missionsselskaps forlag, 1915); Myklebust, 'Sør-Afrika'.

18. Hans Kristian Leisegang, *Vor Zulumission* (Stavanger: Det Norske Missionsselskaps forlag, 1921); *Misjonsalbum: Syd-afrika: 109 billeder og et kart fra Det Norske Misjonsselskaps arbeidsmark i Zulu og Natal* (Stavanger: Det Norske Misjonsselskaps forlag, 1928); Johan Kjelvei, ed., *Zulu: Evangeliets landvinning* (Stavanger: Det Norske Misjonsselskaps trykkeri, 1932).

19. Myklebust, 'Sør-Afrika', 17.

20. Stavem, *Et bantufolk og kristendommen*, 42.

21. Kjelvei, ed., *Zulu: Evangeliets landvinning*, 43.

22. Andrew Burgess, *Zulufolket: Evangeliet blant zuluerne* (Oslo: Schreudermisjonens forlag, 1944), 43.

23. Sommerfelt, *Den Norske Zulumission*, 72.

24. Sommerfelt claimed that Zululand was the healthiest region of the world, and that Western physicians who tried to establish an enterprise in Zululand became jobless and either had to return or make a living out of farming.

25. Myklebust, 'Sør-Afrika', 17.

26. Sommerfelt, *Den Norske Zulumission*, 80–3. Ishmael was Abraham's illegal son, born by the female thrall Hagar. According to Genesis 25, Ishmael had 12 sons who were all chiefs ruling in the Suez area. Sommerfelt claimed that Ishmael's descendants had immigrated to central and southern areas of Africa and saw many similarities between Jewish and Zulu religious belief and practice.

27. The Anglican missionary Allen Gardiner compared Zulu spirituality to Hebrew worship. See Benedict Carton, 'Awaken *Nkulunkulu*, Zulu God of the Old Testament: Pioneering Missionaries during the Early Stage of Racial Spectacle', in *Zulu Identities: Being Zulu, Past and Present*, ed. Benedict Carton, John Laband and Jabulani Sithole (Scottsville: University of KwaZulu-Natal Press, 2008), 142–45.

28. Nils Astrup, *En Missionsreise til Limpopo* (Kristiania: Th. Steens Forlagsexpedition, 1891); Nils Astrup, *Zulumissionens Maal – Afrikas Hjerte* (Christiania: Johannes Bjørnstads bogtrykkeri, 1903).

29. Stavem, *Et bantufolk og kristendommen*, 11–28.

30. Extracts of Stavem's collection were published in a Cape Town Folklore Journal; see e.g. Ole Stavem, *USomamekutyo* (Cape Town: Folklore Journal, 1879). He furthermore translated some of the fairy tales into the Norwegian language; see *NMT* 40, no. 21 (1885): 421–24; Ole Stavem, *Intela jolimi i lojelwe abafana ba kwa Zulu, aba funda esikoleni* (Kristiania: Steenske, 1886).

31. Homi K. Bhabha, 'The Other Question: The Stereotype and Colonial Discourse', *Screen* 24, no. 4 (1983): 18–36.

32. Sommerfelt, *Den Norske Zulumission*, 74–5; *NMT* 39, no. 21 (1884), 405–06; *Misjonsalbum: Syd-afrika: 109 billeder og et kart fra Det Norske Misjonsselskaps arbeidsmark i Zulu og Natal*, 7, 9; Kjelvei, ed., *Zulu: Evangeliets landvinning*, 14; Myklebust, 'Sør-Afrika', 17.

33. South African historians are currently reinvestigating the historical truth of Shaka and his so-called 'devastations'; see John Wright, 'Revisiting the Stereotype of Shaka's "Devastations"', in *Zulu Identities: Being Zulu, Past and Present*, ed. Benedict Carton, John Laband and Jabulani Sithole (Scottsville: University of KwaZulu-Natal Press, 2008); Carolyn Hamilton, *Terrific Majesty: The Powers of Shaka Zulu and the Limits of Historical Invention* (Cape Town/ Johannesburg: David Philip Publishers, 1998).

34. Sommerfelt, *Den Norske Zulumission*, 63.

35. John Laband, '"Bloodstained Grandeur": Colonial and Imperial Stereotypes of Zulu Warriors and Zulu Warfare', in *Zulu Identities: Being Zulu, Past and Present*, ed. Benedict Carton, John Laband and Jabulani Sithole (Scottsville: University of KwaZulu-Natal Press, 2008), 168.

36. Ole Stavem, 'Zulufolket, dets Stammeslægtskab og dets Nationalkarakter', in *NMT* 41, no. 11 (1886), 212–17; no. 12, 232–40.

37. Myklebust, 'Sør-Afrika', 17–19.

38. See, e.g., Olav Guttorm Myklebust, 'Syd-Afrika: Motsetningenes og misjonenes land', *Nordisk Missionstidsskrift* 51 (1940): 243–70; Olav Guttorm Myklebust, 'Negerpsyke: Streiflys over sort sjeleliv', *Kirke og Kultur* 84 (1941): 338–54; Olav Guttorm Myklebust, 'Fra frykt til fred: Afrikansk religion – afrikansk kristendom', *Kirke og Kultur* 84 (1941): 413–28.

39. Odd Magne Bakke, '"Negro psyche": The Representation of Black People in the Writings of Missionary Olaf Guttorm Myklebust', *Studia Historiae Ecclesiasticae. Journal of Church History Society of Southern Africa* 36, no. 1 (2010): 37–52.

40. Jørgensen asserts that even if traditional Zulu life was characterised as 'darkness' by the NMS missionaries, they did not have aspects such as racial inferiority or evolutionary backwardness in mind. The reports of the Norwegian missionaries lacked the stereotypes typical of colonial writings, according to Jørgensen, and the missionaries, due to the close and long-lasting contact with the Zulus, rendered a 'much more nuanced and detailed description of Africans than was the case elsewhere'. See Jørgensen, *Contact and Conflict*, 141. See also Torstein Jørgensen, 'Norske misjonærer, samtid og forståelse i det 19. århundre', *Norsk Tidsskrift for Misjon* 39, no. 2 (1985): 75–85; Torstein Jørgensen, 'Misjon som med- og motkultur under kulturimperialismen', in *Misjon og kultur: Festskrift til Jan-Martin Berentsen*, ed. Thor Strandenæs (Stavanger: Misjonshøgskolens forlag, 2006).

41. Myklebust, 'Negerpsyke', 347.

42. Morrell, 'Of Boys and Men', 616.

43. Thirteen letters from 'famous men' in Durban regarding Christian Zulu men, in MA-MHS, HA/G.sekr.92/Box 182/Jacket 19. See also the NMS's 53rd annual report (Stavanger, 1895), 59–62; *NMT* 50, no. 21 (1895): 417–24.

44. Minutes from MC 1926, MA-MHS, 3.

45. Hanna Mellemsether, 'African Women in the Norwegian Mission in South Africa', in *Gender, Race and Religion: Nordic Missions 1860–1940*, ed. Inger Marie Okkenhaug (Uppsala: Swedish Institute of Missionary Research, 2003), 167–70.

46. Deborah Gaitskell, 'Devout Domesticity? A Century of African Women's Christianity in South Africa', in *Women and Gender in Southern Africa to 1945*, ed. Cherryl Walker (Cape Town/London: David Philip/James Currey, 1990), 253.

47. Mellemsether, 'African Women in the Norwegian Mission in South Africa', 160.

48. Paul la Hausse de Lalouvière, '"Death is not the End": Zulu Cosmopolitanism and the Politics of the Zulu Cultural Revival', in *Zulu Identities: Being Zulu, Past and Present*, ed. Benedict Carton, John Laband and Jabulani Sithole (Scottsville: University of KwaZulu-Natal Press, 2008), 258.

49. Mellemsether, 'African Women in the Norwegian Mission in South Africa', 159–66.

50. Walker, 'Women and Gender in Southern Africa to 1945', 13–16; Heather Hughes, '"A Lighthouse for African Womanhood": Inanda Seminary, 1869–1945', in *Women and Gender in Southern Africa to 1945*, ed. Cherryl Walker (Cape Town/London: David Philip/James Currey, 1990).

51. Line Nyhagen Predelli's research on NMS missionaries in Madagascar reveals that Malagasy women according to the missionary reports were 'oppressed, subjugated and alienated from their womanly nature'; see Line Nyhagen Predelli, *Issues of Gender, Race, and Class in the Norwegian Missionary Society in Nineteenth-Century Norway and Madagascar* (Lewiston, NY: Edwin Mellen Press, 2003), 96. Also Lisbeth Mikaelsson, in her study of Norwegian missionaries' autobiographical writings, registers that the narratives of 'heathen' women's cruel life conditions 'abound' in the texts; see Lisbeth Mikaelsson, 'Gender Politics in Femal Autobiography', in *Gender, Race and Religion: Nordic Missions 1860–1940*, ed. Inger Marie Okkenhaug (Uppsala: Swedish Institute of Missionary Research, 2003), 40–3.

52. E.g. Jeff Guy, 'Gender Oppression in Southern Africa's Precapitalist Societies', in *Women and Gender in Southern Africa to 1945*, ed. Cherryl Walker (Cape Town/London: David Philip/James Currey, 1990).

53. E.g. Kumari Jayawardena, *The White Woman's Other Burden: Western Women and South Asia during British Colonial Rule* (New York: Routledge, 1995); Susan Thorne, 'Mission-imperial Feminism', in *Gendered Missions: Women and Men in Missionary Discourse and Practice*, ed. Mary Taylor Huber and Nancy Lutkehaus (Ann Arbor, MI: University of Michigan Press, 1999).

54. Sheila Meintjes, 'Family and Gender in the Christian Community at Edendale, Natal, in Colonial Times', in *Women and Gender in Southern Africa to 1945*, ed. Cherryl Walker (Cape Town/London: David Philip/James Currey, 1990), 132.

55. Hughes, '"A lighthouse for African womanhood"', 203.

56. Minutes from MC 1902, MA-MHS, HA/G.sekr.40/Box 42/Jacket 7.

57. Kjelvei, ed., *Zulu: Evangeliets landvinning*, 69–71.

58. Minutes from MC 1902, MA-MHS, HA/G.sekr. 40/Box 42/Jacket 7.

59. Minutes from MC 1909, MA-MHS, 15–18.

60. Gaitskell, 'Devout domesticity?' 254.

61. Leisegang, *Vor Zulumission*, 5–11.

62. Jarle Simensen, Thomas Børhaug, Per Hernæs and Endre Sønstabø, 'Christian Missions and Socio-Cultural Change in Zululand 1850–1906: Norwegian Strategy and African Response', in *Norwegian Missions in African History, Vol. 1:*

South Africa 1845–1906, ed. Jarle Simensen (Oslo: Norwegian University Press, 1986), 198.

63. Norman Etherington, *Preachers Peasants and Politics in Southeast Africa, 1835–1880: African Christian Communities in Natal, Pondoland and Zululand* (London: Royal Historical Society, 1978), 24.

64. Gaitskell, 'Devout domesticity?' 254.

65. Simensen et al., 'Christian Missions and Socio-Cultural Change in Zululand 1850–1906', 223–9.

66. Although the NMS missionaries' support of British occupation and conquest of Zululand was shared by most Western missionaries in the area, Simensen finds that their attitude can also be explained by the Norwegians' special frustrations under an independent Zulu kingdom. After all, the NMS, and from 1873 Schreuder's mission, were the only missionary societies with their 'nerve centre' in Zululand, and not in the British colony of Natal. The Norwegians' attitude could further be related to their pietistic view of conversion, where distress, crisis and humiliation were regarded as 'positive' factors which could create an awareness of sin and thus lead to salvation.

67. Peder Aage Rødseth, 'Våre kristne', in *Zulu: Evangeliets landvinning,* ed. Johan Kjelvei (Stavanger: Det Norske Misjonsselskaps trykkeri, 1932), 63.

68. Etherington, *Preachers Peasants and Politics in Southeast Africa,* 24–46; Robert Morrell, John Wright and Sheila Meintjes, 'Colonialism and the Establishment of White Domination, 1840–1990', in *Political Economy and Identities in KwaZulu-Natal: Historical and Social Perspectives,* ed. Robert Morrell (Durban: Indicator Press, 1996), 42–45.

69. Per O. Hernæs, *Norsk misjon og sosial endring: Norske misjonærer i Zululand/Natal 1887–1906* (Unpublished MA thesis, University of Trondheim, 1978), 234–40.

70. Norman Etherington, 'Education and Medicine', in *Missions and Empire,* ed. Norman Etherington (Oxford: Oxford University Press, 2005), 264.

71. See, e.g., *NMT* 28, no. 11 (1873): 401–08, where Schreuder elaborates the 'falls' of many concrete Christian Zulu men at the mission stations of Entumeni, Eshowe and Empangeni.

72. *NMT* 28, no. 1 (1873): 10–17.

73. Torstein Jørgensen, 'Zibokjana Ka Gudu Moses: Student fra Zululand ved Misjonshøgskolen 1866–69', in *Nordmenn i Afrika – Afrikanere i Norge,* ed. Anne K. Bang and Kirsten Alsaker Kjerland (Bergen: Vigmostad & Bjørke AS, 2002).

74. Knut Holter, 'Did Prince Cetshwayo Read the Old Testament in 1859? The Role of the Bible and the Art of Reading in the Interaction between Norwegian Missionaries and the Zulu Elite in the Mid-19th Century', *Old Testament Essays* 22, no. 3 (2009): 580–88.

75. *NMT* 26, no. 1 (1871): 7–9; no. 7: 251–6; *NMT* 27, no. 7 (1872): 252; no. 10: 361–6; no. 12: 441–3.

76. *NMT* 31, no. 1 (1876): 11–17.

77. Before Jan Kielland left South Africa in 1874, he received a letter from Moses in which he was asked to greet the congregations in Norway and also Moses' previous teachers at the mission school in Stavanger. Parts of the letter were printed in *NMT* 29, no. 8 (1874): 315.

78. Norman Etherington, 'Outward and Visible Signs of Conversion in Nineteenth-century KwaZulu-Natal', *Journal of Religion in Africa* 32, no. 4 (2002), 422.

79. For a broad discussion, see Jean and John Comaroff, *Of Revelation and Revolution: Christianity, Colonialism, and Consciousness in South Africa* (Chicago/London: University of Chicago Press, 1991); Jean and John Comaroff, *Of Revelation and Revolution: The Dialectics of Modernity on a South African Frontier* (Chicago/London: University of Chicago Press, 1997). For a discussion of religious conversion in the case of NMS missionaries to the Dii people in Cameroon in the mid-twentieth century see Tomas Sundnes Drønen, *Communication and Conversion in Northern Cameroon: The Dii People and Norwegian Missionaries, 1934–60* (Leiden: Brill, 2009).

80. Leisegang, *Vor Zulumission*, 5–11.

81. Rødseth, 'Våre Kristne'.

82. Cited from Robert J. Houle, 'The American Mission Revivals and the Birth of Modern Zulu Evangelism', in *Zulu Identities: Being Zulu, Past and Present*, ed. Benedict Carton, John Laband and Jabulani Sithole (Scottsville: University of KwaZulu-Natal Press, 2008). Houle finds that in the case of the American Zulu Mission, the holiness movement which swept over South Africa in the 1890s, liberated urbanised Christian Zulu from the expectations of their *amakholwa* parents, and from the many warnings of the cities and towns as 'universities of vice'.

83. Georg Scriba and Gunnar Lislerud, 'Lutheran Missions and Churches in South Africa', in *Christianity in South Africa: A Political, Social & Cultural History*, ed. Richard Elphick and Rodney Davenport (Oxford: James Currey, 1997), 190.

84. Letter from the NMS's Home Board of 05.5.1890, MA-MHS, South Africa/Box 1A/Jacket 16.

85. Paul Maylam, 'The Changing Political Economy of the Region, 1920–1950', in *Political Economy and Identities in KwaZulu-Natal: Historical and Social Perspectives*, ed. Robert Morrell (Durban: Indicator Press, 1996), 102–07.

86. La Hausse de Lalouvière, *Restless Identities: Signatures of Nationalism, Zulu Ethnicity and History in the Lives of Petros Lamula (c. 1881–1948) and Lymon Maling (c. 1889–c. 1936)* (Pietermaritzburg: University of Natal Press, 2000).

87. Hanna Mellemsether, *Misjonærer, settlersamfunn og afrikansk opposisjon: Striden om selvstendiggjøring i den norske Zulukirken, Sør-Afrika ca. 1920–1930* (Dr Art dissertation, University of Trondheim, 2001), 171–248.

88. Statement from the discussion at MC 1903, MA, HA/G.sekr.40/Box 42/Jacket 15.

89. Eleven stations in 1885. In 1890 the NMS established a station in Durban, and in 1915 Kangelani mission station was established.

90. Myklebust, 'Sør-Afrika', 32.

91. Myklebust, 132.

92. Peggy Brock, 'New Christians as Evangelists', in *Missions and Empire*, ed. Norman Etherington (Oxford: Oxford University Press, 2005), 132.

93. Myklebust, 'Sør-Afrika', 108–09. The NMS gave priority to the successful field of Madagascar, and from 1901 China became a new and promising mission field.

94. Mission statistics were presented in the superintendent's annual report which was published as a section of the NMS's official annual report. In the case of South Africa, the quality of the statistics improved considerably after Ole Stavem took over as superintendent in 1888.

95. For a general overview of mission societies' education of indigenous clergy in Protestant South Africa, see Joan Millard, 'Educating Indigenous Clergy in Some South African Protestant Churches during the Nineteenth Century', in *The Making of an Indigenous Clergy in Southern Africa: Proceedings of the International Conference held at the University of Natal, Pietermaritzburg, 25–27 October 1994*, ed. Philippe Denis (Pietermaritzburg: Cluster Publications, 1995).

96. Minutes from MC 1881, MA-MHS, HA/G.sekr.40/Box 34/Jacket 21.

97. Ole Stavem reported from the Catechist School in a letter of 30.9.1884, MA-MHS, HA/G.sekr.90/Box 136/Jacket 3.

98. Minutes from MC 1884, MA-MHS, HA/G.sekr.40/Box 35/Jacket 8.

99. Ingolf Edward Hodne, *Missionary Enterprise in African Education: The Co-operating Lutheran Missions in Natal, South Africa, 1912–1955* (Stavanger: Misjonshøgskolens forlag, 1997).

100. Minutes from MC 1905, MA-MHS, HA/G.sekr.40/Box 43/Jacket 11; Letter from the NMS's Home Board to the missionaries in Natal and Zululand of 6.11.1905, MA-MHS, HA/G.sekr.91/Box 171/Jacket 2.

101. Jørgensen, *Contact and Conflict*, 217–23.

102. Etherington, *Preachers Peasants and Politics in Southeast Africa*, 145–75; Philippe Denis, ed., *The Making of an Indigenous Clergy in Southern Africa: Proceedings of the International Conference held at the University of Natal, Pietermaritzburg, 25–27 October 1994* (Pietermaritzburg: Cluster Publications, 1995).

103. Richard Elphick, 'Evangelical Missions and Racial "Equalization"', in *Converting Colonialism: Visions and Realities in Mission History, 1709–1914*, ed. Dana L. Robert (Grand Rapids, MI/Cambridge: Wm. B. Eerdmans Publishing Co., 2008), 112–33. Elphick bases his calculation on the statistics of the 1911 *World Atlas of Christian Missions*.

104. See also Bengt Sundkler, *Bantu Prophets in South Africa* (London: Lutterworth Press, 1948); Bengt Sundkler, *Zulu Zion and Some Swazi Zionists* (London, Oxford University Press, 1976); Erhard Kamphausen, 'Unknown Heroes: The Founding Fathers of the Ethiopian Movement in South Africa', in *The Making of an Indigenous Clergy in Southern Africa: Proceedings of the International Conference held at the University of Natal, Pietermaritzburg, 25–27 October 1994*, ed. Philippe Denis (Pietermaritzburg: Cluster Publications, 1995); Simon Moripe, 'Indigenous Clergy in the Zion Christian Church', in *The Making of an Indigenous Clergy in Southern Africa*, ed. Denis.

105. Etherington, *Preachers Peasants and Politics in Southeast Africa*, 25, 28. Lars Berge found the same to be true in the case of the first black pastor in the Church of Sweden Mission. Josef kaMataka Zulu was ordained in Uppsala, Sweden, in 1901, after a Home Board resolution. See Lars Berge, *The Bambbatha Watershed: Swedish Missionaries, African Christians and an evolving Zulu Church in rural Natal and Zululand 1902–1910*, (Uppsala: SIM, 2000), 260–63.

106. Minutes from MC 1884, MA-MHS, HA/G.sekr.40/Box 35/Jacket 8.

107. Ole Gjerløw, *Beretning vedkommende Sekretærens Reise til Missionsmarken i Zululand og Natal 1887–88* (Stavanger: Det Norske Missionsselskab, 1888), 48.

108. Minutes from MC 1889, MA-MHS, NMS/HA/G.sekr.40/Box 36/Jacket 11.

109. Minutes from MC 1890, MA-MHS, NMS/HA/G.sekr.40/Box 36/Jacket 15.
110. The superintendent's annual report of 1890, MA-MHS, HA/G.sekr.40/Box 37/Jacket 6.
111. Minutes from MC 1892, MA-MHS, HA/G.sekr.40/Box 37/Jacket 14.
112. By the mid-1870s Anglican missionaries paid their evangelists £2 per month and a salary of £50 per annum was thought sufficient for an ordained priest. The highest salary paid to any African by Christian missionaries in the 1870s was £75 per annum. Etherington, *Preachers Peasants and Politics in Southeast Africa*, 148.
113. The NMS's 52nd annual report (Stavanger 1894), 53–72.
114. Minutes from MC 1903, MA-MHS, HA/G.sekr.40/Box 42/Jacket 15.
115. It is not reported in the superintendent's annual report of 1903, nor in Lars Dahle's official report from his inspection trip; see Lars Dahle, *Inspektionsreisen til Zulu og Madagaskar i 1903: Indberetning til Generalforsamlingen i Bergen 1904* (Stavanger: Det norske Missionsslskabs Forlag, 1904).
116. Shula Marks, *Reluctant Rebellion: The 1906–8 Disturbances in Natal* (Oxford: Clarendon Press, 1970), 51–82.
117. Marks, *Reluctant Rebellion*, 80–1; Clement Tsheloane Keto, 'Race Relations, Land and the Changing Missionary Role in South Africa: A Case Study of the American Zulu Mission, 1850–1910', *International Journal of African Historical Studies* 10, no. 4 (1977): 600–27; Kristin Norseth, 'To alen av hvilket stykke? Tvillingsøstrene LMF og KMA i norsk, nordisk og internasjonalt perspektiv', *Norsk tidsskrift for misjon* 56, no. 2 (2002): 91–106; Kristin Fjelde Tjelle, 'Lærerinnenes Misjonsforbund gjennom 100 år', *Norsk tidsskrift for misjon* 56, no. 2 (2002): 67–89; Inger Marie Okkenhaug, '"Herren har givet mig et rigt virkefelt": Kall, religion og arbeid blant armenere i det osmanske riket', *Historisk tidsskrift* 88, no. 1 (2009): 39–60.
118. Minutes from MC 1902, MA-MHS, HA/G.sekr.40/Box 42/Jacket 7. See also Zulu, 'The Ministry of the Black People in the Lutheran Norwegian Mission Stations in Zululand and Natal from 1875 to 1963', where he recounts that Simon Ndlela was hit by the severe agrarian crises of the 1890s, like droughts, infestations of locusts and rinderpest.
119. Minutes from MC 1903, MA-MHS, HA/G.sekr.40/Box 42/Jacket 15.
120. Rødseth does not mention the newspaper's name, but John Langalibalele Dube established the first Zulu/English newspaper *Ilanga lase Natal* in 1903.
121. Some asked whether Simon really had written that article personally, or whether he was protecting his sons or others who may have done it. They found Simon to be influenced by 'unfavourable surroundings' – his sons and his wife. He could also have been influenced by 'the Ethiopian movement', some said. Others emphasised that the concept of 'lie' and 'lying' was understood differently among Zulus and Norwegians.
122. Minutes from MC 1904, MA-MHS, HA/G.sekr.40/Box 43/Jacket 7.
123. Minutes from MC 1905, MA-MHS, HA/G.sekr.40/Box 43/Jacket 11.
124. Letter from the NMS's Home Board of 6.11.1905, MA-MHS, HA/G.sekr.91/ Box 171/Jacket 2.
125. Ole Stavem, *The Norwegian Missionary Society: A Review of its Work among the Zulus* (Stavanger: The Norwegian Missionary Society, 1918), 60.
126. Zulu, 'The Ministry of the Black People in the Lutheran Norwegian Mission Stations in Zululand and Natal from 1875 to 1963'.

127. Mellemsether, *Misjonærer, settlersamfunn og afrikansk opposisjon*.
128. Jørgensen, 'Zibokjana Ka Gudu Moses'.
129. *NMT* 15, no. 2 (1860): 50–1.
130. Minutes from MC 1927, MA-MHS, 67.
131. Minutes from MC 1903, MA-MHS, HA/G.sekr.40/Box 42/Jacket 15.

6 Missionary Masculinity versus Missionary Femininity

1. The couple suggested a separation of their private household economy from the school's economy. And, they asked for a reconstruction of the school building, claiming their right for more private rooms. They furthermore asked for more staff in the boarding section of the institution.
2. Minutes from MC 1886, MA-MHS, HA/G.sekr.40/Box 35/Jacket 13. The documents in the case consist of several hundred handwritten pages.
3. Minutes from MC 1887, MA-MHS, HA/G.sekr.40/Box 36/Jacket 3.
4. Letter from Martinius Borgen to Gundvall Gundersen of of 20.7.1886, MA-MHS, HA/G.sekr.90/Box 137/Jacket 1.
5. For an overview of international research on women and mission in the modern Western mission movement see note 24 in Chapter 1.
6. Robert William Connell, *Masculinities*, 2nd edition (Berkeley/Los Angeles: University of California Press, 2005), 68.
7. Connell, *Masculinities*, 71.
8. Øystein Gullvåg Holter, 'Social Theories for Researching Men and Masculinities', in *Handbook of Studies on Men & Masculinities*, ed. Michael S. Kimmel, Jeff Hearn, and R. W. Connell (Thousand Oaks, CA: Sage Publications, 2005), 21–2.
9. Karin Sarja, 'The Missionary Career of Baroness Hedvig Posse 1887–1913', in *Gender, Race and Religion: Nordic Missions 1860–1940*, ed. Inger Marie Okkenhaug (Uppsala: Swedish Institute of Missionary Research, 2003), 106.
10. Line Nyhagen Predelli, 'Contesting the Mission's Patriarchal Gender Regime: Single Missionary Women in 19th Century Madagascar', in *Gender, Race and Religion: Nordic Missions 1860–1940*, ed. Inger Marie Okkenhaug (Uppsala: Swedish Institute of Missionary Research, 2003).
11. Ingie Hovland, *Mission Station Christianity: Norwegian Missionaries in Colonial Natal and Zululand, Southern Africa 1850–1890* (Leiden/Boston: Brill, 2013). See also Kristin Fjelde Tjelle, 'Misjonærenes barn – foreldrenes eller misjonens ansvar? Misjonærbarn i NMS, ca 1840–1940', in *Med hjertet på flere steder: Om barn, misjon og flerkulturell oppvekst*, ed. Tomas Sundnes Drønen and Marianne Skjortnes (Trondheim: Tapir Akademisk Forlag, 2010), 32–3.
12. *NMT* 11, no. 11 (1856): 180–82.
13. Schreuder married Jakobine Emilie Adelheid Løwenthal in 1858. After her death in 1878 he married Johanne Margrethe Vedeler. Øystein Rakkenes, *Himmelfolket. En norsk høvding i Zululand* (Oslo: Cappelen, 2003), 161–67, 282–84, 306.
14. Inger Hammar, *Emancipation och religion: Den svenska kvinnorörelsens pionjärer i debatt om kvinnans kallelse ca 1860–1900* (Stockholm: Carlssons, 1999), 23–6; Inger Hammar, 'Protestantism and Women's Liberation in 19th Century Sweden', in *Gender, Race and Religion: Nordic Missions 1860–1940*,

ed. Inger Marie Okkenhaug (Uppsala: Swedish Institute of Missionary Research, 2003), 20–3; Lise Nyhagen Predelli, 'Marriage in Norwegian Missionary Practice and Discourse in Norway and Madagascar, 1880–1910', *Journal of Religion in Africa* 31, no. 1 (2001): 5–8.

15. *NMT* 30, no. 3 (1875): 111–14.
16. *NMT* 31, no. 10 (1876): 465–73.
17. *NMT* 31, no. 10 (1876): 473.
18. For a study of Catholic missionary masculinity in a Nordic context, see Yvonne Maria Werner, 'Alternative Masculinity? Catholic Missionaries in Scandinavia', in *Christian Masculinity: Men and Religion in Northerns Europe in the 19th and 20th Centuries*, ed. Yvonne Maria Werner (Leuven: Leuven University Press, 2011).
19. Patricia Grimshaw and Peter Sherlock, 'Women and Cultural Exchanges', in *Missions and Empire*, ed. Norman Etherington (Oxford: Oxford University Press, 2005), 181.
20. E. E. Thommesen (in service 1844–47), Arnt Tønnesen (in service 1854–57) and Thomas Conrad Hirsch Borgen (in service 1893–95) stayed unmarried during their service in the NMS. Gundvall Gundersen (in service 1865–1902) and Peder Aage Rødseth (in service 1893–1939) were married twice.
21. Olav Guttorm Myklebust, C. M. Doke and Ernst Dammann, *Én var den første: Studier og tekster til forståelse av H. P. S. Schreuder* (Oslo: Land og kirke/ Gyldendal, 1986), 74; Øystein Rakkenes, *Himmelfolket: En norsk høvding i Zululand* (Oslo: Cappelen, 2003), 161–67, 282–84, 306.
22. Line Nyhagen Predelli, *Issues of Gender, Race, and Class in the Norwegian Missionary Society in Nineteenth-Century Norway and Madagascar* (Lewiston, NY: Edwin Mellen Press, 2003), 45–94; Predelli, 'Marriage in Norwegian Missionary Practice and Discourse in Norway and Madagascar, 1880–1910'.
23. Men educated as medical doctors or theologians from the University of Oslo were allowed to marry before being posted abroad, and they could bring their wives on the first trip to Madagascar. Also, men working as assistant missionaries were allowed to bring their families to the field.
24. Predelli, *Issues of Gender, Race, and Class*, 57–9. The same was the case in other European missionary societies as well, such as the British Church Missionary Society and the Swiss Basel Mission; see Line Nyhagen Predelli and Jon Miller, 'Piety and Patriarchy: Contested Gender Regimes in Nineteenth-Century Evangelical Missions', in *Gendered Missions: Women and Men in Missionary Discourse and Practice*, ed. Mary Taylor Huber and Nancy Lutkehaus (Ann Arbor, MI: University of Michigan Press, 1999), 80–1.
25. Predelli, *Issues of Gender, Race, and Class*, 57–9.
26. Dana L. Robert, 'The "Christian Home" as a Cornerstone of Anglo-American Missionary Thought and Practice', in *Converting Colonialism: Visions and Realities in Mission History, 1706–1914*, ed. Dana L. Robert (Grand Rapids, MI/ Cambridge: Wm. B. Eerdmans Publishing Co., 2008).
27. Grimshaw and Sherlock, 'Women and Cultural Exchanges', 179.
28. Hilde Margrethe Voll, *Fra oppdragelse til forkynnelse: Kvinner i Det Norske Misjonsselskap i Norge og på Madagaskar 1879–1920. Praksis og debatt* (Unpublished thesis in theology, University of Oslo, 1977), 26–33; Ingvild Osberg, *Pikeasylet på Antsahamanitra, Antananarivo 1872–1912* (unpublished thesis in theology, University of Oslo, 1988); Predelli, *Issues of Gender, Race,*

and Class in the Norwegian Missionary Society in Nineteenth-Century Norway and Madagascar, 189–202, 95–132; Kristin Norseth, '*La os bryte over tvert med vor stumhet!' Kvinners vei til myndighet i de kristelige organisasjonene 1842–1912* (Dr Theol. dissertation, Norwegian School of Theology, 2007), 93–101.

29. Ingeborg Hovland, *Distance Destroys and Kills: An Anthropological Inquiry into the Nature of Faith in a Lutheran Norwegian Missionary Society* (PhD dissertation, University of London, 2006), 49; Ingie Hovland, *Mission Station Christianity*.

30. *NMT* 45, no. 21(1890): 402.

31. *NMT* 45, no. 22 (1890): 428.

32. *MFK* 1, no. 4 (1884): 29–32. See also articles by Inga Eriksen in *MKF* 2, no. 7 (1885): 49–53; 5, no. 11 (1888): 83–7; 13, no. 7 (1896): 53–5; 16, no. 6 & 7 (1899): 47–51; 17, no. 7 (1900): 49–53; 18, no. 7 (1901): 49–53.

33. *MKF* 4, no. 6 (1887): 48–50.

34. Rannveig Naustvoll, *Kvinner i misjonen: Kvinneliv og hverdagsliv på de norske misjonsstasjonene i Natal og Zululand 1900–1925* (unpublished MA thesis, University of Trondheim, 1998).

35. The payment a married man received from the NMS should provide for the sustenance of his wife and children, and an intricate wage system was developed on this basis. If a married missionary died, the wife received a widow's pension from the NMS. If she was still young and capable of work, she could be offered employment in the NMS. This was the case with Dortha Tvedt who lost her husband in 1910 but continued her service for the NMS in South Africa from 1912 to 1946. See minutes from MC 1912, MA-MHS, 22.

36. Markus Dahle's remarks in a letter from the missionaries in South Africa to Martinius Borgen of 31.7.1887, MA-MHS, HA/G.sekr.90/Box 137/Jacket 1.

37. *NMT* 84, no. 42 (1929): 335.

38. In his memoirs Braatvedt praises the work of the missionary wives; see Nils Torbjørnsen Braatvedt, *Erindringer fra mitt misjonsliv* (Stavanger: Boye og Hinnas boktrykkeri, 1930), 105–07.

39. Grimshaw and Sherlock, 'Women and Cultural Exchanges', 182.

40. *MKF* 4, no. 6 (1887): 48–50.

41. *NMT* 84, no. 42 (1929): 335.

42. Letter from Karl Larsen Titlestad to the NMS's Home Board of 1.7.1871. A copy of the letter is found in the Killie Campbell Africana Library, *Diary of Karl Larsen Titlestad 1865–1891*, file 1.

43. See Gundersen's report in *NMT* 31, no. 9 (1876): 385–7.

44. Kristin Norseth finds that the first three unmarried women in the Norwegian mission field all went 'by private initiatives and by private means', and they were all supposed to serve in the household of Schreuder. The unmarried Schreuder needed female assistance, and Jakobine Emilie Adelheid Løwenthal was originally recruited as a housekeeper by faithful supporters in Norway. As soon as she disembarked in Durban she received Schreuder's letter of proposal. Anna Catrine von Elye came to assist Mrs Schreuder in the house in 1860 but married assistant missionary Erik Ingebrektsen the following year. The teacher Johanne Margrethe Vedeler came to assist Mrs Schreuder in the mission school at Entumeni mission station in 1866. After the death of Mrs Schreuder in 1878 she became Schreuder's next wife. See Kristin Norseth, '*La os bryte over tvert med vor stumhet!*', 93–6.

45. Titlestad emphasised in a letter to Schreuder in 1871 that his sister-in-law, Marthe Haaland, was the only relative he dared to ask to come and assist them, this because of her 'Christian life and mission-friendly attitude'. See letter from Karl Larsen Titlestad to Bishop Schreuder of 5.10.1871. A copy of the letter is found in the Killie Campbell Africana Library, *Diary of Karl Larsen Titlestad 1865–1891*, file 1. According to Marthe Haaland's nephew, Lars Martin Titlestad, both his aunt and his mother were influenced in their youth by Christian revivals and felt a calling to serve in the mission, see *NMT* 77, no. 18 (1922): 278–9.

46. John Nome, 'Det Norske Misjonsselskaps historie i norsk kirkeliv: Fra syttiårene til nåtiden', in *Det Norske Misjonsselskap 1842–1942*, ed. John Nome (Stavanger: Dreyer, 1949), 121; Voll, *Fra oppdragelse til forkynnelse*, 33–6; Predelli, *Issues of Gender, Race, and Class*, 172–73, 178–79, 194.

47. *NMT* 23, no. 9 (1868): 257.

48. *NMT* 26, no. 3 (1871): 105–07.

49. Karina Hestad Skeie, *Building God's Kingdom in Highland Madagascar: Norwegian Lutheran Missionaries in Vakinankaratra and Betsileo 1866–1903* (Dr Art. dissertation, University of Oslo, 2005), 119–22.

50. Minutes from MC 1882, MA-MHS, HA/G.sekr.40/Box 35/Jacket 3.

51. Karin Sarja, '*Ännu en syster till Afrika*': *Trettiosex kvinnliga missionärer i Natal och Zululand* (Uppsala: Studia Missionalia Svecana LXXXVIII, 2002), 53–111; Karin Sarja, 'The Missionary Career of Baroness Hedvig Posse 1887–1913'.

52. See *NMT* 26, no. 12 (1871): 457–62; 31, no. 9 (1976): 409–28. Johanne Carlsen, the wife of the assistant missionary Georg Fredrik Carlsen, was an educated midwife. As long as her husband was employed by the NMS (1860–68) she served the NMS families during confinements.

53. See letter from Ingeborg Jordal to the NMS's Home Board of 7.9.1885; enclosed are also the missionaries' statements regarding her application, MA-MHS, HA/G.sekr.90/Box 136/Jacket 10.

54. Letter from the NMS's Home Board to the missionaries in South Africa of 4.12.1885, MA-MHS, SA/Box 1 A/Jacket 11.

55. Minutes from MC 1884, MA-MHS, HA/G.sekr.40/Box 35/Jacket 8.

56. Letter from Elsebeth Kahrs to the NMS's Home Board of 22.8.1884, MA-MHS, HA/G.sekr.90/Box 136/Jacket 1.

57. Letter from the Home Board to the missionaries in South Africa of 30.5.1885, MA-MHS, SA/Box 1 A/Jacket 11.

58. Dana L. Robert, ed., *Gospel Bearers: Missionary Women in the Twentieth Century* (Maryknoll, New York: Orbis Books, 2002), 7.

59. Kristin Fjelde Tjelle, '*Kvinder hjælper Kvinder*': *Misjonskvinneforeningsbevegelsen i Norge 1860–1910* (unpublished MA thesis, University of Oslo, 1990).

60. Lisbeth Mikaelsson, '"Kvinne, ta ansvar og ledelse i dine egne hender": Historien om Henny Dons', *Norsk tidsskrift for misjon* 56, no. 2 (2002): 107–37; Kristin Norseth, 'To alen av hvilket stykke? Tvillingsøstrene LMF og KMA i norsk, nordisk og internasjonalt perspektiv', *Norsk tidsskrift for misjon* 56, no. 2 (2002): 91–106; Kristin Fjelde Tjelle, 'Lærerinnenes Misjonsforbund gjennom 100 år', *Norsk tidsskrift for misjon* 56, no. 2 (2002): 67–89; Inger Marie Okkenhaug, '"Herren har givet mig et rigt virkefelt": Kall, religion og arbeid blant armenere i det osmanske riket', *Historisk tidsskrift* 88, no. 1 (2009): 39–60.

61. Dana L. Robert, *Christian Mission: How Christianity became a World Religion* (Chichester: Wiley-Blackwell, 2009), 124.
62. The Norwegian case resembled the development in international missions; see, e.g., the works of Ruth Compton Brouwer, *Modern Women Modernizing Men: The Changing Missions of three Professional Women in Asia and Africa, 1902–69* (Vancouver: UBC Press, 2002); Rhonda Anne Semple, *Missionary Women: Gender, Professionalism and the Victorian Idea of Christian Mission* (Woodbridge: Boydell Press, 2003).
63. Predelli, *Issues of Gender, Race, and Class*, 185–88.
64. Tor Berger Jørgensen, 'Japan', in *I tro og tjeneste: Det norske misjonsselskap 1842–1992*, ed. Torstein Jørgensen and Nils Kristian Høimyr (Stavanger: Misjonshøgskolen, 1992), 283–84.
65. Superintendent Lars Martin Titlestad presented in 1924 a proposal which granted female missionary workers the right to speak and vote at the annual missionary conferences. See minutes from MC 1924, MA-MHS, 3. Only one of the missionaries, Otto Alfred Aadnesgaard, opposed the proposal.
66. It should be noticed, however, that while women in the Norwegian political society got the right to vote in 1913, white women in South Africa were enfranchised first in 1930; see Cherryl Walker, 'The Women's Suffrage Movement: The Politics of Gender, Race and Class', in *Women and Gender in Southern Africa to 1945*, ed. Cherryl Walker (Cape Town/London: David Philip/James Currey, 1990).
67. *MKF* 4, no. 7 (1887): 53–5.
68. Minutes from MC 1888, MA-MHS, HA/G.sekr.40/Box 36/Jacket 6.
69. Minutes from MC 1898, MA-MHS, HA/G.sekr.40/Box 39 B/Jacket 7.
70. Letter from Therese Aaagard to Ole Stavem of 15.12.1896, MA-MHS, HA/G.sekr.90, Box 140 B/Jacket 8.
71. Henny Dons, *Den kristne kvinne og hedningemisjonen: En historisk oversikt* (Oslo: Lutherstiftelsen, 1925), 35.
72. *MKF* 14, no. 3 (1897): 19–21; 15, no. 4 (1898): 30–2; 17, no. 5 (1900): 38–40; 23, no. 11 (1906): 85–7; 24, no. 5 (1907): 33–6; 25, no. 4 (1908): 29–30; 26, no. 7 (1909): 51–3; 27, no. 3 (1910): 17–20; 28, no. 3 (1911): 18–21.
73. See minutes from MC 1905, MA-MHS, HA/G.sekr.40/Box 43/Jacket 11; MC 1906, 10–11; MC 1908, 16–17 and the Home Board's letter of response to the missionary conference in South Africa 1906, MA-MHS, 2–3 and 1908, 3–4.
74. Letter from Ole Stavem to Lars Dahle of 19.7.1910, MA-MHS, HA/G.sekr.90/Box 144 B/Jacket 3.
75. Minutes from MC 1919, MA-MHS, 19.
76. Hanna Mellemsether, *Kvinne i to verdener: En kulturhistorisk analyse av afrikamisjonæren Martha Sannes liv i perioden 1884–1901* (Trondheim: Senter for kvinneforsknings skriftserie, 1994); Sarja, *'Ännu en syster till Afrika'*.
77. Heather Hughes, '"A Lighthouse for African Womanhood": Inanda Seminary, 1869–1945', in *Women and Gender in Southern Africa to 1945*, ed. Cherryl Walker (Cape Town/London: David Philip/James Currey, 1990). In the CSM female missionary workers had by 1900 established boarding institutions for girls – or orphanages – at Applesbosh, Dundee, Ekutuleni, Emtulwa and Oscarsberg mission stations. Sarja, *'Ännu en syster till Afrika'*, 193–99; Sarja, 'The Missionary Career of Baroness Hedvig Posse 1887–1913'.
78. *MKF* 18, no. 7 (1901): 50.

79. Ole Stavem, *Et bantufolk og kristendommen: Det norske missionsselskaps syttiaarige zulumission* (Stavanger: Det norske missionsselskaps forlag, 1915), 325.
80. Minutes from MC 1902, MA-MHS, HA/G.sekr.40/Box 42/Jacket 7.
81. *MKF* 22, no. 1 (1905): 7–8; 22, no. 7 (1905): 49–54; 23, no. 10 (1906): 74–6.
82. Minutes from MC 1916, MA-MHS, 11–17.
83. Minutes from MC 1926, MA-MHS, 47–55; Johan Kjelvei, ed., *Zulu: Evangeliets landvinning* (Stavanger: Det Norske Misjonsselskaps trykkeri, 1932), 69–71.
84. For an overview of the history of the Female Teachers' Missionary Association see Tjelle, 'Lærerinnenes Misjonsforbund gjennom 100 år'.
85. See minutes from MC 1924, MA-MHS, 34–9; MC 1925, 37–9; MC 1926, 47–55; MC 1927, 79–83; MC 1928, 56–65. See also the Home Board's answer to the missionary conference in South Africa 1926, MA-MHS, 14–6; and in 1928, 16–17.
86. Kjelvei, ed., *Zulu: Evangeliets landvinning*, 69–70.
87. Minutes from MC 1902, MA-MHS, HA/G.sekr. 40/Box 42/Jacket 7.
88. Minutes from MC 1909, MA-MHA, 15–18.
89. The Home Board's answer to the missionary conference in South Africa 1910, MA-MHS, 6–7.
90. Ingolf Edward Hodne, *Missionary Enterprise in African Education: The Co-operating Lutheran Missions in Natal, South Africa, 1912–1955* (Stavanger: Misjonshøgskolens forlag, 1997), 35. Bertha Nerø was the first Norwegian female missionary teacher employed at the institution (1910–13), she was followed by Sofie Kyvik (1915–16, 1917–18) and Bertha Gilje (1925–44).
91. E. g. minutes from MC 1911, MA-MHS, 19–25.
92. See minutes from MC 1921, MA-MHS, 26–9; MC 1922, 21–6; MC 1923, 18–20; MC 1925, 28–9; MC 1926, 55–64; MC 1927, 34–44; MC 1928, 88–96; MC 1929, 111–13; MC 1930, 46–9. See also the Home Board's answer to the missionary conference in South Africa 1926, MA-MHS, 16–20 and 1928, 20–1.
93. Ivar A. Andersen, 'Sør-Afrika', in *I tro og tjeneste: Det Norske Misjonsselskap 1842–1992*, ed. Torstein Jørgensen (Stavanger: Misjonshøgskolen, 1992), 332–34.
94. Minutes from MC 1922, MA-MHS, 6; the Home Board's letter of answer to the missionary conference in South Africa 1922, MA-MHS, 2.
95. Elida Fykse, *Til Sydkorsets land: Studiebrev til norske gjenter og gutar fra misjonær Elida Fykse.*, vol. 3 (Stavanger: Det norske misjonsselskaps Bibel- og misjon-skurs pr. korrespondanse, 1946), 5–10.
96. Martha Palm, 'Vår hospitalsvirksomhet', in *Zulu: Evangeliets landvinning*, ed. Johan Kjelvei (Stavanger: Det Norske Misjonsselskaps trykkeri, 1932), 86–94.
97. Strømme was accepted as a student at the NMS's mission school in 1997 and ordained in 1903. He had also applied for admission in 1893. According to the historian Gunnar Stave, several of the young men who were refused by the NMS as missionary candidates in 1893 were recommended to apply for admission at the newly established institution (1890) for male deacons in Christiania. Strømme was a student at the Deacons' Home from 1893 to 1897. Both the mission school and the Deacons' Home recruited students among the same social groups: men from lower social classes who lacked

secondary education but still had strong commitments to serve in church or mission. Gunnar Stave, *Mannsmot og tenarsinn. Det norske Diakonhjem i hundre år* (Oslo: Det Norske Samlaget, 1990), 105–06.

98. Minutes from MC 1927, MA-MHS, 15–17.
99. See Ingrid Wyller, *Sykepleiernes Misjonsring S.M.R. 50 år* (Oslo: Sykepleiernes Misjonsring 1971), 31–4. While Borghild Magnussen finished missionary courses in Oslo and midwife training in Edinburgh, the SMR paid the wages for Bertha Nerø who from 1926 assisted Elida Ulltveit-Moe at the Ekombe mission hospital. Magnussen served at Ekombe from 1929 to 1935 and established in 1935 the NMS's third mission hospital at Umphumulo.
100. *NMT* 84, no. 34 (1929): 267.
101. *NMT* 83, no. 19 (1928): 150; Palm, 'Vår hospitalsvirksomhet'; Vesla Hafstad, *The History of Nkonjeni Hospital Mahlabatini District, Kwa Zulu, South Africa: From 1925–1978* (Norway: Vesla Hafstad, 2000).
102. Minutes from MC 1929, MA-MHS, 111–13.
103. Minutes from MC 1925, MA-MHS, 28.
104. *NMT* 84, no. 10 (1929): 396.
105. Minutes from MC 1927, MA-MHS, 37.
106. Minutes from MC 1923, MA-MHS, 22–33.
107. Dana L. Robert, *American Women in Mission: A Social History of their Thought and Practice* (Macon, GA: Mercer University Press, 1997), 255–316; Dana L. Robert, ed., *Gospel Bearers, Gospel Barriers*, 8–16.
108. Minutes from MC 1924, MA-MHS, 19.
109. Minutes from MC 1926, MA-MHS, 57.

7   Missionary Men

1. Inger Hammar, 'Några reflexioner kring "religionsblind kvinnoforskning"', *Historisk tidsskrift*, no. 1 (1998): 19–34.
2. Roald Berg, 'Misjonshistorie og samfunnsforskning', *Nytt Norsk Tidsskrift*, no. 3–4 (2009): 322–44.
3. Anders Olsen, *Misjonsprest Karl Larsen Titlestad: Det Norske Missionsselskaps senior* (Bergen: A/S Lunde & Co.s Forlag, 1929).
4. By a decree of 1739 the Danish government had guaranteed elementary schooling for all Norwegian children. The curriculum consisted mostly of education in the Evangelical-Lutheran faith and was supposed to prepare children for the obligatory church rite of confirmation at the age of 15. Besides the confessional education, some elementary skills in reading, writing and arithmetic were taught. Hans-Jørgen Dokka, *En skole gjennom 250 år* (Oslo: NKS-forlaget, 1988).
5. It was common practice for municipalities to recruit school teachers among intelligent, local young men, and thereafter send them to the teachers' seminaries, which were established in Norway from the 1830s, to gain further qualifications.
6. The class of 1859–64 is regarded in the 'annals' of the NMS's mission school as 'the First Class', and the class of 1843–48 (Ommund Oftebro, Lars Larsen, Tobias Udland) has been described as 'a first attempt'. From 1859 to 1864 the school rented a house in Verksgaten 33 in central Stavanger. In 1862 property

for a new school was purchased, and the school building was finished in 1864. Emil Birkeli and C. Tidemann Strand, *Kallet og veien: Det Norske Misjonsselskaps misjonsskole 1850–1959* (Stavanger: Misjonsselskapets Forlag, 1959).

7. *NMT* 20, no. 3 (1865): 49–61.

8. *NMT* 26, no. 7 (1871): 244–47.

9. Ole Stavem, *Et bantufolk og kristendommen: Det norske missionsselskaps syttiaarige zulumission* (Stavanger: Det norske missionsselskaps forlag, 1915), 217–23.

10. *NMT* 35, no. 6 (1880): 109–15.

11. Jeff Guy, *The Destruction of the Zulu Kingdom: The Civil War in Zululand, 1879–1884* (Pietermaritzburg: University of Natal Press, 1994), 73–4.

12. According to NMS superintendent Ole Stavem, 'it did not look nice that the missionaries of the Church of England occupied Titlestad's previous houses', see Stavem, *Et bantufolk og kristendommen*, 230.

13. Olsen, *Misjonsprest Karl Larsen Titlestad*, 59–76.

14. *NMT* 41, no. 5 (1886): 89–93.

15. Karl Titlestad wrote several letters to the NMS's Home Board and also to the principal of the mission school pleading with them to accept his sons Lars Martin and Lauritz as missionary candidates. The brothers, who were 18 and 20 respectively, were elected from 39 applicants. Letter from Karl Larsen Titlestad to the NMS's mission school of 1.8.1885, MA-MHS, Mission school archive 1843–1977/Box 1852/Jacket 4. See also letters of 12.1.1886, 20.3.1886, 5.10.1886, MA-MHS, Mission school archive 1843–1977/Box 1925/Jacket 1. In the letter dated 20.3.1886, Lars Martin's letter of application and samples of his student work are enclosed.

16. Lars Dahle, *Tilbakeblik paa mit liv – og særlig paa mit missionsliv: Tredje del* (Stavanger: Det Norske Missionsselskabs trykkeri, 1923), 86–9.

17. *The life story of Thora-Margaretha Titlestad Brodin*, unpublished manuscript. Thora-Margaretha Titlestad Brodin's private archive.

18. Letters from Karl Michael Titlestad to Lars Dahle of 2.1.1917 and 11.3.1917, MA-MHS, HA/G.sekr.90/Box 125/Jacket 11.

19. Hege Roaldset finds that in the 1879–1940 period 36 of the male NMS missionaries in South Africa were ordained theologians. Twenty-eight were educated at the NMS's mission school in Stavanger, two were educated in South Africa, and six had obtained the academic degree *candidatus theologiae* at the University of Kristiania or at the School of Theology. Of the latter group, who had the highest level of education, four out of six were sons of NMS Zulu missionaries, and Roaldset claims this to be evidence of missionaries' 'aspirations of elevated social status'. Karl Michael belonged to the latter group. Hege Roaldset, 'Norwegian missionaries and Zulu converts: A case for Bakhtinian dialogue', *Studia Historiae Ecclesiasticae. Journal of the Church History Society of Southern Africa* 36, no. 1 (2010), 132.

20. Birkeli and Tidemann Strand, *Kallet og veien: Det Norske Misjonsselskaps misjonsskole 1850–1959*, 212.

21. Simensen and Gynnild, Jarle Simensen and Vidar Gynnild, 'Norwegian Missionaries in the Nineteenth Century: Organizational Background, Social Profile and World View', in *Norwegian Missions in African History, Vol 1: South Africa 1845–1906*, ed. Jarle Simensen (Oslo: Norwegian University Press, 1986), 26–32.

22. Ingeborg Hovland, *Distance Destroys and Kills: An Anthropological Inquiry into the Nature of Faith in a Lutheran Norwegian Missionary Society* (PhD dissertation, University of London, 2006), 197.

23. Hovland, *Distance destroys and kills*, 26.

24. Some examples from the Norwegian discussion: Kirsti Mosvold, *Misjonærkallet i misjonsteologisk perspektiv* (unpublished thesis in theology, Norwegian School of Theology, 1981); Tarald Rasmussen, 'Lutherdom og misjonsethos: Om norsk lekmannskristendom i det 19. århundre', *Norsk Teologisk Tidsskrift* 86, no. 3 (1985): 169–83; Jan-Martin Berentsen, *Teologi og misjon: Trekk fra protestantismens historie fram til vårt århundre* (Oslo: Luther, 1990), 32–67; Øyvind M. Eide, *Skatten og leirkaret: Sjelesørgeriske perspektiv på erfaringer i en misjonærs liv* (Stavanger: Misjonshøgskolens forlag, 2002), 33–41; Lisbeth Mikaelsson, *Kallets ekko: Studier i misjon og selvbiografi* (Kristiansand: Høyskoleforlaget, 2003); Kari Løvaas, 'Her er jeg, send meg!', *Nytt Norsk Tidsskrift*, no. 3–4 (2009): 337–51; Knut Alfsvåg, 'Misjonærkall og foreldrekall – fruktbar spenning eller uløselig konflikt?' in *Med hjertet på flere steder: Om barn, misjon og flerkulturell oppvekst*, ed. Tomas Drønen and Marianne Skjortnes (Trondheim: Tapir Akademisk Forlag, 2010); Lisbeth Mikaelsson, 'Fortellinger om kallet' in Drønen and Skjortnes, ed., *Med hjertet på flere steder*.

25. According to his grandson Karl Michael he was suicidal by this time. See *Kamp og Seier* 17, no. 30 (1916): 235.

26. Karl Larsen Titlestad's letters of application, MA-MHS, HA/G.sekr.90/Box 81/Jacket 7.

27. Bjørg Seland, *Religion på det frie marked: Folkelig pietisme og bedehuskultur* (Kristiansand: Høyskoleforlaget AS – Norwegian Academic Press, 2006), 93–6.

28. Simensen and Gynnild, 'Norwegian Missionaries in the Nineteenth Century', 32–4.

29. The conversion experience is described in letters to the NMS but also in later sermons and testimonies. See Olsen, *Misjonsprest Karl Larsen Titlestad*, 11–12. The conversion experience must also have been a noted family narrative considering how vividly it was retold by his son Elias about 80 years later: 'What he saw was a most remarkable sight, colossal, filling the dark valley before him, a perfect image of the crucifixion reflected in a shining light, clear-cut within the surrounding darkness! The scene stood out clearly before his eyes and remained long enough for him to absorb it fully and it made a definite and lasting impression on his mind. He interpreted this as a divine sign, accepting him as a servant of the Saviour.... He was filled with a deep happiness and his persistent restlessness left him at once. He soon regained his former health and strength.' Lawrence Titlestad, *Under the Zulu Kings*, 25. Killie Campbell Africana Library.

30. His younger brother Elias described the experience in Titlestad, *Under the Zulu Kings*, 70. Killie Campbell Africana Library; his son Karl Michael in *Kamp og Seier* 17, no. 30 (1916): 285–86.

31. Letter from Karl Michael Titlestad to the NMS's Home Board of 2.5.1923, MA-MHS, HA/G.sekr.92/Box 190/Jacket 2.

32. *Kamp og Seier* 17, no. 30 (1916): 236.

33. *NMT* 80, no. 32 (1925): 269.

34. Letter from Karl Michael Titlestad to the NMS's Home Board of 2.5.1923, MA-MHS, HA/G.sekr.92/Box 190/Jacket 2.

35. Letter from Einar Amdahl to Karl Michael Titlestad of 13.11.1923, MA-MHS, HA/G.sekr.91/Box 494/Jacket 8.
36. Letter from Karl Michael Titlestad to Einar Amdahl of 3.10.1923, MA-MHS, HA/G.sekr.90/Box 433/Jacket 1.
37. See e.g. letter to Peder Blessing of 27.12.1867 in *Diary of Karl Larsen Titlestad 1865–1891*, file 1, Killie Campbell Africana Library.
38. See, e.g., draft of a letter to the Home Board of 18.11.1868, in *Diary of Karl Larsen Titlestad 1865–1891*, file 1, Killie Campbell Africana Library. Complaints about Larsen's stubbornness were expressed in a paragraph which in the end was deleted.
39. Lars Larsen apparently had difficulties in distributing pastoral responsibilities to junior missionaries. When Lars Berge arrived at Nhlazatshe in 1880 he complained about Larsen's controlling style of leadership. Both at the missionary conference in 1881 and in 1882 Berge asked for a transfer. See minutes from MC 1881, MA-MHS, HA/G.sekr.40/Box 34/Jacket 21; Minutes from MC 1882, MA-MHS, HA/G.sekr.40/Box 35/Jacket 3. See also letter from Lars Berge to the NMS's Home Board of 12.2.1883, MA-MHS, HA/G.sekr.90/ Box 135 B/Jacket 10.
40. Letter to the Home Board of April 1869, in *Diary of Karl Larsen Titlestad 1865–1891*, file 1, Killie Campbell Africana Library.
41. *NMT* 25, no. 4 (1870): 155–66.
42. *NMT* 25, no. 8 (1870): 338–39.
43. *NMT* 25, no. 12 (1870): 513.
44. In Titlestad's diary there are copies of several letters to Schreuder in which he invites him to come and visit him. See letters of 25.3.1870; 23.8.1870; 26.8.1870 in *Diary of Karl Larsen Titlestad 1865–1891*, file 1, Killie Campbell Africana Library.
45. *NMT* 26, no. 7 (1871): 244–47.
46. *NMT* 30, no. 4 (1875): 133–36.
47. *NMT* 31, no. 10 (1876): 444–46.
48. *NMT* 30, no. 10 (1875): 373–77.
49. *NMT* 36, no. 7 (1881): 130.
50. *NMT* 35, no. 19 (1880): 378–80.
51. *NMT* 36, no. 7 (1881): 130. Titlestad's narrative was later repeated in several NMS texts. See Stavem, *Et bantufolk og kristendommen*, 235–36; Olsen, *Misjonsprest Karl Larsen Titlestad*, 43–4; Elida Fykse, *Til Sydkorsets land: Studiebrev til norske gjenter og gutar fra misjonær Elida Fykse*, 11th letter (Stavanger: Det norske misjonsselskaps Bibel- og misjonskurs pr. korrespondanse, 1946).
52. *NMT* 36, no. 7 (1881): 133.
53. *MKF* 1, no. 7 (1884): 49–52.
54. Minutes from the NMS's Home Board meeting of 08.1.1894, in The Home Board's Journal of Negotiations 1894–1896, MA-MHS, HA/G.sekr.10.
55. Minutes from MC 1894, issue 2, MA-MHS, HA/G.sekr.40/Box 38/Jacket 11.
56. *NMT* 50, no. 24 (1895): 466–69.
57. Olsen, *Misjonsprest Karl Larsen Titlestad*, 75.
58. Letter from Martin Titlestad to the NMS's Home Board of 29.12.1892, MA-MHS, HA/G.sekr.90/Box 104/Jacket 5. He was actually allowed to travel second-class by steamboat, and he also paid part of the ticket himself, whereas

the rest of his class waited another six months for the mission ship *Paulus* to be ready for departure.

59. *NMT* 48, no. 15 (1893): 289–92.
60. *NMT* 50, no. 24 (1895): 466–69.
61. Mission statistics, Ekombe Mission District, 1895–1919

Year	Baptisms since the establishment of the station	Baptisms in this particular year	Zulu church personnel (pastors, evangelists and teachers)	Preaching places	Schools	Students in the mission schools
1895	109	9	3	3	1	20
1900	272	32	4	3	4	81
1904	449	64	6	6	5	70
1910	699	50	7	6	6	122
1915	1146	88	16	12	13	320
1919	–	156	30	16	20	488

62. *NMT* 59, no. 5 (1904): 111–13.
63. *MKF* 31, no. 10 (1914): 73.
64. *NMT* 73, no. 1 (1918): 6–8.
65. *Kamp og Seier* 21, no. 12 (1920): 93; *NMT* 75, no. 13 (1920): 198–200.
66. Minutes from MC 1916, MA-MHS, 18.
67. *NMT* 73, no. 1 (1918): 6–8; Minutes from MC 1917, MA-MHS, 90.
68. Minutes from MC 1919, MA-MHS, 7–12; MC 1921, 32–36; MC 1926, 21–25; MC 1927, 30–34. See also the Home Board's response to the missionary conference in South Africa 1919, MA-MHA, 2 and 1926, 6.
69. *Kamp og Seier* 23, no. 46: 364–65.
70. Letter from Lars Martin Titlestad to Lars Dahle of 2.4.1902, MA-MHS, HA/G. sekr.90/Box 142/Jacket 5. In the first half of the 1920s when he functioned as the superintendent of the field, he was frustrated by the many reductions in the budget forced on them by the NMS which were caused by economic depression in Norway and a corresponding decline in mission donations. Titlestad sometimes felt disappointed and discouraged by the priorities set by NMS's Home Board, and at such times feelings of unfair and unreasonable treatment of the Zulu mission, compared with the missions in Madagascar and China, came to the surface. See, e.g., letter from Lars Martin Titlestad to the NMS's Home Board of 5.1.1925, MA-MHS, HA/M.sekr.90/Box 703/Jacket 2.
71. *NMT* 72, no. 5 (1917): 103–4; *Kamp og Seier* 21, no. 12 (1920): 93.
72. *MKF* 31, no. 10 (1914): 73–4.
73. *NMT* 81, no. 49 (1926): 436–37.
74. *NMT* 51, no. 21 (1896): 416–20; *Kamp og Seier* 22, no. 11 (1921): 84–5.
75. The first association for 'Christian young men' in Norway, inspired by the German movement of *Jünglingsvereine* (the 1820s) and the British movement of the Young Men's Christian Association (YMCA) (the 1840s), saw the light

in 1867, and a national YMCA organisation was established in 1880; see Per Voksø and Erik Kullerud, *I trekantens tegn: Norges Kristelige Ungdomsforbund gjennom hundre år* (Oslo: Triangelforlaget, 1980). The YMCA in Norway became an important supporter of the NMS's mission work, providing the organisation with financial means and missionaries; see Anders Tangeraas, *Ungdom og misjon* (Oslo: Norges Kristelige Ungdomsforbund, 1944); Ingmar Areklett, *Ungdomsmisjonen: En biografi* (Torvastad: KFUK-KFUM Global, 2008).

76. Revivalist nineteenth-century Christians initiated soldiers' homes in a number of countries such as Great Britain and Germany. As the YMCA was often involved, this inspired a local YMCA group in Norway to establish a first soldier's home at Værnesmoen military base in 1901. Voksø and Kullerud, *I trekantens tegn*, 100–02, 239.

77. Elin Malmer, who studied the soldiers' homes run by the youth organisation of Swedish Mission Covenant (Svenska Missionsförbundet) in the early twentieth century, finds that evangelical male identity was preserved at the homes. Christian youth organisations asserted that the conscription period was particularly suited for the recruitment of young men, and the military training grounds were thus regarded as a field of mission. According to Malmer, the soldiers' missions should be regarded as attempts at the re-Christianisation of young men. Elin Malmer, 'The Making of Christian Men: An Evangelical Mission to the Swedish Army, c. 1900–1920', in *Christian Masculinity: Men and Religion in Northern Europe in the 19th and 20th Centuries*, ed. Yvonne Maria Werner (Leuven: Leuven University Press, 2011), 191–211.

78. Michael Parker, *The Kingdom of Character: The Student Volunteer Movement for Foreign Missions (1886–1926)* (Lanham, MD/New York/Oxford: American Society of Missiology and University Press of America, 1998), 1–21.

79. Letter from Karl Michael Titlestad to the NMS's General Secretary Jørgen Nilssen of 21.2.1921, MA-MHS, HA/G.sekr.90/Box 430/Jacket 6; Karl Michael Titlestad, 'Norges A.F.M.F.: En kort utsigt', in *Missionsuppgifter och missionsproblem: Akademiska Frivilliges Missionsförbunds 25-årsskrift* (Stockholm: Sveriges Kristliga Studentrörelses Förlag, 1921).

80. *Kamp og Seier* 18, no. 21 (1917): 169–70.

81. Parker, *The Kingdom of Character*, 105.

82. Mott worked for the YMCA internationally and in the 1890s incorporated the YMCA and SVM. Largely responsible for the formation of the World Student Christian Federation in 1895, he became a leading evangelist among students across the world, and his books gained wide circulation. In particular, Mott became the Master Chairman of the Conference of World Mission in Edinburgh in 1910, and at the two succeeding conferences at Jerusalem in 1928 and Tambaram, Madras in 1938. He was also the Chairman of the International Missionary Council established at the Edinburgh conference. See Timothy Yates, *Christian Mission in the Twentieth Century* (Cambridge: Cambridge University Press, 1994), 7–33.

83. The Norwegian female mission leader Henny Dons participated at a mission summer school in Mundesley in Norfolk, England in 1909. When she returned she contacted the managements of several Norwegian mission organisations, and the first Norwegian mission summer school was arranged

at Framnes in 1911 with 500 youths, both men and women, participating. Lars Dahle comments on this new trend of mission studies in NMT, no. 14 (1911): 331–34.

84. *Kamp og Seier* 25, no. 9 (1925): 71; NMT 85, no. 24 (1930): 189.

85. Letter from Karl Michael Titlestad to Lars Dahle of 15.5.1919, MA-MHS, HA/G. sekr.90/Box 90/Jacket 12. He planned to study the Zulu language, to visit mission stations, and to receive medical training at his uncle Karl Titlestad's medical practice at Nkandla. The journey lasted for almost a year, and during his stay in Zululand he also had the opportunity to follow his father and superintendent Hans Kristian Leisegang on an inspection in Ekombe mission district, visiting all outstations. *Kamp og Seier* 21, no. 3 (1920): 20–2.

86. Application from Karl Michael Titlestad of 2.5.1923, MA-MHS, HA/G.sekr.92/ Box 190/Jacket 2. He was accepted as a missionary by a Home Board decision of 15.5.1923.

87. Letter from Karl Michael Titlestad to Einar Amdahl of 20.2.1923; 5.3.1923, MA-MHS, HA/G.sekr.90/Box 433/Jacket 1.

88. Letters from Karl Michael Titlestad to Einar Amdahl of 3.10.1923; 17.10.1923; 3.11.1923; 10.11.1923; 15.12.1923, MA-MHS, HA/G.sekr.90/Box 433/Jacket 1. Letters from Amdahl to Titlestad of 13.11.1923, 23.11.1923; 1.12.1923; 17.12.1923; 18.12.1923 MA-MHS, HA/G.sekr.91/Box 494/Jacket 8.

89. Letter from Karl Michael Titlestad to Einar Amdahl of 28.2.1925, MA-MHS, HA/M.sekr.90/Box 703/Jacket 2.

90. Obituary by Peder Aa. Rødseth in *Fram* 18, no. 196 (1930): 7–8.

91. *NMT* 85, no. 30 (1930): 237.

92. Like his father and grandfather he looked after his mission supporters in Norway, and with previous peers and friends he raised funds for the restoration of Schreuder's old stone church at Umphumulo, which was used as a college chapel. Letter from Karl Michael Titlestad to Einar Amdahl of 4.10.1926, MA-MHS, HA/M.sekr.90/Box 703/Jacket 7. See also the obituary written by Peder Aa. Rødseth in *Fram* 18, no. 196 (1930): 7–8.

93. The many letters Signe Titlestad received after the death of her husband (Thora-Margaretha Titlestad Brodin's private archive), displayed his broad network in Natal. There were letters from influential Zulu church leaders and politicians as well as mission leaders representing diverse nationalities and denominations.

94. *NMT* 85, no. 30 (1930): 237.

95. NMT 85, no. 30 (1930): 237.

96. Anna Prestjan, 'The Man in the Clergyman: Swedish Priest Obituaries, 1905–1937', in *Christian Masculinity: Men and Religion in Northern Europe in the 19th and 20th Centuries*, ed. Yvonne Maria Werner (Leuven: Leuven University Press, 2011), 117–18.

97. Anders Olsen and Ole Stavem, 'Misjonsprest Karl Titlestad. 1832–1924', *Norvegia Sacra* 5 (1925), 145–51.

98. Olsen and Stavem, 'Misjonsprest Karl Titlestad', 151.

99. Letter from Karl Larsen Titlestad of 25.12.1874 to Hans P.S. Schreuder, in *Diary of Karl Larsen Titlestad 1865–1891*, file 1, Killie Campbell Africana Library. When Schreuder married Miss Vedeler in 1879 he actually asked Titlestad to conduct the wedding service; see *NMT* 35, no. 6 (1880): 112. After the death of Schreuder in 1882 the NMS negotiated with Schreuder's widow about the

rights to Entumeni mission station. Mrs Schreuder stated that Titlestad was the only NMS missionary she would allow to settle at Entumeni; see minutes from MC 1882, MA-MHS, HA/G.sekr.40/Box 35/Jacket 3.

100. Ole Gjerløw, *Beretning vedkommende Sekretærens Reise til Missionsmarken i Zululand og Natal 1887–88* (Stavanger: Norwegian Missionary Society, 1888), 21.

101. See minutes from MC 1882, MA-MHS, HA/G.sekr.40/Box 35/Jacket 3, where Christian Oftebro stated that Karl L. Titlestad had little thought for himself.

102. Letter from Karl L. Titlestad to Lars Dahle of 24.2.1891, in *Diary of Karl Larsen Titlestad 1865–1891*, file 1, Killie Campbell Africana Library.

103. Letter from K.L. Titlestad of 11.5.1891, NMS/G.sekr.90/Box 139/Jacket 10.

104. Olsen, *Misjonsprest Karl Larsen Titlestad*, 59–76.

105. *MKF* 38, no. 7–8 (1921): 50–1.

106. See, e.g., his report from the construction work of a chapel at Fongosi in *NMT* 65, no. 8 (1910): 180–82.

107. In an article of 1916 called 'The Missionary as a Doctor', Titlestad presented many examples from his medical practice. He admitted to being more of a 'quack' and that he was called 'Dr Helpless' by relatives in Norway. Still, in a district with no physicians, he claimed to have healed a lot of people and saved some lives. *NMT* 71, no. 4 (1916): 73–6.

108. Strømme deputised for Titlestad at Ekombe mission station when the latter was on furlough in Norway from 1904 to 1906, and Strømme also took over as the station manager at Ekombe in 1920 when Titlestad was relocated to Eshowe. It is no coincidence that the first mission hospital in the NMS's Zulu mission was established at Ekombe in 1923 by the nurse Elida Ulltveit-Moe in close cooperation with Kirsten and Peder Aa. Strømme.

109. *NMT* 53, no. 16 (1898): 317–20; no. 17 (1899): 329–32; *MKF* 16, no. 6 (1899): 41. The response from the Norwegian donators was overwhelming; see *NMT* 59, no. 20 (1904): 477–78.

110. *NMT* 96, no. 38 (1941): 5; no. 41: 5.

111. Minutes from MC 1942, MA-MHS, 2–3.

112. Minutes from MC 1922, MA-MHS, 4. He received only four out of 12 votes. Leisegang, who was still in Norway, was re-elected as superintendent. Also, when a vice-superintendent had to be elected, Titlestad got only one-third of the votes. The Home Board reprimanded the missionary community for their reluctance to trust Titlestad, and since Leisegang was still in Norway it did commissioned Titlestad for a second time to serve as temporary superintendent. See the Home Board's response to the missionary conference in South Africa 1922, MA-MHS, 1–2.

113. Minutes from MC 1927, MA-MHS, 20.

114. Minutes from MC 1926, MA-MHS, 81–89.

115. Letter from Lars Martin Titlestad to Einar Amdahl of 11.7.1927, MA-MHS, HA/M.sekr.90/Box 704/Jacket 5.

116. *NMT* 100, no. 16 (1945): 4.

117. *NMT* 85, no. 31 (1930): 247.

8 Family Men

1. John Tosh, *A Man's Place: Masculinity and the Middle-Class Home in Victorian England* (New Haven, CT: Yale University Press, 1999), 2.

2. Michele Adams and Scott Coltrane, 'Boys and Men in Families: The Domestic Production of Gender, Power, and Privilege', in *Handbook of Studies on Men & Masculinities*, ed. Michael S. Kimmel, Jeff Hearn and R. W. Connell (Thousand Oaks, CA: Sage Publications, 2005), 230.
3. Karl Larsen Titlestad's letters of application, MA-MHS, HA/G.sekr.90/Box 81/ Jacket 7.
4. Anders Olsen, *Misjonsprest Karl Larsen Titlestad: Det Norske Missionsselskaps senior* (Bergen: A/S Lunde & Co.s Forlag, 1929), 14–16.
5. Elias Titlestad, *Under the Zulu Kings*, 28–9. Killie Campbell Africana Library.
6. When Ole Z. Norgaard went to Norway on furlough in 1899, it became known that he owed a considerable debt to the NMS, his congregation at Empangeni, and also to private creditors in Durban. The NMS dismissed him from service in 1900. See the 'Norgaard-file' in MA-MHS, HA/G.sekr.93/Box 192/Jacket 12.
7. Letter from Karl L. Titlestad of 27.12.1867 to Peder Blessing, *Diary of Karl Larsen Titlestad 1865–1891*, file 1, Killie Campbell Africana Library.
8. Titlestad, *Under the Zulu Kings*, 34. Killie Campbell Africana Library.
9. Titlestad, *Under the Zulu Kings*, 28.
10. Annual report 1867, *Diary of Karl Larsen Titlestad 1865–1891*, file 1, Killie Campbell Africana Library.
11. Jørgen Lorentzen, 'Fedrene', in *Män i Norden: Manlighet och modernitet 1840–1940*, ed. Claes Ekenstam and Jørgen Lorentzen (Hedemora: Gidlund, 2006), 150–54.
12. Letter from Karl L. Titlestad to Peder Blessing of 27.12.1867, *Diary of Karl Larsen Titlestad 1865–1891*, file 1, Killie Campbell Africana Library.
13. *NMT* 25, no. 12 (1879): 515; Letter to Schreuder of 23.8.1870 in *Diary of Karl Larsen Titlestad 1865–1891*, file 1, Killie Campbell Africana Library.
14. *NMT* 26, no. 7 (1871): 249.
15. *NMT* 28, no. 10 (1873): 375.
16. Letter from Karl Larsen Titlestad to the NMS's Home Board of 1.7.1871, *Diary of Karl Larsen Titlestad 1865–1891*, file 1, Killie Campbell Africana Library; *NMT* 27, no. 12 (1872): 453–5.
17. Letter from Karl L. Titlestad of 29.12.1873 to the NMS's Home Board, *Diary of Karl Larsen Titlestad 1865–1891*, file 1, Killie Campbell Africana Library.
18. Letter from Karl Larsen Titlestad to the NMS's Home Board of 4.1.1877, MA-MHS, HA/G.sekr.90/Box 134/Jacket 6. When Karl Titlestad negotiated with Chief Hlube regarding the possibility of a return to the mission station of Umzinyathi, he begged the Chief not to destroy the little grave. See *NMT* 36, no. 7 (1881): 130.
19. *MKF* 3, no. 4 (1886): 25.
20. Letter from Karl L. Titlestad to Ommund Oftebro of 22.5.1878, *Diary of Karl Larsen Titlestad 1865–1891*, file 1, Killie Campbell Africana Library.
21. Letter from Karl Larsen Titlestad to the NMS's Home Board of 1.3.1879, MA-MHS, HA/G.sekr.40/Box 135 A/Jacket 1.
22. *NMT* 30, no. 4 (1875): 135.
23. Paul Peter Wettergren in 1870, Jan Olaus Kielland in 1874, Johannes Larsen Kyllingstad in 1878.
24. Kristin Fjelde Tjelle, 'Misjonærenes barn – foreldrenes eller misjonens ansvar? Misjonærbarn i NMS, ca 1840–1940' in *Med hjertet på flere steder: Om barn,*

misjon og flerkulturell oppvekst, ed. Tomas Drønen and Marianne Skjortnes (Trondheim: Tapir Akademisk Forlag, 2010), 36–40.

25. *NMT* 36, no. 7 (1881): 131.
26. Tjelle, 'Misjonærenes barn – foreldrenes eller misjonens ansvar?' 40–2.
27. Letter from Nils T. Braatvedt to the NMS's Home Board of 18.1.1881, MA-MHS/HA/G.sekr.90/Box 135 A/Jacket 13; *NMT* 42, no. 5 (1886), 93–7.
28. Tjelle, 'Misjonærenes barn – foreldrenes eller misjonens ansvar?' 44–5.
29. The same happened at the NMS's institutions for missionary children in Madagascar, China and Stavanger; see Kristin Fjelde Tjelle, 'Misjonærbarna på Solbakken', in *Med hjertet på flere steder: Om barn, misjon og flerkulturell oppvekst*, ed. Tomas Drønen and Marianne Skjortnes (Trondheim: Tapir Akademisk Forlag, 2010), 86. Inga Fergstad, who retired in 1910 from her position as matron of the Durban-located institution for missionary children, criticised the prevailing arrangement of female management. Boys and girls should not live together in a boarding institution that lacked a male principal, she claimed; the teenage boys in particular needed male guidance and supervision. Fergstad's worries were ignored by the missionaries, who asked the Home Board to send them 'a couple of ladies' to succeed Fergstad and the housekeeper Kristine Knudsen at the home for missionary children; see minutes from MC 1910, MA-MHS, 24. Female management continued until the institution was closed in the early 1950s.
30. *MKF* 3, no. 4 (1986): 25–8. Karen Titlestad described in this article how hard it was to leave their seven-year-old son Peder at the school.
31. Michael S. Kimmel, *Manhood in America: A Cultural History*, 2nd edn (New York/Oxford: Oxford University Press, 2006), 80–104.
32. Titlestad, *Under the Zulu Kings*, 66–70. Killie Campbell Africana Library.
33. Titlestad, *Under the Zulu Kings*, 86.
34. Joy Wilkins, *Titlestad Family History*, MA-MHS, Personer SA/Box 2.
35. Letter from the NMS's Home Board to Karl Larsen Titlestad of 17.8.1908, MA-MHS, HA/G.sekr.91/Box 171/Jacket 6. See also Olsen, *Misjonsprest Karl Larsen Titlestad*, 72–4.
36. Gunhild Pedersen Oftebro served as a midwife in the NMS's Zulu mission from 1890 until 1899, and according to Lars Martin she assisted his wife both during labour and in the weeks after childbirth; *NMT* 82, no. 45 (1927): 384.
37. *MKF* 15, no. 10 (1898): 73–6; *MKF* 21, no. 9 (1904): 65–7.
38. *MKF* 21, no. 9 (1904): 67.
39. *NMT* 52, no. 24 (1897): 467–9; 53, no. 1 (1898): 7–10.
40. Karina Hestad Skeie, 'Building God's Kingdom: The Importance of the House to Nineteenth Century Norwegian Missionaries in Madagascar', in *Ancestors, Power and History in Madagascar*, ed. Karen Middleton (Leiden: Brill Academic Publishers, 1999), 88.
41. Erik Sidenvall, *The Making of Manhood among Swedish Missionaries in China and Mongolia, c. 1890–c. 1914* (Leiden/Boston: Brill, 2009), 159.
42. *MKF* 37, no. 7–8 (1920): 52.
43. *NMT* 80, no. 22 (1925): 182–83; *MKF* 15, no. 10 (1898): 73–4; 39, no. 4 (1922): 26.
44. *MKF* 19, no. 7 (1902): 53–6.

45. Letter from Lars Martin Titlestad to the NMS's Home Board of 15.5.1907, MA-MHS, HA/G.sekr.90/Box 144 A/Jacket 2.
46. Tosh, *A Man's Place*, 55.
47. Lars Martin Titlestad's notice about his wife's sixtieth anniversary, *NMT* 80, no. 30 (1925): 256.
48. See Margaretha Titlestad in *NMT* 80, no. 32 (1925): 269 and Lars Martin Titlestad in *NMT* 80, no. 29 (1925): 247; 81, no. 7 (1926): 54–5.
49. Hanna Mellemsether, *Misjonærer, settlersamfunn og afrikansk opposisjon: Striden om selvstendiggjøring i den norske Zulukirken, Sør-Afrika ca. 1920–1930* (Dr Art dissertation, University of Trondheim, 2001), 229.
50. Minutes from MC 1897, MA-MHS, HA/G.sekr.40/Box 39 A/Jacket 4. A home for Norwegian missionary children was first purchased in Greyville. It was sold some years later and a new home built in Bellevue Road. In 1928 a house was bought in Seaforth Avenue. Ernst Hallen, *Nordisk Kirkeliv Under Sydkorset: Festskrift i anledning Den Norsk Lutherske Kirkes 50 Aarsjubileum i Durban 14 mars 1880–14 mars 1930* (Durban: The Mission Press, 1930), 58.
51. The NMS's 56th annual report (Stavanger, 1898), 6.
52. Mellemsether, *Misjonærer, settlersamfunn og afrikansk opposisjon*, 89–116.
53. Robert Morrell, *From Boys to Gentlemen: Settler Masculinity in Colonial Natal, 1880–1920* (Pretoria: University of South Africa, 2001), 48–77.
54. *NMT* 81, no. 7 (1926): 54.
55. The Madagascar missionary wife Oline Birkeli, who in 1915 reported from her recreation stay in South Africa, admitted begrudging the missionary families in South Africa, see *MKF* 32, no. 10 (1915): 73–4. Edle Solberg, a missionary wife in South Africa, discussed the same issue in a 1942 article, 'Misjonærlodd: Far og mor der ute – barna igjen her hjemme', *Korsmerket. Blad for norsk misjonsungdom*, 1942, no. 14: 1, 3.
56. Mellemsether, *Misjonærer, settlersamfunn og afrikansk opposisjon*, 108–10.
57. *MKF* 39, no. 4 (1922): 30.
58. Karl Michael Titlestad's bible, Thora-Margaretha Titlestad Brodin's private archive.
59. He moved in on 18 August 1912 and moved out on 2 July 1914. MA-MHS/ Forretningsfører 60/Box 333/Jacket 1.
60. In the period 1889–1952 177 children lived at Solbakken for shorter or longer periods. 156 children (88.1 per cent) had parents in Madagascar, 12 (6.8 per cent) were children of missionaries to China, six (3.4 per cent) were children of missionaries to South Africa and three (1.7 per cent) were children of missionaries to the Cameroons.
61. Tjelle, 'Misjonærbarna på Solbakken', 71–104.
62. *NMT* 1856, no. 11, 180–82.
63. Tjelle, 'Misjonærenes barn – foreldrenes eller misjonens ansvar? 36–7.
64. Anna Fredén, *Missionärernas barn* (Stockholm: Svenska Kyrkans Diakonistyrelses Bokförlag, 1918), 36–7.
65. Lars Dahle visited these mission organisations during a study trip in 1869, and his report describes the conditions at the boarding institutions for missionary children; see *NMT* 25, no. 7 (1870): 325.
66. Walthamstow Hall, Home and School for the Daughters of Missionaries, and Eltham College, School for the Sons of Missionaries; see Elizabeth Buettner,

Empire Families: Britons and Late Imperial India (Oxford: Oxford University Press, 2004), 154–62.

67. Buettner, *Empire Families*, 154–62.
68. Buettner, *Empire Families*, 144.
69. Cited in Buettner, *Empire Families*, 112.
70. Adams and Coltrane, 'Boys and Men in Families', 238.
71. In the NMS's Mission Archive it has not been possible to find any documents originating from Signe Brekke.
72. Letter from Karl Michael Titlestad to General Secretary Jørgen Nilssen of 23.9.1921, MA-MHS, HA/G.sekr.90/Box 430/Jacket 6.
73. Letter from Karl Michael Titlestad to Einar Amdahl of 1.5.1923, MA-MHS, HA/G.sekr.90/Box 433/Jacket 1.
74. *Kamp og Seier* 25, no. 1924: 147–48.
75. Letter from Karl Michael Titlestad to Einar Amdahl of 31.8.1924, MA-MHS, HA/M.sekr.90/Box 702/Jacket 5.
76. Letter from Karl Michael Titlestad to Einar Amdahl of 28.2.1925, MA-MHS, HA/M.sekr.90/Box 703/Jacket 2.
77. Letter from Karl Michael Titlestad to Einar Amdahl of 28.2.1925, MA-MHS, HA/M.sekr.90/Box 703/Jacket 2.
78. *The life story of Thora-Margaretha Titlestad Brodin,* unpublished manuscript. Thora-Margaretha Titlestad Brodin's private archive.
79. Letter from Karl Michael Titlestad to Einar Amdahl of 17.10.1929, MA-MHS, HA/M.sekr.90/Box 705/Jacket 5.
80. *The life story of Thora-Margaretha Titlestad Brodin,* unpublished manuscript. Thora-Margaretha Titlestad Brodin's private archive.
81. A central work has been Leonore Davidoff and Catherine Hall, *Family Fortunes: Men and Women of the English Middle Class, 1780–1850* (London: Hutchinson, 1987).
82. See the case of Norway in Gro Hagemann, 'De stummes leir? 1800–1900', in *Med kjønnsperspektiv på norsk historie: Fra vikingtid til 2000-årsskiftet,* ed. Ida Blom and Sølvi Sogner (Oslo: Cappelen akademisk forlag, 2005), 157–250.
83. Tosh, *A Man's Place*; Shawn Johansen, *Family Men: Middle-Class Fatherhood in Early Industrializing America* (New York: Routledge, 2001).
84. Tomas Berglund, *Det goda faderskapet i svenskt 1800-tal* (Stockholm: Carlssons, 2007); Lorentzen, 'Fedrene'; Jørgen Lorentzen, '"Først mor og barn, derefter Faderen": Om fedrene i norsk historie fra 1850–1920', *Tidsskrift for kjønnsforskning* 32, no. 3 (2008).
85. Skeie, 'Building God's Kingdom', 92.
86. See report from Lars Larsen in *NMT* 30, no. 4 (1875): 126–33; from Ole Stavem in *NMT* 28, no. 11 (1873): 419–22.
87. For the cases of the Braatvedt and Steenberg families, see Chapter 6.
88. Ingie Hovland, *Mission Station Christianity: Norwegian Missionaries in Colonial Natal and Zululand, Southern Africa 1850–1890* (Leiden/Boston: Brill, 2013).
89. Tosh, *A Man's Place*, 17.
90. Studies on mission have until recently paid little attention to the role of the missionary family. In 2010 Emily Manktelow of King's College London submitted the PhD thesis *Missionary Families and the Formation of the Missionary Enterprise: The London Missionary Society and the Family, 1795–1875.* The thesis

is an exploration and analysis of family life in the global context of mission, and how it was shaped and directed by both official policy in London, and the realities in the mission field.

9 Men in the World

1. R. W. Connell, 'Globalization, Imperialism, and Masculinities', in *Handbook of Studies on Men & Masculinities*, ed. Michael S. Kimmel, Jeff Hearn and Robert William Connell (Thousand Oaks, CA: Sage Publications, 2005), 72.
2. Connell, 'Globalization, Imperialism, and Masculinities', 74.
3. Robert Morrell, 'Of Boys and Men: Masculinity and Gender in Southern African Studies', *Journal of Southern African Studies* 24, no. 4 (1998), 605–30.
4. Belinda Bozzoli, 'Marxism, Feminism and South African Studies', *Journal of Southern African Studies* 9, no. 2 (1983), 139–71.
5. John Tosh, *A Man's Place: Masculinity and the Middle-Class Home in Victorian England* (New Haven, CT: Yale University Press, 1999), 2.
6. Per Hernæs, 'The Zulu Kingdom, Norwegian Missionaries, and British Imperialism, 1845–1879', in *Norwegian Missions in African History, Vol. 1: South Africa 1845–1906*, ed. Jarle Simensen (Oslo: Norwegian University Press, 1986), 117–36.
7. Hernæs, 'The Zulu Kingdom, Norwegian Missionaries, and British Imperialism', 138–39.
8. *NMT* 25, no. 4 (1870): 160–61.
9. *NMT* 25, no. 12 (1870): 513.
10. Letter from Karl Larsen Titlestad to the NMS's Home Board of 4.1.1877, MA-MHS, HA/G.sekr.90/Box 134, Jacket 6.
11. *NMT* 33, no. 6 (1878): 108–13.
12. Letter from Karl Larsen Titlestad to the NMS's Home Board of 1.7.1878, MA-MHS, HA/G.sekr.90/Box 134, Jacket 12.
13. Ole Stavem, *Et bantufolk og kristendommen: Det norske missionsselskaps sytti-aarige zulumission* (Stavanger: Det norske missionsselskap forlag, 170).
14. Jeff Guy, *The Destruction of the Zulu Kingdom: The Civil War in Zululand, 1879–1884* Pietermaritzburg: University of Natal Press, 1994), 48–9, 73–4. The ultimatum made known to the King on 11 December demanded payment of fines and the surrender of certain Zulu men – Sihayo's sons – to the colonial authorities, but also the abolition of the Zulu military system within thirty days.
15. Hernæs, 'The Zulu Kingdom, Norwegian Missionaries, and British Imperialism, 1845–1879', 136–86.
16. Jarle Simensen et al., 'Christian Missions and Socio-Cultural Change in Zululand 1850–1906: Norwegian Strategy and African Response', in *Norwegian Missions in African History, Vol. 1: South Africa 1845–1906*, ed. Jarle Simensen (Oslo: Norwegian University Press, 1986), 223–29.
17. Letter from Karl Larsen Titlestad to the NMS's Home Board of 8.1.1879, MA-MHS, HA/G.sekr.40/Box 135 A/Jacket 1.
18. The historian Bjørg Seland also claims that positive evaluation of suffering and crisis characterised the ideology of the pietistic movements in Norway; see Bjørg Seland, *Religion på det frie marked: Folkelig pietisme og bedehuskultur*

(Kristiansand: Høyskoleforlaget AS – Norwegian Academic Press, 2006), 96–9.

19. Roald Berg claims in his masculinity study of polar aviators in the 1920s, that the meaning of emotions in human relationship should be taken more seriously in historical research; see Berg, 'Gender in Polar Air: Roald Amundsen and his Aeronautics', *Acta Borealia* 23, no. 2 (2006): 130–44. See also Jan Eivind Myhre, 'Feeling One's Way: Emotions in History and Historiography', in *Pathways of the Past: Essays in Honour of Sølvi Sogner,* ed. Hilde Sandvik, Kari Telste and Gunnar Thorvaldsen (Oslo: Novus, 2002).

20. Guy, *The Destruction of the Zulu Kingdom*, 73–4.

21. Stavem, *Et bantufolk og kristendommen*, 228–30, 233–35.

22. Dahle, *Inspektionsreisen til Zulu og Madagaskar i 1903: Indberetning til Generalforsamlingen i Bergen 1904* (Stavanger: Det norske Missionsselskabs Forlag, 1904), 29–31.

23. Olav Guttorm Myklebust, 'Sør-Afrika', in *Det Norske Misjonsselskap 1842–1942*, ed. John Nome, vol. 3 (Stavanger: Dreyer, 1949), 107–08.

24. Umphumulo Mission Reserve (500 acres) was donated to the NMS by the Natal government in 1850. During the short Boer Republic (Provisio B) in Northern Zululand, the NMS had received title deed for their 'mission farm' at Nhlazatsche (3 000 acres). Also, Imfule mission station had been granted 3 000 acres of land by the Boer government, but a title deed was still missing.

25. Stavem's application to the Colonial Secretary of Natal in February 1898, MA-MHS, HA/G.sekr.92/Box 182/Jacket 16.

26. Dahle, *Inspektionsreisen til Zulu og Madagaskar i 1903*, 25–31.

27. The original documents signed by Shepstone are archived in MA-MHS, South Africa Archive/Box 1 B/Jacket 6.

28. In 1898, Stavem applied for official recognition of the station borders of Ekombe, but failed to receive it. See Stavem's application to the Colonial Secretary of Natal in February 1898, MA-MHS, HA/G.sekr.92/Box 182/Jacket 16.

29. Minutes from MC 1905, MA-MHS, HA/G.sekr.40/Box 43/Jacket 11.

30. Letter from Lars Martin Titlestad to Lars Dahle of 28.10.1908, MA-MHS, HA/G.sekr.90/Box 144 A/Jacket 8.

31. According to Titlestad, much of the original mission land was sold in 1904 as 'Farm no. 15' to William Law, a white farmer. In Titlestad's opinion, Law was 'not a good man', and there were rumours that the government would remove him from the farm and sell it. Letter from Lars Martin Titlestad to Lars Dahle of 28.10.1908, MA-MHS, HA/G.sekr.90/Box 144 A/Jacket 8.

32. Letter from Lars Martin Titlestad to Lars Dahle of 14.1.1909, MA-MHS, HA/G. sekr.90/Box 144 A/Jacket 8.

33. The NMS Home Board's letter of response to MC 1909, MA-MHS, 1–2.

34. Elias Titlestad, *Under the Zulu Kings*, 73. Killie Campbell Africana Library.

35. Hanna Mellemsether, '"Misjonærsettlerne i Sør-Afrika"', in *Nordmenn i Afrika – Afrkanere i Norge*, ed. Kirsten Alsaker Kjerland and Anne K. Bang (Bergen: Vigmostad & Bjørke, 2002), 66–8.

36. Philippe Denis, Thulani Mlotshwa, and George Mukuka, ed., *The Casspir and the Cross: Voices of Black Clergy in the Natal Midlands* (Pietermaritzburg: Cluster Publications, 1999), 43.

37. Minutes from MC 1942, MA-MHS, 2–3.

38. *NMT* 50, no. 24 (1895): 466–69.
39. John M. MacKenzie, 'The Imperial Pioneer and Hunter and the British Masculine Stereotype in Late Victorian and Edwardian Times', in *Manliness and Morality: Middle-class Masculinity in Britain and American 1800–1940*, ed. J.A. Mangan and James Walvin (Manchester: Manchester University Press, 1987); Allen Warren, 'Popular Manliness: Baden-Powell, Scouting, and the Development of Manly Character', in *Manliness and Morality: Middle-class Masculinity in Britain and America 1800–1940*, ed. J.A. Mangan and James Walvin (Manchester: Manchester University Press, 1987).
40. *NMT* 59, no. 1 (1904): 10–12.
41. *NMT* 59, no. 1 (1904): 11.
42. Carolyn Hamilton, *Terrific Majesty: The Powers of Shaka Zulu and the Limits of Historical Invention* (Cape Town/Johannesburg: David Philip Publishers, 1998), 130–67; John Laband, '"Bloodstained Grandeur": Colonial and Imperial Stereotypes of Zulu Warriors and Zulu Warfare', in *Zulu Identities: Being Zulu, Past and Present*, ed. Benedict Carton, John Laband and Jabulani Sithole (Scottsville: University of KwaZulu-Natal Press, 2008).
43. *MKF* 14, no. 1 (1898): 2.
44. Minutes from MC 1914, MA-MHS, 46–8.
45. *NMT* 88, no. 22 (1914): 523.
46. Letter from Lars Martin Titlestad to Einar Amdahl of 25.9.1927, MA-MHS, HA/M.sekr.90/Box 704/Jacket 5; Minutes from MC 1927, MA-MHS, 65–6.
47. *NMT* 63, no. 5 (1908); 100–02.
48. La Hausse de Lalouvière, *Restless Identities: Signatures of Nationalism, Zulu Ethnicity and History in the Lives of Petros Lamula (c. 1881–1948) and Lymon Maling (1889–c. 1936)* (Pietermaritzburg: University of Natal Press, 2000), 124–34; Hanna Mellemsether, *Misjonærer, settlersamfunn og afrikansk opposisjon: Striden om selvstendiggjøring i den norske Zulukirken, Sør-Afrika ca. 1920–1930* (Dr Art dissertation, University of Trondheim, 2001), 227–31.
49. Mellemsether, *Misjonærer, settlersamfunn og afrikansk opposisjon*, 249–72.
50. Minutes from MC 1924, MA-MHS, 18.
51. *Kamp og Seier* 25, no. 19 (1924): 147–48.
52. See, e.g., Karl Larsen Titlestad in *NMT* 28, no. 10 (1873), 373–75.
53. *NMT* 31, no. 5 (1876): 226–27.
54. Titlestad, *Under the Zulu Kings*, 73. Killie Campbell Africana Library.
55. Stavem, *Et bantufolk og kristendommen*, *134*; *NMT* 8, no. 8 (1890): 150.
56. See *NMT* 29, no. 4 (1874): 124–31 where Larsen reported that 16 'foreigners', Britons, Boers, Germans, during the last month had visited his station and stayed overnight. See also *NMT* 39, no. 8 (1884): 150–6.
57. *NMT* 40, no. 18 (1885): 346–53; *NMT* 41, no. 6 (1886): 106–13; *NMT* 43, no. 19 (1888): 377–80.
58. Lars Berge and Ole Steenberg's reports in *NMT* 45, no. 10 (1890): 186–88, no. 18: 346–49; no. 22: 427–28.
59. Connell, 'Globalization, Imperialism, and Masculinities', 74.
60. *NMT* 59, no. 5 (1904): 111–13; *NMT* 81, no. 51–2: 444.
61. See e.g. *NMT* 59, no. 1 (1904): 12–15; *NMT* 63, no. 8 (1908): 170–2.
62. Letter from Karl Larsen Titlestad to the NMS's Home Board of 25.7.1907, MA-MHS, HA/G.sekr.90/Box 144 A/Jacket 2.
63. *NMT* 66, no. 7 (1911): 150.

64. *MKF* 25, no. 11 (1908): 82.
65. Mellemsether, '"Misjonærsettlerne i Sør-Afrika"', 65.
66. *Kamp og Seier* 17, no. 30 (1917): 235–36. See also *Kamp og Seier* 25, no. 4 (1924): 28–9.
67. *NMT* 81, no. 7 (1926): 54–5.
68. *NMT* 84, no. 25 (1929): 196.
69. Mellemsether, '"Misjonærsettlerne i Sør-Afrika"'.
70. Dag Ingemar Børresen, '"The Boys will die like flies": Afrikanere på hval-fangst i Antarktis 1908–1920', in *Kolonitid: Nordmenn på eventyr og big business i Afrika og Stillehavet*, ed. Kirsten Alsaker Kjerland and Knut M. Rio (Oslo: Scandinavian Academic Press, 2009).
71. Alan H. Winquist, *Scandinavians and South Africa: Their Impact on the Cultural, Social and Economic Development of Pre-1902 South Africa* (Cape Town/ Rotterdam: A.A. Balkema, 1978), 148–57.
72. H. P. Braatvedt, *Roaming Zululand with a Native Commissioner* (Pietermaritzburg: Shuter & Shooter, 1949).
73. Peter H. Rodseth, *Mission Station to Mayor's Parlour: An Autobiography* (1980); Fred Rodseth, *Ndabazabantu. The Life of a Native Affairs Administrator* (Volda: Fred Rodseth, 1984).
74. Cited in Mellemsether, '"Misjonærsettlerne i Sør-Afrika"', 65.
75. Ernst Hallen, *Nordisk Kirkeliv Under Sydkorset: Festskrift i anledning Den Norsk Lutherske Kirkes 50 Aarsjubileum i Durban 14 mars 1880 – 14 mars 1930* (Durban: The Mission Press, 1930), 58.
76. The NMS's annual missionary conference of 1914 was in Durban, so that everyone could participate in the national celebrations.
77. *NMT* 93, no. 30/31 (1938): 4.
78. Roald Berg, *Norge på egen hånd 1905–1920* (Oslo: Universitetesforlaget, 1995).
79. The networks between Norwegian religious, commercial and diplomatic enterprises in a colonial context have recently been examined by Svein Ivar Angell in Svein Ivar Angell, 'Konsulatspørsmålet og Kolonialismen', in *Kolonitid: Nordmenn på eventyr og big business i Afrika og Stillehavet*, ed. Kirsten Alsaker Kjerland and Knut M. Rio (Oslo: Scandinavian Academic Press, 2009).
80. *Kamp og Seier* 17, no. 30 (1917): 235–6. See also *Kamp og Seier* 25, no. 4 (1924): 28–9.
81. Letter from Karl Larsen Titlestad to the NMS's Home Board of 25.7.1907, MA-MHS, HA/G.sekr.90/Box 144 A/Jacket 2.
82. Rhonda Semple, 'Missionary Manhood: Professionalism, Belief and Masculinity in the Nineteenth-Century British Imperial Field', *Journal of Imperial and Commonwealth History* 36, no. 3 (2008): 410.
83. The term 'white heathen' was used by Ommund Oftebro in *NMT* 25, no. 7 (1870): 293–300.
84. The hospital bills of £30 and £50 were considerable considering a mission-ary's annual salary of £150. Titlestad, *Under the Zulu Kings*, 105. Killie Campbell Africana Library. See also letters from Lars Martin Titlestad to the NMS's Home Board of 12.9.1901 and 2.4.1902, MA-MHS, HA/G.sekr.90/ Box 142/Jacket 5; and of 15.5.1907, MA-MHS, HA/G.sekr.90/Box 144 A/ Jacket 2.

85. Letter from Ole Stavem to Lars Dahle of 20.6.1901, MA-MHS, HA/G.sekr.90/ Box 144 A/Jacket 2.
86. Minutes from MC 1921, MA-MHS, 26.
87. Letter from Lars Martin Titlestad of 24.9.1922, MA-MHS, HA/M.sekr.90/ Box 701/Jacket 5.
88. See Peder Aage Rødseth's letter of 9.9.1922, MA-MHS, South Africa Archive, Box 1 B/Jacket 6.
89. Arne Gunnar Carlsson, 'Norge og boerkrigen', in *Nordmenn i Afrika – Afrikanere i Norge*, ed. Kirsten Alsaker Kjerland and Anne K. Bang (Bergen Vigmostad & Bjørke, 2002). A Scandinavian corps was established in Transvaal in 1899 to support the Boers, whereas the Umzimkulu Mounted Rifles established among Norwegian settlers in Marburg supported the British side. See Anna Halland, Andrew Halland, and Ingeborg Kjønstad, *Norsk Nybyggerliv i Natal: Festskrift i anledning De Norske Settleres 50-aarsjubileum i Marburg. 29de august 1882–29de august 1932.* (Port Shepstone: South Coast Herald Ltd., 1932), 60–8. See also Winquist, *Scandinavians and South Africa*, 158–92.
90. Martinius Borgen was stationed at Nhlazatsche and Martin Borgen and Ole S. Steenberg at Mahlabatini.
91. Report from Ole Stavem in the NMS's 58th annual report (Stavanger, 1900), 3–4.
92. Report from Ole Stavem in the NMS's 58th annual report (Stavanger, 1900, 3
93. Shula Marks, *Reluctant Rebellion: The 1906–8 Disturbances in Natal* (Oxford: Clarendon Press, 1970); Jeff Guy, *Remembering the Rebellion: The Zulu Uprising of 1906* (Scottsville: University of KwaZulu-Natal Press, 2006).
94. Hernæs, 'The Zulu Kingdom, Norwegian Missionaries, and British Imperialism', 177–8. See also Hernæs's unpublished paper 'Lydighet mot Øvrigheten: Norske misjonærer i Natal og Zululand under Bambatha-opprøret i 1906', (Center for Afrikastudier, Københavns universitet, juni 1975).
95. Lars Berge, *The Bambatha Watershed: Swedish Missionaries, African Christians and an evolving Zulu Church in rural Natal and Zululand 1902–1910*, Vol. 78 Studia Missionalia Upsaliensia (Uppsala: SIM, 2000), 381.
96. *NMT* 61, no. 17 (1906): 390–94.
97. See for instance Tvedt's report from Eotimati in *NMT* 61, no. 23 (1906): 542–48.
98. Titlestad, *Under the Zulu Kings*, 109–38. Killie Campbell Africana Library.
99. Guy, *Remembering the Rebellion*, 168–79.
100. Laurits Aadnesgaard, 'Rasespørsmålet', in *Zulu: Evangeliets landvinning*, ed. Johan Kjelvei (Stavanger: Det Norske Misjonsselskaps trykkeri, 1932).
101. Myklebust, 'Sør-Afrika', 154–56.
102. Aadnesgaard, 'Rasespørsmålet', 103.
103. Myklebust, 'Sør-Afrika', 155.
104. Mellemsether, *Misjonærer, settlersamfunn og afrikansk opposisjon*, 171–248.
105. Mellemsether, *Misjonærer, settlersamfunn og afrikansk opposisjon*, 249–72.
106. Berit Hagen Agøy, *Den tvetydige protesten: Norske misjonærer, kirker og apartheid i Sør-Afrika, 1948 – ca. 1970* (Unpublished Ma thesis, University of Oslo, 1987).

107. Scriba and Lislerud, 'Lutheran Missions and Churches in South Africa', in *Christianity in South Africa: A Political, Social & Cultural History*, ed. Richard Elphick and Rodney Davenport (Oxford: James Currey, 1997).

108. Richard Elphick, 'The Benevolent Empire and the Social Gospel: Missionaries and South African Christians in the Age of Segregation', in *Christianity in South Africa: A Political, Social & Cultural History*, ed. Richard Elphick and Rodney Davenport (Oxford: James Currey, 1997).

109. The lecture was printed in the minutes from MC 1929, MA-MHS, 122–59: 'En historisk, social og religiøs analyse av den indfødte sydafrikaner av idag. (Spesielt zulueren.)'

110. For a review of the Jerusalem conference, see Timothy Yates, *Christian Mission in the Twentieth Century* (Cambridge: Cambridge University Press, 1994), 65–70.

111. Letter from Karl Michael Titlestad to Einar Amdahl of 17.10.1929, MA-MHS, HA/M.sekr.90/Box 705/Jacket 5.

112. *NMT* 85, no. 24 (1930): 189.

113. Einar Amdahl's lecture was printed in the minutes from MC 1929, MA-MHS, 1–44.

114. See Einar Amdahl's reports from the conference in Jerusalem 1928 in *NMT* 83, no. 7 (1928): 60; no. 8: 69; no. 10: 85; no. 17: 139, 142; no. 18: 147; no. 19: 157; no. 20: 164; no. 22: 177; no. 25: 205–06; no. 26: 212–13.

Concluding Remarks

1. Michael Kimmel, *Manhood in America: A Cultural History*, 2nd edn (New York/Oxford: Oxford University Press, 2006).

2. Erik Sidenvall, *The Making of Manhood among Swedish Missionaries in China and Mongolia, c. 1890–c. 1914* (Leiden/Boston: Brill, 2009).

3. Anna Prestjan, *Präst och karl, karl och präst* (Lund: Sekel Bokförlag, 2009).

4. Tjeder, *The Power of Character: Middle-Class Masculinities, 1800–1900* (PhD dissertation, Stockholm University, 2003).

5. Berg, 'Misjonshistorie og samfunnsforskning', *Nytt Norsk Tidsskrift*, no. 3–4 (2009): 322–3.

6. Text by NMS missionary in China, Karl Ludvig Reichelt, melody by Johann Michael Haydn, 1822.

7. Claes Ekenstam, 'Mansforskningens bakgrund och framtid: Några teoretiska reflexioner', *Norma* 1, no. 1 (2006): 6–23; Claes Ekenstam, 'Män, manlighet och umanlighet i historien', in *Män i Norden: Manlighet och modernitet 1840–1940*, ed. Claes Ekenstam and Jørgen Lorentzen (Hedemora: Gidlund, 2006).

8. Tjeder, *The Power of Character*.

9. Connell, *Masculinities*, 2nd edn (Berkeley/Los Angeles: University of California Press, 2005).

Unprinted Sources

The NMS Mission Archive (MA), School of Mission and Theology (MHS):

Hjemmearkivet (HA), *Forretningsfører 60*:
Box 333
Hjemmearkivet, Generalsekretæren 10:
Styreprotokoll nr. 8 (1862–1875), nr. 9 (1875–1881), nr. 10 (1881–1886), nr. 11 (1886–1889), nr. 12 (1889–1893), nr. 13 (1893–1896)
Hjemmearkivet, Generalsekretæren 40:
Boxes 34, 35, 36, 37, 38, 39 A, 42, 43
Hjemmearkivet, Generalsekretæren 90:
Boxes 81, 90, 104, 125
Hjemmearkivet, Generalsekretæren 90:
Boxes 131, 134, 135 A, 135 B, 136, 137, 138, 139, 140 B, 142, 144 A, 144 B, 430, 433
Hjemmearkivet, Misjonssekretæren 90:
701, 702, 703, 704, 705
Hjemmearkivet, Generalsekretæren 91:
Boxes 165, 171, 494
Hjemmearkivet, Generalsekretæren 92:
Boxes 182, 190
Hjemmearkivet, Generalsekretæren 93:
Boxes 191, 192
Misjonsskolen 1843–1977:
Boxes 1852, 1925
Sør Afrika arkivet:
Boxes 1 A, 1 B
Uordnet arkiv:
Personer SA, box 2: Joy Wilkins, *Titlestad Family History*.

Killie Campbell Africana Library

Diary of Karl Larsen Titlestad 1865–1891, file 1.
Lawrence Titlestad, *Under the Zulu Kings,* Cape Town 1939, unpublished manuscript.

Torstein Oftebro's Private Archive

Ommund Oftebro's letter to his brother Tobias Oftebro of 5.06.1888.

Thora-Margaretha Titlestad Brodin's Private Archive

The Life Story of Thora-Margaretha Titlestad Brodin, unpublished manuscript.
Letters and newspaper articles regarding the death of Karl Michael Titlestad.
Karl Michael Titlestad's bible.

Printed Sources

Mission magazines

Norsk Missionstidende, 1870–1930
Missionslæsning for Kvindeforeninger, 1884–1925
Kamp og Seier, 1900–1925

Mission reports

Aktstykker til belysning af Forholdet mellom Biskop Schreuder og det Norske Missionsselskab: Fra Biskopens Ordination indtil generalforsamlingen 1873. Stavanger: Kielland, 1876.

Amdahl, Einar. *Under sydkorset og i Sinims land: Beretning om inspeksjonen til Madagaskar, Zulu og Kina 1928–30*. Stavanger: Det Norske Misjonsselskaps trykkeri, 1930.

Gjerløw, Ole. *Beretning vedkommende Sekretærens Reise til Missionsmarken i Zululand og Natal 1887–88*. Stavanger: Det Norske Missionsselskab, 1888.

Dahle, Lars. *Inspektionsreisen til Zulu og Madagaskar i 1903: Indberetning til Generalforsamlingen i Bergen 1904*. Stavanger: Det norske Missionsselskabs Forlag, 1904.

The NMS annual reports, 1870–1930.

The NMS missionary conference minutes, 1905–30.

The NMS Home Board's letter of response to the missionary conference, 1905–30.

Mission autobiographies and biographies

Braatvedt, Nils T. *Erindringer fra mitt misjonsliv*. Stavanger: Boye og Hinnas boktrykkeri, 1930.

Fløttum, Ole S. *Arvesølv: Boka om biskop Schreuder*. Stavanger: Misjonsselskapets forlag, 1951.

Gilje, Kåre. *Høvdingen*. Stavanger: Misjonsselskapets forlag, 1949.

Igland, Alf K. *Tante Marit: Zulumisjonær og mor for tretten*. Oslo: Luther Forlag, 1977.

Olsen, Anders. *Hjem fra kamppladsen: Livsbilleder af vore afdøde missionærer og kvindelige missionsarbeidere i Zulu og paa Madagaskar*. Kristiania: Steen'ske Bogtrykkeri og Forlag, 1906.

Olsen, Anders. *Missionsprest Karl Larsen Titlestad: Det Norske Missionselskaps senior*. Bergen: A/S Lunde & CO.s forlag, 1929.

Olsen, Anders and Ole Stavem. 'Misjonsprest Karl Titlestad. 1832–1924'. In *Norvegia Sacra*. Oslo: Steenske Forlag, 1925.

Skadberg, Karten. *Under regnbuen*. Stavanger, Misjonsselskapets forlag, 1947.

Mission travel accounts

Astrup, Nils. *En Missionsreise til Limpopo gjennem Zululand, Swaziland og Togaland ind i Riget Umgaza*. Kristiania: Th. Steens Forlagsexpedition, 1891.

Astrup, Nils. *Zulumissionens Maal – Africas Hjerte*. Christiania: Johannes Bjørnstads bogtrykkeri, 1903.

Mission study books

Fykse, Elida. *Til Sydkorsets land: Studiebrev til norske gjenter og gutar fra misjonær Elida Fykse*. Volume 1–3. Stavanger: Det norske misjonsselskaps Bibel- og misjonskurs pr. korrespondanse, 1946.

Kjelvei, Johan (ed.). *Zulu: Evangeliets landvinning*. Stavanger: Det Norske Misjonsselskap trykkeri, 1932.

Leisegang, Hans Christian. *Vor Zulumission*. Stavanger: Det Norske Missionsselskaps forlag, 1921.

Misjonsalbum: Syd-afrika: 109 billeder og et kart fra Det Norske Misjonsselskaps arbeidsmark i Zulu og Natal. Stavanger, Det Norske Missionsselskaps forlag, 1928.

Mission narratives

Fergstad, Inga. *Fortellinger fra Zululand*. Oslo: Schreudermisjonens forlag, 1946.

Larsen, Hanna. *Skisser fra Zululand*. Debora, Iowa: Lutheran Publishing House, 1905.

Leisegang, Hans Kristian. *Høvdingens Søn*. Bergen: A/S Lunde & Co.'s Forlag, 1929.

Titlestad, Lars Martin. *En Zuluers Omvendelse, Kamp og Seier*. Stavanger: Det Norske Missionsselskabs Forlag, 1904.

Mission novels

Helander, Gunnar. *Zulu møter hvit mann*. Stavanger: Misjonsselskapets forlag, 1950.

Mission histories

Burgess, Andrew. *Zulufolket: Evangeliet blant zuluerne*. Oslo: Schreudermisjonens forlag, 1944. Norsk oversettelse av *Unkulunkulu in Zululand*. Minneapolis: Augsburg Publishing House, 1934, ved Osvald Granborg.

Dahle, Lars and Simon Emanuel Jørgensen. *Festskrift til Det Norske Missionsselskabs Jubilæum i 1892*. Stavanger: Det Norske Missionsselskabs Forlag, 1892.

Jørgensen, Simon Emanuel. *Vidnesbyrd fra Det norske Missionsselskabs Missionsgjerning*. Stavanger: P.T. Mallings Boghandels Forlag, 1887.

Landmark, Nils. *Det Norske Missionsselskab, dets Oprindelse og historiske Udvikling, dets Arbeidsmarker og dets Arbeidere*. Stavanger: Det Norske Missionsselskabs Forlag, 1889.

Myklebust, Olav Guttorm. 'Sør-Afrika'. In *Det Norske Misjonsselskap 1842–1942*, ed. John Nome, vol. 3. Stavanger: Dreyer, 1949.

Nome, John. 'Det Norske Misjonsselskaps historie i norsk kirkeliv: Fra stiftelsestiden til Schreuders brudd'. In *Det Norske Misjonsselskap 1842–1942*, ed. John Nome, vol. 1. Stavanger: Dreyer, 1943.

Nome, John. 'Det Norske Misjonsselskaps historie i norsk kirkeliv: Fra syttiårene til nåtiden'. In *Det Norske Misjonsselskap 1842–1942*, ed. John Nome, vol. 2. Stavanger: Dreyer, 1943.

Sommerfelt, Halfdan E. *Den Norske Zulumission: Et Tilbageblik paa de første 20 Aar af det Norske Missionsselskabs Virksomhed.* Christiania: Wm. Gram, 1865.

Stavem, Ole. *The Norwegian Missionary Society: A Short Review of Its Work among the Zulus.* Stavanger: The Norwegian Missionary Society, 1918.

Stavem, Ole. *Et bantufolk og kristendommen: Det norske missionsselskaps syttiaarige zulumission.* Stavanger: Det norske missionsselskaps forlag, 1917.

Stavem, Ole. *Lys over det mørke fastland.* Stavanger: Det Norske misjonsselskaps trykkeri, 1923.

Bibliography

Aadnesgaard, Laurits. 'Rasespørsmålet'. In *Zulu: Evangeliets landvinning*, ed. Johan Kjelvei, 102–08. Stavanger: Det Norske Misjonsselskaps trykkeri, 1932.

Aasen, Ivar. 'Misjonssommerskolene'. In *Norsk Misjonsleksikon*, ed. Fridtjov Birkeli, Trygve Bjerkrheim, Alfred K. Dahl, Johannes Gausdal, Halvor Hjertvik, Arnfinn Nordbø, Gunnar Rødahl, Martin Ski, Christian Tidemann Strand and Johan Straume. Stavanger: Nomi forlag – Runa forlag, 1967.

Adams, Michele and Scott Coltrane. 'Boys and Men in Families: The Domestic Production of Gender, Power, and Privilege'. In *Handbook of Studies on Men & Masculinities*, ed. Michael S. Kimmel, Jeff Hearn and R. W. Connell, 230–48. Thousand Oaks, CA: Sage Publications, 2005.

Agøy, Berit Hagen. *Den tvetydige protesten: Norske misjonærer, kirker og apartheid i Sør-Afrika, 1948–ca.1970*. Unpublished MA thesis, University of Oslo, 1987.

Aktstykker til belysning af Forholdet mellom Biskop Schreuder og det Norske Missionsselskab: Fra Biskopens Ordination indtil generalforsamlingen 1873. Stavanger: Kielland, 1876.

Alfsvåg, Knut. 'Misjonærkall og foreldrekall – fruktbar spenning eller uløselig konflikt?' In *Med hjertet på flere steder: Om barn, misjon og flerkulturell oppvekst*, ed. Tomas Drønen and Marianne Skjortnes, 295–312. Trondheim: Tapir Akademisk Forlag, 2010.

Amdahl, Einar. *Under sydkorset og i Sinims land: Beretning om inspeksjonen til Madagaskar, Zulu og Kina 1928–30*. Stavanger: Det Norske Misjonsselskaps trykkeri, 1930.

Amdahl, Einar and Otto Chr. Dahl. 'Lars Dahle'. In *Norsk Misjonsleksikon*, ed. Fridtjov Birkeli, Trygve Bjerkrheim, Alfred K. Dahl, Johannes Gausdal, Halvor Hjertvik, Arnfinn Nordbø, Gunnar Rødahl, Martin Ski, Christian Tidemann Strand and Johan Straume. Stavanger: Nomi forlag – Runa forlag, 1967.

Andersen, Ivar A. 'Sør-Afrika'. In *I tro og tjeneste: Det Norske Misjonsselskap 1842–1992*, ed. Torstein Jørgensen. Stavanger: Misjonshøgskolen, 1992.

Angell, Svein Ivar. 'Konsulatspørsmålet og Kolonialismen'. In *Kolonitid: Nordmenn på eventyr og big business i Afrika og Stillehavet*, ed. Kirsten Alsaker Kjerland and Knut M. Rio, 111–27. Oslo: Scandinavian Acdemic Press, 2009.

Areklett, Ingmar. *Ungdomsmisjonen: En biografi*. Torvastad: KFUK-KFUM Global, 2008.

Astrup, Nils. *En Missionsreise til Limpopo*. Kristiania: Th. Steens Forlagsexpedition, 1891.

Astrup, Nils. *Zulumissionens Maal – Afrikas Hjerte*. Christiania: Johannes Bjørnstads bogtrykkeri, 1903.

Bakke, Odd Magne. '"Negro psyche": The Representation of Black People in the Writings of Missionary Olav Guttorm Myklebust'. *Studia Historiae Ecclesiasticae. Journal of the Church History Society of Southern Africa* 36, no. 1 (2010): 37–52.

Ballard, Charles. 'From Sovereignty to Subjection: The Political Economy of Zululand 1820–1906'. In *Norwegian Missions in African History, Vol. 1: South Africa 1845–1906*, ed. Jarle Simensen, 56–100. Oslo: Universitetsforlaget 1986.

Beaver, R. Pierce. *All Loves Excelling: American Protestant Women in World Mission.* Grand Rapids, MI: Eerdmans, 1968.

Bederman, Gail. '"The Women Have Had Charge of the Church Long Enough": The Men and Religion Forward Movement of 1911–1912 and the Masculinization of Middle Class Protestantism'. *American Quarterly* 41, no. 3 (1989): 432–65.

Berentsen, Jan-Martin. *Teologi og misjon: Trekk fra protestantismens historie fram til vårt århundre.* Oslo: Luther, 1990.

Berg, Roald. *Norge på egen hånd 1905–1920.* Oslo: Universitetsforlaget, 1995.

Berg, Roald. 'Gender in Polar Air: Roald Amundsen and His Aeronautics'. *Acta Borealia* 23, no. 2 (2006): 130–44.

Berg, Roald. 'Misjonshistorie og samfunnsforskning'. *Nytt Norsk Tidsskrift*, no. 3–4 (2009): 322–33.

Berg, roald. 'The Missionary Impulse in Norwegian History'. *Studia historiae ecclesiasticae. Journal of the Church History Society of Southern Africa* 36, no. 1 (2010): 1–13.

Berge, Lars. *The Bambbatha Watershed: Swedish Missionaries, African Christians and an Evolving Zulu Church in rural Natal and Zululand 1902–1910*, vol. 78, Studia Missionalia Upsaliensia. Uppsala: SIM, 2000.

Berglund, Tomas. *Det goda faderskapet i svenskt 1800-tal.* Stockholm, Carlssons, 2007.

Bhabha, Homi K. 'The Other Question: The Stereotype and Colonial Discourse'. *Screen* 24, no. 4 (1983): 18–36.

Birkeli, Emil. *Misjonshistorie: Kirken og Misjonsproblemet.* Oslo, Selskapet til Kristelige Andagtsbøkers Utgivelse, 1935.

Birkeli, Emil and C. Tidemann Strand. *Kallet og veien: Det Norske Misjonsselskaps misjonsskole 1850–1959.* Stavanger: Misjonsselskapets Forlag, 1959.

Blaschke, Olaf. 'Das 19. Jahrhundert: Ein zweites konfessionelles Zeitalter'. In *Geschichte und Gesellschaft. Zeitschrift für historische Socialwissenschaft* 26, no. 1 (2000): 38–75.

Blaschke, Olaf, ed. *Konfessionen im Konflikt: Deutchland zwischen 1800 und 1970: Ein zweites konfessionelles Zeitalter.* Göttingen: Vandenhoeck & Ruprecht, 2002.

Blaschke, Olaf. 'Fältmarskalk Jesus Kristus: Religiös remaskulinisering i Tyskland'. In *Kristen manlighet: Ideal och verklighet 1830–1940*, ed. Yvonne Maria Werner, 23–50. Lund: Nordic Academic Press, 2008.

Blom, Ida and Sølvi Sogner, eds. *Med kjønnsperspektiv på norsk historie: Fra vikingtid til 2000-årsskiftet*, 2nd edition. Oslo: Cappelen akademisk forlag, 2005.

Bowie, Fiona, Deborah Kirkwood and Shirley Ardner, ed. *Women and Missions: Past and Present: Anthropological and Historical Perceptions.* Oxford: Berg, 1993.

Bozzolini, Belinda. 'Marxism, Feminism and South African Studies'. *Journal of Southern African Studies* 9, no. 2 (1983): 139–71.

Braatvedt, H. P. *Roaming Zululand with a Native Commissioner.* Pietermaritzburg: Shuter & Shooter, 1949.

Braatvedt, Nils Torbjørnsen. *Erindringer fra mitt misjonsliv.* Stavanger: Boye og Hinnas boktrykkeri, 1930.

Breistein, Ingunn Folkestad. *'Har staten bedre borgere?' Dissenternes kamp for religiøs frihet 1891–1969.* Trondheim: Tapir Akademisk Forlag, 2003.

Brock, Peggy. 'New Christians as Evangelists'. In *Missions and Empire*, ed. Norman Etherington, 132–52. Oxford: Oxford University Press, 2005.

Brouwer, Ruth Compton. *Modern Women Modernizing Men: The Changing Missions of three Professional Women in Asia and Africa, 1902–69*. Vancouver: UBC Press, 2002.

Brown, Callum G. *The Death of Christian Britain: Understanding Secularisation, 1800–2000*. London: Routledge, 2001.

Buettner, Elizabeth. *Empire Families: Britons and Late Imperial India*. Oxford: Oxford University Press, 2004.

Burgess, Andrew. *Zulufolket: Evangeliet blant zuluerne*. Oslo: Schreudermisjonens forlag, 1944.

Burton, Antoinette. *Burdens of History: British Feminists, Indian Women, and Imperial Culture, 1865–1915*. Chapel Hill, NC: University of North Carolina Press, 1994.

Børhaug, Thomas M. *Imperialismens kollaboratører? En analyse av norske misjonærers holdning og rolle under den europeiske etableringsfase i Zululand 1873–1890*. Unpublished MA thesis, University of Trondheim, 1976.

Børresen, Dag Ingemar. '"The Boys Will Die Like Flies": Afrikanere på hvalfangst i Antarktis 1908–1920'. In *Kolonitid: Nordmenn på eventyr og big business i Afrika og Stillehavet*, ed. Kirsten Alsaker Kjerland and Knut M. Rio, 77–110. Oslo: Scandinavian Acdemic Press, 2009.

Carlsson, Arne Gunnar. 'Norge og boerkrigen'. In *Nordmenn i Afrika – Afrkanere i Norge*, ed. Kirsten Alsaker Kjerland and Anne K. Bang, 107–16. Bergen Vigmostad & Bjørke, 2002.

Carrigan, Tim, Robert William Connell and John Lee. 'Toward a New Sociology of Masculinity'. *Theory and Society* 14, no. 5 (1985): 551–604.

Carrington, Tyler. 'Instilling the "Manly" Faith: Protestant Maculinity and the German *Jünglingsvereine* at the *fin de siècle*'. *Journal of Men, Masculinities and Spirituality* 3, no. 2 (2009): 142–54.

Carton, Benedict. 'Awaken *Nkulunkulu*, Zulu God of the Old Testament: Pioneering Missionaries During the Early Stage of Racial Spectacle'. In *Zulu Identities: Being Zulu, Past and Present*, ed. Benedict Carton, John Laband and Jabulani Sithole, 133–52. Scottsville: University of KwaZulu-Natal Press, 2008.

Carton, Benedict, John Laband and Jabulani Sithole, ed. *Zulu Identities: Being Zulu, Past and Present*. Scottsville: University of KwaZulu-Natal Press, 2008.

Cleall, Esme. 'Missionaries, Masculinities and War: The London Missionary Society'. *South African Historical Journal* 61, no. 2 (2009): 232–53.

Cleall, Esme. *Missionary Discourses of Difference: Negotiating Otherness in the British Empire, 1840–1900*. Basingstoke: Palgrave Macmillan, 2012.

Comaroff, Jean and John. *Of Revelation and Revolution: Christianity, Colonialism, and Consciousness in South Africa*. Chicago/London: University of Chicago Press, 1991.

Comaroff, Jean and John. *Of Revelation and Revolution: The Dialectics of Modernity on a South African Frontier*. Chicago/London: University of Chicago Press, 1997.

Connell, Robert William. 'Globalization, Imperialism, and Masculinities'. In *Handbook of Studies on Men & Masculinities*, ed. Michael S. Kimmel, Jeff Hearn and Robert William Connell, 71–89. Thousand Oaks, CA: Sage Publications, 2005.

Connell, Robert William. *Masculinities*, 2nd edition. Berkeley/Los Angeles: University of California Press, 2005.

Connell, Robert William and James W. Messerschmidt. 'Hegemonic Masculinity: Rethinking the Concept'. *Gender & Society* 19, no. 6 (2005): 829–59.

Cooper, Fredrick. *Colonialism in Question: Theory, Knowledge, History*. Berkeley, CA: University of California Press, 2005.

Daa, Ludvig Kristensen. 'Om den Norske Hedning-Omvendelse'. *Tids-tavler* 2 (1873): 129–58.

Dahle, Lars. *Inspektionsreisen til Zulu og Madagaskar i 1903: Indberetning til Generalforsamlingen i Bergen 1904*. Stavanger: Det norske Missionsselskabs Forlag, 1904.

Dahle, Lars. '"Et smaalig og sneversynt Missionsstyre"'. *Norsk Kirkeblad* (1917): 626–33.

Dahle, Lars. *Tilbakeblik paa mit liv – og særlig paa mit missionsliv: Første del*. Stavanger: Det Norske Missionsselskabs trykkeri, 1922.

Dahle, Lars. *Tilbakeblik paa mit liv – og særlig paa mit missionsliv: Tredje del*. Stavanger: Det Norske Missionsselskabs trykkeri, 1923.

Dahle, Lars and Simon Emanuel Jørgensen. *Festskrift til Det Norske Missionsselskabs Jubilæum i 1892*. Stavanger: Det Norske Missionsselskabs Forlag, 1892.

Dahle, Markus. 'Christian Oftebro'. In *Hjem fra Kamppladsen: Livsbilleder af norske missionærer*, ed. Anders Olsen, 22–25. Kristiania: Steen'ske Bogtrykkeri og Forlag, 1906.

Danbolt, Erling. 'Det Norske Misjonsselskaps forhistorie'. *Norsk Teologisk Tidsskrift* 44, no. 1 (1943): 22–57.

Danbolt, Erling. 'Det Norske Misjonsselskaps misjonærer 1842–1948'. In *Det Norske Misjonsselskaps historie i hundre år*, ed. John Nome, vol. 5. Stavanger: Dreyer, 1948.

Davidoff, Leonore and Catherine Hall. *Family Fortunes: Men and Women of the English Middle Class, 1780–1850*. London: Hutchinson, 1987.

Denis, Philippe, ed. *The Making of an Indigenous Clergy in Southern Africa: Proceedings of the International Conference Held at the University of Natal, Pietermaritzburg, 25–27 October 1994*. Pietermaritzburg: Cluster Publications, 1995.

Denis, Philippe, Thulani Mlotshwa and George Mukuka, ed. *The Casspir and the Cross: Voices of Black Clergy in the Natal Midlands*. Pietermaritzburg: Cluster Publications, 1999.

Dokka, Hans-Jørgen. *En skole gjennom 250 år*. Oslo: NKS-forlaget, 1988.

Dons, Henny. *Den kristne kvinne og hedningemisjonen: En historisk oversikt*. Oslo: Lutherstiftelsen, 1925.

Driver, Felix. *Geography Militant: Cultures of Exploration and Empire*. Oxford: Blackwell, 2001.

Drønen, Tomas Sundnes. 'Misjonshistorie: Fagets akademiske egenart og forhold til samfunnsvitenskapelige metoder'. *Norsk tidsskrift for misjon* 63, no. 1 (2009): 3–18.

Drønen, Tomas Sundnes. *Communication and Conversion in Northern Cameroon: The Dii People and Norwegian Missionaries, 1934–60*. Leiden: Brill, 2009.

Edgar, Robert. 'New Religious Movements'. In *Missions and Empire*, ed. Norman Etherington, 216–37. Oxford: Oxford University Press, 2005.

Edland, Sigmund. 'Lars Dahle og den gassisk-lutherske kyrkjas frihet og sjølvstendighet'. *Norsk tidsskrift for misjon* 60, no. 2 (1982): 97–104.

Edland, Sigmund. 'Lars Dahle's 'regime' og sjølvstendighetstrongen i den gassisk-lutherske kyrkja (1889–1902)'. *Norsk tidsskrift for misjon* 60, no. 3 (1982): 171–83.

Edland, Sigmund. *Evangelists or Envoys? The Role of British Missionaries at Turning Points in Malagasy Political History, 1820–1840: Documentary and Analysis*. PhD dissertation, School of Mission and Theology, 2006.

Eide, Øyvind M. *Skatten og leirkaret: Sjelesørgeriske perspektiv på erfaringer i en misjonærs liv*. Stavanger: Misjonshøgskolens forlag, 2002.

Ekenstam, Claes. 'Män, manlighet och omanlighet i historien'. In *Män i Norden: Manlighet och modernitet 1840–1940*, ed. Claes Ekenstam and Jørgen Lorentzen, 13–47. Hedemora: Gidlund, 2006.

Ekenstam, Claes. 'Mansforskningens bakgrund och framtid: Några teoretiska reflexioner'. *Norma* 1, no. 1 (2006): 6–23.

Ekenstam, Claes. 'Klämda män: Föreställningar om manlighet & umanlighet i det samtida Norden'. In *Män i rörelse: Jämställdhet, förändring och social innovation i Norden*, ed. Øystein Gullvåg Holter. Stockholm: Gidlund, 2007.

Ekenstam, Claes, Jonas Frykman, Thomas Johansson, Jari Kuosmanen, Jens Ljunggren and Arne Nilsson. *Rädd att falla: Studier i manlighet*. Stockholm: Gidlund, 1998.

Ekenstam, Claes, Thomas Johansson and Jari Kuosmanen. *Sprickor i fasaden: Manligheter i förändring: En antologi*. Hedemora: Gidlund, 2001.

Ellingsen, Terje. 'Lars Dahle som misjonær, teolog og kirkemann'. *Norsk tidsskrift for misjon* 27, no. 3 (1973): 147–61.

Elphick, Richard. 'The Benevolent Empire and the Social Gospel: Missionaries and South African Christians in the Age of Segregation'. In *Christianity in South Africa: A Political, Social & Cultural History*, ed. Richard Elphick and Rodney Davenport. Oxford: James Currey, 1997.

Elphick, Richard. 'Evangelical Missions and Racial "Equalization"'. In *Converting Colonialism: Visions and Realities in Mission History, 1706–1914*, ed. Dana L. Robert, 112–33. Grand Rapids, MI/Cambridge: Wm. B. Eerdmans Publishing Co., 2008.

Etherington, Norman. *Preachers Peasants and Politics in Southeast Africa, 1835–1880: African Christian Communities in Natal, Pondoland and Zululand*. London: Royal Historical Society, 1978.

Etherington, Norman. 'Kingdoms of This World and the Next: Christian Beginnings among the Zulu and Swazi'. In *Christianity in South Africa: A Political, Social and Cultural History*, ed. Richard Elphick and Rodney Davenport, 89–106. Oxford: James Curry, 1997.

Etherington, Norman. 'Outward and Visible Signs of Conversion in Nineteenth-century KwaZulu-Natal'. *Journal of Religion in Africa* 32, no. 4 (2002): 422–38.

Etherington, Norman. 'Education and Medicine'. In *Missions and Empire*, ed. Norman Etherington, 261–84. Oxford: Oxford University Press, 2005.

Etherington, Norman. *Missions and Empire*. Oxford: Oxford University Press, 2005.

Fiedler, Klaus. *The Story of Faith Missions: From Hudson Taylor to Present Day Africa*. Oxford: Regnum Books International, 1994.

Fosseus, Helge. *Mission blir kyrka: Luthersk kyrkobilding i södra Afrika 1957–1961*. Stockholm: Verbum, 1974.

Fredén, Anna. *Missionärernas barn*. Stockholm: Svenska Kyrkans Diakonistyrelses Bokförlag, 1918.

Furberg, Tore. *Kyrka och Mission i Sverige 1868–1901: Svenska Kyrkans Missions tillkomst och förste verksomhetstid*. Uppsala: Svenska Institutet för Missionsforskning, 1962.

Fykse, Elida. *Til Sydkorsets land: Studiebrev til norske gjenter og gutar fra misjonær Elida Fykse*, vol. 1–3. Stavanger: Det norske misjonsselskaps Bibel- og misjonskurs pr. korrespondanse, 1946.

Gaitskell, Deborah. 'Devout Domesticity? A Century of African Women's Christianity in South Africa'. In *Women and Gender in Southern Africa to 1945*, ed. Cherryl Walker, 251–72. Cape Town/London: David Philip/James Currey, 1990.

Gelfand, Michael. *Christian Doctor and Nurse: The History of Medical Missions in South Africa from 1799–1976*. Sandton: Mariannhill Mission Press, 1984.

Gjerløw, Ole. *Beretning vedkommende Sekretærens Reise til Missionsmarken i Zululand og Natal 1887–88*. Stavanger: Norwegian Missionary Society, 1888.

Grimshaw, Patricia. *Paths of Duty: American Missionary Wives in Nineteenth-Century Hawaii* Honolulu: University of Hawai'i Press, 1989.

Grimshaw, Patricia and Peter Sherlock. 'Women and Cultural Exchanges'. In *Missions and Empire*, ed. Norman Etherington, 173–93. Oxford: Oxford University Press, 2005.

Gullestad, Marianne. *Picturing Pity: Pitfalls and Pleasures in Cross-Cultural Communication. Image and Word in a North Cameroon Mission*. New York/Oxford: Berghahn, 2007.

Guy, Jeff. *The Heretic: A Study of the Life of John William Colenso: 1814–1883*. Johannesburg: Ravan Press, 1983.

Guy, Jeff. 'Gender Oppression in Southern Africa's Precapitalist Societies'. In *Women and Gender in Southern Africa to 1945*, ed. Cherryl Walker, 33–47. Cape Town/London: David Philip/James Currey, 1990.

Guy, Jeff. *The Destruction of the Zulu Kingdom: The Civil War in Zululand, 1879–1884*. Pietermaritzburg: University of Natal Press, 1994.

Guy, Jeff. *Remembering the Rebellion: The Zulu Uprising of 1906*. Scottsville: University of KwaZulu-Natal Press, 2006.

Gynnild, Vidar. *Norske misjonærer på 1800-tallet: Geografisk, sosial og religiøs bakgrunn*. Unpublished MA thesis, University of Trondheim, 1981.

Hafstad, Vesla. *The History of Nkonjeni Hospital Mahlabatini District, Kwa Zulu, South Africa: From 1925–1978*. Norway: Vesla Hafstad, 2000.

Hagemann, Gro. 'De stummes leir? 1800–1900'. In *Med kjønnsperspektiv på norsk historie: Fra vikingtid til 2000-årsskiftet*, 2nd edition, ed. Ida Blom and Sølvi Sogner, 157–250. Oslo: Cappelen akademisk forlag, 2005.

Hale, Frederick. *The History of Norwegian Missionaries and Immigrants in South Africa*. Doctoral thesis, University of South Africa, 1986.

Hale, Frederick. *Scandinavian Free Church Missions in Southern Africa, 1889–1960*. Doctoral thesis, University of South Africa, 1988.

Hale, Frederick. *The Missionary Career and Spiritual Odyssey of Otto Witt*. Unpublished doctoral thesis, University of Cape Town, 1991.

Hale, Frederick. *Norwegian Missionaries in Natal and Zululand: Selected Correspondance 1844–1900*. Cape Town: Van Riebeeck Society, 1997.

Hale, Frederick. 'Scandinavian Urban Evangelisation in Southern Africa: The Free East Africa Mission in Durban, 1889–1999'. *Swedish Missiological Themes* 86, no. 2 (1998): 227–50.

Hall, Donald E. *Muscular Christianity: Embodying the Victorian Age*. Cambridge/New York/Melbourne: Cambridge University Press, 1994.

Halland, Anna, Andrew Halland and Ingeborg Kjønstad. *Norsk Nybyggerliv i Natal: Festskrift i anledning De Norske Settleres 50-aarsjubileum i Marburg. 29de august 1882–29 de august 1932.* Port Shepstone: South Coast Herald Ltd., 1932.

Hallen, Ernst. *Nordisk Kirkeliv Under Sydkorset: Festskrift i anledning Den Norsk Lutherske Kirkes 50 Aarsjubileum i Durban 14 mars 1880–14 mars 1930.* Durban: The Mission Press, 1930.

Hamilton, Carolyn. *Terrific Majesty: The Powers of Shaka Zulu and the Limits of Historical Invention.* Cape Town/Johannesburg: David Philip Publishers, 1998.

Hammar, Inger. 'Några reflexioner kring "religionsblind" kvinnoforskning'. *Historisk tidsskrift,* no. 1 (1998): 3–29.

Hammar, Inger. *Emancipation och religion: Den svenska kvinnorörelsens pionjärer i debatt om kvinnans kallelse ca 1860–1900.* Stockholm: Carlssons, 1999.

Hammar, Inger. 'Protestantism and Women's Liberation in 19th Century Sweden'. In *Gender, Race and Religion: Nordic Missions 1860–1940,* ed. Inger Marie Okkenhaug, 19–34. Uppsala: Swedish Institute of Missionary Research, 2003.

Handeland, Oscar. *Det Norske Lutherske Kinamisjonsforbund gjennom 50 år.* Oslo: Forbundets Forlag, 1941.

Handeland, Oscar. *Fram kristmenn, korsmenn! Hovedlinjer og førerskikkelser i norsk hedningemisjon.* Bergen: Lunde, 1963.

Hardiman, David. 'Introduction'. In *Healing Bodies, Saving Souls: Medical Missions in Asia and Africa,* ed. David Hardiman, 5–58. Amsterdam/New York: Editions Rodopi B.V., 2006.

Harris, Paul William. *Nothing but Christ: Rufus Anderson and the Ideology of Protestant Foreign Mission.* New York: Oxford University Press, 1999.

Hastings, Derek K. 'Fears of a Feminized Church: Catholicism, Clerical Celibacy, and the Crisis of Masculinity in Wilhelmine Germany'. *European History Quarterly* 38, no. 1 (2008): 34–65.

Hearn, Jeff. 'Is Masculinity Dead? A Critique of the Concept of Masculinities'. In *Understanding Masculinities: Social Relations and Cultural Arenas,* ed. Mairtin Mac an Ghaill. Buckingham: Open University Press, 1996.

Hemstad, Ruth. *Fra Indian Summer til nordisk vinter: Skandinavisk samarbeid, skandinavisme og unionsoppløsningen.* Oslo: Akademisk publisering, 2008.

Henningsen, Anne Folke. *'En straalende Juvel i Frelserens Krone': Civiliseringsbestræbelser i Den Frie Østafrikanske Missions frelsesvirksomhed i Natal og Zululand 1889–1899.* Unpublished master's thesis, Roskilde Universitetscenter, 2003.

Hernæs, Per O. 'Lydighet mot Øvrigheten: Norske misjonærer i Natal og Zululand under Bambatha-opprøret i 1906'. Unpublished paper, Center for Afrikastudier, Københavns universitet, 1975.

Hernæs, Per O. *Norsk misjon og sosial endring: Norske misjonærer i Zululand/Natal 1887–1906.* Unpublished MA thesis, University of Trondheim, 1978.

Hernæs, Per. 'The Zulu Kingdom, Norwegian Missionaries, and British Imperialism, 1845–1879'. In *Norwegian Missions in African History, Vol. 1: South Africa 1845–1906,* ed. Jarle Simensen, 103–86. Oslo: Norwegian University Press, 1986.

Hestnes, Aslaug. *Fortellinger fra Midtens rike: En studie i Racin Kolnes' barne- og ungdomsbøker med særlig henblikk på misjonssyn, -motivasjon og -metoder.* Unpublished thesis in Theology, School of Mission and Theology, 1987.

Hill, Patricia R. *The World Their Household: The American Woman's Foreign Mission Movement and Cultural Transformation, 1870–1920.* Ann Arbor, MI: University of Michigan Press, 1985.

Hodne, Ingolf Edward. *Missionary Enterprise in African Education: The Co-operating Lutheran Missions in Natal, South Africa, 1912–1955*. Stavanger: Misjonshøgskolens forlag, 1997.

Holter, Knut. 'Did Prince Cetshwayo Read the Old Testament in 1859? The Role of the Bible and the Art of Reading in the Interaction between Norwegian Missionaries and the Zulu Elite in the Mid-19th Century'. *Old Testament Essays* 22, no. 3 (2009): 580–88.

Holter, Øystein Gullvåg. *Gender, Patriarchy and Capitalism: A Social Forms Analysis*. Work Research Institute, 1997.

Holter, Øystein Gullvåg. *Can Men Do It? Men and Gender Equality: The Nordic Experience*. Copenhagen: Nordic Council of Ministers, 2003.

Holter, Øystein Gullvåg. 'Social Theories for Researching Men and Masculinities'. In *Handbook of Studies on Men & Masculinities*, ed. Michael S. Kimmel, Jeff Hearn and R. W. Connell, 15–34. Thousand Oaks, CA: Sage Publications, 2005.

Holter, Øystein Gullvåg. 'Power and Structure in Studies of Men and Masculinities'. *Norma. Nordisk tidsskrift for maskulinitetsstudier* 4, no. 2 (2009): 133–45.

Hopkins, Charles Howard. *The Rise of the Social Gospel in American Protestantism 1865–1915*. New Haven, CT: Yale University Press, 1940.

Houle, Robert J. 'The American Mission Revivals and the Birth of Modern Zulu Evangelism'. In *Zulu Identities: Being Zulu, Past and Present*, ed. Benedict Carton, John Laband and Jabulani Sithole, 222–39. Scottsville: University of KwaZulu-Natal Press, 2008.

Hovland, Ingeborg. *Distance Destroys and Kills. An Anthropological Inquiry into the Nature of Faith in a Lutheran Norwegian Missionary Society*. PhD dissertation, University of London, 2006.

Hovland, Ingie. *Mission Station Christianity: Norwegian Missionaries in Colonial Natal and Zululand, Southern Africa 1850–1890*. Leiden/Boston: Brill, 2013.

Hovland, Thor Halvor. 'Embetssyn og dåpssyn hos Schreuder og Dahle'. *Norsk tidsskrift for misjon* 56, no. 3 (2002): 209–20.

Hovland, Thor Halvor. 'Kirkesyn og konferanseordning'. *Norsk tidsskrift for misjon* 56, no. 3 (2002): 193–208.

Huber, Mary Taylor and Nancy Lutkehaus. *Gendered Missions: Women and Men in Missionary Discourse and Practice*. Ann Arbor, MI: University of Michigan Press, 1999.

Hughes, Heather. '"A Lighthouse for African Womanhood": Inanda Seminary, 1869–1945'. In *Women and Gender in Southern Africa to 1945*, ed. Cherryl Walker, 197–220. Cape Town/London: David Philip/James Currey, 1990.

Hunter, Jane. *The Gospel of Gentility: American Women Missionaries in Turn-of-the-century China*. New Haven, CTt: Yale University Press, 1984.

Høydal, Reidun. *Nasjon – region – profesjon: Vestlandslæraren 1840–1940*. Oslo: Noregs forskingsråd, 1995.

Haanes, Vidar L. *'Hvad skal da dette blive for prester?' Presteutdannelse i spennings-feltet mellom universitet og kirke, med vekt på modernitetens gjennombrudd i Norge*. Trondheim: Tapir, 1998.

Jayawardena, Kumari. *The White Woman's Other Burden: Western Women and South Asia during British Colonial Rule*. New York: Routledge, 1995.

Johansen, Shawn. *Family Men: Middle-Class Fatherhood in Early Industrializing America*. New York: Routledge, 2001.

Jørgensen, Tor Berger. 'Japan'. In *I tro og tjeneste: Det norske misjonsselskap 1842–1992*, ed. Torstein Jørgensen and Nils Kristian Høimyr, vol. 2, 229–93. Stavanger: Misjonshøgskolen, 1992.

Jørgensen, Torstein. 'Norske misjonærer, samtid og forståelse i det 19. århundre'. *Norsk Tidsskrift for Misjon* 39, no. 2 (1985): 75–85.

Jørgensen, Torstein. *Contact and Conflict: Norwegian Missionaries, the Zulu Kingdom, and the Gospel: 1850–1873*. Oslo: Solum, 1990.

Jørgensen, Torstein. 'De første 100 år'. In *I tro og tjeneste: Det norske misjonsselskap 1842–1992*, ed. Torstein Jørgensen and Nils Kristian Høimyr, 11–145. Stavanger: Misjonshøgskolen, 1992.

Jørgensen, Torstein. 'En liten sommerdebatt om misjon: Dikteren Alexander Kielland i diskusjon med generalsekretær Lars Dahle'. *Misjon og teologi* 5/6 (1998/1999): 77–82.

Jørgensen, Torstein. 'Zibokjana Ka Gudu Moses: Student fra Zululand ved Misjonshøgskolen 1866–69'. In *Nordmenn i Afrika – Afrikanere i Norge*, ed. Anne K. Bang and Kirsten Alsaker Kjerland, 221–29. Bergen: Vigmostad & Bjørke AS, 2002.

Jørgensen, Torstein. 'Misjon som med- og motkultur under kulturimperialismen'. In *Misjon og kultur: Festskrift til Jan-Martin Berentsen*, ed. Thor Strandenæs, 141–50. Stavanger: Misjonshøgskolens forlag, 2006.

Kamphausen, Erhard. 'Unknown Heroes: The Founding Fathers of the Ethiopian Movement in South Africa'. In *The Making of an Indigenous Clergy in Southern Africa: Proceedings of the International Conference Held at the University of Natal, Pietermaritzburg, 25–27 October 1994*, ed. Philippe Denis, 83–100. Pietermaritzburg: Cluster Publications, 1995.

Keto, Clement Tsheloane. 'Race Relations, Land and the Changing Missionary Role in South Africa: A Case Study of the American Zulu Mission, 1850–1910'. *International Journal of African Historical Studies* 10, no. 4 (1977): 600–27.

Kimmel, Michael S. *Manhood in America: A Cultural History*, 2nd edition. New York/Oxford: Oxford University Press, 2006.

Kimmel, Michael S., Jeff Hearn and R. W. Connell. *Handbook of Studies on Men & Masculinities*. Thousand Oaks, CA: Sage Publications, 2005.

Kirkley, Evelyn A. 'Is it Manly to be a Christian? The Debate in Victorian and Modern America'. In *Redeeming Men: Religion and Masculinities*, ed. Stephen D. Boyd, M. Longwood and M. Muesse, 80–8. Loisville, KY: Westminster John Knox Press, 1996.

Kjelvei, Johan, ed. *Zulu: Evangeliets landvinning*. Stavanger: Det Norske Misjonsselskaps trykkeri, 1932.

Kjøllesdal, Maria and Gunnar Andreas Meling. *Guds høstfolk: Det Norske Misjonsselskaps misjonærer 1842–1977*. Stavanger: Det Norske Misjonsselskaps forlag, 1977.

Kumari, Jayawardena. *The White Woman's Other Burden: Western Women and South Asia during British Colonial Rule*. New York/London: Routledge, 1995.

Kvaal Pedersen, Odd. 'Misjonslitteratur'. In *Norsk Misjonsleksikon*, ed. Fridtjov Birkeli, Trygve Bjerkrheim, Alfred K. Dahl, Johannes Gausdal, Halvor Hjertvik, Arnfinn Nordbø, Gunnar Rødahl, Martin Ski, Christian Tidemann Strand and Johan Straume. Stavanger: Nomi forlag – Runa forlag, 1967.

Laband, John. '"Bloodstained Grandeur": Colonial and Imperial Stereotypes of Zulu Warriors and Zulu Warfare'. In *Zulu Identities: Being Zulu, Past and Present*, ed. Benedict Carton, John Laband and Jabulani Sithole, 82–6. Scottsville: University of KwaZulu-Natal Press, 2008.

La Hausse de Lalouvière, Paul. *Restless Identities: Signatures of Nationalism, Zulu Ethnicity and History in the Lives of Petros Lamula (c. 1881–1948) and Lymon Maling (c. 1889-c. 1936).* Pietermaritzburg: University of Natal Press, 2000.

La Hausse de Lalouvière, Paul. '"Death is Not the End": Zulu Cosmopolitanism and the Politics of the Zulu Cultural Revival'. In *Zulu Identities: Being Zulu, Past and Present*, ed. Benedict Carton, John Laband and Jabulani Sithole, 256–72. Scottsville: University of KwaZulu-Natal Press, 2008.

Langmore, Diane. *Missionary Lives: Papua, 1874–1914.* Honolulu: University of Hawai'i Press, 1989.

Larsen, Hanna. *Skisser fra Zululand.* Decorah, IA: Lutheran Publishing House, 1905.

Lear, M. F. *The St.Olav Lutheran Church 1880–1980: Its Origin and History Over One Hundred Years.* Durban: Unity Publications, 1980.

Lehmann, Hartmut, ed. *Säkularisierung, Dechristianisierung, Rechristianisierung im neuzeitlichen Europa: Bilanz und Perspektiven der Forschung.* Göttingen: Vanderhoeck & Ruprecht, 1997.

Lehmann, Hartmut. *Säkularisierung: Der europäische Sonderweg in Sachen Religion.* Göttingen: Wallstein, 2004.

Leisegang, Hans Kristian. *Vor Zulumission.* Stavanger: Det Norske Missionsselskaps forlag, 1921.

Liliequist, Jonas. 'Från niding till sprätt: En studie i det svenska omanlighets-begreppets historia från vikingatid till sent 1700-tal'. In *Manligt och umanligt i ett historisk perspektiv*, ed. Ann-Marie Berggren, 73–95. Stockholm: Forskningsrådnämden, 1999.

Lorentzen, Jørgen. 'Fedrene'. In *Män i Norden: Manlighet och modernitet 1840–1940*, ed. Claes Ekenstam and Jørgen Lorentzen, 133–66. Hedemora: Gidlund, 2006.

Lorentzen, Jørgen. '"Først mor og barn, derefter Faderen": Om fedrene i norsk historie fra 1850–1920'. *Tidsskrift for kjønnsforskning* 32, no. 3 (2008): 41–59.

Lorentzen, Jørgen and Wencke Mühleisen. *Kjønnsforskning: En grunnbok.* Oslo: Universitetsforlaget, 2006.

Løgstrup. *Nordisk Missionshaandbog.* København, 1889.

Løvaas, Kari. 'Her er jeg, send meg!' *Nytt Norsk Tidsskrift*, no. 3–4 (2009): 337–51.

MacKenzie, John M. 'The Imperial Pioneer and Hunter and the British Masculine Stereotype in Late Victorian and Edwardian Times'. In *Manliness and Morality: Middle-class Masculinity in Britain and American 1800–1940*, ed. J.A. Mangan and James Walvin, 176–97. Manchester: Manchester University Press, 1987.

Malmer, Elin. 'The Making of Christian Men: An Evangelical Mission to the Swedish Army, c. 1900–1920'. In *Christian Masculinity: Men and Religion in Northern Europe in the 19th and 20th Centuries*, ed. Yvonne Maria Werner, 191–211. Leuven: Leuven University Press, 2011.

Mangan, J.A. and James Walvin, ed. *Manliness and Morality: Middle-class Masculinity in Britain and American 1800–1940.* Manchester: Manchester University Press, 1987.

Manktelow, Emily. *Missionary Families and the Formation of the Missionary Enterprise: The London Missionary Society and the Family, 1795–1875.* PhD dissertation, King's College, 2010.

Marks, Shula. *Reluctant Rebellion: The 1906–8 Disturbances in Natal.* Oxford: Clarendon Press, 1970.

Maughan, Steven. '"Mighty England Do Good": The Major English Denominations and Organisation for the Support of Foreign Missions in the Nineteenth Century'. In *Missionary Encounters: Sources and Issues*, ed. Robert A. Bickers and Rosemary Seton, 11–37. Richmond, UK: Curzon Press, 1996.

Maurits, Alexander. 'Treståndläran och den lutherske prästmannen'. In *Kristen manlighet: Ideal och verklighet 1830–1940*, ed. Yvonne Maria Werner, 51–73. Lund: Nordic Academic Press, 2008.

Maurits, Alexander. 'The Exemplary Lives of Christian Heroes as an Historical Construct'. *Journal of Men, Masculinities and Spirituality* 3, no. 1 (2009): 4–21.

Maylam, Paul. 'The Changing Political Economy of the Region, 1920–1950'. In *Political Economy and Identities in KwaZulu-Natal: Historical and Social Perspectives*, ed. Robert Morrell, 33–61. Durban: Indicator Press, 1996.

McCracken, John. *Politics and Christianity in Malawi 1875–1940*. Cambridge: Cambridge University Press, 1977.

McLeod, Hugh. *Secularisation in Western Europe, 1848–1914*. New York: St. Martin's Press, 2000.

Meintjes, Sheila. 'Family and Gender in the Christian Community at Edendale, Natal, in Colonial Times'. In *Women and Gender in Southern Africa to 1945*, ed. Cherryl Walker, 125–45. Cape Town/London: David Philip/James Currey, 1990.

Meling, Gunnar Andreas. *På tokt med Elieser: Pionermisjonærene og deres skip 1864–1884*. Stavanger: Det Norske Misjonsselskap, 1982.

Meling, Gunnar Andreas. *I fredens kjølvann: Misjonsskipet Paulus i storm og stille 1884–1894*. Stavanger: Det Norske Misjonsselskap, 1984.

Mellemsether, Hanna. *Kvinne i to verdener: En kulturhistorisk analyse av afrika-misjonæren Martha Sannes liv i perioden 1884–1901*. MA thesis, University of Trondheim, 1994.

Mellemsether, Hanna. *Misjonærer, settlersamfunn og afrikansk opposisjon: Striden om selvstendiggjøring i den norske Zulukirken, Sør-Afrika ca. 1920–1930*. Dr Art dissertation, University of Trondheim, 2001.

Mellemsether, Hanna. '"Misjonærsettlerne i Sør-Afrika"'. In *Nordmenn i Afrika – Afrikanere i Norge*, ed. Kirsten Alsaker Kjerland and Anne K. Bang, 63–70. Bergen Vigmostad & Bjørke, 2002.

Mellemsether, Hanna. 'African Women in the Norwegian Mission in South Africa'. In *Gender, Race and Religion: Nordic missions 1860–1940*, ed. Inger Marie Okkenhaug, 157–73. Uppsala: Swedish Institute of Missionary Research, 2003.

Mikaelsson, Lisbeth. '"Kvinne, ta ansvar og ledelse i dine egne hender": Historien om Henny Dons'. *Norsk tidsskrift for misjon* 56, no. 2 (2002): 107–37.

Mikaelsson, Lisbeth. 'Gender Politics in Female Autobiography'. In *Gender, Race and Religion: Nordic Missions 1860–1940*, ed. Inger Marie Okkenhaug, 35–51. Uppsala: Swedish Institute of Missionary Research, 2003.

Mikaelsson, Lisbeth. *Kallets ekko: Studier i misjon og selvbiografi*. Kristiansand: Høyskoleforlaget, 2003.

Mikaelsson, Lisbeth. 'Fortellinger om kallet'. In *Med hjertet på flere steder: Om barn, misjon og flerkulturell oppvekst*, ed. Tomas Drønen and Marianne Skjortnes, 281–93. Trondheim: Tapir Akademisk Forlag, 2010.

Mikaelsson, Lisbeth. '"Self" and "Other" as Biblical Representations in Mission Literature'. In *Protestant Missions and Local Encounters in the Nineteenth and*

Twentieth Centuries: Unto the Ends of the World, ed. Hilde Nielssen, Inger Marie Okkenhaug and Karina Hestad Skeie, 87–99. Leiden/Boston: Brill, 2011.

Millard, Joan. 'Educating Indigenous Clergy in some South African Protestant Churches during the Nineteenth Century'. In *The Making of an Indigenous Clergy in Southern Africa: Proceedings of the International Conference Held at the University of Natal, Pietermaritzburg, 25–27 October 1994*, ed. Philippe Denis, 58–68. Pietermaritzburg: Cluster Publications, 1995.

Misjonsalbum: Syd-afrika: 109 billeder og et kart fra Det Norske Misjonsselskaps arbeidsmark i Zulu og Natal. Stavanger: Det Norske Misjonsselskaps forlag, 1928.

Moripe, Simon. 'Indigenous Clergy in the Zion Christian Church'. In *The Making of an Indigenous Clergy in Southern Africa: Proceedings of the International Conference Held at the University of Natal, Pietermaritzburg, 25–27 October 1994*, ed. Philippe Denis, 102–7. Pietermaritzburg: Cluster Publications, 1995.

Morrell, Robert. 'Of Boys and Men: Masculinity and Gender in Southern African Studies'. *Journal of Southern African Studies* 24, no. 4 (1998): 605–30.

Morrell, Robert. *From Boys to Gentlemen: Settler Masculinity in Colonial Natal, 1880–1920*. Pretoria: University of South Africa, 2001.

Morrell, Robert. *Changing Men in Southern Africa*. Pietermaritzburg: University of Natal Press, 2001.

Morrell, Robert, John Wright and Sheila Meintjes. 'Colonialism and the Establishment of White Domination, 1840–1990'. In *Political Economy and Identities in KwaZulu-Natal: Historical and Social Perspectives*, ed. Robert Morrell, 33–61. Durban: Indicator Press, 1996.

Mosse, George L. *The Image of Man: The Creation of Modern Masculinity*. New York: Oxford University Press, 1996.

Mosvold, Kirsti. *Misjonærkallet i misjonsteologisk perspektiv*. Unpublished thesis in Theology, Norwegian School of Theology, 1981.

Mott, John R. *Den afgørende Time i den kristne Mission*. København: Det Danske Missionsselskabs forlag, 1911.

Munthe, Ludvig. *Venstrehandsmisjon? Misjonslegar på Madagaskar frå 1860-åra og ut hundreåret*. Oslo: Luther, 1985.

Myhre, Jan Eivind. 'Feeling One's Way: Emotions in History and Historiography'. In *Pathways of the Past: Essays in Honour of Sølvi Sogner: On Her 70th Anniversary 15. March 2002*, ed. Hilde Sandvik, Kari Telste and Gunnar Thorvaldsen, 162–78. Oslo: Novus, 2002.

Myklebust, Olav Guttorm. 'Syd-Afrika: Motsetningenes og misjonenes land'. *Nordisk Missions-tidsskrift* 51 (1940): 243–70.

Myklebust, Olav Guttorm. 'Fra frykt til fred: Afrikansk religion – afrikansk kristendom'. *Kirke og Kultur* 84 (1941): 413–28.

Myklebust, Olav Guttorm. 'Negerpsyke: Streiflys over sort sjeleliv'. *Kirke og Kultur* 84 (1941): 338–54.

Myklebust, Olav Guttorm. 'Sør-Afrika'. In *Det Norske Misjonsselskap 1842–1942*, ed. John Nome, vol. 3. Stavanger: Dreyer, 1949.

Myklebust, Olav Guttorm. 'Bekjennelsesspørsmålet i den protestantiske misjonsbevegelsens gjennombruddstid'. *Norsk tidsskrift for misjon* 13, no. 3 (1959): 148–61.

Myklebust, Olav Guttorm. 'Bekjennelsesspørsmålet og Det Norske Misjonsselskap i 1840- og 1850-årene'. *Norsk tidsskrift for misjon* 13, no. 4 (1959): 237–46.

Myklebust, Olav Guttorm. 'Norsk misjon og britisk imperialisme i Syd-Afrika'. *Norsk tidsskrift for misjon* 31, no. 2 (1977): 65–72.

Myklebust, Olav Guttorm. *H. P. S. Schreuder: Kirke og misjon*. Oslo: Land og kirke/ Gyldendal, 1980.

Myklebust, Olav Guttorm, C. M. Doke and Ernst Dammann. *Én var den første: Studier og tekster til forståelse av H. P. S. Schreuder*. Oslo: Land og kirke/Gyldendal, 1986.

Naustvoll, Rannveig. *Kvinner i misjonen: Kvinneliv og hverdagsliv på de norske misjonsstasjonene i Natal og Zululand 1900–1925*. Unpublished MA thesis, University of Trondheim, 1998.

Nielsen, Hilde. 'From Norway to the Ends of the World: Missionary Contributions to Norwegian Images of "Self" and "Other"'. In *Encountering Foreign Worlds. Experiences at Home and Abroad: Proceedings from the 26th Nordic Congress of Historians*, ed. Christina Folke Ax, Anne Folke Henningsen, Niklas Thode Jensen, Leila Koivunen and Taina Syrjämaa. Reykjavik, 2007.

Nielssen, Hilde, ed. *Til jordens ender: Fortellinger om norsk misjon*, Bergen Museums skrifter nr. 23. Bergen: Bergen Museums forlag, Universitetet i Bergen, 2008.

Nielssen, Hilde. 'James Sibree and Lars Dahle: Norwegian and British Missionary Ethnography as a Transnational and National Activity'. In *Protestant Missions and Local Encounters in the Nineteenth and Twentieth Centuries: Unto the Ends of the World*, ed. Hilde Nielssen, Inger Marie Okkenhaug and Karina Hestad Skeie, 23–42. Leiden/Boston: Brill, 2011.

Nielssen, Hilde, Inger Marie Okkenhaug and Karina Hestad Skeie. 'Introduction'. In *Protestant Missions and Local Encounters in the Nineteenth and Twentieth Centuries: Unto the Ends of the World*, ed. Hilde Nielssen, Inger Marie Okkenhaug and Karina Hestad Skeie, 1–22. Leiden/Boston: Brill, 2011.

Nome, John. 'Det Norske Misjonsselskaps historie i norsk kirkeliv: Fra stiftelsestiden til Schreuders brudd'. In *Det Norske Misjonsselskap 1842–1942*, ed. John Nome, vol. 1. Stavanger: Dreyer, 1943.

Nome, John. 'Det Norske Misjonsselskaps historie i norsk kirkeliv: Fra syttiårene til nåtiden'. In *Det Norske Misjonsselskap 1842–1942*, ed. John Nome, vol. 2. Stavanger: Dreyer, 1943.

Nordberg, Marie. 'Hegemonibegreppet och hegemonier inom mansforskingsfältet'. In *Hegemoni och mansforskning*, ed. Per Folkeson, Marie Norberg and Goldina Smirtwaite. Karlstad: University of Karlstad, 2000.

Norseth, Kristin. '… at sætte sig imod vilde være som at stoppe Elven'. Unpublished MA thesis, Norwegian School of Theology, 1997.

Norseth, Kristin. 'To alen av hvilket stykke? Tvillingsøstrene LMF og KMA i norsk, nordisk og internasjonalt perspektiv'. *Norsk tidsskrift for misjon* 56, no. 2 (2002): 91–106.

Norseth, Kristin. *'La os bryte over tvert med vor stumhet!': Kvinners vei til myndighet i de kristelige organisasjonene 1842–1912*. Dr Theol. dissertation, Norwegian School of Theology, 2007.

O'Brien, Anne. 'Missionary Masculinities, the Homoerotic Gaze and the Politics of Race: Gilbert White in Northern Australia, 1885–1915'. *Gender & History* 20, no. 1 (2008): 66–85.

Okkenhaug, Inger Marie. *The Quality of Heroic Living, of High Endeavour and Adventure: Anglican Mission, Women and Education in Palestine, 1888–1948*. Leiden: Brill, 2002.

Okkenhaug, Inger Marie. *Gender, Race and Religion: Nordic Missions 1860–1940*. Uppsala: Swedish Institute of Missionary Research, 2003.

Okkenhaug, Inger Marie. 'To Give the Boys Energy, Manliness, and Self-Command in Temper: The Anglican Male Ideal and St. George's School in Jerusalem, c. 1900–40'. In *Gender, Religion and Change in the Middle East: Two Hundred Years of History*, ed. Inger Marie Okkenhaug and Ingvild Flaskerud, 47–65. Oxford: Berg Publishers, 2005.

Okkenhaug, Inger Marie. 'Herren har givet mig et rigt virkefelt: Kall, religion og arbeid blant armenere i det osmanske riket'. *Historisk tidsskrift* 88, no. 1 (2009): 39–60.

Okkenhaug, Inger Marie. 'Refugees, Relief and Restoration of a Nation: Norwegian Mission in the Armenian Republic, 1922–1925'. In *Protestant Missions and Local Encounters in the Nineteenth and Twentieth Centuries: Unto the Ends of the World*, ed. Hilde Nielssen, Inger Marie Okkenhaug and Karina Hestad Skeie, 207–32. Leiden/Boston: Brill, 2011.

Olsen, Anders, ed. *Hjem fra Kamppladsen: Livsbilleder af norske missionærer*. Kristiania: Steen'ske Bogtrykkeri og Forlag, 1906.

Olsen, Anders. *Misjonsprest Karl Larsen Titlestad: Det Norske Missionsselskaps senior*. Bergen: A/S Lunde & Co.s Forlag, 1929.

Olsen, Anders and Ole Stavem. 'Misjonsprest Karl Titlestad. 1832–1924'. *Norvegia Sacra* 5 (1925): 145–51.

Osberg, Ingvild *Pikeasylet på Antsahamanitra, Antananarivo 1872–1912*. Unpublished thesis in Theology, University of Oslo, 1988.

Osselaer, Tine Van. *The Pious Sex: Catholic Constructions of Masculinity and Femininity in Belgium c. 1800–1940*. Doctor in History dissertation, University of Leuven, 2009.

Osselaer, Tine Van and Thomas Buerman. '"Feminisation" Thesis: A Survey of International Historiography and a Probing of Belgian Grounds'. *Revue d'histoire ecclesiastique* 103, no. 2 (2008): 497–544.

Ouzgane, Lahoucine and Robert Morrell. *African Masculinities: Men in Africa from the Late Nineteenth Century to the Present*. New York: Palgrave Macmillan, 2005.

Palm, Martha. 'Vår hospitalsvirksomhet'. In *Zulu: Evangeliets landvinning*, ed. Johan Kjelvei, 86–94. Stavanger: Det Norske Misjonsselskaps trykkeri, 1932.

Parker, Michael. *The Kingdom of Character: The Student Volunteer Movement for Foreign Missions (1886–1926)*. Lanham/New York/Oxford: American Society of Missiology and University Press of America, 1998.

Petrusic, Christopher. 'Violence as Masculinity: David Livingstone's Radical Racial Politics in the Cape Colony and the Transvaal, 1845–1852'. *International History Review* 26, no. 1 (2004): 20–55.

Porter, Andrew. *Religion Versus Empire? British Protestant Missionaries and Overseas Expansion, 1700–1914*. Manchester: Manchester University Press, 2004.

Predelli, Line Nyhagen. *Contested Patriarchy and Missionary Feminism: The Norwegian Missionary Society in Nineteenth Century Norway and Madagascar*. PhD dissertation, University of Southern California, 1998.

Predelli, Line Nyhagen. 'Marriage in Norwegian Missionary Practice and Discourse in Norway and Madagascar, 1880–1910'. *Journal of Religion in Africa* 31, no. 1 (2001): 4–48.

Predelli, Line Nyhagen. 'Contesting the Mission's Patriarchal Gender Regime: Single Missionary Women in 19th Century Madagascar'. In *Gender, Race and Religion: Nordic Missions 1860–1940*, ed. Inger Marie Okkenhaug, 53–80. Uppsala: Swedish Institute of Missionary Research, 2003.

Predelli, Line Nyhagen. *Issues of Gender, Race, and Class in the Norwegian Missionary Society in Nineteenth-Century Norway and Madagascar*. Lewiston, NY: Edwin Mellen Press, 2003.

Predelli, Line Nyhagen and Jon Miller. 'Piety and Patriarchy: Contested Gender Regimes in Nineteenth-Century Evangelical Missions'. In *Gendered Missions: Women and Men in Missionary Discourse and Practice*, ed. Mary Taylor Huber and Nancy Lutkehaus, 67–112. Ann Arbor, MI: University of Michigan Press, 1999.

Prestjan, Anna. *Präst och karl, karl och präst: Prästmanlighet i tidigt 1900-tal*. Lund: Sekel Bokförlag, 2009.

Prestjan, Anna. 'The Man in the Clergyman: Swedish Priest Obituaries, 1905–1937'. In *Christian Masculinity: Men and Religion in Northern Europe in the 19th and 20th Centuries*, ed. Yvonne Maria Werner, 115–26. Leuven: Leuven University Press, 2011.

Putney, Clifford. *Muscular Christianity: Manhood and Sports in Protestant America 1880–1920*. Cambridge, MA: Harvard University Press, 2001.

Rakkenes, Øystein. *Himmelfolket: En norsk høvding i Zululand*. Oslo: Cappelen, 2003.

Rasmussen, Tarald. 'Lutherdom og misjonsethos: Om norsk lekmannskristendom i det 19. århundre'. *Norsk Teologisk Tidsskrift* 86, no. 3 (1985): 169–83.

Reeser, Todd W. *Masculinities in Theory*. Malden, MA: Wiley-Blackwell, 2010.

Roaldset, Hege. 'Norwegian Missionaries and Zulu Converts: A Case for Bakhtinian Dialogue'. *Studia Historiae Ecclesiasticae. Journal of the Church History Society of Southern Africa* 36, no. 1 (2010): 123–39.

Robert, Dana L. *American Women in Mission: A Social History of Their Thought and Practice*. Macon, GA: Mercer University Press, 1997.

Robert, Dana L., ed. *Gospel Bearers, Gospel Barriers: Missionary Women in the Twentieth Century*. Maryknoll, New York: Orbis Books, 2002.

Robert, Dana L., ed. *Converting Colonialism: Visions and Realities in Mission History, 1706–1914*. Grand Rapids, MI/Cambridge: Wm. B. Eerdmans Publishing Co., 2008.

Robert, Dana L. 'The "Christian Home" as a Cornerstone of Anglo-American Missionary Thought and Practice'. In *Converting Colonialism: Visions and Realities in Mission History, 1706–1914*, ed. Dana L. Robert, 134–65. Grand Rapids, MI/Cambridge: Wm. B. Eerdmans Publishing Co., 2008.

Robert, Dana L. *Christian Mission: How Christianity Became a World Religion*. Chichester: Wiley-Blackwell, 2009.

Rodseth, Fred. *Ndabazabantu: The Life of a Native Affairs Administrator*. Volda: Fred Rodseth, 1984.

Rodseth, Peter H. *Mission Station to Mayor's Parlour: An Autobiography*, 1980.

Rotundo, E. Anthony. *American Manhood: Transformations in Masculinity from the Revolution to the Modern Era*. New York: Basic Books, 1993.

Rutherdale, Myra. *Women and the White Man's God: Gender and Race in the Canadian Mission Field*. Vancouver: UBC Press, 2002.

Rødseth, Peder Aage. 'Våre kristne'. In *Zulu: Evangeliets landvinning*, ed. Johan Kjelvei, 58–65. Stavanger: Det Norske Misjonsselskaps trykkeri, 1932.

Said, Edward W. *Orientalism*. NY: Pantheon Books, 1978.

Sarja, Karin. *'Ännu en syster till Afrika'*: *Trettiosex kvinnliga missionärer i Natal och Zululand*. Uppsala: Studia Missionalia Svecana LXXXVIII, 2002.

Sarja, Karin. 'The Missionary Career of Baroness Hedvig Posse 1887–1913'. In *Gender, Race and Religion: Nordic Missions 1860–1940*, ed. Inger Marie Okkenhaug, 104–53. Uppsala: Swedish Institute of Missionary Research, 2003.

Schlyter, Herman. *The History of the Co-operating Lutheran Missions in Natal 1912–1951*. Durban: Lutheran Publishing House, 1953.

Schreuder, H. P. S. *Nogle ord til Norges Kirke om christelig Pligt med Hensyn til Omsorg for ikke-christne Medbrødres Salighed*. Christiania, 1842.

Schreuder, H. P. S. *Beretning om Missionspræst Schreuders Ordination til Biskop over den Norske Kirkes Missionsmark i Bergens domkirke den 8de juli 1866 samt Prædikener og Foredrag af Biskop Schreuder, holdte under hans Nærværelse i Hjemmet* Stavanger: Det Norske Missionsselskabs Forlag, 1868.

Scriba, Georg and Gunnar Lislerud. 'Lutheran Missions and Churches in South Africa'. In *Christianity in South Africa: A Political, Social & Cultural History*, ed. Richard Elphick and Rodney Davenport, 173–94. Oxford: James Currey, 1997.

Seidler, Victor J. *Unreasonable Men: Masculinity and Social Theory*. London: Routledge, 1994.

Seip, Jens Arup. 'Kirkelig historieteori og kirkelig historieforskning'. *Historisk tidsskrift* 34 (1944): 372–98.

Seland, Bjørg. *Religion på det frie marked: Folkelig pietisme og bedehuskultur*. Kristiansand: Høyskoleforlaget AS – Norwegian Academic Press, 2006.

Semple, Rhonda Anne. *Missionary Women: Gender, Professionalism and the Victorian Idea of Christian Mission*. Woodbridge: Boydell Press, 2003.

Semple, Rhonda A. 'Missionary Manhood: Professionalism, Belief and Masculinity in the Nineteenth-Century British Imperial Field'. *Journal of Imperial and Commonwealth History* 36, no. 3 (2008): 397–415.

Sidenvall, Erik. '"Gap men": Manlighet och mission i 1800-talets Kina'. In *Kristen manlighet: Ideal och verklighet 1830–1940*, ed. Yvonne Maria Werner, 75–91. Lund: Nordic Academic Press, 2008.

Sidenvall, Erik. *The Making of Manhood among Swedish Missionaries in China and Mongolia, c. 1890–c. 1914*. Leiden/Boston: Brill, 2009.

Simensen, Jarle, ed. *Norwegian Missions in African History, Vol. 1: South Africa 1845–1906*. Oslo: Norwegian University Press, 1986.

Simensen, Jarle. 'Norsk misjonsforskning: Faser i utviklingen av historiske studier'. *Norsk tidsskrift for misjonsvitenskap* 61, no. 4 (2007): 227–48.

Simensen, Jarle, Thomas Børhaug, Per Hernæs and Endre Sønstabø. 'Christian Missions and Socio-Cultural Change in Zululand 1850–1906: Norwegian Strategy and African Response'. In *Norwegian Missions in African History, Vol. 1: South Africa 1845–1906*, ed. Jarle Simensen, 187–275. Oslo: Norwegian University Press, 1986.

Simensen, Jarle and Vidar Gynnild. 'Norwegian Missionaries in the Nineteenth Century: Organizational Background, Social Profile and World View'. In *Norwegian Missions in African History, Vol. 1: South Africa 1845–1906*, ed. Jarle Simensen, 11–55. Oslo: Norwegian University Press, 1986.

Sinha, Mrinalini. *Colonial Masculinity: The 'Manly Englishman' and the 'Effeminate Bengali' in the Late Nineteenth Century*. Manchester and New York: Manchester University Press, 1995.

Skeie, Karina Hestad. 'Building God's Kingdom: The Importance of the House to Nineteenth Century Norwegian Missionaries in Madagascar'. In *Ancestors, Power and History in Madagascar*, ed. Karen Middlton. Leiden: Brill Academic Publishers, 1999.

Skeie, Karina Hestad. *Building God's Kingdom in Highland Madagascar: Norwegian Lutheran Missionaries in Vakinankaratra and Betsileo 1866–1903*. Dr Art. dissertation, University of Oslo, 2005.

Skeie, Karina Hestad. 'Misjonsmateriale som historisk materiale'. *Norsk tidsskrift for misjonsvitenskap* 62, no. 2 (2008): 89–100.

Solberg, Edle. *I misjonærfart: Med kaptein Landmark og Elieser*. Stavanger: Nomi, 1965.

Solberg, Terje. '1877–1902: "Og nu staar os intet tilbage … "'. In *Midt i livet. Den Evangelisk Lutherske Frikirke 1877–2002*, ed. Ole Angell, Per Eriksen and Terje Solberg, 13–86. Oslo: Norsk Luthersk Forlag, 2002.

Sommerfelt, Halfdan E. *Den Norske Zulumission: Et Tilbageblik paa de første 20 Aar af det Norske Missionsselskabs Virksomhed*. Christiania: Wm. Gram, 1865.

Stave, Gunnar. *Mannsmot og tenarsinn: Det norske Diakonhjem i hundre år*. Oslo: Det Norske Samlaget, 1990.

Stavem, Ole. *USomamekutyo*. Cape Town: Folk-Lore Journal, 1879.

Stavem, Ole. *Intela jolimi i lojelwe abafana ba kwa Zulu, aba funda esikoleni*. Kristiania: Steenske, 1886.

Stavem, Ole *Et bantufolk og kristendommen: Det norske missionsselskaps syttiaarige zulumission*. Stavanger: Det norske missionsselskaps forlag, 1915.

Stavem, Ole. *The Norwegian Missionary Society: A Short Review of Its Work among the Zulus*. Stavanger: The Norwegian Missionary Society, 1918.

Stavem, Ole. 'Lars Dahle som missionselev'. In *Fra Norges indsats i verdensmissionen: Festskrift ved Lars Dahles femtiaars-jubilæum*, 9–12. Stavanger: Det norske missionsselskaps trykkeri, 1921.

Stoler, Ann Laura. *Carnal Knowledge and Imperial Power: Race and the Intimate Colonial Rule*. Berkeley, CA: University of California Press, 2002.

Strandenæs, Thor. 'Misjonsdiakonien som kulturuttrykk i Kina: En tekst- og billeddokumentasjon fra Hunanprovinsen'. In *Misjon og kultur: Festskrift til Jan-Martin Berentsen*, ed. Thor Strandenæs, 167–206. Stavanger: Misjonshøgskolens forlag, 2006.

Strömberg, C. 'Hednamissionens återverkan på hemlandskyrkans religiøsa lif'. *Nordic Journal of Mission* 1 (1890): 97–120.

Summers, Carol. 'Mission Boys, Civilized Men, and Marriage: Educated African Men in the Missions of Southern Rhodesia, 1920–1945'. *Journal of Religious History* 23, no. 1 (1999): 75–91.

Sundkler, Bengt. *Bantu Prophets in South Africa*. London: Lutterworth Press, 1948.

Sundkler, Bengt. *Zulu Zion and Some Swazi Zionists*. London: Oxford University Press, 1976.

Sundkler, Bengt and Christopher Steed. *A History of the Church in Africa*. Cambridge: Cambridge University Press, 2000.

Sønstabø, Endre. *Fortropper for europeisk imperialisme: Norske misjonærer i Zululand 1850–1880*. Unpublished MA thesis, University of Trondheim, 1973.

Tangeraas, Anders. *Ungdom og misjon*. Oslo: Norges Kristelige Ungdomsforbund, 1944.

Thorne, Susan. *Congregational Missions and the Making of an Imperial Culture in Nineteenth-century England*. Stanford, CA: Stanford University Press, 1999.

Thorne, Susan. 'Mission-imperial Feminism'. In *Gendered Missions: Women and Men in Missionary Discourse and Practice*, ed. Mary Taylor Huber and Nancy Lutkehaus, 39–65. Ann Arbor, MI: University of Michigan Press, 1999.

Thrap, Daniel. *Biskop H.P.S. Schreuders Liv og Virksomhed i korte Træk fremstillet*. Christiania: Nils Lunds Forlag, 1877.

Thrap, D. *Til vore 3 store Missionærers Karakteristik: Foredrag ved Missionsmødet i Skien 22. August 1903*. Skien, 1903.

Titlestad, Karl Michael. 'Norges A.F.M.F.: En kort utsigt'. In *Missionsuppgifter och missionsproblem: Akademiska Frivilliges Missionsförbunds 25-årsskrift*. Stockholm: Sveriges Kristliga Studentrörelses Förlag, 1921.

Tjeder, David. *The Power of Character: Middle-Class Masculinities, 1800–1900*. PhD dissertation, Stockholm University, 2003.

Tjeder, David. 'Borgerlighetens sköra manlighet'. In *Män i Norden: Manlighet och modernitet 1840–1940*, ed. Claes Ekenstam and Jørgen Lorentzen, 48–76. Hedemora: Gidlund, 2006.

Tjelle, Kristin Fjelde. *'Kvinder hjælper Kvinder': Misjonskvinneforeningsbevegelsen i Norge 1860–1910*. Unpublished MA thesis, University of Oslo, 1990.

Tjelle, Kristin Fjelde. 'Lærerinnenes Misjonsforbund gjennom 100 år'. *Norsk tidsskrift for misjon* 56, no. 2 (2002): 67–89.

Tjelle, Kristin Fjelde. 'Misjonærbarna på Solbakken'. In *Med hjertet på flere steder: Om barn, misjon og flerkulturell oppvekst*, ed. Tomas Drønen and Marianne Skjortnes, 71–104. Trondheim: Tapir Akademisk Forlag, 2010.

Tjelle, Kristin Fjelde. 'Misjonærenes barn – foreldrenes eller misjonens ansvar? Misjonærbarn i NMS, ca 1840–1940'. In *Med hjertet på flere steder: Om barn, misjon og flerkulturell oppvekst*, ed. Tomas Drønen and Marianne Skjortnes, 31–70. Trondheim: Tapir Akademisk Forlag, 2010.

Tjora, Svein Ragnvald. *Valg eller vigsel: En undersøkelse av Lars Dahles syn på kirkeforfatningsspørsmål med særlig henblikk på innføringen av misjonærkonferansen på Madagaskar 1877 og på diskusjonen ved århundreskiftet om den gassisk lutherske kirkes selvstendiggjøring*. Unpublished thesis in Theology, School of Mission and Theology, 1985.

Tosh, John. *A Man's Place: Masculinity and the Middle-Class Home in Victorian England*. New Haven, CT: Yale University Press, 1999.

Tosh, John. 'Manliness, Masculinities and the New Imperialism, 1880–1900'. In *Manliness and Masculinities in Nineteenth-Century Britain: Essays on Gender, Family and Empire* ed. John Tosh, 192–214. Harlow: Longman, 2005.

Vance, Norman. *The Sinews of the Spirit: The Ideal of Christian Manliness in Victorian Literature and Religious Thought*. Cambridge: Cambridge University Press, 1985.

Voksø, Per and Erik Kullerud. *I trekantens tegn: Norges Kristelige Ungdomsforbund gjennom hundre år*. Oslo: Triangelforlaget, 1980.

Voll, Hilde Margrethe. *Fra oppdragelse til forkynnelse: Kvinner i Det Norske Misjonsselskap i Norge og på Madagaskar 1879–1920: Praksis og debatt*. Unpublished thesis in Theology, University of Oslo, 1977.

Walker, Cherryl. 'Women and Gender in Southern Africa to 1945: An Overview'. In *Women and Gender in Southern Africa to 1945*, ed. Cherryl Walker, 1–32. Cape Town/London: David Philip/James Currey, 1990.

Walker, Cherryl. 'The Women's Suffrage Movement: The Politics of Gender, Race and Class'. In *Women and Gender in Southern Africa to 1945*, ed. Cherryl Walker, 313–45. Cape Town/London: David Philip/James Currey, 1990.

Warren, Allen. 'Popular Manliness: Baden-Powell, Scouting, and the Development of Manly Character'. In *Manliness and Morality: Middle-class Masculinity in Britain and American 1800–1940*, ed. J.A. Mangan and James Walvin, 199–217. Manchester: Manchester University Press, 1987.

Werner, Yvonne Maria. 'Kristen manlighet i teori och praxis'. In *Kristen manlighet: Ideal och verklighet 1830–1940*, ed. Yvonne Maria Werner, 9–21. Lund: Nordic Academic Press, 2008.

Werner, Yvonne Maria, ed. *Kristen manlighet: Ideal och verklighet 1830–1940*. Lund: Nordic Academic Press, 2008.

Werner, Yvonne Maria. 'Religious Feminisation, Confessionalism and Re-masculinisation in Western European Society 1800–1960'. In *Pieties and Gender*, ed. Lene Sjørup and Hilda Rømer Christensen, 143–62. Leiden: Brill, 2009.

Werner, Yvonne Maria. 'Alternative Masculinity? Catholic Missionaries in Scandinavia'. In *Christian Masculinity: Men and Religion in Northerns Europe in the 19th and 20th Centuries*, ed. Yvonne Maria Werner, 165–87. Leuven: Leuven University Pres, 2011.

Werner, Yvonne Maria, ed. *Christian Masculinity – a Paradox of Modernity: Men and Religion in Northern Europe in the 19th and 20th century*. Leuven: Leuven Univerity Press, 2011.

Wettergren, Paul Peter. *Brev til mine Venner i Anledning af min Udtrædelse af Statskirken den 27.de Marts 1877*. Risør: J.G. Fryxell, 1877.

Williams, C. Peter. *The Ideal of the Self-Governing Church: A Study in Victorian Missionary Strategy*. Leiden: E.J. Brill, 1990.

Williams, C. Peter. 'The Church Missionary Society and the Indigenous Church in the Second Half of the Nineteenth Century: The Defense and Destruction of the Venn Ideals'. In *Converting Colonialism: Visions and Realities in Mission History, 1706–1914*, ed. Dana L. Robert, 86–111. Grand Rapids, MI/Cambridge: Wm. B. Eerdmans Publishing Co., 2008.

Winquist, Alan H. *Scandinavians and South Africa: Their Impact on the Cultural, Social and Economic Development of Pre-1902 South Africa*. Cape Town/Rotterdam: A.A.Balkema, 1978.

Wright, John. 'Revisiting the Stereotype of Shaka's "Devastations".' In *Zulu Identities: Being Zulu, Past and Present*, ed. Benedict Carton, John Laband and Jabulani Sithole, 82–6. Scottsville: University of KwaZulu-Natal Press, 2008.

Wyller, Ingrid. *Sykepleiernes Misjonsring S.M.R. 50 år*. Oslo: Sykepleiernes Misjonsring, 1971.

Yates, Timothy. *Christian Mission in the Twentieth Century*. Cambridge: Cambridge University Press, 1994.

Zulu, Prince Bongani kaShelemba. 'The Ministry of the Black People in the Lutheran Norwegian Mission Stations in Zululand and Natal from 1875 to 1963'. Unpublished conference paper, University of Stellenbosch, 2009.

Index

Printed and bound in the United States of America